AMBROSE BIERCE

AMBROSE BIERCE

Alone
in
Bad
Company

✝

Roy Morris, Jr.

Oxford University Press
New York   Oxford

Oxford University Press

Oxford   New York
Athens   Auckland   Bangkok   Bogotá   Buenos Aires   Calcutta
Cape Town   Chennai   Dar es Salaam   Delhi   Florence   Hong Kong   Istanbul
Karachi   Kuala Lumpur   Madrid   Melbourne   Mexico City   Mumbai
Nairobi   Paris   São Paulo   Singapore   Taipei   Tokyo   Toronto   Warsaw

and associated companies in

Berlin   Ibadan

Copyright © 1995 by Roy Morris, Jr.

First published in 1996 by Crown Publishers, Inc.,
201 East 50th Street, New York, New York 10022

First issued as an Oxford University Press paperback, 1998

Oxford is a registered trademark of Oxford University Press

Library of Congress Cataloging-in-Publication Data
Morris, Roy.
    Ambrose Bierce : alone in bad company / Roy Morris, Jr.
        p.   cm.
    Originally published: New York : Crown Publishers, c1995.
    Includes bibliographical references (p.   ) and index.
    ISBN 0-19-512628-9
    1. Bierce, Ambrose, 1842-1914?   2. Authors, American--19th
century--Biography.   3. Journalists--United States--Biography.
I. Title.
PS1097.Z5M67   1998
813'.4--dc21
    [B]   98-33467

10 9 8 7 6 5 4 3 2 1

Printed in the United States of America
on acid-free paper

To Lucy,
With Love,
From Daddy

Contents

Acknowledgments

*I*n the commission—if not necessarily the conclusion—of this new biography of Ambrose Bierce, I am greatly indebted to the pioneering work of such previous biographers as Carey McWilliams, Paul Fatout, and M. E. Grenander, all of whom labored valiantly to preserve and extend the historical record of a most perplexing, provoking, and private individual. To Professor Grenander, especially, I want to add my personal thanks for her patient response to numerous uninvited questions, and for a lifetime of work spent nurturing the often flickering flame of Ambrose Bierce's posthumous reputation. I would also like to thank Colonel James D. Stephens, president of Kentucky Military Institute, Inc., for his helpful assistance on Bierce's short-lived career at KMI; Judith C. Ferrell, reference assistant at the Elkhart, Indiana, public library; Michael R. Gannett, president and town historian, Cornwall Historical Society; Judith Ellen Johnson, reference librarian and genealogist, Connecticut Historical Society; and Mitchell Yockelson of the National Archives, for their help in tracing Bierce's early life.

Special thanks to my agent, Robert Gottlieb, senior vice president and member of the board of directors of William Morris Agency, for his always cogent professional advice; and to my editor, James O'Shea Wade, for sharing, behind his courtly Southern demeanor, a truly devilish appreciation of Biercian wit.

Thanks to my fellow Chattanoogans Jan Strunk, Mike Bullock of Computer Cove, and Jerry Sanders of Beeline Printing for their much-needed technical support.

And finally, thanks beyond thanks to my parents, Roy and Margaret Coode Morris, for their love and support; to my father-in-law, G. Burton Pierce, for his continued and much-appreciated generosity; to my fellow author and neighbor Nat Hughes, for his personal and professional commiseration; and to my long-suffering wife, Leslie, who had to listen repeatedly to much-chortled-at selections from the Bierce canon, for all this and then some.

AMBROSE BIERCE

Prologue

When seventy-one-year-old Ambrose Bierce disappeared without a trace into the smoke and dust of revolutionary Mexico in late December 1913, he probably had more enemies than any man alive. This was only fair, as even he might have admitted: He had labored long and hard to make himself hateful, and in the end he succeeded all too well. The various targets of his printed abuse, extraordinary even by the eye-gouging standards of the day, ranged from the mightiest and most rapacious robber baron to the meekest and least-offensive female poet. His erstwhile friend George Sterling, himself a victim of the Biercian lash, described the older man's brutal literary criticism—after his death—as "breaking butterflies on a wheel." And certainly there were dozens of such ethereal victims, whose only transgressions were those of writing poorly (by Bierce's rather Augustan standards), or of recklessly entering the public arena and thus exposing themselves, like scurrying mice, to the columnist's fierce and predatory gaze. Great or small, his victims qualified, at least in Bierce's eyes, by virtue of being representative examples of what he termed, with tart dissatisfaction, "that immortal ass, the average man." Such fools, he predicted, were everlasting, and would continue to flourish long after "the rest of us shall have retired for the night of eternal oblivion."

His own oblivion came in depressingly regular installments: deaths, suicides, emotional estrangements; the painful eclipse of his creative powers; and the failure of his remarkable short stories (at least during his lifetime) to reach a widespread national audience. Even his heroic service in the Union army during the Civil War came in the end to seem almost meaningless. History, he wrote in that most caustic of lexicons, *The Devil's Dictionary*, is "an account mostly false, of events mostly unimportant, which are brought about by rulers mostly knaves, and soldiers mostly fools." When, at the height of the Gilded Age, he looked back at the nation he had fought for four years to preserve, it somehow did not seem worth saving anymore. The slaves did not deserve their freedom, the businessmen did not deserve their fortunes, and the Confederate soldiers who had broken his head "like a walnut" at Kennesaw Mountain did not deserve their defeat. "They were brave and courageous foemen," he wrote of the Southerners, "having little in common with the political madmen who persuaded them to their doom." To his Virginia-born publisher, Walter Neale, he wondered aloud if he had fought on the right side.

Whatever his doubts about the rightness of the war, there is no question that it marked him, as it did all the 4 million who fought in it, deeply and for life. Little more than a boy when he enlisted in the army during the first week of the war, Bierce quickly found himself in the front ranks of "hardened and impenitent man-killers, to whom death in its awfulest forms is a fact familiar to their every-day observation; who sleep on hills trembling with the thunder of great guns, dine in the midst of streaming missiles, and play cards among the dead faces of their dearest friends." Gloomy and saturnine to begin with, he discovered in the war a bitter confirmation of his darkest assumptions about man and his nature. It did not necessarily make him a pacifist—he cared too little about himself and others to place much value on individual human life—but it did disabuse him, painfully and forever, of any childish notions about the romance of war. And when, three decades later, he began translating his wartime experiences into fictional form, it was for the express purpose of showing the lethal arbitrariness of life, for both soldiers and civilians, in the modern world. As with Ernest Hemingway, whose work he influenced to an even greater degree than has been generally recognized, the war in Bierce's stories kills the best soldiers first, while still managing to get around to the rest in due time. Many former soldiers have felt this way, and many writers have written this way, but it is important to note for the sake of the record that Bierce did it first—before Stephen Crane, before e. e. cummings, before Robert Graves, before Wilfred Owen, before Siegfried Sassoon, before John Dos Passos, before Norman Mailer, before Joseph Heller, before Kurt Vonnegut, before Tim O'Brien, before any of the long cavalcade of Anglo-American authors who have variously sought to chronicle and curse the world's long descent into atavistic darkness. It does not mean that Bierce was a better writer than the others, but it does give him an honorable place at the head of their table.

Having survived—just barely—the Civil War, he sometimes had the sense, like the dying Keats, of living a posthumous existence. It is significant that several of his stories, including his greatest, "An Occurrence at Owl Creek Bridge," concern characters who are at, or a little beyond, the point of death. "When I ask myself what has become of Ambrose Bierce the youth, who fought at Chickamauga," he told a friend, "I am bound to answer that he is dead. Some little of him survives in my memory, but many of him are absolutely dead and gone." Freed in a sense from his prior life, Bierce would spend the next fifty years rejecting the comfortable hypocrisies and spirit-killing compromises that enabled his fellow countrymen to live with themselves. "My future programme," he announced early in his career, "will be calm disapproval of human institutions in general, including all forms of government, most laws and customs, and all contemporary literature; enthusiastic belief in the Darwinian theory, intolerance of intolerance, and war upon every man with a mission . . . human suffering and human injustice in all their forms to be contemplated with a merely curious interest, as one looks into an anthill." It was a philosophy he followed doggedly the rest of his life, but it was one that carried with it a great personal price in loneliness, rancor, and spiritual isolation.

Having lost so much for so long—he was a master of the Pyrrhic moral victory—Bierce proceeded at last to lose himself. And despite the best efforts of countless investigators over the last eighty-odd years to find him, he has remained resolutely, and no doubt happily, lost, a doom-haunted old man whose own death, occurring, as it were, offstage, may be said in a way not to have happened at all, since to die unnoticed is to cheat death of its usual audience of mourners, kibitzers, and curiosity-seekers. "Nobody will find my bones," he promised, and nobody ever has. As John Lennon is supposed to have said when Elvis Presley died (the same could also be said for Lennon), Bierce's spectacular disappearance in the winter of 1913 was a "good career move." If, in the end, the mystery seems insolvable, that has not stopped the legion of speculators from writing their own versions of Bierce's death. And if such speculation has helped in any way to keep his name alive, then it has served a valuable purpose, for Ambrose Bierce is a writer who, however limited and uncharitable his talent, still deserves to be read today.

It is no longer necessary, as it was for decades following his death, to plead the case for Bierce's importance. At least two of his Civil War stories, "Chickamauga" and "An Occurrence at Owl Creek Bridge," as well as his groundbreaking nonfictional work, "What I Saw of Shiloh," will last for as long as anyone cares about good writing in general, or that bad war in particular. His ghost stories, too, are still worth reading for their skin-prickling supernatural effects and their sepulchrally black humor. Dozens of his definitions from *The Devil's Dictionary* have already entered the national consciousness, even if their author is not always given credit for them: "MARRIAGE, n. The state or condition of a community consisting of a master, a mistress, and two slaves, making in all two"; "SELF-ESTEEM, n. An erroneous appraisement"; "ALONE, adj. In bad company"; "ONCE, adv. Enough"; "DIPLOMACY, n. The patriotic art of lying for one's country"; "PEACE, n. In international affairs, a period of cheating between two periods of fighting"; "BRIDE, n. A woman with a fine prospect of happiness behind her"; "POSITIVE, adj. Mistaken at the top of one's voice"; "YEAR,

n. A period of 365 disappointments." Then there is the perfect battle-of-the-sexes formulation: "Oh that we could fall into woman's arms without falling into her hands." He also wrote the shortest and most lethal book review on record: "The covers of this book are too far apart." The list could, and does, go on and on.

Like many complicated individuals, Bierce is best defined by his contradictions. He was an essentially good man who amused himself by pretending to be a bad one; a kind man who concealed his many private acts of kindness behind a public posture of cruelty; a sensitive man who assumed in print a callousness toward human suffering that he did not always maintain in private; a generous man who patiently read and corrected the works of dozens of young and unproven writers, even as he publicly pilloried artists as variously gifted and personally unoffending as Henry James, William Dean Howells, Stephen Crane, Charles Dickens, and Oscar Wilde. (Told once that Howells, the reigning dean of American letters, had called him one of the country's three best writers, Bierce immediately responded, "I suppose Mr. Howells is the other two.") He was also on occasion a ruthless man, particularly to friends who he felt, often with some justice, had let him down. He enjoyed the company of talented, intelligent, and independent women, yet denounced to the point of fixation the newly "liberated" woman. A successful seducer with numerous amatory conquests on his record, he claimed never to have taken another man's wife or lover, or ever to have been seen naked by a woman. He was a republican with a lowercase *r*, but not a democrat with a lowercase *d*. Neither was he, as some revisionist critics maintain, a protofascist. To him, all organized governments were suspect, since all were comprised unavoidably of men. He cared enough about his country to fight bravely for it in one war, and to criticize it, equally bravely, during another, when he came to believe, as do most modern historians, that it was unnecessary, unmerited, and ungentlemanly. A good drinking companion, careful listener, and witty conversationalist, he confided very little of himself to others. A health fanatic and fitness freak, he was also a lifelong asthmatic who spent more than one smothering night draped over a chair in a lonely hotel room, fighting for his next—or last—breath. He suffered blinding headaches and frequent dizzy spells as a result of his war wound, yet he once refused a substantial offer of back pay from the government, noting archly that "when I hired out as an assassin for my country, that wasn't part of the contract."

If, in today's politically correct, habitually aggrieved world, Bierce sometimes seems almost lunatically combative, at least he fought his battles in the open, and not all of them were petty or insignificant. When California railroad magnate Collis P. Huntington set out in 1896 to supervise personally a lifetime extension of his railroad's $75 million debt to the federal government, in effect absolving himself of all liability, Bierce rushed to Washington to cover the proceedings for William Randolph Hearst's San Francisco *Examiner*. Huntington—"an inflated old pigskin," in one of the columnist's milder formulations—was the perfect target for a frustrated idealist like Bierce. An unrepentant capitalist who once said that "everything that is not nailed down is mine, and anything I can pry loose is not nailed down," Huntington did not even pretend to care about the public interest. For once in his career given a target worthy of his dark disdain, Bierce spent months savagely lambasting "the swine of the century" in articles that have since entered journalistic legend. Yet if Huntington was an easy target, Bierce also took on less popular causes. A resident of San Francisco during a ferocious nativist backlash against Asian immigration, he publicly decried the murder of a Chinese woman as an example of "galloping Christianity of the malignant California type." And when a handful of Mormons were waylaid and lynched on their way to Utah, he condemned the lynching as "one of the most hateful and sneaking aggressions that has ever disgraced the generally straightforward and forthright course of religious persecution." He repeatedly spoke out against racial intolerance, political malfeasance, and government corruption, often at the risk of violent retaliation. At all times, he wrote with such force and authority that when he signed his columns with his first two initials, "AG," many people simply assumed, a fellow journalist joked, that the letters stood for "Almighty God."

Almighty or not, Bierce would have had trouble finding a place in today's more squeamish and thin-skinned society—he could scarcely find a place in his own. The epithets he acquired over the course of his tumultuous forty-year career were almost entirely negative: Bitter Bierce, the Devil's Lexicographer, the Wickedest Man in San Francisco, the Rascal with the Sorrel Hair. Even the more flattering sobriquet, the West Coast Samuel Johnson, loses a bit of its luster in the wake of Bierce's famous complaint that the good doctor had gotten it all wrong: Patriotism isn't the last refuge of the scoundrel; it is the first. Whatever they called him, Bierce professed not to care what people thought, and perhaps he did not. Nevertheless, he carried a loaded .45-caliber revolver under his coat and kept a much-handled human skull on his desk—one of his former friends, he said—as a talisman to ward off evil spells. And when, at the height of his journalistic career, a few of his more fastidious readers objected to the level of his personal invective, he brusquely advised them to "continue selling shoes, selling pancakes, or selling themselves. As for me, I sell abuse." In a way, he was being modest. Any fishwife can hurl abuse; few have ever written it as piercingly—and as unrepentantly—as Ambrose Bierce.

1

Direst of All Disasters

*I*n the early spring of 1882, all San Francisco was abuzz over the rarefied presence of London's reigning literary lion, Oscar Wilde, in town for a series of public lectures on the future of art in the philistine world. The flamboyant Wilde was then in the midst of a 105-city tour of darkest America, spreading his gospel of transcendent estheticism to a degraded people who could not even make a decent cup of tea. In a specially tailored black velvet dress coat, knee-length breeches, and sheer silk stockings, he was the walking embodiment of what he humbly termed "the science of the beautiful," and he inspired in his wake an army of limpid-eyed, flower-toting followers and a blizzard of favorable press clippings fit, he noted proudly, for a *petit roi*. Not all journalists, however, were such willing subjects, even in historically live-and-let-live San Francisco. One in particular was quite clearly not amused. Ambrose Bierce, editor of the aptly named weekly *Wasp* and Wilde's closest American counterpart in the near-lethal practice of aphorism and retort, noted the visit in his March 31 column. "That sovereign of insufferables, Oscar Wilde," he groused to his readers, "has ensued with his opulence of twaddle and his penury of sense. He has mounted his hind legs and blown crass vapidities through the bowel of his neck, to the capital edification of circumjacent fools and fooleses. The ineffable dunce has nothing to say and says it with a liberal embellishment of bad delivery, embroidering it with reasonless vulgarities of attitude, gesture and attire. There never was an impostor so hateful, a blockhead so stupid, a crank so variously and offensively daft. He makes me tired."[1]

Wilde had unwittingly irritated Bierce from a continent away by calling satire, upon his arrival in New York, an art form that was "as sterile as it is shameful, and as impotent as it is insolent." Bierce, who was neither sterile nor impotent, knew no shame, but he was nevertheless insolent enough to take offense at the new arrival's casual dig at his own preferred method of verbal warfare. "This gawky gowk," he wrote in *Wasp*, "has the divine effrontery to link his name with those of Swinburne, Rossetti and Morris—this dunghill he-hen would fly with eagles. This littlest and looniest of a brotherhood of simpletons, whom the wicked wits of London, haling him dazed from obscurity, have crowned and crucified as King of the Cranks, has accepted the distinction in stupid good faith and our foolish people take him at his word." Bierce's own crankiness was equally regal, and his literary eminence was at least as self-confirmed as Wilde's, but the foppish young Irishman was not alone in tiring him. Many things wearied Ambrose Bierce: preachers, politicians, doctors, lawyers, capitalists, socialists, jingoists, anarchists, immigrants, women, bohemians, and dogs. Indiana rhymester James Whitcomb Riley—a particular Biercian bête noire—was close to the point when he archly observed that "Bierce edits God."[2]

It was not so much that Bierce edited God, as that he audited Him. In an age of gilded ritual and reflexive cant overlying a slippery social network of hypocrisy and greed, Bierce had given himself the task of telling the truth. It was a lonely and thankless role, and one that would eventually wear him (and those around him) out. But until it did, not even the perfumed eloquence of Oscar Wilde could daunt this teller of unpopular truths. For forty fierce and contentious years, as a newspaper columnist, short-story writer, and tireless moral arbiter, Bierce prowled his territory as ceaselessly and unforgivingly as a church deacon scans the pews, ever vigilant for backsliding and fallings-off. And if, in his "private system of morality," such sins were literary rather than spiritual, it was nevertheless his duty to denounce and decry. A nonbelieving puritan, he came from a long line of churchgoing New Englanders, men whose fundamental values—honesty, hard work, and personal rectitude—he consistently honored through his actions, even as he frequently mocked them with his words.[3]

Not that Bierce looked to his ancestors for guidance. "I know a man," he once said, speaking of himself, "to whose character not an ancestor since the seventeenth century appears to have contributed an element." Given the fact that the first Bierce to walk upright on American soil arrived from England at precisely that time, he would seem to be rejecting the entire paternal branch of the family. Certainly he rejected their overt religiosity. His great-great-great-great-grandfather, Augustin Bearse (as the name was then spelled), had once carried his newborn son two miles through a swirling snowstorm to have the baby baptized in the local church to save its soul from infant damnation. Ambrose, his most famous descendant, doubtless heard the story of that wintry walk of faith, but if it was intended to instill a similar piety in him, it had rather the opposite effect. All his life, Bierce savagely skewered organized religion, which he defined in his book *The Devil's Dictionary* as "a daughter of Hope and Fear, explaining to Ignorance the Unknowable." Likewise, he considered *faith* "belief without evidence in what is told by one who speaks without knowledge, of things without parallel." As for *Christians,* he considered them to be, his ancestors included, men who "follow the teachings of Christ in so far as they are not inconsistent with a life of sin." Bierce himself was many things, but he was seldom inconsistent, particularly when it came to religion, or his lack thereof. He never missed an opportunity to scoff and scorn.[4]

Had it somehow been possible for Bierce to meet the founder of the American branch of the family, Augustin would doubtless have disowned him at once. In 1638, at the age of twenty, Augustin (later shortened to Austin) Bearse had immigrated to Massachusetts from Southampton, England, the southernmost tip of Thomas Hardy's Wessex and a Royalist stronghold with little of the fundamentalist fervor that young Bearse brought with him, like a virus, to the New World. That fervor had long since abated by the time Ambrose arrived on the scene. Between Austin, described in ancient Massachusetts histories as "one of the very few against whom there was no complaint," and Ambrose, against whom there were multitudinous complaints, lay an unbridgeable gulf of philosophy and experience. Young Goodman Bearse, one of 110 passengers to sail from Southampton on Master John Jobson's good ship *Confidence,* was hardworking, God-fearing, and family-loving. He met his future wife, Mary Wilder, on the voyage across the Atlantic, and, in accordance with the fashion of the day, he honored his mother-in-law, Martha, by naming his second-born daughter after her. He settled on twelve acres of stony land in Barnstable, Massachusetts (on Cape Cod), and within a few years' time, he had expanded his ownership to an even fifty acres of land and two small islands, still known locally as Bearse's Islands. As a charter member of the Reverend John Lothrop's Baptist Church, Austin was said to have "brought up his family to be like himself—useful members of society." Against this backdrop of rock-ribbed New England piety (Lothrop, who was once literally thrown into the Clink for his religious views, considered Boston's flinty Puritans too liberal for his taste), Austin founded a family tradition of long lives, large families, and financial success. In the all-too-common American way, his descendants also served loyally in King Philip's War, the French and Indian War, the Revolutionary War, and the Mexican War, rendering unto various Caesars the same devotion to duty that they faithfully exhibited in their churches on Sunday. When the time came for Ambrose Bierce to pick up a rifle in the Civil War, he had a long military tradition behind him, and an even longer religious one to justify it.[5]

But family traditions meant little to Bierce, and family trees even less. His one recorded bow to his ancestors reads, in part: "My country, 'tis of thee,/Sweet land of felony,/Of thee I sing—/Land where my fathers fried/Young witches and applied/Whips to the Quaker's hide/And made him spring." Genealogy itself, the study of those fryers, he considered an "account of one's descent from an ancestor who did not particularly want to trace his own." Actually, it would have been quite easy for Bierce to trace himself back to his upright forebears; he never tried. It is safe to say that if any child could have entered the world without the unwanted encumbrance of inconvenient relatives, Bierce would have been the first. His parents were as much an embarrassment to him as he was, no doubt, a puzzlement to them— "unwashed savages," he called them. Given their strict fundamentalist upbringing and his own lifelong obsession with cleanliness, it is unlikely that they were that. Instead, they were humble, devout, sin-defying frontier people, saddled already with nine hungry children by the time Ambrose came along on June 24, 1842, to add his somewhat dandified name to the long list of *A*'s in the well-thumbed family Bible. His father, for unfathomable reasons probably having to do with his own extravagant name—Marcus Aurelius— amused himself by giving each of his progeny names beginning with the letter *A*: Abigail, Amelia, Ann, Addison, Aurelius, Augustus, Almeda, Andrew, Albert, and Ambrose.[6]

At the time of his birth, Bierce's family was living in the ramshackle religious community of Horse Cave Creek, Ohio, having made its way across the intervening two centuries from Barnstable, Massachusetts, through Cornwall, Connecticut, to the old Western Reserve of northern Ohio, and thence southward for a time to Horse Cave Creek. The region was a hotbed of revivalist frenzy, full of spirit-rappers, tongue-talkers, stump-shouters, and psalm-singers. Some early Bierce biographers have maintained that his parents somehow stood apart from the nightly open-air revels out of a more fastidious approach to the practice of religion. But this ignores the fact that back in Cornwall, where they were born, they had been raised in an equally fervid, albeit somewhat more refined, religious environment. As members of the First Congregational Church of Christ, Marcus Bierce and Laura Sherwood had regularly flinched and shied along with other Cornwallian children under the never-sleeping eye of the Reverend Timothy Stone, a Jonathan Edwards acolyte whose proudest boast was of stamping out youthful dancing for the entire twenty years of his pastorage. Stone, who labored under the rather serious professional handicap of a partially paralyzed mouth, was considered—unsurprisingly—a poor preacher. He made up for his oratorical shortcomings with ferocious week-long revivals that literally scared hell out of his young charges, many of whom would tearfully descend on the altar, begging to know what they could do to be saved. (To begin with, Stone insisted, they should remove their hats in his presence.) Given that mortifying background, and their later attendance at similar fire-and-brimstone revivals in Indiana, it is unlikely that the Bierces simply stayed home knitting when the holy spirit was working on their neighbors.[7]

Marcus, the son of a Revolutionary War veteran who had been with Washington at Valley Forge, married well; Laura Sherwood was the daughter of the head deacon of the Reverend Stone's church and a direct descendant of William Bradford of *Mayflower* fame. (On Marcus's side, too, there seems to have been a *Mayflower* connection, through his great-great-grandmother, Experience Howland Bierce.) His marriage, unfortunately, was about the only successful event in Marcus Bierce's life. Tall, shambling, and slow to speak, he dutifully excelled at the two family distinctions: making babies and living long lives. It was the more prosaic business in between that seemed to baffle him. At various times a farmer, a shopkeeper, a property assessor, and—somewhat hilariously, given his own lifelong struggle against poverty—a county overseer of the poor, Marcus dutifully labored in the vineyards and churches of mid-nineteenth-century America. His heart, however, was somewhere else—specifically, in his library. For Marcus Bierce, calloused hands and all, was something of an esthete, at least by contemporary midwestern standards. His personal collection of books was said to be the largest in the county; and it was in that library, reading alone, that his tenth child, Ambrose, first became acquainted with the enduring consolations of serious literature. A possibly apocryphal story has young Ambrose, aged ten, poring over a copy of Pope's translation of the *Iliad* in his father's far meadow, the wind gently rustling his sandy blond hair. It is a pleasant, if somewhat implausible, image, more appropriate to a budding romantic poet than an unexceptional Hoosier farm boy. But indoors or out, Ambrose did avail himself of the old man's surprisingly worldly library (Marcus was a closet admirer of Byron and the reigning gothic novelists of the day). He may even have read the penny-dreadful play that gave him his name, *Ambrose Gwinett; or A Sea-Side Story,* by the little-known English dramatist Douglas Jerrold, since Bierce's most famous short story, "An Occurrence at Owl Creek Bridge," shares the play's basic plot contrivance of a young man miraculously surviving—or seeming to survive—a hanging. Where his family was concerned, Bierce was notably frugal with compliments, but he later called his father, apparently without irony, "a man of considerable scholarship," adding, "All that I have I owe to his books."[8]

His mother was another matter. Although she did, presumably, transmit some of William Bradford's writing genes to her youngest surviving child, Laura Bierce gave Ambrose little else—at least by his own after-the-fact accounting. Bierce never wrote his memoirs, and few of his acquaintances ever heard him mention his family or his childhood. But like other writers before and since, he managed from time to time to sneak into his stories a certain amount of unassimilated autobiographical baggage. And judging by the psychological implications of such hair-raising tales as "My Favorite Murder," "Oil of Dog," "An Imperfect Conflagration," and "The Hypnotist," collected by Bierce under the pointed rubric *The Parenticide Club,* it would seem that their author was—to say the least—a man with a less-than-normal relationship with his parents. "Having murdered my mother under circumstances of singular atrocity," he starts one story. Another begins: "Early one June morning in 1872 I murdered my father—an act which made a deep impression on me at the time." The singularly ugly story "The Hypnotist" ends with the title character entrancing his parents into thinking they are wild stallions; they then kick and stomp each other to death while the narrator looks on impassively, noting with a certain mordant satisfaction that now "the author of the strife was an orphan." The fact that these stories were intended to be—and are, in a somewhat grisly way—funny makes them seem, if anything, even more terrible. A writer capable of turning his pious, family-centered parents into slack-jawed abortionists and child-murderers, as Bierce does in jest in "Oil of Dog," is not exactly a model of filial devotion.[9]

Relatives of Bierce later insisted that the writer did not really hate his parents, and probably he did not, at least on an active, day-to-day basis. Instead, he seems to have held them in, or slightly beneath, contempt, blaming them for the poverty he felt he had suffered, both physically and emotionally, when he was a child. To be sure, life in Kosciusko County, Indiana, where the family removed when he was four, was hardly a soft and leisurely existence. Warsaw, the closest settlement, was three miles away, and the fledgling northern Indiana town supported only a sawmill, a log schoolhouse, the inevitable church, and a few rough cabins. (Ironically, by the time a second noted American writer, Theodore Dreiser, moved to Warsaw four decades later, the town, with its surfeit of clear lakes and good fishing, had become something of a vacation resort. This was no consolation to Dreiser: He and his family were socially ostracized after one of his sisters ran off with the local pharmacist and a second got herself pregnant by a wealthy man-about-town, the banal and sordid genesis of his great novels *Sister Carrie* and *An American Tragedy.*) Marcus and the older boys immediately took to the fields, clearing land for a permanent dwelling alongside Goose Creek, within sight of the Tippecanoe River two miles away. In the time-honored way of the American frontier, work was plentiful and luxuries scarce. Still, the Bierces lived no more meanly than most of their neighbors, and better than some. Given the fact that Bierce himself was spared much of the physical labor, then and later, and was untypically permitted to attend school until the age of fourteen, his later remark, "In the wilds of the 'far West' we had to grub out a very difficult living," should be taken with a certain pinch of salt. His own impoverishment was more psychic than physical, and it appears to have been largely self-induced. Simply put—such things, of course, are never truly simple—Bierce blamed his mother for not loving him enough.[10]

Feeling deprived, or at least ignored, the boy reacted in a typical way: He withdrew. Whereas his older brothers and sisters seemed to have enjoyed reasonably pleasant relations with their parents (one brother, Andrew, lived with his mother and father all their lives), Ambrose gloomily kept to himself, spending as little time as possible around the family home. In a parody of the sunny tripe that fellow Hoosier James Whitcomb Riley was then foisting shamelessly on the American public, Bierce apostrophized "the malarial farm, the wet fungus-grown wildwood,/The chills then contracted that since have remained./The scum-covered duck pond, the pigsty close by it,/The ditch where the sour-smelling house drainage fell;/The dark, shaded dwelling, the foul barnyard nigh it"—and so on. Unmediated loathing of his boyhood surroundings stayed with Ambrose all his life.[11]

His parents, no doubt, did their best by him, but they were harried by debts and grief-stricken over the deaths of their three youngest children: Arthur, who died in 1846 at the age of nine months, and the twin girls, Adelia and Aurelia, who succumbed separately within two years of their birth in 1848. Infant mortality, of course, was no stranger to American families of the time, and the Bierces, as Christians, were fully reconciled to God's inscrutable will. But the couple had never lost a child until their eleventh died, and it is likely that the household was even heavier with consolatory religion than might ordinarily have been the case. Ambrose, typically, never spoke of his siblings' deaths or admitted any sympathy for his suffering parents. Instead, he satirized his grieving mother as "the pious old lady at home after service singing 'Plunged in a Gulf of Dark Despair.'" For his father, he had slightly more sympathy, though colored always by a contingent wit. In a later short story, "Three and Three Are One" (which ends with the hero's entire family being killed by an artillery shell), Bierce gives a thinly disguised description of Marcus: "The elder Lassiter had that severity of manner that so frequently affirms an uncompromising devotion to duty, and conceals a warm and affectionate disposition. He was of the iron of which martyrs are made, but in the heart of the matrix had lurked a nobler metal, fusible at a milder heat, yet never coloring nor softening the hard exterior." Perhaps in frustration at his son's surly nature, or perhaps in reaction to his own unassuaged grief, Marcus frequently took a rod to Ambrose's back—with the predictable result of making the boy even more fractious and slow to obey. "Disobedience," Bierce jeered forty years later, "is the silver lining to the cloud of servitude. Had not our pious parent administered daily rebukes with such foreign bodies as he could lay his hands on, we might have grown up a Presbyterian deacon. Look at us now!"[12]

Bierce's mother, in particular, could do little right in her son's eyes. Once, when he was small, Ambrose asked her if there really was a Santa Claus. She assured him, as parents will, that there was, but he soon found out the truth, probably from his older brothers. Then, said Bierce, "I proceeded forthwith to detest my deceiver with all my little might and main. And even now I cannot say that I experience any consuming desire to renew my acquaintance with her in that other life to which, she also assured me, we hasten hence." Most children do not permanently fall out with their mothers over the question of Santa Claus, but Bierce had a lengthy memory. John Dos Passos once said that Ernest Hemingway was the only man he had ever met who truly hated his mother, but Dos Passos never met Ambrose Bierce. Ever afterward, Bierce despised Christmas as a particularly bogus holiday. His idea of a properly festive meal, he wrote, was "just a baby's body/Done to a nutty brown," and "as to drink/About a half a jug of blood, I think." The real nub of the problem, of course, was not Christmas or Santa Claus—it was his mother. As Bierce himself described it, "The human heart has a definite quantity of affection. The more objects it is bestowed upon, the less each object will get." There were a lot of children in Laura Bierce's household.[13]

Such intense, conflicted feelings toward one's mother must find a psychic outlet somewhere. For Bierce, his sense of familial estrangement manifested itself in a series of vivid nightmares, dreams so terrible that he could still recall them half a century later. In one, he found himself traveling at night through a fire-ravaged countryside. Pools of dark water lay on the ground, as though an apocalyptic fire had been followed immediately by a drenching rain. To the west, a crimson light burned inside a ruined fortress. Reaching the ruins, he wandered through the deserted works until he came to a large vacant room where a body lay abandoned on a bed. Gazing down, he saw with horror that the corpse's staring eyes and frozen features were his own. A second dream was even more frightening. He was walking alone—"in my bad dreams, I am always alone"—through a weird forest within which a dark brook flowed sluggishly with blood. The stream's source he traced to a white marble tank filled with blood, around which scores of dead bodies had been symmetrically arranged, each lying on its back with its throat cut, oozing still more blood. He had the unshakable sense that the murders were the direct result of some crime he had committed but could not remember, "a natural and necessary result of my offense." In such dreams, Bierce experienced the Nietzschean vision of a God-abandoned universe, one in which "Man is long ago dead in every zone,/The angels are all gone in graves unknown;/The devils, too, are cold enough at last,/And God lies dead before a great white throne!"[14]

It doesn't take a trained psychologist to find in these dreams a deep sense of self-loathing, alienation, and unlovableness, resulting in a violent pathological reaction against one's parents for giving one birth, defined by Bierce as "the first and direst of all disasters." They are, in a way, the dreams of a serial killer, the only difference being that, in Bierce's case, the killings take place on the written page, in a succession of gory, macabre, and heartless stories in which more or less innocent people are variously hanged, strangled, shot, stomped, roasted, toasted, and boiled in oil. A few even die, perhaps mercifully, of fright. For a child such as Bierce, who had seen three younger siblings die in quick succession and his parents withdraw into broodful mourning, the sense of personal vulnerability must have been at times overwhelming.[15]

This existential sense of aloneness carried over to his no doubt mystified family. Only his brother Albert, who was closest to him in age, became anything like a boon companion. Albert, nicknamed "Grizzly," was as easygoing and openhearted as Ambrose was closed off and wound tight. The two once scandalized their parents at an outdoor revival by draping straw over an unfortunate horse, setting the straw afire, and driving the frantic animal into the tent about the time the traveling preacher was reaching his well-practiced peroration about "Saul of Catarrhsus." In what probably qualifies as an understatement, Albert later observed that where their mother was concerned, he and Ambrose "did not make life as pleasant for her as we might have." As for his other brothers and sisters, Bierce considered them either too old, too obedient, too straitlaced, or too conventional for his own hotly blooming rebelliousness. The girls, like their mother, were the picture of virtue; one, Almeda, later became a missionary in Africa, where she died, it was rumored, after reading a collection of brother Ambrose's irreligious musings. (A second legend has it that she was eaten by cannibals—either way, it was an unlikely death.) The other boys, wrote Bierce, were "as nice, well-behaved a bevy of boys as ever you saw. They always attended Sunday School regularly, waiting with pious patience for the girls to come forth. They were an obedient seven, too; they knew well enough the respect due to parental authority, and when their father told them what was what, and which side up it ought to lie, they never tarried until he had more than picked up a hickory cudgel before tacitly admitting the correctness of riper judgment."[16]

Not even Gus, who later topped the scales at an epic three hundred pounds, or Addison, who became a strongman in a traveling circus, much impressed their sharp-tongued younger brother. And after a third brother, Aurelius, died in a carpentering accident at the early age—particularly for a Bierce—of thirty-two, a less-than-grief-stricken Ambrose memorialized him in a newspaper column as "Mr. Bildad Snobblepopkin, whose life furnishes an instructive lesson to fast livers." Aurelius/Snobblepopkin, wrote Bierce, "never tasted ardent spirits, ate spiced meats, or sat up later than nine o'clock. [He] rose, summer and winter, at two a.m., and passed an hour and three quarters immersed in ice water. For the last twenty years he has walked fifteen miles daily before breakfast, and then gone without breakfast. Up to the time of his death he had never spoken to a doctor, never had occasion to curse a dentist. If he had not been cut off by a circular saw at the early age of thirty-two, there is no telling how long he might have weathered it through. A life like this is so bright and shining an example that we are almost sorry he died." The resemblance, both physical and spiritual, between Aurelius and their father may have prompted the heavy-handed outburst, which even for Bierce was rather excessive.[17]

Outside the family, Bierce found the social pickings equally sparse. Although he dutifully trudged three miles to school each day from Walnut Creek in country-bumpkin brogans and homespun shirts, Ambrose made few close friends among his classmates. Even the girl who would later become his first sweetheart, Bernice Wright, could muster only a vague memory of the younger Ambrose (whom she called Brady) during their schooling. It was understandable; in the rough-and-tumble milieu of the rustic schoolyard Bierce resolutely stood apart, taking no interest in organized athletics, autumn hayrides, or winter dances. He later observed, with a certain wistful defiance, that he could never tell the difference between "Tick-tack-toe, Blind-man's bluff, and Simon-says-wig-wag." As for baseball and other popular sports, they were merely "the last shifts of intellectual vacuity militant against the Siren song of natural stagnation." He preferred to exercise alone, taking long walks in the woods around Warsaw, where he acquired a lifelong affinity for small animals, particularly those that were typically unloved—snakes and lizards being among his favorites. Dogs, on the other hand, with their slavish need for affection and approval, he always loathed; they were, he grumbled, "reekers, leakers, smilers and defilers." Nor did he much like cats. In one tall tale, "Cargo of Cat," he happily dispatched six thousand of the ship's felines by drowning. In typical adolescent fashion, Bierce walked abroad, brooding about his parents, his teachers, his classmates, and himself. Fifty years later, he still recalled the overwhelming disgust he felt within for the outside world. "Youth sees the nasty world stretched out before him," he told his publisher, Walter Neale. "He can go far in no direction without stepping into a cesspool. To him it is astonishing that his predecessors had not cleaned it up." Revealingly, the only surviving relic of his isolate schooldays is a handwritten copy of a child's epitaph, taken off a headstone in the local cemetery: "She tasted of life's bitter cup/Refused to drink her potion up/But turned her little head aside/Disgusted with the taste and died." One senses that Bierce, like Thomas Gray, spent a lot of time in country graveyards.[18]

When he turned fifteen, Ambrose left the family farm for good. Apparently with his parents' blessing, he moved into Warsaw and went to work as a printer's devil on editor Reuben Williams's newly minted abolitionist newspaper, the *Northern Indianan*. At the same time, he also moved into the Williams household, taking his meals with the family. This was a traditional step for bookish, literary-minded youths, as the fond reminiscences of Mark Twain, Benjamin Franklin, William Dean Howells, and other beginning American writers attest. It also had—for what it was worth—Marcus Bierce's wholehearted support, since Marcus was an early antislavery advocate who carefully pasted articles from other abolitionist newspapers into his home-made scrapbook, alongside such excruciatingly banal domestic verses as

"Daughter's First Walking," "The Little Girl's Lament for Her Country Home," and—perhaps pointedly—"Cheerfulness in a Young Wife." Surprisingly, Bierce never mentioned his professional apprenticeship, an omission that may be explained by the local legend that he left the newspaper after being falsely accused (and subsequently cleared) of theft.[19]

Whatever the reason for his abrupt departure from Warsaw journalism, the troubled teen was now taken in hand by his uncle, the family's resident great man, Lucius Verus Bierce. Lucius was Marcus's younger brother, but in all matters save the order of their births, Lucius was clearly the dominant male. He was the first to leave home, heading out at the precocious age of fifteen with a mere nickel to his name in search of a college education. For the next five years, he attended Ohio University in Athens, Ohio, graduating with a bachelor of arts degree in 1822. Then, perhaps foreshadowing his famous nephew's subsequent writing career and restless, wandering spirit, he embarked on a year-long walking tour of the South, a trek he later chronicled in a book, *Travels in the Southland.* Returning to Ohio, he studied law, opened a practice, and entered wholeheartedly into the breezy political give-and-take of Whig-dominated upstate Ohio. By the time Ambrose turned up on his doorstep in early 1859, Lucius had been mayor of Akron four different times, and he was a founding member of the state Republican party.[20]

Colorful, combative Uncle Lucius was everything Bierce's father was not, and it is likely that Ambrose modeled himself, at least in part, after his rowdy, larger-than-life relative. As far back as his great-great-great-uncle Joseph, who had fought with the British in King Philip's War, there was a family tradition of military service; and Lucius, despite the unfortunate handicap of living in an era of national peace, managed to find, by looking hard enough, his own war to fight. As a boy, Ambrose must have heard many times the story of Uncle Lucius's dramatic role in the abortive "liberation" of Canada. A longtime member of the Ohio militia and a leading figure in the secret military society known variously as the Hunters and Chasers of the Eastern Frontier, the Patriots, and the Grand Eagles, Lucius helped raise a ragtag force of five hundred disaffected Canadians, Americans, and Polish adventurers to invade Windsor, Ontario, and free the country from the presumably hateful British yoke. On December 3, 1838, "General" Bierce, as he now styled himself, led a contingent of volunteers across Lake Erie aboard a captured passenger steamer and set fire to the British barracks at Windsor. Then, foolishly dividing his forces, he moved into town with thirty men while the rest of the attackers incautiously bivouacked in a nearby apple orchard. Later that morning, an Anglo-Canadian militia force fell on the orchard, killing or capturing all the invaders camping there. Lucius and the others managed to commandeer a few canoes and paddle back across the Detroit River to U.S. territory, their return trip rather less grand than their embarkation.[21]

Subsequently, five of the captured invaders were hanged, and the rest were transported to Van Diemen's Land, Tasmania, which was about as far from Lake Erie as one could physically get. Lucius himself was prosecuted for violating American neutrality laws, but the indictments were quashed by popular demand. He returned to Akron with a new nickname, "The Hero of Windsor," and a captured British officer's sword that he carried with him for the rest of his life. Politically, the fiasco did him little harm, although one unfriendly Whig newspaper later groused that the only reason he had been nominated for the post of public prosecutor was because his supporters "supposed he would *run* well in Summitt because he [had] *run* so well at Windsor."[22]

By the mid-1850s, Lucius had another noble cause to espouse, this one somewhat closer to home: abolishing slavery in the American South. Since first seeing a slave auction in Charleston, South Carolina, on his youthful journey across the region, Lucius had been an ardent abolitionist, ever willing to put his money and his mouth to good use in the ongoing struggle against the "peculiar institution." By a curious coincidence, in 1855 he found himself in a position to aid materially the abolitionist cause. One of his friends and neighbors in Akron was a wild-haired, cold-eyed fellow-Connecticut emigrant named John Brown. As an attorney, Lucius was well acquainted with the chronically litigious Brown, who also happened to be a coreligionist in the local Congregational church (although much more fervent—fanatical, really—than the increasingly skeptical Lucius). Following passage of the Kansas-Nebraska Act in 1854 and the subsequent outbreak of violence in the affected territories, Brown determined to follow his erratic star and join the antislavery forces there. When he left Ohio, he took with him, compliments of Lucius Bierce, a wagonload of arms and ammunition somewhat questionably appropriated from a disbanded militia store in Tallmadge. Included in the haul were the broadswords carried by Lucius and his men in the Windsor campaign, the same broadswords that Brown and his henchmen would use to butcher a family of proslavery settlers on the banks of Pottawatomie Creek, Kansas, a few months hence. If Lucius felt any complicity in the crime, he never let it bother him. When Brown was hanged in December 1859 for the bloody fiasco at Harpers Ferry, Lucius urged that Akron's courts and businesses be closed, and mourning bells tolled for a solid hour across the town. At a rally that evening, he gave his old friend a rousing send-off, praising him as "the first martyr in the irrepressible conflict of liberty with slavery." Said Lucius: "Thank God I furnished him with arms, and right good use did he make of them. Men like Brown may die, but their acts and principles will live forever." Unlike, one might add, their victims.[23]

It is unclear how long Ambrose spent with his uncle in Akron (Lucius Bierce's donated papers burned up in a fire at Buchtel College, now the University of Akron, in 1899), but by the latter part of 1859, he was away at military school in Kentucky. Somehow, Lucius had persuaded the recalcitrant youth to enroll in the Kentucky Military Institute at Franklin Springs, a few miles west of the state capital at Frankfort. The school had been founded in 1847 by Col. Robert Thomas Pitcairn Allen, an 1834 graduate of West Point whose only previous claim to fame had been to burn down an old building on Academy grounds and thus get himself expelled for his troubles. Allen managed to win reinstatement from President Andrew Jackson (he eventually married Old Hickory's niece), and he later served without particular distinction in the Seminole War. Under Allen, KMI became one of the South's most prestigious military schools, training a number of future Confederates, including Maj. Gen. Robert F. Hoke, one of Robert E. Lee's seemingly endless legion of brave and talented junior officers.[24]

The school featured a demanding curriculum of Latin composition, English grammar, and American history, along with supplemental courses in architecture, political science, physiology, mathematics, constitutional law, and physical education. It also advertised, as an added attraction, "the distance of its location from the tempting and corrupting influences of the city"—that is, Frankfort. It was here, presumably, that Bierce acquired his characteristic military bearing and the useful skills of draftsmanship and cartography that would stand him in good stead in the years to come. Again, however, the documentary record is blank. The school, perhaps cursed by Allen's undergraduate caper, suffered two major fires in the decade of the 1850s, the second coming in Bierce's lone year of attendance, and the only tangible record of his presence at KMI is a catalog card listing him as "Bierce, Ambrose G., Ohio." The state reference might be to his place of birth, or it might signify his last known residence with his uncle in Akron. Either way, Bierce never referred to his undergraduate days at KMI, and by the summer of the next year, he was back in Indiana, although not back with his family.[25]

The period between his leaving Kentucky Military Institute and the beginning of the Civil War nine months later was the first of several times in his normally crowded life when Bierce, perhaps clinically depressed, drifted without energy through a series of menial—not to say demeaning—jobs. Settling in Elkhart, thirty miles due north of Warsaw, he marked time for a while as a common laborer in a brickyard, then went to work as a combination waiter and clerk at A. E. Faber's all-purpose ice cream parlor, oyster bar, dry goods store, and tavern. Serving up sandwiches and beers to the boys in the back room, and bolts of fabric, tenpenny nails, and five-cent dishes of ice cream to the more respectable citizens up front, Bierce struck his new neighbors as a "rather queer and different" young man whose future prospects were a decidedly "poor chance," according to town historian Maurice Frink. If he followed the momentous presidential election that fall and the accelerating breakup of the national union, he left behind no record of personal involvement. He must have gone back and forth between Elkhart and Warsaw several times, however, as he managed to renew his acquaintance with former classmate Bernice Wright, whose father operated a Warsaw boardinghouse. Bernice, whom Bierce had taken to calling, for some reason, Fatima, apparently took Brady's attention a good deal less seriously than he supposed; when he later sent her a rather delirious anonymous poem extolling the paradisaical nectar of her lips, she could not for the life of her puzzle out who it was she was supposed to have kissed, as the poet made clear, "twice…and only twice."[26]

How long Bierce might have drifted along, swotting out a humdrum blue-collar existence as a military school dropout turned soda jerk, is anyone's guess. But in the spring of 1861, for the first time in his life, he got lucky, even if the rest of the country did not: The Civil War erupted at Fort Sumter. Inspired perhaps by his uncle's abolitionist leanings—to say nothing of his likely desire to escape a dead-end job in a lonely new town—Bierce became the second man in Elkhart County to enlist in the Union army after Abraham Lincoln's call to arms in April 1861. On the nineteenth day of that month, he signed his name to the enlistment rolls of Company C, Ninth Indiana Volunteers, commanded by local attorney Robert H. Milroy. The jaundiced young man who disliked his parents, his siblings, his schoolmates, his neighbors, and the world at large now had found, if only temporarily, a calling greater than his own inverted bitterness. "At one time in my green and salad days," he later wrote, "I was sufficiently zealous for Freedom to engage in a four years' battle for its promotion. There were other issues involved, but they did not count for much with me." Albert, too, soon joined the fold, enlisting in the Eighteenth Ohio Light Artillery, which Uncle Lucius personally raised after his appointment as the state's assistant adjutant general.[27]

The regiment was due in Indianapolis in a week to start drilling, and Bierce, flushed with the sort of romanticized patriotism that was inducing young men on both sides of the Mason-Dixon line to pick up a rifle and march blithely off to war, had little time for long good-byes. He did, however, deliver himself of a transparently Keatsian sonnet that he secretly sent to Bernice Wright. It was a rather strange conjoining of love and sin, understandable perhaps in a boy who was still struggling to recover from a severe childhood bout with organized religion. No doubt he was proud of the poem, as young poets usually are of their silly and derivative verses, and Bernice was probably flattered, if mystified, to read:

> *Fatima, should an angel come from heaven,*
> *Bright with celestial ardor from above,*
> *And say no sin of mine should be forgiven,*
> *Till I should cease to sigh for thy dear love,—*
> *Though I'd acknowledge just was the decree,*
> *(For how can I love God adoring thee),*
> *I'd proudly point him back to heaven, and say*
> *"Give me her love,—wash not my sins away*

> *But double them upon my head, and bid me go*
> *When life is ended to the realms below."*
> *Thy love, dear girl, is worth eternal woe,*
> *And wouldst thou know whose heart thus yearns for thee*
> *And if thou knew couldst deign to pardon me*
> *Two moments sweet I've known in paradise:*
> *Thy lips have twice met mine and only twice.*[28]

All across the country, thousands of would-be Sir Richard Lovelaces were similarly bidding adieu to childhood sweethearts in that first fatal season of civil war. All the young men were marching off to war—or what they naïvely took war to be, a kind of high-spirited shoving match between two chivalrous and sporting opponents—and the only mercy in that childish image was that none of them could know how wrong it was, or how few of them would ever come marching home again once the war was over. Bierce would, but not for years, and by then he would be another person entirely from the callow, countrified teen who had reflexively answered his nation's call to arms. In the meantime, he would undergo an all-too-familiar rite of passage for American youths, a kind of reverse metamorphosis from carefree butterfly to cocooned moth, from boys playing tag in summer meadows to soldiers stalking death on ravaged fields. Still, in a curious though not entirely unpredictable way, the war would be good for Ambrose Bierce, as other wars have been good for other budding writers—those who survive them, anyway: It would give him a voice. And if anyone may be said to have been prepared for the human catastrophe about to occur, it was the dream-haunted, God-hating, graveyard-tromping Bierce. The whole country was about to turn into a cemetery, its best and its least lying down together on an impious altar of pride and hate. And somewhere in between, like Ishmael bobbing on Queequeg's coffin, the scarred survivor of a nightmare voyage, was eighteen-year-old Ambrose Bierce—seeing, feeling, and remembering.

2

What I Saw of Shiloh

hile obscure, unfavored Ambrose Bierce was en route from Elkhart to Indianapolis to begin training as a full-fledged member of Company C, Ninth Indiana Volunteer Infantry Regiment, thousands of other young men throughout the country—many of them with more to lose than Bierce—were making their own decisions for peace or war. In Cambridge, Massachusetts, Harvard senior Oliver Wendell Holmes, Jr., son of the famous New England poet, enlisted in the Twentieth Massachusetts Regiment four days after Bierce signed up in Indiana. Holmes's decision, coming mere weeks before his class was due to graduate, elicited a bemused and somewhat defensive letter from a distant acquaintance named William Dean Howells, who wondered, "I hear by circuitous route that you have enlisted. If so, how? why? when?" Howells, a Columbus, Ohio, journalist who had just written a campaign biography of Abraham Lincoln and thus was in line for a coveted appointment as American consul to Venice, gave a meteorological reason for not enlisting himself: "The hot weather comes on. The drill will be very hot and oppressive. And whatever valor I have had in earlier years has been pretty well metaphysicked out of me, since I came of thought." A few months later, from the safety of Venice, Howells would complain to another friend, "Aren't you sorry the Atlantic goes so gun-powerfully into the war? It's patriotic; but do we not get enough in the newspapers? I would rather have the honey of Attic bees."[1]

In New York City, another newspaperman turned esthete, forty-two-year-old poet Walt Whitman, quickly decided that war was a young man's game and settled instead for a personal pledge to abjure liquor, fat meats, and late-night dinners in order to give himself "a purged, cleansed, spiritualized, invigorated body." His younger brother George Washington Whitman, however, did sign up after joining a quarter of a million other New Yorkers at Union Square in welcoming Maj. Robert Anderson, the hero of Fort Sumter, to their fair city. Whitman would later hurry to his brother's side after George had been wounded at the Battle of Fredericksburg; and there, in the rank, fever-ridden hospitals of Washington, D.C., he would render his own form of service—changing bandages, writing letters, telling stories, and holding the hands of dozens of sick and dying young soldiers. Asked after the war if he ever went back to those "Specimen Days," Whitman responded, "I have never left them."[2]

In the exclusive seaside resort of Newport, Rhode Island, bookish, delicate Henry James, Jr., celebrated his eighteenth birthday on the same day that newly sworn President Abraham Lincoln called for 75,000 volunteers, Bierce and Holmes among them, to put down the rapidly spreading Southern rebellion. James, soon to fall victim to an "obscure hurt" that would conveniently leave him unfit for military service (although not for Harvard Law School), contented himself with watching the state militia sail off into the distance. Also taking to the seas, but bound for London, not the Virginia front, was twenty-four-year-old Henry Adams, the grandson and great-grandson of American presidents. The younger Adams was en route to the Court of St. James's, where his father had just been appointed Lincoln's minister to Great Britain. Unlike Howells, Adams would occasionally regret—although not too much—his absence from the battlefield, but he would come to see his service at court as its own kind of "fury of fire," one in which he had shown himself to be "confident in times of doubt, steady in times of disaster, cool and quiet at all times, and unshaken under any pressure."[3]

In the South, too, young men awaited the coming of war. At Oglethorpe University, then located in Milledgeville, Georgia, poet-musician Sidney Lanier took time away from his duties as a postgraduate tutor to watch a crowd of fellow students raise a new Confederate flag over the campus. A few weeks later, Lanier would leave school and join his hometown Macon Guards, marching off to Virginia with a jaunty "On to the Field of Glory!" Another southern poet, Charleston-born Henry Timrod, dashed off an ode to the virtues of "The Cotton-Boll," then enlisted in the Thirtieth South Carolina Regiment. Fortunately for Timrod, a lifelong consumptive, the regiment was commanded by a family friend, and he was given the relatively soft post of regimental secretary. Even that quickly proved too much for Timrod, and he exchanged his warrior's uniform for a correspondent's pass, although he was so nearsighted and night-blind that a colleague "had to carry him around, at dusk, as if he were sightless." Meanwhile, on the Mississippi River, a carrot-topped young riverboat pilot named Sam Clemens was enduring a nervous trip upriver from New Orleans to St. Louis, in constant fear that one side or the other would conscript him into service on a naval warship. Clemens eventually made it home to Hannibal, Missouri, and secretly joined the pro-Southern Marion Rangers before lighting out for the territories a few weeks later and gratefully leaving the Civil War and all its attendant terrors behind him.[4]

Howells, Adams, James, and Clemens, "the four malingerers," in literary critic Daniel Aaron's pungent phrase, would sit out the war in European drawing rooms, Back Bay student's quarters, or, in Clemens's case, a Nevada mining camp. They were, said Aaron, "the men probably best endowed, if not the most temperamentally suited, to record the War in history or fiction." The only trouble was, they "never got close enough to the fighting to write about it." That honor, dubious though it was, ultimately would fall to less gifted, less learned, but physically braver Ambrose Bierce, who, of all the Boys of '61, would be the only one to make anything approaching great art out of the looming national calamity. But first, he would have to make himself a soldier, and—more to the point—he would have to survive the war. For he would certainly get close enough to the fighting to learn all that anyone would want to know about how men fought and died, suffered and bled, in defense of abstract political concepts and vague, high-sounding calls to glory.[5]

The nascent regiment debarked at Camp Morton, on the outskirts of Indianapolis. The camp was named for the state's new Republican governor, Oliver P. Morton. Like Bierce's uncle Lucius, Morton was one of the GOP's founding members and a rabid supporter of Abraham Lincoln. "If it was worth a bloody struggle to establish this nation," Morton thundered in April 1861, "it is worth one to preserve it." In response to the President's call for troops, Morton obligingly produced nearly three times the requested number of Hoosier recruits, who were hastily jammed into the state fairgrounds to begin their brief passage from farm boys to soldiers. Indiana was ill-prepared for war, the state's arsenal containing a grand total of thirteen vintage 1812 muskets and two rusty horse pistols, and the twelve thousand new recruits drilled somewhat self-consciously in civilian clothes, armed only with broom handles, during the first chaotic weeks at camp. At night, they slept in the fairground's stock barns—which, given their subsequent role in the war, was an irony worthy of Bierce himself. By war's end, some 24,400 Indianans, roughly 12 percent of all Union losses, would fall to rebel bullets or epidemic diseases; and the indefatigable Morton would see to it that 57 percent of the state's eligible men were in uniform, second only to Kansas's total of 59.4 percent.[6]

The Ninth Indiana, like most midwestern regiments, was composed mainly of farmers, with a smattering of shop clerks, schoolboys, and the odd prairie-sown individualist like Bierce who did not fall neatly into any particular category. Robert H. Milroy, an attorney from Salem, was chosen the regiment's commanding colonel. Unlike many of the political appointees at the beginning of the war, Milroy at least had some formal military training and experience to go along with his bureaucratic clout: a master of military science degree from Partridge's Academy in Norwich, Vermont, and a stint as captain in the First Indiana Volunteers in the Mexican War. A stern, bearded, vaguely biblical-looking figure, Milroy would later live up to his daunting appearance by suppressing pro-Southern guerrillas in West Virginia so ruthlessly that the Confederate government would put a price on his head. A less august, but no doubt welcome, member of the regiment was Oliver Wright, Fatima's brother, who kept his sister apprised of Company C's progress and, perhaps guilelessly, urged her to show Bierce a good time if and when he made it back to Warsaw.[7]

After five weeks of slogging through sodden late-spring rains, the regiment was deemed ready for offensive action. Governor Morton personally accompanied Maj. Gen. George B. McClellan, commander of the Department of the Ohio, to the campground for a formal review, then bade the regiment a ringing farewell when it left camp at midnight on May 29 to entrain for the front in western Virginia, the first Indiana unit to march away to war. After a nine-hour wait at the railway station, the regiment finally began rumbling across central Ohio, where it was met by wildly cheering crowds and flower-strewing maidens. "It is said," wrote a delirious Indianapolis *Sentinel* correspondent, "that more than one gallant patriot received kisses from the 'rosy mouths' of some of Ohio's fairest daughters. In the name of heaven, what can not men do when thus prompted to defend the best constitution and happiest country in the world from destruction?"[8]

What indeed? Two days later, the stalwart defenders, in new blue uniforms with real muskets at their sides, reached Grafton, Virginia, near Tygart Lake. Here they learned that a Confederate force had taken up residence in the little town of Philippi, eighteen miles south on the Beverly-Fairmont Pike. The rebels were a mixed bag, at best. The green-as-grass infantry, which had just received a shipment of unusable cartridges and rusted rifles, was being trained by a group of sixteen-year-old Virginia Military Institute cadets. Meanwhile, the cavalry could boast a goodly supply of military tents, but scarcely any weapons (one company was armed with forty sabers and one pistol). Nevertheless, under a hard-pressed young colonel named George A. Porterfield, the Southerners had managed to burn two important railroad bridges above Grafton before pulling back to Philippi. There, warned by a couple of pro-Confederate young ladies that the Yankees were planning to attack them forthwith, Porterfield and his men loaded their meager supplies onto a few creaky wagons and prepared to retreat at the first sign of danger.[9]

Back at Grafton, the Union high command—Milroy, Brig. Gen. Thomas A. Morris, Col. Benjamin F. Kelley, and Brig. Gen. Frederick W. Lander, an aide-de-camp of McClellan, who was directing operations from far-off Cincinnati—met to make their battle plans. While they fumed, formulated, and strategized, Bierce and his comrades took stock of their new surroundings. "It was a strange country," wrote Bierce. "Nine in ten of us had never seen a mountain, nor a hill as high as a church spire, until we had crossed the Ohio River. To a member of a plains-tribe, born and reared on the flats of Ohio or Indiana, a mountain region was a perpetual miracle. Space seemed to have taken on a new dimension." The officers decided to divide their forces and fall on Philippi from two directions, above and below the town. After a miserable night-long march through pouring rain, the Federals reached their jumping-off points before dawn and waited for the prearranged signal of a lone pistol shot to begin the attack. Unfortunately, another female Confederate sympathizer, Mrs. Thomas Humphreys, was awakened by well-soaked Yankee soldiers trudging through her yard and attempted to send her son racing into town to spread the alarm. When the Union forces quite logically objected to Mrs. Humphreys's plan, she took a potshot at them with her own pistol. Northern artillerists, hearing what sounded to them like the signal, helpfully unleashed a barrage of cannon fire in the general direction of Philippi, without undue reference to the respective positions of friend or foe.[10]

Milroy's regiment, Bierce included, ducked and shimmied beneath the random shelling. Fortunately for them, the Confederates inside Philippi, already standing with one foot out the door, so to speak, swiftly followed with the other, and the first battle of the Civil War degenerated into its mocking historical tag name, "the Philippi Races." One Ohio gunner gloated over the marvelous effect a round or two of his hardware seemed to have on the startled enemy. "Out they swarmed, like bees from a molested hive," he wrote. "This way and that the chivalry flew, and yet scarcely knew which way to run." Bierce, for his part, was less impressed by the shelling, perhaps because he had been under it. "We shot off a Confederate leg at Philippi," he remarked offhandedly in his postwar memoir, "On a Mountain." Actually, the Southern casualty was rather significant, in both a military and a medical sense. The wounded reb, a Washington College student named James E. Hanger, had been sheltering inside a stable with the rest of the Churchville (Virginia) Cavalry when the first solid Union cannon shot of the war, a six-pound ball, hit nearby, ricocheted off the barnyard turf, and bounded malignly into the stable, striking him squarely in the leg. That night, at the hands of a Union doctor, Hanger underwent the first battle-field amputation of the war. During his subsequent recuperation, the resourceful convalescent designed and built an artificial leg from barrel staves, and he later convinced the Confederate government in Richmond to give him an all-too-lucrative business fashioning artificial limbs for Southern soldiers. His firm, the J. E. Hanger Company, remains the world's largest manufacturer of artificial limbs. Forty-two years later, Bierce looked in on Hanger at Philippi, typically noting that he was "still minus the leg; no new one had grown on."[11]

Another casualty of the battle made a more meaningful impression on Bierce. Colonel Kelley, commander of the First Virginia (Union) Infantry, had ridden after the retreating rebels, firing off a few complimentary rounds with his sidearm. A Rebel private, John Shefee, answered back, hitting the reckless Kelley squarely in the chest. While General Lander took the marksman into custody, Kelley was carried into a nearby tavern to die. Bierce got a good look at his first Union casualty—a colonel, no less. Kelley, he remembered, had been shot "spang through the breast, a hole that you could have put two fingers in. And, bless my soul! how it bled! Wounds were new to my observation in those golden days, and I said to myself, with Lady Macbeth: 'Who would have thought the old man [Kelley had just turned fifty-four] to have had so much blood in him!'" Surprisingly, Kelley recovered from his wound; indeed, it earned him a brigadier's star. He would spend the rest of the war safeguarding the Baltimore & Ohio Railroad in West Virginia. His exasperated superior, Maj. Gen. Phil Sheridan, would later complain that "General Kelley is very cautious about that which is in little danger, and not remarkably so about that which is," a remark that was given added weight when Kelley managed to get himself captured by Southern guerrillas, along with fellow Union general George Crook, in a Cumberland, Maryland, hotel in early 1865.[12]

As for the Union artillerists who had given him and his comrades a nasty few minutes at the start of the battle, Bierce later exacted an indirect revenge. His short story "One Kind of Officer" concerns a Northern artillery captain literally trapped in the fog of war (a heavy white mist obscures the battlefield) who is brusquely ordered to fire on anything moving in front of him. Insulted by the dismissive manner of the brigadier general giving him the order—"Captain Ransome, it is not permitted to you to know anything. It is sufficient that you obey my order"—Ransome obtusely allows his men to fire on their own army, even after a lieutenant in his battery informs him of the tragic error. When a higher-ranking general rides up and demands to know why Ransome has been killing his own men, the captain airily replies, "That I am unable to say. In my orders that information was withheld. It appeared to be none of my business." Ransome apparently hopes to embarrass the general who gave him the order. Unfortunately for him, that officer has already been killed in the fighting, and the young lieutenant who witnessed the initial order (and whom Ransome gratuitously insulted in turn) refuses to confirm that the captain had been acting under direct, peremptory orders. Trapped by his own vindictiveness, Ransome foresees his inevitable execution—a fate that Bierce and the rest of his regiment probably wished on all the Federal gunners at Philippi.[13]

After their tragicomic initiation into the fraternity of war, the men of the Ninth Indiana spent a somewhat sylvan next few weeks camping out atop Cheat Mountain below Philippi. Ever afterward, Bierce saw his days in western Virginia through an uncharacteristically golden glow. "Looking back upon it through the haze of near half a century," he wrote, "I see that region as a veritable realm of enchantment; the Alleghenies as the Delectable Mountains. I note again their dim, blue billows, ridge after ridge interminable, beyond purple valleys full of sleep 'in which it seemed always afternoon.'" He and his tentmates wandered the countryside like city boys away at summer camp, carving rings and pipes out of laurel roots and avidly gathering spruce gum to mail to the folks back home. "The flatlanders who invaded the Cheat Mountain country had been suckled in another creed," he wrote, "and to them western Virginia—there was, as yet, no West Virginia—was an enchanted land. How we reveled in its savage beauties!"[14]

In one sense, at least, Bierce's memory was faulty. There was, or shortly would be, a West Virginia, thanks in large part to the skirmish at Philippi. On June 11, eight days after the battle, pro-Union delegates from Virginia's western counties convened at Wheeling and voted to secede from the Old Dominion and set up their own provisional state government. This decision delighted George McClellan, confirming his choice of the railroad-rich region as the logical starting place for offensive operations, but it put Bierce and his fellow volunteers squarely back in harm's way. Responding to the Confederate defeat at Philippi, Southern general Robert E. Lee sent reinforcements racing through the Allegheny Mountains to hold the vital Parkersburg-Staunton Turnpike. As a measure of Lee's concern, he chose his own adjutant, forty-one-year-old Brig. Gen. Robert S. Garnett, to direct the holding operation. Garnett, a graduate and former commandant of the United States Military Academy at West Point, threw his 4,500 troops across two key passes at Rich Mountain and Laurel Hill, near the town of Beverly. McClellan rushed to the scene as well, arriving in Grafton on June 23 and issuing a grandiloquent declaration to the troops that was struck off on his own handy printing press: "Soldiers! I have heard there was danger here. I have come to place myself at your head and share it with you. I fear now but one thing—that you will not find foemen worthy of your steel."[15]

What, if anything, he and his messmates made of McClellan's fiery pronouncement Bierce did not say, but its immediate effect was to put an end to their month-long summer idyll. Behind their new brigadier, Thomas Morris—"a timid old woman," in McClellan's private opinion—they marched off on July 3 to confront Garnett's forces at Laurel Hill. Morris, who, like McClellan, had finished in the top four of his class at West Point, was under orders to "amuse" Garnett while McClellan personally led a larger attacking force against Col. John Pegram's thirteen hundred rebels farther south at Rich Mountain. Upon arriving at the base of the hill, Morris was chagrined to discover that the Confederate force he was supposed to amuse actually outnumbered his own. "I confess I feel apprehensive unless our force could equal theirs," he reported, not without reason, to McClellan. But McClellan was having none of it. He fired back that he had proposed to take "the really difficult & dangerous part of this work on my own hands," not bothering to explain why his 7,000 men were in more danger from 1,300 of the enemy than Morris and his 3,500 men were from 4,000. "I must have Generals under me who are willing to risk as much as I am," McClellan added. Apprehensive or not, Morris would not get any additional troops—what was more, he was given to understand that if he asked for any extra men, he would be duly relieved of duty and sent back to Indiana. Morris wisely took the hint.[16]

While McClellan's column attacked the rebels at Rich Mountain on July 11, Morris's troops peppered away at the Confederate breastworks on Laurel Hill. Bierce and his company found shelter in a convenient clump of trees and traded potshots all afternoon with the Southerner defenders. Just before nightfall, wrote Bierce, "a few dozen of us, who had been swapping shots with the enemy's skirmishers, grew tired of the resultless battle, and by a common impulse, and I think without orders or officers, ran forward into the woods and attacked the Confederate works. We did well enough, considering the hopeless folly of the movement, but we came out of the woods faster than we went in, a good deal. This was the affair in which Corporal Dyson Boothroyd of Company 'A' fell with a mortal wound." As he would do in all his Civil War reminiscences, Bierce was being modest about his own part in the fighting. Actually, he was something of a hero, and an Indianapolis *Journal* reporter happened to be on hand to record Bierce's first public act of distinction. "Privates A. J. [*sic*] Bierce and Boothroyd, Ninth Indiana Volunteers, advanced up the hill to within fifteen paces of the enemy's breastworks when Boothroyd was wounded in the neck by a rifle ball, paralyzing him," the correspondent wrote. "Bierce, in open view of the enemy, carried poor Boothroyd and his gun without other assistance, fully twenty rods, balls falling around him like hail." It was, in a way, oddly similar to Ernest Hemingway's equally brave feat in the First World War, when he single-handedly carried a wounded Italian soldier back to their lines on his back, the signal difference being that Bierce, unlike Hemingway, was not seriously wounded for his troubles. In both cases, the rescued parties soon died, perhaps confirming for the embryonic authors the intrinsic absurdity of valorous deeds. Bierce, again like Hemingway, later returned to his first battlefield and "found the very rock against which [Boothroyd] lay." The old camp, he reported with italicized irony, "is now a *race track*." Both Bierce and Hemingway took for granted their physical courage; Bierce, however, never felt the need to advertise his.[17]

McClellan's forces, after a daylong fight, managed to dislodge the Confederate defenders from Rich Mountain and send them stumbling northward through the rocky darkness in hopes of linking up with Garnett's troops at Laurel Hill. Unknown to them, Garnett had already heard about their mishap and decided to cut his own losses, vacating the hillside and making tracks for the Cheat River ten miles northeast. Bierce and his fellows followed them, catching up with the rebels at Carrick's Ford and shooting Garnett dead on the banks of the river—the first general to be killed in the war. Meanwhile, McClellan surrounded and captured Pegram and half of his dis-integrating force. The Battle of Rich Mountain (Laurel Hill being considered merely a skirmish) gained control of western Virginia for the Union and brought McClellan, in the wake of the Northern debacle at Bull Run eight days later, command of the Army of the Potomac. "Soldiers of the Army of the West!" he exulted. "I am more than satisfied with you. You have annihi-lated two armies, commanded by educated and experienced soldiers, and entrenched in mountain fastnesses fortified at their leisure. I have confidence in you, and I trust you have learned to confide in me." Perhaps they had, but Bierce and the rest of the Ninth Regiment did not linger long enough in West Virginia to try out their newfound intimacy with their commanding general. By the end of the month, they were back in Indianapolis, their three-month enlistments successfully concluded, and were feted with a lavish ban-quet and a dress parade through town. Most of them immediately re-upped when the regiment was reorganized in late August, and Bierce, probably due to his hero's role at Laurel Hill, was promoted to sergeant and then to sergeant major. "The army," wrote one former neighbor a little wonderingly, "seemed to bring out in young Ambrose things that had never been seen in Elkhart"—or Warsaw, either, for that matter.[18]

Despite McClellan's earlier boast that "our success is complete & secession is killed in this country," Bierce and his regiment were soon back in Virginia, making sure that secession—or, at any rate, its stubbornly unburied ghost—remained dead. They found themselves again in the Cheat Mountain Valley, "holding a road that ran from Nowhere to the southeast." As veterans of the summer campaign, Bierce noticed that "we were regarded by the others with profound respect as 'old soldiers.' (Our ages, if equalized, would, I fancy, have given about twenty years to each man.) We gave ourselves, this aristoc-racy of service, no end of military airs; some of us even going to the extreme of keeping our jackets buttoned and our hair combed. We now 'brought to the task' of subduing the Rebellion a patriotism which never for a moment doubted that a rebel was a fiend accursed of God and the angels." Their bur-geoning patriotism would soon be tested. Robert E. Lee, stung by the loss of western Virginia, personally led a new force into the valley, with the stated intention of retaking Cheat Mountain from the Union invaders.[19]

Bierce's regiment, at Elkwater, was too far away to take part in the mis-handled Confederate attack on Cheat Mountain on September 12, but on October 3, it participated in a reconnaissance in force against rebel breastworks near the Greenbrier River. The subsequent skirmish there "has not got into history," wrote Bierce, "but it had a real objective existence. Its short and simple annals are that we marched a long way and lay down before a fortified camp of the enemy at the farther edge of a valley. Our commander had the forethought to see that we lay well out of range of the small-arms of the period. A disadvantage of this arrangement was that the enemy was out of reach of us as well, for our rifles were not better than his. Unfortunately—one might almost say unfairly—he had a few pieces of artillery very well protected, and with those he mauled us to the eminent satisfaction of his mind and heart. So we parted from him in anger and returned to our own place, leaving our dead—not many." One of the dead the regiment left behind was a fellow named Abbott, whose taking off, Bierce remembered with mordant irony, was distinctly unusual. "He was lying flat upon his stomach," Bierce wrote, "and was killed by being struck in the side by a nearly spent cannon-shot that came rolling in among us. The shot remained in him until removed. It was a solid round-shot, evidently cast in some private foundry, whose proprietor had put his 'imprint' upon it: it bore, in slightly sunken letters, the name 'Abbott.'" The nineteen-year-old Bierce was quickly becoming a connoisseur of the grotesque.[20]

Two months later, both his irony and his patriotism were severely challenged by a new engagement at Camp Allegheny, at the southern end of the Tygart Valley. Brig. Gen. Joseph J. Reynolds, the new brigade commander, had determined to probe the enemy defenses at Buffalo Mountain, a move that Bierce, as a rapidly seasoned veteran, justifiably considered one that was being made "more to keep up the appearance of doing something than with a hope of accomplishing a military result." What it accomplished was a stinging Union defeat. "Here," wrote Bierce, "the regiment had its hardest fight in Western Virginia, and was most gloriously thrashed." Revisiting the site decades after the war, Bierce found the rebel breastworks still standing, although so rotten that he could pick through the timber with his fingers for souvenir bullets (to his disappointment, he found none). The works had been admirably constructed to defend both front and rear, a wise choice, since Reynolds divided the attackers into two columns, each led by a guide who was a native of the parts. When the columns predictably failed to converge on the site for a simultaneous attack, the rebels found themselves enjoying "that inestimable military advantage known in civilian speech as being 'surrounded.'" Bierce's column, attacking from the rear, was pinned down behind an obstacle course of fallen timbers, an act that probably saved their lives, said Bierce, since it prevented them from forming into line for a frontal assault. "We took cover," he wrote, "and pot-shotted the fellows behind the parapet all day and then withdrew and began our long retreat in a frame of mind that would have done credit to an imp of Satan."[21]

The regimental mind-set was scarcely improved by the sight that greeted them along their retreat. They had already passed "some things lying by the wayside" on their way to the front. These "things" turned out to be the corpses of Union scouts slain by "Allegheny Ed" Johnson's Confederate troops in an earlier skirmish. Bierce, with his avid eye for the macabre, had already examined the bodies, "curiously lifting the blankets from their yellow-clay faces. How repulsive they looked with their blood-smears, their blank, staring eyes, their teeth uncovered by contraction of the lips!" The sight of their dead comrades left the men of the Ninth speechless—"for an hour afterward the injunction of silence in the ranks was needless." The troops were still as patriotic as ever, observed Bierce, "but we did not wish to be that way."[22]

Repassing the site the next day, "feeble from fatigue and savage from defeat," Bierce and the others were surprised to see that the dead men seemed to have altered their positions and thrown off their covering. The reason— and its effect—was quickly seen. A herd of wild pigs had eaten the faces off the dead men. Years later, in his short story "The Coup de Grace," Bierce gives a graphic rendering of the hideous sight: "Fifty yards away, on the crest of a low, thinly wooded hill, he saw several dark objects moving about among the fallen men—a herd of swine. One stood with his back to him, its shoulders sharply elevated. Its forefeet were upon a human body, its head was depressed and invisible. The bristly ridge of its chine showed black against the red west. The swine, catching sight of him, threw up their crimson muzzles, regarding him suspiciously a second, and then with a gruff, concerted grunt, raced away out of sight." The real-life soldiers quickly shot the pigs— Bierce termed it "a military execution"—but they could not bring themselves to eat the repulsive animals. "The shooting of several kinds was good in the Cheat Mountain country, even in 1861," he noted dryly.[23]

Bierce would make use of the mountainous West Virginia terrain in another postwar story, "A Horseman in the Sky." In it, the civilian guide who led Bierce's column up to the rebel camp at Buffalo Mountain is personified by a young, wellborn Virginian who has impulsively joined the Union army at Grafton. This traitor to Virginia, as his father sorrowfully calls him, finds himself posted as a sentry in a clump of laurel overlooking a sheer drop-off hundreds of feet below. The character's name, Carter Druse, bears a certain euphonic similarity to the author's, and it is perhaps something of a private joke that he is described as "the son of wealthy parents, an only child, [who] had known such ease and cultivation and high living as wealth and taste were able to command." Aware that his regiment is planning a surprise attack on the enemy camp that night, Druse is startled to see a Confederate scout suddenly appear on horseback on the ridge across the way. After a brief internal debate in which Druse struggles to reconcile himself with the act of shooting the horseman from ambush, he remembers his father's parting injunction to "do what you conceive to be your duty." He shoots the rider's horse, sending both man and beast plunging over the sheer precipice, and a Union officer coming up the mountainside witnesses "an astonishing sight—a man on horseback riding down into the valley through the air!" The horseman in the sky turns out to be Druse's own father, and the hardened sergeant to whom he later tells the story can scarcely stomach Druse's act. "Good God!" he says, walking away. The story, like those in *The Parenticide Club,* is another of Bierce's compulsive acts of patricide, and the image of the rider on horseback silently plunging through the air to his death, his long hair streaming upward like a plume, is genuinely eerie and affecting.[24]

The affair at Camp Allegheny was the last fighting Bierce's regiment would see in Virginia. After a frigid winter atop Cheat Mountain, "guard[ing] the pass through which nobody wanted to go," the unit was ordered south to Tennessee, where it joined Brig. Gen. William Nelson's division at Nashville in February 1862. The months in the mountains had had a kind of Rip van Winkle quality about them, an out-of-time experience to which even the preternaturally jaded Bierce responded. Apparently, however, the Virginia campaigning had not made full-grown soldiers out of the Ninth. Their new brigade commander, Ohio-born Col. William B. Hazen, complained upon their arrival that the men "seemed fixed in many vicious habits, acquired while in the three months' service in Western Virginia. To correct this, some severity was indispensable." If severity and discipline were what the regiment needed, they had definitely come to the right man. William Babcock Hazen, then thirty-one, was Regular Army, an 1855 graduate of West Point who had already fought Rogue River Indians in Oregon and been wounded by Comanches in Texas. A boyhood friend of future President James A. Garfield, Hazen had parlayed his Academy background into command of the new Nineteenth Brigade in Nelson's division of Maj. Gen. Don Carlos Buell's Army of the Ohio.[25]

A squat, spruce, rather Prussian-looking soldier with a dandified Vandyke beard (he would later spend a delighted tour as an official observer with the victorious Germans during the Franco-Prussian War), Hazen was a former West Point tactics instructor who was even then developing a career-long habit of criticizing superiors and arguing with equals that would later cause one disgruntled fellow officer to assert that "Hazen was a synonym of insubordination." His opening salutation to Col. Gideon C. Moody, the new commander of the Ninth Indiana (Milroy had been promoted and left behind in western Virginia to commence his persecution of pro-Southern civilians), was a tart injunction to convene his junior officers nightly and read them *The Articles of War* and *The Regulations of the Army* "until they are properly understood by all." The regiment unhappily found itself drilling for an hour and a half each morning, regularly patrolled by "sentinels of the police-guard" who were pointedly enjoined "to prevent any further shouting, such as was faintly heard on the return of the regiment yesterday." Apparently, there were some in the regiment who did not take kindly to Colonel Hazen.[26]

Bierce, in his typical unpredictability, was not among them; he worshiped Hazen from the start. Here was a plain-talking, straight-walking young officer who was not afraid to crack heads, a man who spoke his mind to both private and general alike, the very beau ideal of a congenital naysayer like Bierce. Years afterward, the author would praise Hazen as "my commander and my friend, my master in the art of war. He was aggressive, arrogant, tyrannical, honorable, truthful, courageous, a skillful soldier, a faithful friend, and one of the most exasperating of men"—not a bad description of Bierce himself. In time, Bierce would come to serve on Hazen's personal staff; now he was merely one of four thousand anonymous men in Hazen's brigade, a newly minted sergeant major with a bristling brush mustache and clear blue eyes who was straining to teach his bark-rough company how to properly count cadence and shoulder arms.[27]

The brigade would soon need every bit of the advanced training it received from Hazen at Nashville's Camp Andrew Jackson. On March 29, it moved south with the rest of Nelson's division and three other divisions from Buell's army to join Maj. Gen. Ulysses S. Grant's massive Union force, then encamped on the west bank of the Tennessee River near Pittsburg Landing in southwestern Tennessee. Grant, the recent victor of Fort Donelson, was preparing—somewhat laxly—to move against the remainder of the Confederate army, which had taken refuge at the railroad center of Corinth, Mississippi, just across the state line from the Union camp. Grant's soldiers had pitched their tents on a wide plateau falling away from a one-hundred-foot-high yellow clay bluff overlooking the river landing. The site, bordered on its flanks by Lick and Snake creeks, was marshy and ravine-riddled, and when occupied by the better part of five full divisions, it was as jam-packed as a Chicago stock pen. Nevertheless, it had been chosen by Grant's senior subordinate, Brig. Gen. William Tecumseh Sherman, as a "magnificent plain for camping and drilling." The Northern soldiers did rather more of the first than the second, making themselves tolerably comfortable while they waited for Buell's army to come down from Nashville.[28]

Harking back to his first wartime success at Belmont, Missouri, Grant felt he had learned a valuable lesson; simply put, it was that the enemy was as afraid of him as he was of them, and "from that event to the close of the war, I never experienced trepidation upon confronting an enemy." It would soon prove a costly opinion for an army commander to hold. Foolishly deciding not to fortify his camp, since such precautions might dispirit the men, Grant was aided and abetted in his carelessness by the red-bearded Sherman, who blithely reported that "I do not apprehend anything like an attack on our position." Sherman went on to tell one nervous young colonel to "take your

damn regiment back to Ohio. There is no enemy nearer than Corinth."
Corinth was twenty-three miles away from the Union camp, and Sherman
was off by about twenty-two miles; having marched up from Mississippi in a
downpour of rain, the Confederate army was preparing, even then, for a pre-
emptive predawn attack. The Southern commander, Gen. Albert Sidney
Johnston, had little fear of Grant's forty thousand men. "I would fight them
if they were a million," he declared, urging his own 44,000 troops to throw
back the "agrarian mercenaries sent to subjugate and despoil you of your lib-
erties, property, and honor."[29]

Bierce and his fellow despoilers doubtless would have laughed at Johnston's quaint characterization of them, but on the morning of April 6, they
were too busy marching toward the sound of the guns. The Battle of Shiloh,
named for a nearby Sunday-go-to-meeting place, had begun at dawn, with
Johnston's ragged rebels bursting from the woods beyond the Union camp to
catch the unwary Federals asleep in their tents and spit them on their bayonets like so many ears of corn. Sherman, standing beside an orderly, saw the
first graycoats materializing in the mist beyond. A bullet swiftly toppled the
orderly, and Sherman finally conceded the obvious: "My God, we are
attacked!" Grant was sitting down to breakfast at his headquarters on the east
bank of the river at Savannah when he heard the gunfire in the distance.
Rapidly losing his appetite, he boarded an army steamboat and chugged off
toward Pittsburg Landing, sending a hurried note to William Nelson to bring
his division up to the landing immediately. "If you will get upon the field,
leaving all our baggage on the east bank of the river," Grant added, "it will be
a move to our advantage and possibly save the day to us. The rebel force is
estimated at over 100,000 men."[30]

Although Grant had badly miscounted the strength of the enemy, he was
absolutely right about the danger he was in. Nelson's division—Bierce
included—was a good ten miles away from Pittsburg Landing, drawing three
days' worth of rations, when the summons came, and for some reason it took
the division several costly hours to get under way. In the meantime, the surg-
ing Confederates drove the Union veterans steadily backward toward the
river; and only a brave but doomed stand by Virginia-born Unionist Benjamin Prentiss's division in a shallow wagon trench in the center of the Federal line gave Grant enough time to reform his shaken army in a mile-wide
arc from Snake Creek on the right to Pittsburg Landing on the left. By the
time Bierce's brigade arrived on the opposite side of the river, having lost fully
one-third of its number to sheer exhaustion in the headlong race to the battlefield, it was sundown. Both sides were effectively in shock from the unparalleled bloodletting they had already inflicted upon each other. Before the
battle was over, more Americans would be killed—and kill one another—
than had died in the Revolutionary War, the War of 1812, and the Mexican
War put together.[31]

Bierce and his comrades could not know this, of course, but the milling herd of skulkers and malingerers on the bank across the way were quick to tell them precisely what regions of hell they were about to enter. In his masterful reminiscence of the battle, "What I Saw of Shiloh," published in the San Francisco *Wasp* in December 1881, Bierce vividly recalls the scene at the riverfront: "Along the sheltered strip of beach between the river bank and the water was a confused mass of humanity—several thousands of men. They were mostly unarmed; many were wounded; some dead. All the camp-following tribes were there; all the cowards; a few officers. Not one of them knew where his regiment was, nor if he had a regiment. Many had not. These men were defeated, beaten, cowed. They were deaf to duty and dead to shame. A more demented crew never drifted to the rear of broken battalions. They would have stood in their tracks and been shot down to a man by a provost-marshal's guard, but they could not have been urged up that bank. An army's bravest men are its cowards. The death which they would not meet at the hands of the enemy they will meet at the hands of their officers, with never a flinching."[32]

Death would have to wait another night for the men in Bierce's regiment. They crossed the river on one of two wooden steamboats bobbing like corks between the two banks. Enemy shells fell randomly around them, sending geysers of water spewing from the river, while two small Union gunboats, "looking very much like turtles," answered back to the unseen cannons. A young woman aboard Bierce's boat—"somebody's wife," he guessed—stood on the upper deck of the steamer, holding a small ivory-handled pistol in her hand. With it, she told Bierce, she would do her duty "if it came to the worst." It didn't, for her, but Bierce was "proud to remember that I took off my hat to this little fool." The woman in question may have been Brig. Gen. William H. L. Wallace's wife, Ann, who had rushed to the battlefield from her La Salle, Illinois, home to be with her husband, only to arrive after the battle had started and her husband had taken up position in the killing zone known as the Hornet's Nest. If it was General Wallace's wife whom Bierce encountered, she was soon to be a widow; Wallace died three days after the battle, his wife finally at his side, from the effects of a rebel artillery round to his head.[33]

When the boat docked at the landing, provost guards had to keep back the mob of fugitives with their bayonets; some still jumped on board and were pushed off in midstream "to drown one another in their own way." The men of the Ninth punched and shoved their way through the mob and entered the dusky fields beyond. Inch by inch, through pitch-darkness and face-stinging rain, they filed into line on the Union left. Strange regiments were all around them, whispering in the shadows of the great death beyond. Often, the men would step on dead bodies, or those that were nearly dead. Lightning flared through the Spanish moss above them, and stretcher-bearers incessantly brought the wounded into makeshift hospitals behind the lines, where Bierce observed that "these tents were constantly receiving the wounded, yet were never full; they were continually ejecting the dead, yet were never empty. It was as if the helpless had been carried in and murdered, that they might not hamper those whose business it was to fall tomorrow." The long night wore on to dawn.[34]

The next morning, at daybreak, Bierce led a platoon of riflemen forward across a level meadow dotted here and there with pools of blood. The air was electric with the promise—or threat—of new fighting, but except for one eerie bugle call from the direction of the enemy lines, the countryside was deathly silent as the men made their way across the field. Broken trees "hung their green heads to the ground," their trunks scarred to a height of twenty feet with bullet holes, and angular bits of metal stuck out from the sides of muddy depressions where shells had struck the ground. The detritus of battle was everywhere: "Knapsacks, canteens, haversacks distended with soaken and swollen biscuits, gaping to disgorge, blankets beaten into the soil by the rain, rifles with bent barrels or splintered stocks, waist-belts, hats and the omnipresent sardine-box—all the wretched debris of the battle still lingered on the spongy earth as far as one could see, in every direction." Also strewn about, and even more troubling to the new men in line, were stiffened horses, disabled caissons, broken-down ammunition wagons, and dead bodies. Bierce halted the platoon to wait for other Union troops to swing even with them in line, and here they came upon the first of the new day's legion of horrors. A Federal sergeant lay faceup on the ground, "a fine giant in his time." Now he was dying slowly and terribly, "taking his breath in convulsive, rattling snorts, and blowing it out in sputters of froth which crawled creamily down his cheeks, piling itself alongside his neck and ears. A bullet had clipped a groove in his skull, above his temple; from this the brain protruded in bosses, dropping off in flakes and strings." Bierce marveled that someone "could get on, even in this unsatisfactory fashion, with so little brain." One of his men offered to run his bayonet through the wounded sergeant to end his suffering, but Bierce turned down the humanitarian request—"it was unusual, and too many were looking."[35]

Ahead of the Union line, Confederate scouts galloped out of rifle range, leading Bierce and the others to believe that the main enemy line had fallen back during the night. Pushing up a slight incline into the open, the Federal skirmishers halted again to wait for the others. Bierce, however, had other plans. He ordered his platoon forward at a run to strengthen the distant skirmish line, which was now approaching the opposite end of the open field. "Then—I can't describe it—the forest seemed all at once to flame up and disappear with a crash like that of a great wave upon the beach—a crash that expired in hot hissings, and the sickening 'spat' of lead against flesh. A dozen of my brave fellows tumbled over like ten-pins. Some struggled to their feet, only to go down again, and yet again. Those who stood fired into the smoking brush and doggedly retired." The men had expected to find, at worst, a line of rebel skirmishers in the trees; instead, "what we had found was a line of battle, coolly holding its fire till it could count our teeth." There was nothing to do but retreat, and Bierce led his men back the way they had come as enemy bullets kicked up little jets of mud at their heels. Although profoundly stunned by the quick turn of events—a quiet morning walk turning into a deadly ambush—Bierce retained his keen sense of the ridiculous, noting that a young officer who had taken part in the advance had solemnly walked up to Colonel Hazen and reported, as though he was the only one who had noticed: "The enemy is in force just beyond this field, sir."[36]

Back inside the main line, Bierce and the others lay down between several pieces of field artillery that Hazen had brought up to support his advance. For the next three hours, the two sides bombarded each other with canister and grapeshot while the infantrymen hunkered facedown on the wet ground, alternately showered by enemy shrapnel or deafened by the roar of their own "cursed guns." At length, pulled out of line for a momentary rest, Bierce's regiment fell back to a hill overlooking a deep ravine at the rear of the Union position. Here, the day before, men from the Fifty-fifth Illinois had been caught and butchered as they attempted to retreat through the ravine; Rebel marksmen had lined both sides of the depression and shot them down like sheep as they scrambled futilely up the steep, rocky sides. Now, Bierce, surveying the ghastly scene, "obtained leave to go down into the valley of death and gratify a reprehensible curiosity." Once again, his obsessional interest in the macabre led him to a sight he would never forget: hundreds of Federal soldiers, wounded or dead, had been burned to ashes by a quick-moving brushfire ignited by gunfire. Ankle-deep in their ashes, Bierce observed the charred remains of his brother regiment, "some in the unlovely looseness of attitude denoting sudden death by the bullet, but by far the greater number in postures of agony that told of the tormenting flame. Their clothing was half burnt away—their hair and beard entirely; the rain had come too late to save their nails. Some were swollen to double girth; others shriveled to manikins. According to degree of exposure, their faces were bloated and black or yellow and shrunken. The contraction of muscles which had given them claws for hands had cursed each countenance with a hideous grin." Strong stuff, even for Bierce, and he breaks off his compulsive description of the carnage with a dismissive: "Faugh! I cannot catalogue the charms of these gallant gentlemen who had got what they enlisted for." Again he foreshadows, by a good fifty years, the attraction/repulsion to violent, ugly death that Ernest Hemingway displays in such charnel works as "A Natural History of the Dead," which lingers almost voyeuristically over the dead, twisted bodies of Italian women killed in a munitions plant explosion.[37]

Bierce's regiment returned to the front in time to help beat back three separate Confederate assaults as the enemy attempted to turn the Union flank.
The noise of the gunfire was so loud at one point that it somehow seemed
soundless—"the ear could take in no more"—and the rebels fell back in disarray. "Lead had scored its old-time victory over steel," wrote Bierce, "the
heroic had broken its great heart against the commonplace." Hazen, on
horseback, led a counterattack that brought the brigade back to the original
campsites abandoned by Grant's men the day before, only to be counter-
attacked in turn by fresh Southern troops, which sent Bierce and his comrades scurrying back to the safety of their now "beloved guns." Ironically,
Hazen became separated from his command during the retreat and left himself open to postwar charges that he had abandoned his men under fire. He
subsequently devoted nineteen pages in his memoirs to refuting the ground-
less accusation, before noting resignedly that "since that time, whenever I
have had an adversary he always repeats the falsehood."[38]

For the rest of the regiment, however, the Battle of Shiloh ended after their
brief afternoon advance and retreat. General Nelson himself, a great profane
ex-navy midshipman with a scalding tongue and a brutal manner that had
earned him the not entirely fond nickname of "Bull," personally rode up and
thanked the regiment for its gallantry. The entire brigade had fought well, as
evidenced by its 399 casualties, twice the average for Buell's army. Bierce, in
the forefront of the fighting, somehow escaped wounding—at least physically. But Shiloh exacted a certain toll on everyone who fought there. Even
such experienced soldiers as William Sherman were shocked by the level of
human devastation. "The scenes on this field would have cured anybody of
war," he said. Future President James A. Garfield, Hazen's friend, wrote to his
wife: "The horrible sights that I have witnessed on this field I can never
describe. No blaze of glory, that flashes around the magnificent triumphs of
war, can ever atone for the unwritten and unutterable horrors of the scene."
Grant's army had won a narrow victory, holding the field as the Confederates
retreated, but it had been a near thing. No one was prepared for the casualty
lists—23,741 in all, more than twice the number of the war's four other
major battles to date, Bull Run, Wilson's Creek, Fort Donelson, and Pea
Ridge. Grant, ever the realist, "gave up all idea of saving the Union except by
complete conquest." Southern writer George Washington Cable pronounced
a fitting epitaph for the thousands who had fought and died in the battle
when he wrote: "The South never smiled again after Shiloh."[39]

The battle marked a watershed in the Civil War, and it also represented a
significant shift in experience for Ambrose Bierce. The almost fairy-tale fighting in Virginia had been replaced, at disorienting speed, by a maddened,
blood-soaked butchery the likes of which had never before been seen in
American history. The sights and sounds of Shiloh would stay with Bierce for
the rest of his life, occasioning some of his finest writing and foreshadowing

and directly influencing an entire generation of American writers, men whose own take on war owed a great deal to his seminal works. The callow Indiana teenager who had dreamed horrific dreams of death and haunted country cemeteries in the thrall of some clammy anxiety had now witnessed organized death on a scale not even he had previously imagined. The nighttime crossing of the shell-tossed river, the mob of fear-crazed deserters, the confused, rain-soaked march into line, the dying sergeant with his brains oozing "creamily" down his cheek, the sudden ambush in a quiet field, the ravine of roasted bodies, the whir of shrapnel and the soft thud of bullets striking warm bodies—it is perhaps not too much to claim that the working prototype of all modern war literature, at least as seen by Americans, is Ambrose Bierce's "What I Saw of Shiloh." He and his comrades would fight other battles, nearly three years' worth, but none of them would ever experience anything like what they had known that April morning in Tennessee. It was the end of the world, in a way; the new world that followed would be a colder, harsher, and deadlier place, one in which all the fine rhetoric of fire-breathing politicians would be forever devalued, for Bierce and for others, by what their incautious, ill-considered words had wrought.

3

The Woods of Chickamauga

A few weeks after Shiloh, Indiana governor Oliver P. Morton traveled to the front to see for himself what had happened to his fine levy of troops in Tennessee. What he found upon his arrival in northern Mississippi was an archaic eighteenth-century siege in the process of being wound around the Confederate stronghold at Corinth by the new Union commander on the scene, Maj. Gen. Henry "Old Brains" Halleck, who had superseded the temporarily discredited Grant at the head of the army. Morton was no military man, but he worried to Secretary of War Edwin Stanton that "the enemy are in great force at Corinth, and have recently received reinforcements. They evidently intend to make a desperate struggle at that point, and from all I can learn their leaders have utmost confidence in the result. It is fearful to contemplate the consequences of a defeat at Corinth." Fortunately for the Federals, Confederate general P. G. T. Beauregard had his own supply of fears just then. His enemies were not merely the thousands of Northern soldiers industriously digging, shoveling, and tunneling ever nearer to the town but also the oldest scourges of the human race: measles, dysentery, typhoid fever, and other common infectious diseases. The town's water supply had become hopelessly compromised by unsafe sanitary practices; by the middle of May, over a third of the Confederate soldiers at Corinth, some eighteen thousand, were on sick call. Thousands more, wounded at Shiloh, jammed the town's houses, hotels, churches, businesses, and railroad station, making the town more hospital than citadel. Ambrose Bierce, on the outside looking in, accurately termed the overburdened village "a wretched place—the capital of a swamp."[1]

Bad weather and worse roads slowed the Union advance—not that Halleck was in any particular hurry to get to Corinth as it was. Well aware of the near disaster that Shiloh had been for the North, Halleck did not intend to let himself be similarly surprised by a dangerous and unpredictable opponent whose overall strength he consistently put at three times its actual size. Caution, if not indeed outright timidity, characterized his generalship. He had only to look at the downcast Grant shuffling about headquarters with a stricken look on his face to see firsthand what a fatal lack of precaution could do to a promising career. (Grant, reduced to the meaningless post of second in command after his erratic performance at Shiloh, strongly considered resigning from the army, and he might have done so had not William Sherman, his partner in unpreparedness, even more strongly urged him to stay.) Bierce, who would always have a rather qualified view of Grant's wartime accomplishments, felt along with other members of Don Carlos Buell's Army of the Ohio that Buell's crucial contribution at Shiloh had been purposely downplayed by Grant and his supporters. Thirty-six years after the battle, he was still complaining about the lack of attention Buell had suffered at the hands of historians. "Buell's most notable service," Bierce wrote in the San Francisco *Examiner* in December 1898, "was the rescue of Grant's army from the consequences of its commander's astonishing fatuity at Shiloh. The facts are simple. At the close of the first day's battle Grant's camps were held by the enemy and his army had been driven (withdrawn, he says) to the river. Night had put an end to the fighting. Buell arrived that evening and crossing thirty thousand men attacked next morning. It required an all day's fight of incomparable severity for the united Federal armies to retake the lost ground and win a victory which was merely not a defeat. These facts are conceded by all."[2]

Such *après la guerre* controversies were beyond Bierce's limited ken in May 1862. It was enough, just then, for him to have survived the Battle of Shiloh in one piece, which was more than could be said for 170 others of the Ninth Indiana Regiment, whose combined loss in that battle would prove to be its greatest of the war. Colonel Hazen soon joined the list of absentees, falling prey to malaria and missing five weeks' service. As it turned out, Hazen did not miss very much. On May 29, following an all-day bombardment by Union artillery, Beauregard's Confederates slipped unnoticed out of Corinth, leaving behind little except a few dummy guns manned by rebel straw men sporting—a nice touch—broad painted grins. "At dawn on May 30th," noted Union general Lew Wallace, "we marched into its deserted works, getting nothing—nothing—not a sick prisoner, not a rusty bayonet, not a bite of bacon—nothing but an empty town and some Quaker guns." It was the sort of ridiculous anticlimax that Bierce always relished; he must have howled with laughter at Halleck's after-the-fact announcement to the troops that they had just won "a victory as brilliant and important as any recorded in history." The soldiers in the field knew better, and so did the newspaper correspondents on the scene. "General Halleck has achieved one of the most barren triumphs of the war," the Chicago *Tribune* asserted. "In fact it is tantamount to a defeat." That was probably overstating things a bit; the Confederates, after all, had retreated. Bierce was closer to the truth when he judged that the Corinth campaign had been "a solemn farce," conducted by a sluggish and irresolute commander. "Foot by foot," he wrote of Halleck, "his troops, always deployed in line-of-battle to resist the enemy's bickering skirmishers, always entrenching against the columns that never came, advanced across the thirty miles of forest and swamp toward an antagonist prepared to vanish at contact, like a ghost at cock-crow. It was a campaign of 'excursions and alarums,' of reconnaissances and countermarches, of cross-purposes and countermanded orders." Given his assiduous avoidance of battle, Halleck was no doubt speaking from the heart when he notified Washington that "the result is all I could possibly desire."[3]

Bierce later fictionalized Governor Morton's trip to the front in a bitterly ironic short story, "An Affair of Outposts." In it, "our friend the Governor" joins a stream of "distinguished civilians" who have been drawn to the scene of the fighting by a desire "to see what they safely could of the horrors of war." Attended by his personal staff, faultlessly tailored and top-hatted amid the inevitable rabble of an army camp, the governor is a handy target of derision for the bedraggled soldiers laboriously digging away in their trenches, his "ornamental irrelevance" contrasting vividly with their own tatterdemalion circumstances. Visiting one of his state's regiments at the front, the governor is startled by the appearance of Captain Armisted, whom he had personally commissioned a few months earlier. Armisted, though young, has already been badly marked by the war: "His hair, which but a few months before had been brown, was streaked with gray. His face, tanned by exposure, was seamed as with age. A long livid scar across the forehead marked the stroke of a sabre; one cheek was drawn and puckered by the mark of a bullet. Only a woman of the loyal North would have thought the man handsome."[4]

Behind that last observation is a bitter joke: Armisted, a Southerner fighting for the North, has only joined the army to get himself killed after discovering that his wife has been unfaithful to him. The governor, with whom he pointedly declines to shake hands, soon flees to the rear at the first sign of danger, while Armisted conducts a fighting retreat with marked coolness and resolution. Throughout the story, Bierce is at pains to contrast the soldier's unromantic lot with the foppish politician's ridiculous preconceptions. Seeing a trooper shot down nearby, the governor shudders. "In all this was none of the pomp of war—no hint of glory," he complains. "Even in his distress and peril the helpless civilian could not forbear to contrast it with the gorgeous parades and reviews held in honor of himself—with the brilliant uniforms, the music, the banners, and the marching. It was an ugly and sickening business; to all that was artistic in his nature, revolting, brutal, in bad taste." When the governor, racing away from the front, sprains his ankle and finds himself in immediate danger of capture, Armisted orders his men forward to save the cringing politico. In the short, sharp fight that follows, Armisted and several of his men are killed, but the governor survives, to find a letter from the captain's wife lying beside the dead officer—"nothing very remarkable—merely a weak woman's confession of unprofitable sin—the penitence of a faithless wife deserted by her betrayer." The betrayer, of course, is the governor, whom Armisted, knowing the truth, nevertheless has died defending.[5]

"An Affair of Outposts," one of Bierce's better stories, is a bitter denunciation of both romantic betrayal and fatuous patriotism. Its unusual mixture of the two can be read on one level as an old soldier's disgusted farewell to arms, his hard-earned realization that impassioned appeals to patriotism are in a way the ultimate seduction, and often as faithless as a wayward wife. It is a theme that Bierce would reiterate in several of his stories, and one that foreshadows—and may directly have influenced—William Dean Howells's great 1905 story, "Editha," with its similar plot of a thoughtless young girl goading her reluctant fiancé into joining the army and getting himself killed in the Spanish-American War. (One thinks inevitably of English schoolgirls scornfully handing out white feathers to draft-age civilians on the street during World War I.) It also recalls the treacly art of the Civil War period, richly embodied by George C. Lambdin's 1865 painting *The Consecration, 1861,* in which a Northern girl sporting a conspicuous engagement ring softly kisses—what symbolism—her flower-toting young officer's sword. On a more personal level, it harks back to Bierce's uncharacteristically idealistic enlistment immediately after the start of the war, and his subsequent jilting—not to get ahead of the story—by Bernice Wright. Certainly, Bierce had a lifelong obsession with unfaithful women, many of whom figure prominently in his stories; and it may be that heedless, bubble-headed Fatima had a more direct influence on his own rush to arms—and subsequent disavowal thereof—than previously has been suspected.

Following the fall of Corinth, the Ninth Indiana helped pursue the retreating Confederates into central Mississippi before being detached to repair and guard the Memphis & Charleston Railroad in northern Alabama later that spring. The railroad, called by the South's secretary of war, Leroy Walker, "the vertebrae of the Confederacy," was a vital link to train-rich Chattanooga, Tennessee, and through it to Nashville, Knoxville, and the sister cities of Virginia. It had been seized in early May by Brig. Gen. Ormsby Mitchel, who in so doing had brought upon himself the unenviable task of patrolling some four hundred miles of hostile territory with a force of barely eight thousand men. The area was swarming with armed bands of pro-Southern guerrillas who styled themselves "partisan rangers" and roamed the countryside at will, ambushing Union couriers and terrorizing suspected Northern sympathizers. Clashes between the rangers and Union-leading "tories" occurred with exasperating regularity, and atrocities were common to both sides. To complicate the situation further, resourceful thieves supporting neither side had taken to sporting blue uniforms similar to those worn by Mitchel's troops. These "homemade Yankees" robbed and killed indiscriminately, with scant regard for their victims' politics. Union officers understandably had trouble distinguishing between the various outlaw gangs and properly commissioned Confederate cavalrymen, who frequently employed the same hit-and-run tactics. The tendency was to regard all hostile forces as guerrillas and to deal with them accordingly—which is to say, at the end of a rope. This led, in turn, to Southern reprisals against captured Union soldiers and increased bitterness between the army and the civilian population. (Bierce's most famous story, "An Occurrence at Owl Creek Bridge," with its peremptory execution of an accused rebel spy, is set, appropriately enough, in northern Alabama.)

A notable example of such ill feelings was still smoldering—figuratively, if not literally—when Bierce's regiment moved into new quarters at Athens, Alabama, in early June. A few weeks earlier, the rather pretty little town, the seat of Limestone County, had suffered the malign attentions of Russian émigré turned colonel John Basil Turchin, né Turchininoff, and his Union Eighth Brigade. The colorful Turchin, known variously as "the Russian Thunderbolt," or "the Mad Cossack," depending on one's point of view, had learned his soldiering as a member of the czar's army during the Crimean War. With typical European sangfroid regarding the proper treatment of noncombatants, Turchin had turned his brigade loose on Athens after one of his regiments had been run out of town the day before by a Confederate cavalry regiment. "I shut my eyes for two hours," Turchin had told his soldiers, who, taking the hint, had proceeded to rampage through various homes and businesses, looting, burning, trampling, and assaulting anyone who got in their way. At least one black servant girl was gang-raped, and a pregnant woman was so ill-treated that she subsequently suffered a miscarriage and died. The "Rape of Athens" galvanized public opinion in both North and South, and the Union army itself split into pro- and anti-Turchin camps, General Buell coming down definitely in the latter category and ordering up a court-martial to examine charges against the erstwhile czarist. At the same time, Buell instituted strict new guidelines regulating the protection of civilians and their property. Turchin haughtily dismissed the directives as "guarding potato patches"; and Cincinnati *Gazette* correspondent William S. Furay denounced Buell for having a policy that "cares more for guarding a rebel cabbage patch, or reenslaving a liberated negro, than he does for gaining a triumph over the enemy." Three months after its signal showing at Shiloh, Buell's army found itself riddled with dissension.[6]

Bierce did not venture an opinion on Turchin and his acts, but he later gave his considered judgment on the necessary characteristics of a good soldier. Responding to the overt religiosity that President William McKinley and the rest of the country were then using to cloak their imperialistic ambitions during the Spanish-American War, Bierce complained that "a fellow can't get into this war unless he has a certificate of all the virtues, signed by a majority of the freeholders in his precinct, and is pronounced pious by his pastor. Why, if the best fighters in my old company were spaded out of a half-hundred Southern battlefields, their lives restored and their youth renewed, they would be contumeliously rejected at the recruiting station for moral unfitness to stop Spanish bullets! They were a bad lot in an incalculable number of ingenious ways; but they could everlastingly lick ten times their weight of the churchly dudes and psalming eligibles of this degenerate day. Pah! a soldier should be able to quaff great bumpers of brandy, swear good mouth-filling oaths and play a famous game of cards to win his comrade's monthly wage. He should know how to loot a farm, sack a town and harry the thrifty civilian generally, 'without regard to political affiliations.'" Bierce's as yet unspaded comrades presumably met such qualifications. In August, the hometown Elkhart *Review* praised the "Bloody Ninth" for being able to "do more hard marching and fighting than any other regiment in the service," adding proudly that "the boys can steal, dress and eat a hog, while on march, without breaking rank."[7]

It was well that the regiment was so variously accomplished, for its martial prowess would soon be put to the test. After moving north to Murfreesboro, Tennessee, in mid-August, the Ninth and its brother regiments were hastily dispatched to Kentucky a month later to block Confederate general Braxton Bragg's bold invasion of the state. By now the division had a new commander, Brig. Gen. William Sooy Smith. Bull Nelson had already proceeded to Kentucky to take command of a new division of volunteers from Indiana and Ohio, neighboring states that feared they would be next in line should Kentucky fall to the advancing rebel horde. While Union reinforcements were rushing to Louisville, Nelson fought and lost the Battle of Richmond (Kentucky), subtracting in the bargain nearly 6,000 of the 7,000 men in his over-matched and undertrained division, an astonishing 4,300 of whom simply surrendered at the first approach of the enemy. Mortified by his poor showing, Nelson complained loudly and profanely about the gross insufficiency of his Indiana troops. Hazen had dinner with Nelson upon his arrival in Louisville and noted immediately that the general "had taken a violent dislike to Indiana and to all the people who came from it. Excepting Governor Morton, of whom he always spoke in the highest praise, I never heard him say a kind word of any person from that State, and the mere mention of it was like shaking the red rag at a bull. I have often heard him describe the origin of its colonization as coming from the 'poor trash' of the mountains of Kentucky, Tennessee, and North

Carolina; and he would refer to his brother Tom, Minister to Mexico, of whom he was fond, as having lost his good manners by living in Indiana."[8]

Nelson would soon lose more than his manners through his own exposure to homegrown Hoosiers in the person of Indiana-born Brig. Gen. Jefferson C. Davis, who, accompanied by the peripatetic Morton, breasted Nelson in the lobby of the Galt House about his derogation of Indiana soldiers in general and Jefferson C. Davis in particular. Nelson, who was not called Bull for nothing, responded to Davis's quietly stated complaint by backhanding the smaller man across the room and offering to do the same for Morton, the governor hastily declining the offer. Davis, with Nelson's handprint spreading pinkly across his cheek, borrowed a pistol from someone in the lobby and fatally shot Nelson point-blank in the chest on the first-floor landing of the hotel's elegant stairway. "Tom, I am murdered," Nelson gasped to fellow general Thomas Crittenden, and despite reassurances to the contrary, quickly proceeded to prove his point.[9]

The intramural bloodletting between the two generals would have profound, if indirect, consequences for Bierce and his regiment. Buell, already under fire from Washington for his too-soft policy toward Southern civilians in Alabama and his perceived lack of haste in coming to the rescue of Abraham Lincoln's home state, now faced a major battle in Kentucky, with his best divisional commander lying dead in a Louisville morgue and his notably uncontrite slayer under house arrest in the very hotel where he had done the deed. Buell's subsequent handling of the Battle of Perryville, eight days later, although a narrow Union victory, did nothing to raise his standing with the Lincoln administration. Hampered by a meteorological fluke known as "acoustic shadow," Buell could not hear the sound of gunfire a few miles away, and in consequence, he allowed half his army to be overrun by Bragg's Confederates before he even knew there was a battle going on. Only the opportune arrival of a fresh corps of reinforcements, among them Bierce's regiment, prevented a renewal of fighting the next day, and the rebels sullenly withdrew from the battlefield after having forcibly removed another 4,200 names from Northern unit rosters.

A few days later Buell, too, was gone, summarily sacked by the President for failing to follow up his victory and thus allowing the rebels to retreat unmolested into east Tennessee. His replacement was Maj. Gen. William S. Rosecrans of Cincinnati, "many kinds of a brilliant crank," in Bierce's later evaluation. As for Buell, not least of whose shortcomings was his membership in the wrong political party, his military career was at an end. Upon the occasion of Buell's death three decades later, Bierce memorialized his old commander as "a notable person in his day, and by many of the old Army men regarded as the ablest soldier of the War." Hazen said bluntly that "General Buell was the best general the war produced," adding that "the army was never again as good."[10]

Rosecrans, as yet unburdened by such rank-and-file opinions concerning his advent, immediately took his command back southward into Tennessee, setting up camp outside Nashville and renaming his force the Army of the Cumberland to denote its new territorial imperative (the Cumberland flowing through the heart of the Volunteer State). "Old Rosy," as he was called, was not the only one to receive a promotion that fall. Ambrose Bierce, barely twenty, found himself somewhat surprisingly promoted to second lieutenant on December 1, 1862. Since his Hemingwayesque actions at Laurel Hill the year before, he had performed no notable—or at least officially noted—acts of heroism, but he had been present for duty every day, no mean accomplishment in itself, given the carnage of Shiloh and the rampant illness outside of Corinth. Besides, as he noted in another context, bloody battles such as Shiloh were always "great for those in line for promotion." Despite his seemly humility, Bierce's promotion did not sit well with his old colleagues in Company C. His inherent aloofness, which many interpreted as simple arrogance, had not won him the usual number of foxhole buddies. One searches in vain through his wartime reminiscences for any mention of personal friends; in fact, the only nonsuperiors he mentions at all are, revealingly, the unfortunate Privates Abbott and Boothroyd, both of whom merited his passing attention merely by dying in his immediate vicinity. Otherwise, as he noted with a certain satisfaction, "in military life one may keep to one's self if one wish to." Within days of his promotion, the Elkhart *Review* began receiving letters from the front complaining about Bierce's abrupt ascension and describing him, somewhat unfairly, as "an individual very obnoxious to the Company." Bierce personally responded to the charges in a letter that was paraphrased but unfortunately not published in whole by the newspaper, accusing the journal of doing him a "great injustice." The *Review* reacted in the usual backhanded way of the Fourth Estate, conceding that "Lieut. Bierce has earned a reputation for daring and discipline that he may well be proud of, but we would not justify him in wrongdoing the men under his command if he possessed the skill and courage of Napoleon Bonapart [*sic*]."[11]

Apparently, the problem stemmed from the fact that Bierce had been promoted from above, not elected to the post by his fellow camp mates. In this, he was not exceptional, at least by standards prevailing in late 1862. The democratic election of regimental officers, previously encouraged as a way of promoting interunit pride, preserving cohesion, and—not incidentally—giving the new volunteers the false sense that they in any way controlled their own destinies, was being replaced by a more professional meritocracy. Bierce was a worthy candidate (even one of the disgruntled letter writers conceded that he was "a good and brave soldier who knows no fear"), and he had the added advantage of not belonging to a special clique, since he manifestly kept his own counsel. Years later, perhaps recalling the unpopularity of his promotion, he derided the typical Civil War volunteer as a man who "wants to be a little general, deciding for himself, and is resentful of the despotism necessary to his success and his welfare." From commanding general to second lieutenant, promotions within the Army of the Cumberland were controversial that fall.[12]

Bierce's regiment had missed the Battle of Perryville, but it would not be so lucky under Old Rosy. On the day after Christmas, 1862, the army broke camp and moved south toward Murfreesboro, thirty miles below Nashville, where the Confederate army was believed to be massing for an imminent attack. Hazen's brigade, now part of Maj. Gen. John M. Palmer's division, was posted in a cotton field on the Union left, its flank protecting the Nashville Turnpike and the Nashville & Chattanooga Railroad, which ran parallel to each other at that point, before diverging northward in a widening V. Rosecrans, who was much given to dramatic pronouncements, had told his officers the night before that he intended to attack the rebels, "drive them from their nests [and] make them fight or run!" He punctuated his boast by slamming his coffee mug down on the table in front of him. It made for good theater, but unfortunately, the Confederates had equally bad intentions. Worse yet, they beat the Federals to the punch, attacking the Union right at daybreak on December 31 and bending it backward like a sprung gate.[13]

At the opposite end of the line, Bierce and his charges were hunched over their cooking fires, throwing together the prebattle breakfast that Rosecrans had thoughtfully reserved them the right to eat, apparently acting under the trustful assumption that any rebels in the general vicinity would similarly be dining before engaging the foe. Breakfast was interrupted at half past six by heavy cannonading and rifle fire, followed by an antic Keystone Kops interlude in which Bierce's regiment was first ordered forward, then about-faced to the rear, then moved to the left, then to the right, and finally told to face to the rear again, all as a result of the enemy's rapidly developing attack. At length, Col. W. H. Blake simply had the regiment lie down and wait. Even this sensible order came too late to save five members of the unit from being bowled over by a single cannonball.[14]

Soon the regiment was up again, moving forward to occupy a three-foot-high elevation of cedar and oak trees known in subsequent battle accounts as the Round Forest or, more colorfully, Hell's Half-Acre. The barely noticeable elevation, slight though it was, quickly became the commanding topographical feature on the battlefield. Rosecrans, desperately trying to stabilize his lines in the aftermath of the surprise attack that had already swept half his army off the field, fixed on the Round Forest as the only remaining salient of his original position. All morning, the Ninth Indiana and its brother regiments in Hazen's brigade beat back waves of Confederate attacks, including one by the Eighth Tennessee that cost the Southern unit a phenomenal 68 percent casualty rate, the highest suffered by a Confederate regiment in the western theater during the entire war. Meanwhile, fugitive Northern regiments began reforming alongside Hazen's men. The Ninth Indiana was supported on the right by the Second and Fifteenth Missouri, under the leadership of Brig. Gen. Phil Sheridan, whose division was the only one on the Union right to maintain its cohesion in the aftermath of the initial rebel attack.[15]

The Confederates, forced by the sheer weight of their earlier success to attack across an eight-hundred-yard-deep open space where the missing Union regiments had been, ultimately gave out, as they had done at Perryville in October. Late that afternoon, in a final despairing burst, two more brigades of Tennessee and Florida troops charged across the blood-soaked cotton field in front of the Round Forest, only to be driven back by Hazen's troops in an action that utterly beggared their brigade commander's descriptive powers. "The battle was hushed," wrote Hazen, "and the dreadful splendor of this advance can only be conceived, as all my description must fall vastly short." Colonel Blake, too, was rendered speechless—if not entirely adjectiveless—by the regiment's performance at Hell's Half-Acre. "For the brave men who stood by their colors from seven a.m. until four p.m. continually under fire," reported Blake, "no word of mine could do justice to their unfaltering courage. The officers of the Ninth Indiana Infantry I regard as among the bravest of the brave." They paid dearly for their gallantry: A lieutenant colonel, a captain, and four lieutenants were killed or wounded during the day. One of the latter was Elkhart blacksmith J. D. Braden, who was shot in the head by a rebel bullet while directing a defense of the railroad embankment in the rear of the Union position. Braden, choking in his own blood, was surprised to see Ambrose Bierce kneeling beside him; like others in the regiment, he had always thought Bierce "cold and unapproachable." Now, said Braden, Bierce "gripped my hand in what we both thought was a last goodbye. I tell you he was crying like a little girl." Perhaps so—Bierce typically said nothing about the incident—but crying or not, Bierce picked up the wounded officer and carried him to safety under heavy fire, later winning for himself a promotion to first lieutenant, if not exactly the unqualified praise of the rescued party.[16]

The battle featured another of those gothic incidents that so nourished Bierce's taste for the macabre. At one point during the height of the fighting, Rosecrans and his staff were galloping along behind the regiment's position when a rebel cannonball came crashing through the air, whizzed hotly past the general's ear, and sheared the head off Col. Julius Garesché, his aide-de-camp. Blood and brains spattered Rosecrans's clothing, and Garesché's headless body rode on for another twenty paces before sliding limply off its horse. Whether Bierce witnessed the incident or merely heard about it later, he could not resist commenting on it in a postwar newspaper column. "At the battle of Stone[s] River," he wrote in the *Examiner,* "Gen. Rosecrans sought to hearten up his hard pressed army by riding with his staff along the front,

immediately in rear of the 'firing line.' Unfortunately, he deprived the performance of its expected effect by riding at a wild gallop, which, however, did
not prevent his Chief-of-Staff from losing his head by a cannon-shot. It was
not the only head of that group which was lost that day, but it was the best
one."[17]

Stones River was one of the fiercest battles of the war, and one of the few
that was fought in the dead of winter. A steady sleet fell throughout the
night, and the bitter cold froze to death many of the wounded, while ironically saving the lives of others by stopping their bleeding. Colonel Blake sent
out relief parties from the Ninth Indiana to locate the wounded, but most of
their work was done straightening the limbs of the newly dead. For both
sides, it was a hellish night, perhaps the worst of the entire war. Confederate
general William Preston, sounding very much like Ambrose Bierce, observed:
"The frost, the dead and dying and the dark cedars among which we
bivouacked were wild enough for a banquet of ghouls." As for Bierce himself,
once again he came through a brutal and ill-managed battle unscathed, while
others of the regiment who had joined up with him in Indiana fell by the
dozens in Hell's Half-Acre. In all, the regiment lost 113 dead and wounded,
and the brigade as a whole lost 429. Hazen, who was not easily given to
superlatives, said simply that "the best service rendered by my command in
the war was at the battle of Stone[s] River." To commemorate that service,
Hazen took the unprecedented step a few months later of staking out a private cemetery on the site of his defense of the Round Forest and erecting in
its center a ten-foot-by-ten-foot limestone monument bearing the inscription: "Hazen's Brigade. To the memory of its soldiers who fell at Stone River,
December 31st, 1862. Their faces toward Heaven, their feet to the foe." A
few of Hazen's brother officers later questioned the propriety of a general
placing his own monument on a battlefield, but there it remains, the first
such monument among the thousands that later would dot the various
killing fields, and the only one erected before the war was over.[18]

The Hazen monument figures strongly in another of Bierce's eerie stories,
"A Resumed Identity." In it, a man standing on a hillside just before dawn—
an odd state of affairs in itself—is startled to see a great column of soldiers
moving down a road a quarter of a mile away. More alarming still is the fact
that the soldiers, a full contingent of infantry, cavalry, and artillery, are
absolutely silent in their march. The man, evidently a soldier himself, is
unsettled by the quiet, as well as by the unnatural timbre of his own voice
when he speaks. He attributes the mute passage of the army (which at this
point he is unable to distinguish as friend or foe) to the phenomenon of
acoustic shadows, marking him perhaps as a veteran of Buell's army. He is
even more disturbed by the notion that the passing army might be Confederate, which would mean that his own side, now revealed to be the Union, had
lost the Battle of Stones River. Hiding out, significantly, in "a clump of

cedars," the man waits for the phantom army to move past, absentmindedly gazing about the countryside and passing his hand through his hair in an apparent search for a bullet hole.[19]

The focus of the story shifts to a second man, a Murfreesboro doctor who is returning home at dawn from an overnight house call when he is accosted on the side of the road by a somewhat confused old man in civilian clothes who is loitering in the vicinity of the Stones River battlefield. The man tells the doctor that he is "a lieutenant, of the staff of General Hazen," and wants to know "what has happened here. Where are armies? Which has won the battle?" The doctor answers the question with his own question. "Are you wounded?" "Not seriously," says the man. "I was struck by a bullet and have been unconscious. It must have been a light, glancing blow: I find no blood and feel no pain." The doctor quickly conjectures that the man is suffering from a fuguelike state, "something about lost identity and the effect of familiar scenes in restoring it." He points out to the deluded man that he is "not wearing the uniform of your rank and service" and questions how old the man is. The man replies that he is twenty-three. "You don't look it; I should hardly have guessed you to be just that," says the doctor, whose increasingly skeptical tone irritates the man and sends him stalking off in a huff. Nevertheless, bothered by the doctor's insinuations, the man looks at his hand and feels his face—they do indeed seem old for someone who had suffered merely "a brief unconsciousness." Noting that the countryside is summerlike, and that the Battle of Stones River was fought in the winter, the man assumes that "I must have been a long time in hospital," and he laughingly attributes the doctor's coolness to his thinking that the man was "an escaped lunatic." "I am only an escaped patient," the man declares. At length, passing a small plot of ground inside a low stone wall, the man comes upon a weather-beaten monument. It is, of course, Hazen's monument, and the man, catching sight of his now-aged face in a pool of water, dies of shock, belatedly realizing that he has somehow lost the last forty years of his life due to amnesia induced by his long-ago wounding.[20]

"A Resumed Identity" is quite short—less than five pages—but its implications are large, particularly when read in the context of Bierce's own wartime experience. Recalling the author's often-stated belief that a part of himself had died in the war, the story suggests that, like the aging amnesiac, Bierce and other veterans had indeed lost a significant part of themselves by "hiring out as killers" for the Union cause. The man in the story shares Bierce's age, rank, and brigade affiliation, as well as the physical facts of his subsequent wounding at Kennesaw Mountain, and Bierce himself returned to Stones River battlefield as an old man for one last look at the horrors of his youth. But the story is more than simple autobiography. As Bierce scholar M. E. Grenander has pointed out, "A Resumed Identity" is a good example of the Biercian "mimetic tale," in which a particular sequence of events is skillfully organized to reproduce in the reader a similar emotion that mimics that of the protagonist (a trick that Hemingway would learn from Bierce). In Bierce's war stories, the sequence is typically that of a vague awareness of danger, a quickening fear, and a fateful—and often fatal—reaction based on a crucial misperception of reality. The Bierce protagonist is usually sensitive and intelligent and assumes that he can rationally work through his dilemma. Inevitably, he is misled by his senses, which have been deranged and disoriented by contradictory stimuli in the heat of battle. Often, time itself is out of joint, slowing down or speeding up in ways consistent with the well-documented experience of soldiers in combat.[21]

In "A Resumed Identity," time is off by a good forty years. Bierce, by alternately providing or withholding information from the reader, carefully reproduces the growing terror of a confused and lost old man, one who has probably "escaped," as he himself says early in the story, from a hospital. (There was, and is, a large veterans hospital in Murfreesboro, not far from the battlefield, which may provide a key to how the old man found himself alone at dawn in a strangely familiar landscape.) The story strongly suggests, however, that no one can truly escape the past, even though he may evade it for a time by temporarily forgetting it. Sooner or later, Bierce implies, one must look in a mirror and face—in this case, quite literally— the consequences of one's youthful acts. Like Eliot's Gerontion, whom he strongly resembles, the protagonist in the story, "an old man in a dry month," has been lost in one of history's "cunning passages," and he, too, must demand, if only briefly, at the very end of his life, "After such knowledge, what forgiveness?"

Following Stones River, the army went into winter camp near Readyville, Tennessee. Hazen immediately organized an instructional school for his officers in both theoretical and applied tactics, with daily recitations and regular examinations. Required readings included Jomini's *Art of War* and Hardee's *Tactics* (written in the 1850s by the same William Hardee who was now commanding a corps in the Confederate army quartering a few miles away at Tullahoma). Hazen's usual zeal for education had been reinforced by his unhappy experience at Stones River. "Close observation of the conduct and character of our troops for the past few days, when compared with those I have so carefully taught for more than twelve months, has confirmed me in a long-settled belief that our army is borne down by a lamentable weight of official incapacity in regimental organizations," he wrote in his battle report. "The reasonable expectations of the country can, in my opinion, never be realized until this incubus is summarily removed, and young men of known military ability and faculty for command, without regard to previous seniority, are put in commission. I saw upon the field company officers of over a year's standing who neither had the power nor the knowledge to form their men into two ranks."[22]

In the wake of the heavy casualties suffered by the brigade during the battle, a number of openings had arisen in the officer corps. Among those chosen to fill the vacancies was Ambrose Bierce, promoted to first lieutenant on April 25, 1863. Immediately following his promotion, Bierce served temporarily as provost marshal, helping to police the camp and enforce discipline. One of his duties was to assist at military executions, a typically unwanted duty that Bierce, with his taste for the grotesque, found rather diverting. At one such event, two Union soldiers were to be hanged for "a particularly atrocious murder outside of the issues of war"; they had apparently killed Southern civilians instead of Southern soldiers, a finely drawn distinction often lost on enlisted men, then and now. The brigade was assembled around the scaffold to witness the double execution, and at the critical moment, one of the men suddenly got religion, as condemned men are wont to do. But just as he began to shout that he was "going home to Jesus," the engineer on a nearby train suddenly pulled his whistle, and the man's heartfelt testimony was drowned out by a derisive "Hoot! Hoot!" The irreligious Bierce was not alone in savoring the mockery. It expressed, he said, "the sense of the meeting better than a leg's length of resolutions; and when the drop fell from beneath the feet of that picnic assassin and his mate, the ropes about their necks were practically kept slack for some seconds by the gusts of laughter ascending from below. They are the only persons I know in the other world who enjoyed the ghastly distinction of leaving this to the sound of inextinguishable merriment."[23]

A second execution involved a cavalry officer who had been courtmartialed for desertion in the face of the enemy. The officer was blindfolded and placed astride his own coffin so that he would simply fall into it when shot, thus saving unnecessary labor by the burial party. Prior to sentence being carried out, the man asked to speak to the officer in charge of the firing squad. After a whispered discussion, the officer shook his head and the execution took place. Bierce, curious about the eleventh-hour exchange, asked the officer what the condemned man had wanted. He had, it seemed, requested that a saddle be placed beneath him on the coffin.[24]

Later that spring, Bierce spent a month on detached duty as chief of scouts for Hazen's brigade. During that time, he took part in a midnight raid on the Confederate camp at Woodbury, an event he details in his brief story "A Baffled Ambuscade." The mixed force of infantry and cavalry, including Bierce's old regiment, marched undetected for fourteen miles in an effort to surprise the rebels and drive them into an ambush. The plan failed, largely because a second brigade was late joining the march, but the Third Ohio Cavalry managed to get into the enemy camp and kill or capture a handful of Confederate pickets, while carrying off fifty horses, four wagons, eight mules, and all their provisions. The cavalry was commanded by Maj. Charles B. Seidel, whom Bierce calls by his real name in his fictional account of the raid. The story is nothing special, but it ends with a typically Biercian flourish. The major, advancing down a road toward a dark cedar forest, is unnerved to see a man standing motionless by the side of the road a few yards away. The major recognizes the figure as a trooper named Dunning who had ridden alone ahead of the column. At Dunning's feet is a dead horse, with an equally dead rebel lying at a right angle across the horse's neck. As the major prepares to ride forward, Dunning wordlessly gestures a warning. The major rides back, expecting Dunning to follow him and report what he has seen. After fruitlessly waiting an hour for the scout to appear, the major rides forward again and finds Dunning, "hours dead," lying across his horse's neck, his warning apparently a posthumous one.[25]

In May 1863, Bierce joined Hazen's headquarters staff as acting topographical engineer. By this time, Hazen had been promoted to brigadier general, and apparently he himself selected Bierce for the post. How the commanding general of the brigade had become acquainted with Bierce's attributes in the first place is unknown, since there are no eye-catching encomiums to the obscure young lieutenant in surviving brigade records. Perhaps Bierce's rescue of the wounded Lieutenant Braden at Stones River got back to Hazen; it is not beyond the realm of possibility that Hazen personally witnessed the act, although he doesn't refer to it in his official report of the battle. Bierce was as much in the dark about his selection as anyone else; he attributed it to "some jugglery at department headquarters," noting that Hazen "seemed to think that a position on his staff was a distinction that should be so judiciously conferred as not to beget any sectional jealousies and imperil the integrity of that part of the country which was still an integer." Whatever the case, Bierce left the Ninth Indiana, probably with little fanfare and less regret, and henceforth he bunked down with the other officers on Hazen's staff. One of his new acquaintances was Capt. Sherburne Eaton of the 124th Ohio, a suave young Yale graduate a few years older than Bierce who would cross paths with him on two future and not entirely happy occasions after the war.[26]

It is also something of a mystery how Bierce learned the rather exacting art of military topography in the first place. Probably, he acquired his mapmaking skills at Kentucky Military Institute, since civil engineering, surveying, and topography were all classes offered during his one-year stay. He had also exhibited some rudimentary drawing ability while in school in Warsaw, since Bernice Wright later remembered him entertaining her with satirical drawings of their fellow students and teachers. Certainly it was a handy skill to have, as it removed Bierce from the day-to-day drudgery of army camp, to say nothing of the front-line perils of a combat infantry officer. Not that the duties of a topographical engineer were hazard-free; nothing in war is without its risks. Bierce gave a good description of his newfound responsibilities in his 1883 story "George Thurston," the first Civil War story he ever published. "Whether in camp or on the march," he wrote, "in barracks, in tents, or en bivouac, my duties as topographical engineer kept me working like a beaver—all day in the saddle and half the night at my drawing-table, platting my surveys. It was hazardous work; the nearer to the enemy's lines I could penetrate, the more valuable were my field notes and the resulting maps. It was a business in which the lives of men counted as nothing against the chance of defining a road or sketching a bridge. Whole squadrons of cavalry escort had sometimes to be sent thundering against a powerful infantry out-post in order that the brief time between the charge and the inevitable retreat might be utilized in sounding a ford or determining the point of intersection of two roads."[27]

In short, it was the type of dangerous, solitary, and somewhat elite duty that a young man of Bierce's taciturn nature would have found particularly satisfying. That he did so may be seen by his passing comment in an *Examiner* column from June 1887: "To this day I cannot look over a landscape without noting the advantages of the ground for attack or defense; here is an admirable site for an earthwork, there a noble place for a field battery." As for the mechanical aspects of his work, Bierce probably used a pocket-sized surveyor's compass, also called a circumferentor, which was equipped with two vertical brass plates that were slitted for sighting and fitted with a short tube that allowed the compass to be mounted on a leveling stick thrust into the ground. He likely measured distance by pacing it off at a standard rate, rather than using a sixty-six-foot-long chain, as a handwritten notation on the back of his Civil War–era notebook seems to indicate: "Common paces 18 in 50'=2 7/9' 2 7/9'=2' 9 1/3." Given the precarious nature of his job, the smaller and more easily transportable the topographer's equipment, the better. Back in camp, Bierce drew his maps by hand, often from memory rather than from notes, since "our frequent engagements with the Confederate out-posts, patrols and scouting parties fixed in my memory a vivid and apparently imperishable picture of the locality serving instead of accurate field notes, which, indeed, it was not always convenient to take, with carbines cracking, sabers clashing, and horses plunging all about. These spirited encounters were observations entered in red."[28]

On June 23, 1863, the Army of the Cumberland broke camp at Readyville and finally commenced a southward movement, which the Lincoln adminis-tration had been fruitlessly urging on Rosecrans for several months. The cen-tral objective was Chattanooga, where two of the Confederacy's most important railroads, the East Tennessee & Virginia and the Memphis & Charleston, crisscrossed, linking the upper and lower South. Following a series of masterful feints, Rosecrans maneuvered Braxton Bragg out of his defensive works at Tullahoma and compelled the rebels to fall back to Chat-tanooga. Hazen's brigade took up position at Poe's Tavern, ten miles above the city, while the bulk of Rosecrans's forces continued south to cross the river at Bridgeport, Alabama, and fall on the unsuspecting enemy from the rear. Meanwhile, Hazen kept up a "dumb but noisy show" to divert attention from the crossing. The ruse worked, or so it seemed at the time, and Hazen's brigade joined the rest of the army in fording the river and entering an abandoned and undefended Chattanooga.[29]

Rosecrans would have done well to have halted there and consolidated his already quite creditable gains. His second in command, Maj. Gen. George Thomas, advised him to do just that. But Rosecrans had been the target of a number of threatening and insulting telegrams from the War Department urging him to "give the finishing blow to the rebellion," and he scarcely paused in Chattanooga long enough to catch his breath before dividing his army into three wings and tramping recklessly after Bragg through the mountainous wilds of northwest Georgia. Hazen, with the inestimable advantage of hindsight, maintained in his memoirs that "it was very clear, soon after taking up our march into Georgia, that we were not following a retreating army, but one falling back for strategic purposes." As for his acting topographical engineer, Bierce allowed that "we knew well enough that there was to be a fight: the fact that we did not want one would have told us that, for Bragg always retired when we wanted to fight and fought when we most desired peace. We had manoeuvered him out of Chattanooga, but had not manoeuvered our entire army into it, and he fell back so sullenly that those of us who followed, keeping him actually in sight, were a good deal more concerned about effecting a junction with the rest of our army than to push the pursuit. By the time that Rosecrans had got his three scattered corps together we were a long way from Chattanooga, with our line of communication with it so exposed that Bragg turned to seize it. Chickamauga was a fight for possession of a road."[30]

Bragg did indeed plan to block the Union army's chief line of retreat, the LaFayette Road through Rossville Gap. That done, he intended to destroy the enemy piecemeal, one wing at a time, rather like a fox devouring a chicken. But Rosecrans, at very nearly the last second, belatedly realized his opponent's plan and effected a desperate eleventh-hour juncture of his leg-weary forces on the west side of a deep-sided, ominous-looking creek named Chickamauga, which is Cherokee for "bad water." An immemorial smallpox outbreak had decimated a branch of the tribe when it lived alongside the creek, giving the Chickamauga its inhospitable name and reputation; but historians with more flair for the dramatic than a working command of the Indian language subsequently dubbed the stream the "River of Death." At that, they were not so far off the mark.

The battle erupted at daybreak on September 19, and from the start it was obvious that no previous action—not even Shiloh or Stones River—could rival it for deadly intensity. North to south, the Confederates attacked in swift succession, operating, said Bierce, on "the law of probabilities: of so many efforts one would eventually succeed." The battleground itself, heavy, vine-choked woods interspersed with cleared farmland, invited the slaughter; units would stumble blindly through the trees, already hazy with gunsmoke, and emerge blinking into bright sunlight in an open field, where they would be quickly mowed down by enemy sharpshooters and artillery hidden in the trees beyond. Hazen's brigade first went into action on the Union left and assisted in beating back an attack by Brig. Gen. Preston Smith's Tennesseans, before being relieved by—of all people—John Basil Turchin, now a brigadier general commanding his own brigade. Turchin had been found guilty of "conduct prejudicial to good order and military discipline" following the Rape of Athens sixteen months before, but Abraham Lincoln, responding to pressure from radical Republicans (and unmistakably signaling his own inherent "hard war" sentiments) had reinstated Turchin to the army and given him a promotion. Hazen's men fell back to the LaFayette Road to replenish their ammunition, then rushed back into line farther to the right, near a local landmark known as the Brotherton cabin. Inadvertently, they stepped into the jaws of a looming Union disaster. Maj. Gen. A. P. Stewart's "Little Giants" division was at that moment in the process of splitting the Federal center and heading straight for the barren ridge beyond, where a score of Northern cannon and a few straggly regiments were all that stood between the rebels and an open road to Chattanooga.[31]

Hazen swiftly sent his brigade forward to slow—he did not expect to stem—the Confederate advance, while gathering "with the aid of all the mounted officers and soldiers I could find," including Bierce, a line of rifle-men to support the artillery on the Brotherton ridge. Meanwhile, sensing victory, the Confederates under Brig. Gen. William Bate broke through the flimsy Union line and headed directly toward the ridge across another of Chickamauga's fatally open fields. At a shout, the Northern artillery unleashed a twenty-gun blast of grapeshot and canister. "For perhaps five minutes—it seemed like an hour," wrote Bierce, who was standing behind the guns, "nothing could be heard but the infernal din of their discharge and nothing seen through the smoke but a great ascension of dust from the smitten soil. When all was over, and the dust cloud had lifted, the spectacle was too dreadful to describe. The Confederates were still there—all of them, it seemed—some almost under the muzzles of the guns. But not a man of all these brave fellows was on his feet, and so thickly were all covered with dust that they looked as if they had been reclothed in yellow. 'We bury our dead,' said a gunner grimly."[32]

The almost too-brave Confederates fell back across the LaFayette Road, and the armies spent a sleepless night lying on their guns in the thick under-growth on either side of the turnpike. It was, said Bierce with uncharacteris-tic flatness, "a night of waking." For the thousands of wounded and dying men lying in positions of agony in the stubbled fields and clinging bushes they had fought over like demons from daylight till dark, the frosty, unattended night was much worse than that. Brushfires, like those that had occurred at Shiloh, flared up intermittently and roasted to death anyone who was too badly hurt to crawl away. Thirst—it had been an unusually dry September—tormented the Union side of the line (the Confederates could drink from Chickamauga Creek). Scores of Federals died alongside a stagnant cattle pond near Union headquarters at the Widow Glenn's cabin, their blood staining the scummy surface of the pool and giving it the ghoulish nickname "Bloody Pond." Worse yet were the screams of the wounded, which carried even farther than usual on the icy night air. One Kentucky Unionist remembered with a shudder that "the poor, suffering wounded of friend and foe continued their piteous cries and groans within easy hearing distance of both lines throughout the cold, frosty night. Never before did the horrors of war seem to us so cruel. We could distinctly hear their lamentable cries, 'O, water, water!' and occasionally some poor, half-frantic sufferer calling the name of some familiar comrade or friend to come. This certainly was the most miserable night the Eighth experienced during the war." One dying man called out hourly, in a steadily weakening voice, "O, for God's sake come and help me!" until at last his nerve-shattering petition ceased.[33]

The sun rose red in the hazy sky; undissipated gunsmoke lay across the battlefield like a cloak. Future President James A. Garfield, then serving as Rosecrans's chief of staff, emerged from the Widow Glenn's cabin to announce somewhat unencouragingly, "This will indeed be a day of blood." Hazen's brigade, like the rest of the Union army, had spent the night sliding northward along a line parallel to the LaFayette Road, and by dawn it was busy erecting a set of breastworks at the south end of Kelly's Field to ward off the rebels' anticipated attack. It came soon enough, in the persons of Irish-born Maj. Gen. Patrick Cleburne's superb combat division. For ninety minutes, the Confederates doggedly charged the Union position without making a dent in the makeshift defenses. The effectiveness of the humble breastworks, which division commander Richard W. Johnson had actually argued with Hazen about constructing, can be seen in the enormous discrepancy between Union and Confederate losses in that sector. Southern brigadier general Lucius Polk, for instance, lost 350 men in the first few minutes of his assault, while the target of his bad intentions, Brig. Gen. Charles Cruft, did not lose a man, and Hazen, next to Cruft in line, lost only 13, as opposed to 400 the day before. Said Hazen in something of an understatement: "It was a good example of the advantage of the defensive behind shelter."[34]

By the end of the attack, Hazen's men still had forty rounds left in their ammunition pouches, but the artillery pieces supporting them (which had just killed rebel general James Deshler, literally blowing his heart out of his chest) had run through their limber boxes. Hazen turned to Bierce and sent him galloping toward the right to find some more. Bierce quickly located an ordnance train and a few wagons loaded with shells, but the officer in charge was uneasy about sending them back with Bierce—"he seemed in doubt as to our occupancy of the region across which I proposed to guide them." Bierce, in his new staff position, seemed fated to witness every significant occurrence taking place at Chickamauga. Now came the most dramatic. Accompanied by the leery ordnance officer, Bierce rode to the top of a low ridge directly behind Brig. Gen. Thomas Wood's division on the Union right center. "To my astonishment," wrote Bierce, "I saw the entire country in front swarming with Confederates; the very earth seemed to be moving toward us! They came on in thousands, and so rapidly that we had barely time to turn tail and gallop down the hill and away, leaving them in possession of the train, many of the wagons being upset by frantic efforts to put them about."[35]

What Bierce had just seen was perhaps the most dramatic breakthrough of the war. Wood, obeying a panicky order from Rosecrans to plug a nonexistent gap in the Federal lines, had pulled out of position at exactly the moment that five Confederate divisions charged across the LaFayette Road at the Brotherton cabin and ripped through the now all-too-real opening that the departure of Wood's division had just created in the Union defense. The coincidental timing of the attack could not have been better for the rebels or worse for the Northerners. Half the Union army, including its badly flummoxed commanding general, hurried away from the battlefield, some shouting as they fled, "See you in Ohio!" Rosecrans, at least, refrained from this. He merely told his staff, as enemy bullets zipped past their heads, "If you care to live any longer, you had better get away from here." Few needed any prompting.[36]

Rosecrans, accompanied by James A. Garfield, turned north toward Rossville Gap and Chattanooga, riding along the Dry Valley Road at the rear of the battlefield through a stream of less exalted fugitives hurrying away on foot. Garfield thought Rosecrans looked "abstracted, as if he neither saw nor heard," overcome by mental and physical weakness. Rosecrans, a devout Catholic, maintained that he was praying—as well he might—to the Virgin Mary for divine guidance. At a fork in the road, the two dismounted and put their ears to the ground Indian-style to listen to the muffled firing from the battlefield. Briefly, they discussed what to do next, although their separate versions of the pivotal conversation diverged along predictably self-exculpatory lines. Rosecrans claimed that Garfield had begged off carrying new orders to Chattanooga and thus had forced him, Rosecrans, to go there himself; Garfield maintained that he had merely offered to ride back to the scene to find out what Thomas was doing on the Union left. Whatever the case, Rosecrans remounted and continued toward Chattanooga, where he sent a despairing telegram to Abraham Lincoln: "We have met with a serious disaster; extent not yet ascertained." Garfield, in the meantime, headed for the Union left, where Thomas was holding his position on a horseshoe-

shaped ridge called Snodgrass Hill. Seventeen years later, Garfield's unre-
markable return to the battlefield, romanticized in campaign literature as
"Garfield's Ride," carried the Ohio politician straight into the White House,
where an assassin's bullet swiftly carried him out again.[37]

Meanwhile, Ambrose Bierce made his own twisting way to Thomas's side,
just in time to watch the final chapter in Chickamauga's terrible drama. "A
good deal of nonsense used to be talked about the heroism of General
Garfield, who, caught in the rout of the right, nevertheless went back and
joined the undefeated left under General Thomas," wrote Bierce. "There was
no great heroism in it; that is what every man should have done, including
the commander of the army. I did so myself, and have never felt that it ought
to make me President." At Snodgrass Hill, the unbroken left half of the
Union army was making a desperate last stand, aided by the lay of the land
and the sheer exhaustion of the onrushing Confederates, many of whom
were panting like dogs after chasing the Federals across several miles of broken countryside. Bierce arrived on the scene and attached himself to Thomas,
having first passed Union corps commander James S. Negley going in the
opposite direction. Bierce said later that he "offered to pilot [Negley] back to
glory or the grave. I am sorry to say my good offices were rejected a little
uncivilly, which I charitably attributed to the general's obvious absence of
mind. His mind, I think, was in Nashville, behind a breastwork."[38]

Thomas, a thickset, stolid, and imperturbable Virginian who had stayed
loyal to the Union (having married a New York heiress some years earlier),
directed the Federal resistance with a resigned calm, if not perhaps the heroic,
larger-than-life demeanor that later caused admirers to nickname him, somewhat hyperbolically, "the Rock of Chickamauga." His calm began to break a
little, however, when an approaching column of soldiers suddenly appeared
in his left rear. A great column of dust preceded their arrival, and Thomas
could not make out whether they were Union or Confederate. Once again,
Bierce was on hand for a crucial moment. "Looking across the field in our
rear (rather longingly)," he wrote, "I had the happy distinction of a discoverer. What I saw was the shimmer of sunlight on metal: lines of troops were
coming in behind us! Reporting my momentous 'find' I was directed by the
general to go and see who they were. Galloping toward them until near
enough to see that they were of our kidney I hastened back with the glad tidings and was sent again, to guide them to the general's position."[39]

The fresh troops were Maj. Gen. Gordon Granger's reserve corps, which
had been camped three miles behind the lines near Missionary Ridge.
Marching without orders to the sound of battle, Granger arrived in the nick
of time to reinforce Thomas and beat back yet another Confederate assault
up the ravine-scarred hillside. After leading Granger to Thomas, Bierce,
"unable to think of anything better to do decided to go visiting." His brother
Albert was an officer in the Eighteenth Ohio Light Artillery in Granger's

corps, and the two enjoyed a brief, if perilous, reunion on the back side of Snodgrass Hill. At one point, a rebel bullet unhorsed another artillery officer seated nearby, and the brothers simply propped him against a tree and continued their conversation. Then Bierce went off to find the remains of Hazen's brigade, which had made its own way to Snodgrass Hill after the debacle on the Union right. Hazen, punctilious as always, immediately asked Bierce what had happened to the artillery ammunition he had sent him after three hours earlier.[40]

Ammunition for all arms was in short supply by midafternoon, and Bierce was not alone in believing that one more general Confederate attack could have carried the hill. But the rebels, too, were short of ammunition, and the fighting subsided to sporadic, localized actions involving small knots of soldiers shooting, clubbing, and bayoneting one another to death in smoke so thick that no one could see more than a few steps ahead. Soon, Federal officers began passing the word to their men to prepare to fall back toward Rossville Gap and Chattanooga. "The sun was taking its own time to set," recalled Bierce, and the raddled defenders of Snodgrass Hill "lived through the agony of at least one death each, waiting for [the rebels] to come on." At last it grew too dark to fight, and Bierce and the others began retreating from the hillside. Behind them, they could hear the distinctive, high-pitched rebel yell being taken up by the victorious Confederates. "It was," said Bierce, "the ugliest sound that any mortal ever heard—even a mortal exhausted and unnerved by two days of hard fighting, without sleep, without rest, without food and without hope." The Battle of Chickamauga, the largest battle in the western theater of operations and the bloodiest two-day encounter of the entire war, was over.[41]

Three decades later, Bierce returned imaginatively to the haunted environs of Chickamauga for perhaps his most powerful short story. "Chickamauga" is also, in a way, his most American story, another in a continuum of fictional narratives detailing the ravaging of the young and innocent by the blind forces of violence, warfare, or simply fate. The new man in the new land, often depicted as a child to underscore both the purity and the vulnerability of an America groping its way across a hostile continent, has had many names in the national literature: Natty Bumppo, Goodman Brown, Huck Finn, Henry Fleming, Nick Adams, Jack Crabbe, Jay Gatsby, Tom Joad, Holden Caulfield, Dean Moriarty, Augie March—all of them seekers, in one way or another, of a greater self-knowledge that might somehow validate the pain of their passage. The unnamed protagonist in "Chickamauga" is literally a child, and a quite young one at that. Impelled by the atavistic "warrior-fire" of a thousand years of European exploration, he wanders away from the family farm and enters a dark forest, armed with a flimsy sword he has fashioned in emulation of the soldiers in his father's military picture books. "Made reckless by the ease with which he overcame invisible foes attempting to stay his advance, he committed the common enough military error of pushing the pursuit to a dangerous extreme, until he found himself upon the margin of a wide but shallow brook, whose rapid waters barred his direct advance against the flying foe that had crossed with illogical ease." This is a perfect synopsis of Rosecrans's blunder at Chickamauga, the first of several times in the story when the child's experiences ironically mirror those of the Union army during the battle.[42]

Frightened (somewhat unrealistically) by a rabbit, the child bolts away, stumbling through a tangle of briers into the heart of the forest, where he lies down near the stream and falls into a deep sleep, undisturbed by the "strange, muffled thunder" coming from the woods beyond. Awakening several hours later to a gloomy twilight, the child continues deeper into the forest until he comes upon a procession of men moving with painful slowness back toward the creek. It is an unforgettable image: the blood-streaked wounded of Chickamauga dragging themselves away from the fighting, seeking a quiet place to drink and die, while to the uncomprehending eyes of the child they appear to be so many painted clowns from the circus. Nothing else in Bierce's writings approaches the poignant simplicity of this powerful passage, and it is justly famous: "They were men. They crept upon their hands and knees. They used their hands only, dragging their legs. They used their knees only, their arms hanging idly at their sides. They strove to rise to their feet, but fell prone in the attempt. They did nothing naturally and nothing alike, save only to advance foot by foot in the same direction. They came by dozens and by hundreds; as far on either hand as one could see in the deepening gloom they extended and the black wood behind them seemed inexhaustible. The very ground seemed in motion toward the creek. Occasionally one who had paused did not again go on, but lay motionless. He was dead. Some, pausing, made strange gestures with their hands, erected their arms and lowered them again, clasped their heads; spread their palms upward, as men are sometimes seen to do in public prayer."[43]

Not knowing what he is witnessing, the child jumps atop one of the wounded men, hoping for a piggyback ride like those his father's slaves had often given him. The man he picks collapses from the jolt but somehow flings the boy aside, "then turned upon him a face that lacked a lower jaw— from the upper teeth to the throat was a great red gap fringed with hanging shreds of flesh and splinters of bone. The man shook his fist at the child; the child, terrified at last, ran to a tree near by, got upon the farther side of it and took a more serious view of the situation." Meanwhile, the stream of casualties continues moving forward "like a swarm of great black beetles," reduced in their suffering state to subhuman forms, their "hideous pantomime" made even more terrible by the absolute silence of their suffering. Bierce reinforces the reductive image by likening the trail of discarded equipment left behind by the men to the spoor of wounded animals fleeing their hunters.[44]

Heedless still of what he is witnessing, the child capers to the head of the procession, waving his little wooden sword and urging the men on toward a reddening fire that can be glimpsed in the distance. Supremely confident— like Rosecrans before Chickamauga—the child dashes ahead of his men, ironically "confident of the fidelity of his forces." What he finds is the story's shocking denouncement: the flaming ruins of his own home and the butchered body of his mother, horribly killed by the shell fire: "There, conspicuous in the light of the conflagration, lay the dead body of a woman— the white face turned upward, the hands thrown out and clutched full of grass, the clothing deranged, the long dark hair in tangles and full of clotted blood. The greater part of the forehead was torn away, and from the jagged hole the brain protruded, overflowing the temple, a frothy mass of gray, crowned with clusters of crimson bubbles—the work of a shell." The child, now revealed to be a deaf-mute, has come face-to-face with the terrible reality of warfare that his earlier posturing had denied, an awareness not unlike that of veteran soldiers such as Bierce, whose own rush to enlistment in the first foolish days of the war had now given way to an exhausted disgust at the obscene human cost of such reckless gestures. No longer blind to what has taken place in the fields around his home, the child utters "a series of inarticulate and indescribable cries—something between the chattering of an ape and the gobbling of a turkey—a startling, soulless, unholy sound, the language of a devil." In the face of such insupportable sights, the literal wreckage of his childhood, it is an all-too-appropriate tongue.[45]

Literary critic Vincent Starrett, an early Bierce admirer, has rightly called Bierce's Civil War stories "enduring peace tracts." Certainly, "Chickamauga" is a deeply felt and moving work from a writer usually considered cynical and heartless. More than that, in its young protagonist's physical and metaphorical journey through the dark woods of ignorance to the crimson fields of terrible knowledge, as well as in its ironic use of overt religious imagery and its sophisticated strategy of a double narrative involving a childish (or immature) hero and an older and wiser authorial commentator, the story is a virtual précis of Stephen Crane's more celebrated *The Red Badge of Courage.* Crane, to his credit, readily acknowledged his general debt to Bierce; but the direct link between "Chickamauga" and Crane's great novel has rarely been noted by modern critics. Bierce was not a better writer than Crane—few are, for that matter—but he had been to the war and seen "the great death" close-up, as Crane had not, and he had written his testament a good half decade before Crane wrote his. Pride of place, if not of achievement, must go to Bierce. His experiences at Shiloh, Stones River, and Chickamauga had left him with an irreducible core of vivid sensory images imprinted on his mind's eye in much the same way that it was once believed a killer's face was imprinted on the frozen pupils of his victim. And in both cases, those eyes were open to the horror.[46]

In 1898, a new generation of American soldiers would use the open space of the old battlefield to train for service in the Spanish-American War. Having seen more action in a single hour at Chickamauga than most of the new volunteers would see in their entire lives, Bierce may be forgiven his uncharacteristically sentimental benediction. "To those of us who have survived the attacks of both Bragg and time, and who keep in memory the dear dead comrades whom we left upon that fateful field, the place means much," he wrote. "May it mean something less to the younger men whose tents are now pitched where, with bended heads and clasped hands, God's great angels stood invisible among the heroes in blue and the heroes in gray, sleeping their last sleep in the woods of Chickamauga."[47]

A Brave and Gallant Fellow

*T*he Battle of Chickamauga was over, but the battle for Chattanooga, in a sense, had just begun. Dazed and demoralized, the Army of the Cumberland straggled back into Chattanooga on the evening of September 20, 1863— minus some sixteen thousand of their number left behind, dead or wounded, on the killing fields of northwest Georgia. The exhausted survivors immediately began felling trees and throwing up breastworks for the renewed Confederate onslaught everyone expected would follow soon. But while swarms of Federal engineers literally tore apart the city house by house—a Northern correspondent said it looked like "a town gone to pieces in a heavy sea"—the rebels back at Snodgrass Hill were unsuccessfully urging their commanding general to resume the offensive. Every hour wasted, warned cavalry leader Nathan Bedford Forrest, was worth the lives of ten thousand men. But Braxton Bragg could not be persuaded. For three long days he dithered, counting dead horses and captured artillery pieces, before bringing his army into place along a semicircular six-mile-long siege line running from Missionary Ridge on the east to Lookout Mountain on the south. Against the near-unanimous advice of his subordinates, Bragg decided to try starving the enemy into submission without risking another fight.

Bragg's debatable decision froze the two armies into place for the next eight weeks, while the opposing governments waited impatiently for their generals to act. In Washington, a disappointed Abraham Lincoln sought to bolster William Rosecrans's flagging morale, wiring him encouragement and advice while at the same time receiving secret telegrams from Assistant Secretary of War Charles A. Dana, who had been visiting Rosecrans before Chickamauga and was now trapped alongside him in Chattanooga. A sub rosa partisan of U. S. Grant's, Dana continued to enjoy Rosecrans's personal confidence, even as he industriously set out to undermine the general's position with the President by exaggerating both the immediate peril the army faced at Chattanooga and its supposed disenchantment with Old Rosy for putting it there. To be sure, there was a certain amount of grumbling within the ranks concerning the general's erratic performance at Chickamauga and his subsequent hasty departure therefrom. But most of the men shared Bierce's postwar judgment that "Rosecrans' retirement from the field was not cowardly. He was caught in the rout of the right and naturally supposed that the entire army had given way. His error lay in accepting that view of the disaster without inquiry and endeavoring to repair his broken fortunes by holding the reorganized fugitives at Chattanooga instead of leading them back to support his unbeaten left. There is no reason to doubt that he acted on his best judgment, which, however, was never very good."[1]

But if the rank and file still maintained a residual affection for their commanding general, it was being sorely taxed by their rapidly diminishing food supplies. The Confederate investment of Chattanooga was not complete, and some provisions were carted in from beyond the mountains north of town, but there was never enough food for everyone. Mobs of soldiers trailed each wagon into town, picking through the mud for scraps of food. Guards had to be posted outside stables to keep the men from stealing the animals' grain; one Kansas unit even caught and ate a dog that wandered incautiously into camp. On the black market, crackers were selling for a dollar apiece, cows' tails for ten. The biting chill of an early winter did little to improve the soldiers' lot.

Still, as the weeks went by with no resumption of hostilities, the army began to rebuild and reorganize. Bierce was personally gratified to receive a copy of a request from Hazen to division commander John M. Palmer asking that Bierce and another officer be allowed to join Hazen's staff permanently. "I am instructed by General Palmer to say that he has a high appreciation of both officers named," Lt. Col. Lyne Starling replied for his chief, "considering them among the very best in the service, yet entertaining a sincere desire to gratify and accommodate both them and you your request is most cheerfully complied with." Bierce kept the note from Starling for the rest of his life. He would have been equally pleased by Hazen's official report on the Battle of Chickamauga, in which he singled out Bierce as one who "deserve[d] special mention." His reputation within the army was rising daily.[2]

In late October, following a renewed barrage of telegrams from Dana warning that the city was in imminent peril and that, worse yet, Rosecrans was contemplating a new retreat, Lincoln finally removed the general from command. Ever since Chickamauga, Lincoln said, Rosecrans had been acting "confused and stunned, like a duck hit on the head." This was not entirely fair to Rosecrans, who, in fact, was studiously preparing a plan to reopen supply lines between Chattanooga and the railroad depot at Bridgeport. But Lincoln had grown tired of waiting for Rosecrans to act, and he decided (with a little prodding from Dana) to bring U. S. Grant east from Vicksburg to command the Union forces at Chattanooga, reasoning that Grant, at least, would act quickly and decisively.[3]

Grant wasted little time in proving Lincoln right. Four days after his arrival in the city, he implemented the first phase of Rosecrans's plan, sending Hazen and 1,300 handpicked troops floating surreptitiously down the Tennessee River past rebel sentries at the base of Lookout Mountain to secure a toehold at the key river crossing of Brown's Ferry, while another 3,500 troops, under the ineffable John Turchin, marched overland toward the ferry across Moccasin Point. The secret river voyage, undertaken at 3:00 A.M. on the mist-shrouded morning of October 27, had the makings of a good Bierce story, but it is not known what part, if any, he played in the actual drama. During the trip downriver, one soldier managed to fall overboard and another was knocked into the water by an overhanging branch (the first drowned; the second was successfully fished out of the river), and it seems likely that if Bierce had been riding in one of the boats that night, he would have referred to the mishaps somewhere in his writings, since they were exactly the sort of absurd happenings that always piqued his morbid interest. As it was, the only thing he left behind of the engagement was a topographical map of Brown's Ferry.

One bit of wartime absurdity, however, did find its way into Bierce's writings. Following the Federals' successful seizure of Brown's Ferry, the Confederates attempted to counterattack at Wauhatchie, a railroad depot a few miles south of the river, in Lookout Valley. The surprise attack began with promise, the rebels striking hard at the Union rear guard. But the serious soon gave way to the ridiculous. Union teamsters, afraid that they were about to be overrun, cravenly abandoned their teams, and dozens of terrified mules stampeded under fire and tore into the Confederate lines. In the pitch-black darkness, the Southerners, supposing that they had been charged by a strong force of enemy cavalry, abruptly broke and ran. (One Union officer waggishly recommended that the victorious mules be promoted to horses.) An anonymous poet in the Twenty-ninth Ohio Infantry subsequently immortalized the incident in a six-stanza ditty, "The Charge of the Mule Brigade." With apologies to Tennyson, the poem began:

> Half a mile, half a mile,
> Half a mile onward,

> *Right toward the Georgia troops,*
> *Broke the two hundred.*
> *"Forward, the Mule Brigade,"*
> *"Charge for the Rebs!" they neighed,*
> *Straight for the Georgia troops*
> *Broke the two hundred.*[4]

Bierce no doubt heard the story—it spread quickly through both armies and even traveled northward to the troops in Virginia—and it happily occasioned one of his few comic treatments of the war. "Jupiter Doke, Brigadier-General," written in 1891, recounts in epistolary form the sublimely ridiculous exploits of the title character, a third-rate politician from backwater Illinois who has somehow obtained a generalship in the army. At the start of the war, Doke (whose name, state, and political affiliation tellingly mirror Ulysses S. Grant) is postmaster of Hardpan Crossroads, in Posey County. Responding to the terse note from the secretary of war announcing his appointment, Doke delivers himself of a grandiloquent, cliché-ridden document promising (as did Grant in his first inaugural address) to work for "the greatest good to the greatest number," with a particular eye toward insuring "the triumph of the party in all elections." Wily politico that he is, Doke immediately requests that his son be appointed postmaster in his place.[5]

The secretary of war, recognizing at once the sort of useless papier-mâché soldier he has on his hands, deftly orders Doke to report to the Kentucky front, dressed in full uniform, after first determining from the local commander (the wonderfully named Blount Wardorg) that the area is crawling with rebel guerrillas. Doke, however, innocently manages to avoid a sniper's bullet by dispatching in his place another Hardpan Crossroads politician, his wife's cousin Briller, "the Patrick Henry of Hardpan," who never reaches the Union camp at Distilleryville. Doke lachrymosely reports that Briller "has doubtless been sacrificed upon the altar of his country." Not missing a beat, he then writes to the President requesting—improperly—that he be given the government contract for supplying his command with "firearms and regalia" through his brother-in-law's firm. Then, pointlessly riding out at the head of his entire brigade to greet an incoming artillery company, Doke is nearly killed by an errant cannonball after the new artillerists mistake him for the enemy. Doke immediately petitions the President to appoint him to "the Gubernatorial Chair of the Territory of Idaho."[6]

While Doke is away on his fool's mission, the enemy takes advantage of his absence to raid across the river and steal all his supplies as a prelude to their own rather optimistic intention to "destroy Cincinnati and occupy the Ohio Valley." The ensuing "battle" of Distilleryville—like so many Civil War engagements—is a comedy of errors, one whose turning point is completely misunderstood and misrepresented by the commanding generals on both sides. Doke, typically, favors his hometown newspaper with a self-serving account of the rebel raid, which he credits to his own "strategic ruse." Reasoning that none of the troops engaged (except himself) hails from Posey County, Doke blithely omits any list of casualties. Nor does he describe his subsequent withdrawal to Jayhawk, a nearby Kentucky hamlet from which he has been instructed to fall back at the first sign of the enemy. It is a running gag in the story that Doke habitually sees everything through the prism of politics, and once in Jayhawk, he appoints a Committee on Retreat to duly elect parliamentary officers and pass a ringing resolution "that in case treason again raises her hideous head on this side of the river every man of the brigade is to mount a mule [and] move promptly in the direction of Louisville and the loyal North." True to the name of the hamlet, Doke quickly steals some 2,300 mules from "the resident Democracy"—that is, the Democrats—and keeps them close at hand for a quick getaway.[7]

The Confederates, planning their own advance into the loyal North, set out to round up Doke's brigade, which one Southern general perceptively notes is "apparently without a commander." What happens next is described, *Rashomon*-like, by the three Confederate generals on the scene. To Maj. Gen. Gibeon J. Buxter, "suddenly the head-of-column was struck by one of the terrible tornadoes for which this region is famous, and utterly annihilated." Buxter sets his losses at 14,994 out of a possible 15,000. Maj. Gen. Dolliver Billows reports that the Federals at Jayhawk had "been reinforced by fifty thousand cavalry," which fell upon his division "with astonishing fury." He places his losses at 11,199 out of 11,200—only he has survived—and announces that he is "changing his base to Mobile, Alabama." Brig. Gen. Schneddeker Baumschank, a German convert to the cause, says merely that "somdings occur, I know nod vot it vos," leaving him with no remaining horses, men, or guns, and "I vights no more in a dam gontry vere I gets vipped und knows nod how it vos done." Each Southern general (whose outlandish names are garbled versions of the three Confederate generals Grant defeated at Fort Donelson) dutifully notes that the others have been killed. The story ends with the United States Congress passing a formal resolution urging that the unfit and undeserving Doke be promoted to major general.[8]

It remains, ironically, for a former slave named Hannibal Alcazar Peyton to give the only true account of the battle. Peyton, as befits his Moorish given name (his Christian name, for whatever it is worth, is also the name of the condemned spy in "An Occurrence at Owl Creek Bridge"), is apparently the only vigilant soul in the immediate vicinity. He hears the enemy approaching in the dead of night and awakens Doke, who is sleeping the night away in blissful ignorance, with the shouted warning, "Skin outer dis fo' yo' life!" Doke, needing no further urging, jumps out of the window in his nightshirt and dashes through the mule pen, whereupon the startled animals take him for "de debble hes'f" and tear down the road, directly into the oncoming

Confederates. Like Wauhatchie, the Charge of the Mule Brigade at Jayhawk is a stunning success, and the rebels scatter in disarray.[9]

Admittedly, "Jupiter Doke" is a tall tale intended to make the reader laugh; yet Bierce, as usual, has a more serious and subtle purpose in mind, as well. As the critic G. Thomas Houser has observed, the story is literally a war of words, in which Bierce cleverly lampoons the very process by which history is written, both during and after it has taken place. The story unfolds through a wide variety of written forms: official orders, private letters, diary entries, military reports, newspaper columns, congressional resolutions, and eyewitness accounts. Each writer, in turn, is concerned not merely with telling the simple truth but also with manipulating events and coloring their outcome. The secretary of war attempts to get Doke killed by ordering him to ride conspicuously through enemy territory in his general's uniform, and later he is perfectly willing to sacrifice the general's entire brigade for the greater strategic good. Doke devotes himself either to seeking financial and political favors blatantly or else to distorting the truth of his own manifest incompetence. The Confederate generals are at pains to explain away their own failures. The hometown newspaper pats itself on the back for having had the questionable enterprise to obtain Doke's report from the front (and even endorses Doke for President). Only the two appropriately named individuals, Blount Wardorg and Hannibal Peyton, see the truth for what it is and tell it in an unvarnished and impartial way.

Given the numerous barely concealed digs the story takes at Ulysses S. Grant, it is well to keep in mind that the piece was written not long after Grant's own best-selling memoirs had been published (1885–1886) and taken the country by storm. Other Union and Confederate generals were also in the process of publishing their memoirs, and *Century Magazine* had just collected its well-received series of Civil War articles into an influential four-volume set, *Battles and Leaders of the Civil War*. The government, too, had joined the book wars and begun issuing its multivolume *Official Records of the Union and Confederate Armies*. After two decades of near-total silence regarding the war, it now seemed as though every officer who had ever held a command higher than lieutenant was writing his own version of events. Besides the fact that Bierce, as a professional writer, may have resented the intrusion of well-paid amateurs onto his turf, it is also likely that he was dismayed and disgusted by the self-serving tenor of the various memoirs, as well as by their magisterial posturing. He had already noted, in a previously published nonfiction article, "The Crime at Pickett's Mill," that it was impossible for anyone, general or private, to tell the entire truth about any battle. "The civilian reader must not suppose when he reads accounts of military actions that these were matters of general knowledge to those engaged," he wrote. "Such statements are commonly made, even by those in high command, in the light of later disclosures, such as the enemy's official reports. It is seldom, indeed, that a subordinate knows anything about the disposition of the enemy's forces—except that it is unamiable—or precisely whom he is fighting. As for the rank and file, they can know nothing more of the matter than the arms they carry." Not for nothing did Bierce entitle his own personal reminiscences "What I Saw of Shiloh" and "A Little of Chickamauga."[10]

With Grant's arrival in Chattanooga, Bierce again had the opportunity to view the rising general's war-making ability at close range. As Hazen's aide, he had free entrée to army headquarters, and with the forces still penned down inside the city (although better fed, now that the Cracker Line had been reinstituted between Bridgeport and Chattanooga), there was little call for his scouting or mapmaking skills. For the first and only time during the war, the hallowed Union troika of Grant, William Tecumseh Sherman, and Phil Sheridan was together during the same battle, and Bierce undoubtedly had occasion to observe them firsthand during the siege. Unfortunately, he wrote next to nothing about the Chattanooga campaign, confining himself to a casual remark in a newspaper column about the drinking habits of the Union high command. "They looked upon the wine when it was red, these tall fellows," he wrote in the February 13, 1886, issue of the San Francisco *Wasp*. "The poisoned chalice went about and about. Some of them did not kiss the dragon; my recollection is that Grant commonly did. I don't think he took enough to comfort the enemy—not more than I did myself from another bottle—but I was all the time afraid that he would, which was ungenerous, for he did not appear at all afraid that I would. This confidence touched me deeply." Bierce's apparent dislike of Grant might call into question the accuracy of his observations concerning the general's supposed tippling at Chattanooga, except that Grant's own chief of staff, Brig. Gen. John A. Rawlins, wrote a revealing letter to his fiancée at the same time, complaining about "the free use of intoxicating liquors at the Headquarters," and also drafted, but did not send, a second letter to Grant himself, bluntly warning the general "to immediately desist from further tasting of liquors," lest he earn the "bitterest imprecations of an outraged and deceived people." Apparently, Grant got the message and sobered up sufficiently to conduct the rest of the campaign competently, if not necessarily as brilliantly as his supporters—and he himself—later maintained.[11]

The siege of Chattanooga was lifted in stages, beginning with the capture of Brown's Ferry and the opening of the Cracker Line. Next came the arrival in mid-November of 37,000 reinforcements from Virginia and Mississippi, commanded, respectively, by Maj. Gen. Joseph Hooker and Maj. Gen. William Sherman. The new contingent, in itself, was larger than the entire Confederate force besieging the town, an advantage that Braxton Bragg heedlessly augmented by sending Lt. Gen. James Longstreet and his fifteen-thousand-man corps from the Army of Northern Virginia off on a fruitless expedition to Knoxville, Tennessee, one hundred miles away. Longstreet, whose arrival at Chickamauga had helped turn the tide of that battle, had since alienated Bragg by signing a petition going around among the generals asking Confederate President Jefferson Davis to remove Bragg from command, a request that, unfortunately for the Confederates, fell on deaf ears. Davis was sufficiently alarmed by the petition to visit Missionary Ridge and meet with the unhappy generals, but he still declined to replace Bragg, a longtime friend. Meanwhile, the poorly clothed and inadequately provisioned soldiers under Bragg's command suffered more than the Yankees they were supposedly besieging. A day's rations frequently consisted of nothing more than a few hard crackers and a tablespoon of sugar, and many rebels were so hungry that they could not sleep at night. "We thought of nothing but starvation," one recalled later. Boredom, frostbite, camp lice, and sheer frustration at the seemingly hollow victory at Chickamauga bedeviled the Confederates and sapped their morale. "The men looked sick, hollow-eyed and heartbroken," wrote one Tennessee private. A colonel on Bragg's staff understated the case considerably when he noted, "Our position, it strikes me, is objectionable."[12]

On November 23, the third part of Grant's plan was carried out by the men of General Thomas's command, who rushed forward under the guise of a dress parade to seize the forward Confederate observation post at Orchard Knob, a small hill midway between Chattanooga and Missionary Ridge. In full view of the rebels, Thomas's troops marched impressively out from the city, drums pounding and flags waving. Believing the advance to be merely a feint, the Confederates were stunned when Thomas's two lead divisions suddenly quickened their pace and rushed toward the hill. Hazen's brigade was in the first line of attack and suffered the heaviest casualties—125 killed or wounded—in the short, sharp skirmish that followed. The seizure of Orchard Knob moved the Union forces to within half a mile of Missionary Ridge, thus providing a natural viewing stand for Grant and his staff to watch the subsequent assault on the ridge two days later.

Once again, Hazen's brigade was in the forefront of the fighting, and quite likely it was the first Union force to reach the crest of Missionary Ridge, an honor that was, and is, still hotly debated. In his *Narrative of Military Service,* Hazen marshaled an impressive array of eyewitness testimony from participants in the famous charge to buttress his claim of being the first to carry the ridge. Initially, the men in the Army of the Cumberland had been assigned merely to menace the rebels at the foot of the ridge while Sherman's contingent from Mississippi rolled up the enemy's right flank at the north end of the ridge and Hooker's troops from the Army of the Potomac moved simultaneously against the rebel left from Lookout Mountain, which they had captured the day before in the romantically named action known as the "Battle Above the Clouds." In quick contradiction to Grant's plan, Sherman's men were stopped in their tracks by Maj. Gen. Patrick Cleburne's hard-fighting division at their end of the ridge, and Hooker got bogged down crossing Chattanooga Creek and was late getting into attack position. Meanwhile, watching from Orchard Knob, Grant became increasingly nervous. Sherman, his close friend, sent message after message to headquarters, demanding to know where Thomas was. ("I am here," Thomas wrote back, exasperated.) Finally, late in the afternoon, Grant gave Thomas the order to move forward against the enemy rifle pits at the base of the ridge. Hazen's brigade, in Wood's division, went off first. One of the most storied charges in American history then ensued.[13]

Bierce, as one of Hazen's staff officers, presumably accompanied Hazen during the advance, although neither mentioned it later. According to Hazen, the entire brigade, including servants, cooks, clerks, and musicians, took part in the charge. At the foot of the ridge, the division halted under severe rifle and artillery fire; three other Union divisions on either side of the two-mile line also stopped. Then, in an uncoordinated, impulsive rush, the entire line began climbing the ridge. Grant, who had ordered no such move, was horrified. He asked Thomas who had ordered the charge. "I don't know," said Thomas, rather unhelpfully. "I did not." Corps commander Gordon Granger likewise disavowed the order, but added, "When those fellows get started, all hell can't stop them." Grant muttered something to the effect that heads would roll if the attack failed, then went back to watching the ridge through his binoculars.

Against all logic, the charge succeeded, due in part to the great valor and determination of the Union troops, and in part to the discouragement and dissension of the Confederates. Hazen made the climb on foot and was close at hand when the first troops to breach the line, from the First Ohio Infantry, leapt over the enemy breastworks and seized a rebel cannon that had been firing down at them. The soldiers immediately turned the cannon to the right, and Hazen directed its fire toward Bragg's headquarters a few hundred yards away. Bierce must have been nearby as well, for the only mention of him in action during the entire war occurs at this time, with Maj. Richard T. Whitaker of the Sixth Kentucky reporting that "having gained the crest and breastwork, the enemy fleeing in front of us, a part of the regiment was sent to the right, by order of Lieutenant Bierce, of General Hazen's staff." As more and more members of the brigade reached the top, they began to slide off to one side or the other, enfilading the rebel positions and widening the breech point. Captured Confederate cannons were hastily turned on their erstwhile owners, and an acrimonious dispute later arose between Hazen and Sheridan over the rightful possession of the enemy guns. Again, Hazen solicited numerous eyewitness accounts crediting his brigade with the seizure of the guns, but Sheridan refused to be convinced, then or later. The argument, in fact, would continue intermittently for the next twenty years and severely affect Hazen's postwar career when Sheridan became his superior out west.[14]

Intramural arguing aside, the siege of Chattanooga now was broken. Demoralized Confederates streamed down the back side of Missionary Ridge while deliriously happy Federals swarmed up the front. "Chickamauga! Chickamauga!" they jeered at the retreating rebels. Back at Orchard Knob, Grant and the others were absolutely transfixed. Charles Dana, at least, had the presence of mind to dash off a message to Washington. "Glory to God," he wired the President. "The day is decisively ours. Missionary Ridge has just been carried by a magnificent charge of Thomas's troops." It was, Dana continued, "one of the greatest miracles of military history," a sight "as awful as a visible interposition of God." That was perhaps overstating things a bit, but Dana after all was a military amateur. Grant, the professional, quickly understood what had—and had not—taken place at Missionary Ridge, and afterward he accepted congratulations with notable ill grace. "Damn the battle," he is said to have grumbled, "I had nothing to do with it."[15]

For Bierce and the other soldiers in the Army of the Cumberland who had taken the battle into their own hands and won the day, Missionary Ridge represented the culmination of an eighteen-month-long struggle for Tennessee. In that length of time, they had fought three of the bloodiest battles in American history—at Shiloh, Stones River, and Chickamauga—and endured nine long weeks of siege and starvation in Chattanooga before decisively turning the tables on their Confederate tormentors at Missionary Ridge. For Bierce, who had arrived in Tennessee as a sergeant major and was ending the campaign as a first lieutenant and a valued member of the brigade commander's personal staff, the series of battles was nothing less than a rite of passage from adolescence to maturity. The young man with the bristling blond mustache who returned home to Warsaw on furlough in mid-December 1863 was vastly different from the droopy, indifferent, studiedly world-weary teenager who had left for the front in April 1861. He had "seen the elephant," as the popular phrase then had it, and like other young soldiers before and since, he now looked at the world through a kind of invisible screen, with himself and his fellow soldiers on one side of the partition, and the rest of the world, in its safe civilian cocoon, on the other. Still, he reached out that winter to someone on the other side—his old schoolmate Bernice Wright. And for a time, at least, she seemed to reach back.

Bernice had done some growing of her own in the past two years. She was still something of a tomboy (a photo taken of her at the time in a formal dress shows a young woman with strong, suntanned arms, an equally tanned round face, and a rather wide, sensuous mouth), but she was also pretty, single, and quite likely the only friend Ambrose Bierce still had in Warsaw—his own family, perhaps, aside. He called on her at her father's rooming house, and Bernice, perhaps suspecting the truth, told him about the strange poem she had received in the mail at the start of the war. "If you knew the man that wrote the poem, would you love him?" Bierce asked. "I certainly would love him," she replied. "How could I help but love anyone who loved me so much?" With that somewhat-qualified avowal, Bierce admitted that he had written the poem, and the two old friends began an altogether typical wartime romance. There were long, bracing walks in the woods, bridle-jingling carriage rides, whispered chats in the family parlor, music recitals and book readings to attend—all dutifully chaperoned by Bernice's sister, Clara. Bierce even took her home to meet the folks. It must have seemed, after the twin hells of Shiloh and Chickamauga, rather like a dream; but even in dream time, Bierce's prickly nature inevitably showed through. One day, Bernice came skipping out of the house with her father's old straw hat tied under her chin, jocosely topped by a veil from her bonnet. Bierce furiously yanked the veil from the hat and ordered her to go back inside and change into something more dignified. She did, and they drove off a moment later "in a peaceful and jolly manner," but one wonders whether that ill-humored episode represented the first slight tear in the fabric of life the young lovers were attempting to weave together. Certainly, Bierce's starchy disposition was a poor match for his sweetheart's blithe, devil-may-care demeanor.[16]

Despite any misgivings the two may have had about their compatibility, an understanding of sorts was reached between them before Bierce returned to the front in February 1864. Whether it was a formal engagement, as previous biographers have believed, is ultimately unknowable, since Bernice later destroyed most of their personal correspondence. Bierce apparently considered it one, and he returned to the army in east Tennessee with a reluctance he had not felt before, his newfound loneliness compounded by his veteran's knowledge that the campaign now taking shape to capture Atlanta would be at least as perilous as the one just concluded at Chattanooga. In what was rapidly becoming a personal tradition, Bierce wrote Bernice a farewell poem, an acrostic that spelled out both her nickname and the terrible consequence of losing her love:

> Fate—whose edict oft hath wrung
> Anguish—drops from hearts unstrung—
> Tears of hopeless prayerless pain—
> I now defy thee. Free again,
> My soul though darkened still by thee,
> And 'bittered still, spurns thy decree.

> While she loves me, sheathe thy dart;
> Rob me of that love—and bury
> In this burning passion-heart—
> Gloomy cell of misery—
> Heated toy of woman's art—
> Thy fearful shaft—Insanity.[17]

On May 6, the Army of the Cumberland moved south into Georgia under a new, although hardly unknown, commander—William Tecumseh Sherman. Grant, thanks in large part to the army's showing at Missionary Ridge, had been promoted to lieutenant general (the first American to hold that rank since George Washington) and given command of the entire Union war effort in the field. Grant, in turn, chose Sherman to command the Military Division of the Mississippi, encompassing all the territory east of the Mississippi River and south of the Appalachians. Together, the two had decided to launch coordinated offensives against the major Confederate armies in Georgia and Virginia. Sherman would head due south toward Atlanta, the de facto capital of the Deep South, while Grant would lead the Army of the Potomac into action against Robert E. Lee in the Wilderness section of Virginia. Henceforth, the war would be one of attrition, a hard, grinding contest between two opponents who had learned all too well how to kill each other swiftly and efficiently in the first three years of the war. Grant reasoned—correctly, as it would turn out—that the North had more men to lose than the South, and that by forcing the Confederates to fight unrelentingly on two major fronts, the Union eventually would wear them down. A war of attrition, of course, entails a certain amount of wastage on both sides, and that was where Bierce and his comrades came in. By hammering themselves against the rock that was the Confederate Army of Tennessee, their job was inexorably to grind it down. The fact that they would also inevitably efface a certain number of themselves in the process was a price that Grant and Sherman were only too willing, indeed eager, to pay.

Payment commenced on May 7 at Rocky Face Ridge, just west of Dalton, where the Confederates, now commanded by Gen. Joseph E. Johnston (Bragg had gone into well-deserved exile in Richmond), were drawn up and waiting. The Southern position, on paper, was a strong one, with fifty thousand men in place along an eight-hundred-foot-high ridge, guarding the army's lifeline, the Western & Atlantic Railroad to Atlanta. Under the defensive-minded Johnston's personal supervision, the rebels had laboriously constructed a series of surprises for the expected Union assault. Artillerists had already sighted their guns on carefully measured targets; engineers had dammed railroad culverts along Mill Creek to create an artificial swamp at the base of the ridge; and huge boulders teetered on the edge of the escarpment, ready to be rolled downward at the first enemy approach. Bristling rifle pits glinted silver in the sun, and the Federals gazing across the man-made lake saw flocks of buzzards roosting on the trees beyond. "What do you think they are doing?" one soldier asked a comrade. "Counting us," said the other.

Sherman's overall plan was for two wings of his army to menace the northern approaches to Dalton at Mill Creek Gap and Dug Gap, while a third wing, commanded by his favorite subordinate, Maj. Gen. James McPherson, swung around to the west and moved through undefended Snake Creek Gap, directly opposite the railroad crossing at the flyspeck village of Resaca, thirteen miles to the south. It was essential to the plan that the Federals appear to mount a serious assault on the two northern gaps, the "terrible doors of death," in Sherman's evocative words. Accordingly, his Army of the Cumberland troops made charge after charge up the steep hillside—Missionary Ridge had been good practice, as far as it went—only to be driven back down again. At least twice, elements of the Union army managed to make a lodgment on the crest of the ridge, but they were brusquely shooed away like so many flies from a horse's back. Hazen's brigade, at Mill Creek Gap, was heavily engaged throughout the day on May 9, but it could advance only two-thirds of the way up the side of the ridge. Confederate sharpshooters armed with long-range Whitworth rifles were "very troublesome," Hazen reported, and could strike men down like the hand of God from a mile away. Understandably, he noted, the soldiers were "much worried by sharpshooters," and the next day he pulled them off the ridge and stationed them under a sheltering crest a few hundred yards to the Union rear.[18]

While the Army of the Cumberland was acting as target practice for Confederate snipers at Dalton, McPherson's undisturbed troops easily penetrated Snake Creek Gap. The plan was working like a charm. "I've got Joe Johnston dead!" Sherman exulted when he heard the news. A commander less fond or confident of his subordinate might have detected a troubling note of qualification in McPherson's report that he was within two miles of Resaca and "propose[d] to cut the railroad, if possible, and then fall back to take a strong position near the gorge on this side of the mountain and await your orders." His orders had not been to take a strong defensive position, but to "make a bold attack on the enemy's flank or his railroad at any point between Tilton and Resaca"—something he quite clearly had failed to do. A second message from McPherson later that night made his failure patently obvious. "The enemy have a strong position at Resaca," he reported, "and, as far as we could see, have it pretty well fortified. After skirmishing till nearly dark, and finding that I could not succeed in cutting the railroad before dark, or getting to it, I decided to withdraw the command and take up a position for the night between Sugar Valley and the entrance to the gap." Sherman, who had been expecting something quite different in the way of news, was incredulous. With "twenty-three thousand of the best troops in the army" at his command, Sherman lamented, McPherson "could have walked into Resaca." As it was, the Confederates now knew the Union strategy, and, falling back along interior lines, they easily won the race for Resaca. "Well Mac," said Sherman when he arrived at Resaca, "you have missed the opportunity of your life." It was an even costlier mistake for the Union infantrymen, who now faced the unappetizing prospect of attacking yet another fortified rebel position.[19]

By the time Sherman's army had emerged from Snake Creek Gap and prepared to move on Resaca on the morning of May 14, the Confederates had managed—literally—to scrape together a three-mile-long defensive position on a series of ridges running parallel to the railroad northwest of town. Between the two armies ran waist-deep Camp Creek, fronted on either side by deep gullies, brier-choked underbrush, and thick woods. Hazen's brigade went into position on the Union left, and Bierce made a quick sketch, "drawn on the spot," showing the brigade's position at the start of the battle. Sherman, in a virtual reprise of his earlier plan, intended to hold the rebels in place with a series of frontal assaults while a smaller force of Federals swung around behind the army and cut off the enemy's escape route across the Oostanaula River below Resaca. Accordingly, Hazen's brigade joined the general attack at noon on the Fourteenth, driving to within two hundred yards of the Confederate line. There the attack bogged down, at the cost to Hazen of sixty men. Other Union brigades had similar ill luck—Confederate general Cleburne, displaying an uncharacteristic Gaelic flair for understatement, labeled the Union assaults "uniformly unhappy failures"—and the first day of fighting ended in a stalemate. That night, the two sides bandied words back and forth, the Northerners calling out, "Johnny Reb! Got anything to eat over there?" And the hungry Southerners retorting, "What nigger commands your brigade?"[20]

The next morning, Hazen received orders to join a general attack at the first sign of an enemy withdrawal. Catching sight of rebel skirmishers falling back and rapidly retreating, Hazen obediently ordered his men forward. Unfortunately, no other Union troops joined the advance, and the brigade lost a hundred men in less than a minute before Hazen could recall them. The rest of the day, like the day before, the Federals hunkered down in the red Georgia clay and traded potshots with the enemy, an experience that Hazen said afforded his men "an uninterrupted practice of sharpshooting at close range." One member of the 149th New York, on Hazen's right, unwisely crawled forward to get a closer look at the enemy and was immediately shot dead. When he fell, his body draped over the Union trench, and Confederate snipers literally filled his head with bullets.[21]

That night, after receiving word that two divisions of Federals had crossed the Oostanaula River below Resaca and were in position to block the Confederate line of retreat, Joseph Johnston ordered his army to pull out of line and retreated south along the railroad toward Atlanta. At a cost of eleven thousand Union and Confederate souls, the Battle of Resaca had been a draw. It was also, in its almost matter-of-fact deadliness, a harbinger of the entire campaign. Thousands of men, many of them veterans already of three years' worth of organized slaughter, would fight and die in dozens of pitched battles and nameless skirmishes on the increasingly lethal road to Atlanta.

Attesting to the dreadfulness of the 1864 fighting, several of Bierce's Civil War stories, including three of his best, are set during the Atlanta campaign. The first of these, "Killed at Resaca," concerns a young Union lieutenant named Herman Brayle, an aide-de-camp of an unnamed general (presumably Hazen), who meets the fate implied by the title. Brayle, described as "the best soldier of our staff" by the narrator, is well liked by his comrades, but he has "one most objectionable and unsoldierly quality: he was vain of his courage." During combat, Brayle needlessly exposes himself to fire, sitting motionless on horseback or standing conspicuously in the open while everyone else is taking cover. (In a sardonic aside, Bierce writes that the higher-ranking officers "were loyally preserving behind the crest of a hill lives infinitely precious to their country.") Whenever dispatched with a message to the front, Brayle sends his horse to the rear and walks slowly forward, his figure accentuated by his full-dress uniform. Such behavior, says the narrator, "is easy to condemn and not very difficult to refrain from imitation, but it is impossible not to respect." Other officers remonstrate with him but are turned away with a mild, joking reply.[22]

At Resaca, Brayle is ordered to take a message to one of the regimental colonels at the front, in clear view of the enemy's fortified lines. Disregarding the general's suggestion that he leave his horse behind and take a safe route through the trees at the rear of the position, Brayle canters out into the open and immediately draws fire. Ironically, his suicidal bravado inspires the men on either side to spring to their feet and exchange a blaze of rifle and cannon fire. Meanwhile, Brayle, unhorsed by the firing, "stood awaiting death. It did not keep him long waiting."[23]

The narrator later comes into possession of Brayle's notebook, including a letter from Brayle's fiancée that immediately explains the dead man's extraordinary behavior: "The letter showed evidence of cultivation and good breeding, but it was an ordinary love letter, if a love letter can be ordinary. There was not much in it, but there was something. It was this: 'Mr. Winters, whom I shall always hate for it, has been telling that at some battle in Virginia, where he got his hurt, you were seen crouching behind a tree. I think he wants to injure you in my regard, which he knows the story would do if I believed it. I could bear to hear of my soldier lover's death, but not of his cowardice.'"[24]

After the war, the narrator goes out of his way to return the letter to its author. The woman in question, Miss Mendenhall, mechanically glances through the letter, saying that "it is very good of you, though I am sure it was hardly worth while." Then, noticing a bloodstain on the letter, she disgustedly throws the letter into her fireplace, despite the narrator's injunction that the stain "is the blood of the truest and bravest heart that ever beat." Miss Mendenhall then wants to know how Brayle died. The narrator concludes: "The light of the burning letter was reflected in her eyes and touched her cheek with a tinge of crimson like the stain upon its page. I had never seen anything so beautiful as this detestable creature.

" 'He was bitten by a snake,' I replied."[25]

"Killed at Resaca" is an interesting story on several levels. To begin with, it gives a brief but vivid description of the battle itself, a little-known but decidedly nasty affair that one rebel soldier later characterized, accurately if ungrammatically, as "a heap of hard fiten." Here is how Bierce renders some of that fighting: "Successive scores of rifles spat at him viciously as he came within range, and our own line in the edge of the timber broke out in visible and audible defense. No longer regardful of themselves or their orders, our fellows sprang to their feet, and swarming into the open sent broad sheets of bullets against the blazing crest of the offending works, which poured an answering fire into their unprotected groups with deadly effect. The artillery on both sides joined the battle, punctuating the rattle and roar with deep, earth-shaking explosions and tearing the air with storms of screaming grape, which from the enemy's side splintered the trees and spattered them with blood, and from ours defiled the smoke of his arms with banks and clouds of dust from his parapet."[26]

No less superb is his capsule description of a staff officer's regular duties and dangers: "In such circumstances the life of a staff officer of a brigade is distinctly 'not a happy one,' mainly because of its precarious tenure and the unnerving alternations of emotion to which he is exposed. From a position of that comparative security from which a civilian would ascribe his escape to a 'miracle,' he may be despatched with an order to some commander of a prone regiment in the front line—a person for the moment inconspicuous and not always easy to find without a deal of search among men somewhat preoccupied, and in a din in which question and answer alike must be imparted in the sign language. It is customary in such cases to duck the head and scuttle away on a keen run, an object of lively interest to some thousands of admiring marksmen. In returning—well, it is not customary to return."[27]

The story is also notable for its barely disguised portrait of Bierce himself. Herman Brayle's blatantly Bierce-like name is not the only thing he shares with the author. Like Bierce, he is from Ohio, serves on a general's staff, has light hair and gray-blue eyes, and has seen action at Stones River and in Virginia. Bierce, of course, was not suicidal during the war, although he did perform at least two notable acts of heroism while rescuing others while under fire. But he did recognize the fatalism inherent in a staff officer's job description, both in the story he wrote a quarter of a century after the war, and in a poignant and revealing letter he wrote to Bernice Wright's sister, Clara, a few weeks after the Battle of Resaca. As the only existing letter that Bierce wrote during the war, it deserves to be quoted in full. Dated June 8, 1864, and sent from Acworth, Georgia, it reads:

My Dear Clara:

Will you be very much displeased to hear from me by letter?

If I thought so I would never touch pen again. 'Tis true you never asked me to write to you, but the knowledge that I still live cannot be unwelcome to one who professes to regard me as a friend. *I don't know Clare what the word* friend *means to you who have so many, but to me friendship has a meaning deeper than the definition of Webster or Worcester. And my friendship for you is a feeling which no language can define. Do you call this flattery? If so you do not know me and I forgive you.*

I have not written to you before, but my neglect was not caused by indifference. I knew Tima would sometimes mention my name to you. But I want to hear from you very much; not because you will tell me of Tima, but of yourself. You always seemed to think, Clare, that I never cared for you except as Tima's sister—a sort of necessary evil. (Vide—our carriage ride by Eagle lake. Is it necessary for me to say you were unjust to me?) No, Clare, except our sweet Tima, I love you better than any one on this earth.

Perhaps this is not right;—perhaps my mother and sisters should be first in my affections,—but so it is.

I am getting very tired of my present life and weary of the profession of arms. Not because of its horrors and dangers; not because its hardships affect me, but because I wish to be with you and my darling. The pleasant weeks with you, so like a dream, have nearly spoiled the soldier to make the—pensive individual.

Ask Tima why I get no more letters from her. Have I offended her? I may have written something as heartless and cruel as I used to say to her. If I have I hope she will forgive me. Her last letter was dated May 11th.

Do you think that there is a probability of my letters getting into other hands than hers? Please tell me for the thought troubles me very much. Oh, if I could be with you both again my measure of happiness would be full. I do not see how I could have been so unhappy as I sometimes was when with you.

But I ought rather to be thankful for being allowed so much happiness with you—so much more than I deserved—than to repine at the fate which withholds more. I hardly expect ever to see you again, and perhaps it is better so. Every day some one is struck down who is so much better than I. Since leaving Cleveland, Tenn., my brigade has lost nearly one third of its numbers killed and wounded.

Among these were so many good men who could ill be spared from the army and the world. And yet I am left. But my turn will come in time. Oh, how pleasant death would be were it for you and Tima, instead of for my country—for a cause which may be right and may be wrong. Do you think I lack patriotism for talking this way? Perhaps so. Soldiers are not troubled with that sort of stuff.

May I talk to you about D—? Do you love him yet? or think you do?

Is that a blunt question? You know you told me you did once. Please answer it.

Oh, I wish I could help you. You who have been so good to me. But my hands are tied. I can only warn you. There is a metal among the rocks here which viewed at a distance has all the appearance of gold. A close inspection shows it to be the basest dross. You are an admirer of pebbles I believe.

Do tell me about yourself and Tima. What books you read, what society you have, and if you have lots of fun. Capt. Webster desired to be remembered to you and Tima if I ever wrote you. By the way is Jo Williams at W.? The less you have to do with him the better you will please me. If you require reasons I will give them. Do you know my mother yet, and does Tima call on her as she promised me? How is Lyde C.?

Now Clare if you don't write to me at once I shall take it as proof that you don't wish to hear from me again.

Give my kindest regards to 'Slissa and the girls.

Take my darling in your arms, and kiss her a thousand times for me.

With more love than I can tell, I am

Your friend
A. G. Bierce

P.S. Do you hear from Ol? I can get no word from him.

B——

It is raining very hard and I am very lonely. In looking over my valise just now I found tucked away a little embroidered handkerchief. Do you remember it? Then there were also some little pebbles; common looking things enough, but each one is transparent, and looking into it I see two tiny figures with skirts just slightly elevated, showing such delicate little—feet, stepping along the soft sand, and picking up these little nothings for me. What delicate little tracks they leave behind them. But these tracks will all be erased by the next rain. Not so the impressions left on the hard and stony soil of my heart. Every examination shows me how some mischievous persons have crept into the garden of my soul, and tracked it up worse than a melon patch by school-boys.

But not one of the little tracks shall be blotted out by the rude gardener Time. The amount of it all is, Clare, that I love you and Tima so I can't find language to tell it.

I just wish I could pass my whole life with you both, and have nothing to do but give myself up to the delicious intoxication of your society. For that, I would renounce the whole world and all the ties of kindred; throw away every ambition or aim in life, and make a fool of myself in the most approved style generally.

Brady[28]

A typical letter from a lonely young soldier on a rainy night, but if one deconstructs it like a Bierce short story, it reveals an unusual wealth of information concerning the author's state of mind at the time. Curiously, the apparent purpose of the letter, to ascertain why Bernice has not written him for a month, is obscured and nearly overwhelmed by the numerous indications Bierce gives that he is equally in love with Clara. One does not ordinarily write to the sister of one's lover with such overt displays of affection, unless one is somewhat hedging one's bets, so to speak. Biographer Richard J. O'Connor is probably right when he suggests that "Bierce might have done better with the less frivolous Clara, who apparently took him, and his frequently grim moods, more seriously than the fun-loving, flirtatious Bernie." Certainly, in his letter, Bierce goes to some pains to intimate as much to Clara. A brief aside typically disposes of his mother as someone with an equal claim to his affections; and there is the first indication (later stated openly in his writings) that Bierce questions the moral rightness of the Union cause. His worries about the letter falling into someone else's hands and his blunt warnings about Clara's purported boyfriend "D" and the mysterious Jo Williams are early examples of the jealous paranoia that would darken Bierce's personal relationships with women all his life. In the same way, his rather gratuitous and insulting advice about fool's gold and consorting with "pebbles" is another early sign of his unattractive habit of dispensing magisterial judgments to others on how they should live their lives. And his curious image of Clara and Bernice as mischievous schoolboys tracking up "the garden of my soul" is a perfect example of just how guarded and reticent he could be in matters relating to the human heart.[29]

Of equal interest is Bierce's fatalistic view of his own impending fate—"my turn will come in time." This might be passed off as the overly dramatic posturing of a veteran soldier for the folks back home, except that something had happened to Bierce and his brigade two weeks before that might have given even the bravest soldier pause. It was what Bierce later termed, with bitter accuracy, "The Crime at Pickett's Mill," a murderous frontal assault on an entire Confederate division by Hazen's lone brigade, an incident that Sherman and other Union officers involved in the attack covered up, Vietnam-like, for decades after the war.

The battle at Pickett's Mill took place on the afternoon of May 27, two days after a similar Federal attack had failed miserably at New Hope Church—or "Hell Hole," as survivors of that misbegotten action called it. Sherman, believing that the Confederate line was dangerously overextended, decided to turn the enemy right. Ironically, the man he selected for the task, Maj. Gen. Oliver O. Howard, had some experience at flank attacks; unfortunately, it was the experience of having been outflanked himself, at both Chancellorsville and Gettysburg. Howard, dubbed "the Christian General" for his extreme religiosity (less pious observers called him "Old Prayer

Book"), had lost an arm at the Battle of Seven Pines, an engagement for which he would eventually receive a Medal of Honor, but he had lost none of the purse-lipped sanctimoniousness that caused Sherman to complain later that Howard "should have been born in petticoats." His men, especially those veteran midwesterners he had inherited upon his arrival from Virginia after the Battle of Chickamauga, considered him a bad-luck commander and nicknamed him "Uh-Oh" Howard for his various battlefield misadventures. No one, however, could have guessed the depths to which his inability could sink. At Pickett's Mill, they reluctantly found out just how unlucky he—and they—could be.[30]

Pickett's Mill, on Little Pumpkin Vine Creek, thirty miles northwest of Atlanta, was a water-power facility run by the recently widowed Mrs. Pickett, whose Confederate cavalryman husband had died at Chickamauga. It was Sherman's intention for Howard to swing eastward behind the creek, then wheel south and strike the presumably exposed rebel flank. The extraordinarily rough terrain—no one could see more than fifty yards in any direction—was expected to shield the risky maneuver. Inexplicably, one of Howard's brigade commanders, Col. William Gibson, insisted on having his bugler sound the advance at regular interludes, and Confederate scouts, at any rate, had already picked up the Union trail. By the time Howard moved into position at 4:00 P.M., the enemy was well in place on a rocky, tree-covered ridge directly in front of them.[31]

Compounding his error, Howard determined to attack in columns of brigades, meaning that only one brigade at a time would make the charge, followed closely by the next. The dubious honor of leading the attack fell to Hazen and his brigade. "We will put in Hazen and see what success he has," division commander Thomas Wood told Howard, a remark that Hazen overheard and communicated to Bierce with a quick look that "betray[ed] his sense of the criminal blunder." At exactly 4:30 P.M., Hazen's troops advanced, their progress immediately stymied by a one-hundred-foot-deep ravine that cut diagonally across their path. The underbrush was so thick around them that the color-bearers had to keep their flags furled to prevent them from being torn to pieces by low-lying branches. Bierce, as topographical engineer, had already scouted far enough ahead to hear the distinct murmur of rebel infantrymen waiting for them half a mile away, a fact he duly reported to the grim-faced Hazen. Enemy skirmishers immediately fell back at the Union approach, which caused some of the Federals to shout, erroneously, "Ah, damn you, we have caught you without your logs now!" Southern voices immediately retorted, in reference to published newspaper reports that they were suffering from low morale, "Come on, we are demoralized!"[32]

The brigade labored through the ravine and up the rock-strewn hillside, the color-bearers now breaking out their flags and waving them back and forth in the still dusk air. Then, seemingly as one, the rebels opened up.

Bierce, who was advancing on foot, as were all the officers, heard "a ringing rattle of musketry, the familiar hissing of bullets, and before us the interspaces of the forest were all blue with smoke. Hoarse, fierce yells broke out of a thousand throats. The uproar was deafening; the air was sibilant with streams and sheets of missiles. In the steady, unvarying roar of small-arms the frequent shock of the cannon was rather felt than heard, but the gusts of grape which they blew into that populous wood were audible enough, screaming among the trees and cracking against their stems and branches."[33]

It was the brigade's singular misfortune to be attacking the best division in the Confederate army, that of the redoubtable Cleburne, whose battle-tested troops had stopped Sherman in his tracks at Missionary Ridge the previous November and roughly treated him again at Resaca. Not that it made much difference whom they were attacking; by that time in the war, any veteran troops holding fortified ground could have beaten back the unsupported charge of a single brigade attacking over virtually impassable terrain. Cleburne later gave the Yankees at Pickett's Mill a backhanded compliment, noting that they "display[ed] a courage worthy of an honorable cause." Nevertheless, he said, his men, "needing no logs, were awaiting them, and as they appeared upon the slope, slaughtered them with deliberate aim." It was all over in forty-five minutes. Hazen's brigade lost 467 men, about a third of whom were killed outright, an unusually high proportion, attesting to both the good marksmanship of the Confederates and the fact that once a man was wounded, he had no place to hide. After the battle, one Confederate officer found a dead Yank who had been shot forty-seven times.[34]

During the action, Hazen sent his staff officers dashing to the rear to find out what had happened to the other two brigades that were supposed to have joined the attack at five-minute intervals. Bierce, returning empty-handed like the others, observed a peculiar battlefield phenomenon known as the "dead-line." It was the point, liberally sprinkled with corpses, beyond which no further advance was possible. At Pickett's Mill, the dead-line was about fifteen paces from the enemy position. No one got closer than that, and few got that close. Confederate captain Samuel Foster later counted fifty dead Yankees within a thirty-foot radius of where he stood, most of them "shot in the head, and a great number [with] their skulls bursted open and their brains running out." Without an order being given, the brigade's survivors began falling back. Hazen did not try to stop them. "The battle, as a battle, was at an end," noted Bierce, "but there was still some slaughtering that it was possible to incur before nightfall; and as the wreck of our brigade drifted back through the forest we met the brigade (Gibson's) which, had the attack been made in column, as it should have been, would have been but five minutes behind our heels, with another five minutes behind its own. As it was, just forty-five minutes had elapsed, during which the enemy had destroyed us and was now ready to perform the same kindly office for our successors."[35]

By the time Howard called off the butchery, Wood's division had lost nearly fifteen hundred men. In the grimmest of ironies, Howard received a message from Sherman canceling the attack, but it arrived two hours too late to stop the charge. Never subsequently did Sherman refer to the battle at Pickett's Mill, either in his official reports or in his best-selling memoirs. Howard dismissed it in a single sentence. Bierce noted disgustedly that while the victorious rebels gave various lengthy accounts of the battle, "the vanquished have not thought it expedient to relate it." Only the men who fought there, and the families of those who died there, remembered it.[36]

After Pickett's Mill, Sherman fell back to the railroad depot at Acworth, whence Bierce wrote to Clara Wright a few days later. Having failed to turn the Confederate flanks at New Hope Church and Pickett's Mill, Sherman intended to smash straight down the rail line to Marietta and on into Atlanta. Meanwhile, the sniping and killing continued at a steady rate; 21,000 Union and Confederate troops had been killed and wounded in less than a month since the campaign began. Bierce and his comrades would doubtless have agreed with the Southern private who wrote to his parents that "it is awful hard soldiering up here and takes a right stout man to stand it." Even in camp the soldiers were at risk—in Bierce's brigade, one man was killed by a stray shot that came out of nowhere, completely unheard, and two others were electrocuted by lightning during a severe thunderstorm. Eleven straight days of rain turned the camps into quagmires, and continuous sniping and skirmishing kept everyone's nerves on edge. Sherman, in a letter to his brother, Ohio senator John Sherman, complained that the campaign had turned into "a big Indian war." Confederate general Samuel French, continuing the metaphor, recommended that some Bible society send Sherman a prayer book "instead of shipping them all to a more remote heathen, but it would be the same in either class. The one is uncivilized by nature—the other, I fear, becoming so from habit. Perhaps 'Tecumseh' has something to do with it."[37]

It had now become the "hard war" that Grant and Sherman—with Abraham Lincoln's enthusiastic blessing—had envisioned two months before. There was nothing particularly noble or glorious about it. On June 14, Confederate general Leonidas Polk, the much-beloved churchman turned warrior of the Confederate army, was killed by a purposely aimed artillery round at Pine Mountain, the shell crashing through his body and exploding wetly against the tree behind him. Rebel soldiers spread the rumor that Sherman himself had aimed the gun; one left behind a sign tacked to a tree, reading, "You damned Yankee sons of bitches have killed our old Gen. Polk." Some Southerners talked openly of raising the black flag. In fact, both parties had pretty much done so already, the steady, grinding slaughter having turned the men, in Bierce's words, into "hardened and impenitent man-killers, to whom death in its awfulest forms is a fact familiar to their every-day observation."

In both camps, the soldiers lived with a pervasive sense of impending doom.[38]

Bierce later objectified that feeling of doom in a trio of short stories set in the Atlanta campaign, each dealing, significantly, with literal or figurative suicide. In "One of the Missing," Pvt. Jerome Searing, a Union sniper in the act of taking aim at a retreating column of Confederates at Kennesaw Mountain, finds himself trapped instead by a stray cannon blast in a collapsed building, his hair-trigger rifle pointing directly at his head. Buried in the rubble, Searing suddenly confronts the same fate he had been planning for the enemy. He is now literally staring down the barrel of a gun, a perfect image for the condition in which the two armies found themselves during the murderous summer of 1864. Finally reaching the limits of his endurance, Searing purposely pulls the trigger of the rifle. Ironically, it had gone off when he dropped it, but the sheer terror of the situation overwhelms him, and he dies of fright. What had seemed like hours of torture was actually a mere twenty-two minutes.[39]

In a second Bierce story, "One Officer, One Man," an inexperienced Union captain joyously embarks on his first battle as an opportunity to impress "a pair of dark eyes" back home, as well as the veterans under him who heretofore have regarded him "as one who had shirked his duty, until forced unwillingly into the field." The officer, named Graffenreid, is swiftly disabused of any martial ardor by an enemy shell that startles him into covering his face with his hands, much to the amusement of the men in the ranks. This embarrassment is rapidly compounded when the man standing next to him is shot and killed. The captain immediately throws himself down beside the dead man, while other officers merely dismount casually and send their horses to the rear for safekeeping. Lying beside the dead man, Graffenreid is disgusted by his first encounter with death on the battlefield. From beneath the soldier "flowed a little rill of blood. It had a faint, sweetish odor that sickened him. The face was crushed into the earth and flattened. It looked yellow already, and was repulsive. Nothing suggested the glory of a soldier's death nor mitigated the loathsomeness of the incident." As with Searing in "One of the Missing," the horrors that Graffenreid imagines are far worse than the reality of the situation (the enemy, in fact, has already retreated without a fight). "He fixed his eyes upon the forest, where all again was silent. He tried to imagine what was going on there—the lines of troops forming to attack, the guns being pushed forward by hand to the edge of the open. He fancied he could see their black muzzles protruding from the undergrowth, ready to deliver their storm of missiles. The fire of battle was not now burning very brightly in this warrior's soul." At last, unable to stand the strain of waiting, Graffenreid falls on his sword like a defeated Roman consul. He and the dead man beside him are the only two soldiers to die in the meaningless skirmish.[40]

The third story, "A Son of the Gods," concerns an unnamed young officer who offers himself as a sacrificial victim to ascertain whether the enemy is in force behind a distant hill. Ordinarily, this would be the work of a line of skirmishers, who typically would move forward ahead of the main body of troops. But the young officer, conspicuously mounted on a white horse with a scarlet blanket, inexplicably volunteers to go in their place. "This military Christ," as the narrator calls him, purposely gallops back and forth in front of the concealed enemy, trying to draw their fire. "So long as he advances, the line will not fire—why should it? He can safely ride into the hostile ranks and become a prisoner of war. But this would defeat his object. It would not answer our question; it is necessary either that he return unharmed or be shot to death before our eyes. Only so shall we know how to act." Finally, having caught sight of the enemy's dispositions, the officer rides back toward friendly lines, "speeding like the wind straight down the slope—toward his friends, toward his death!" The rebels fire, unhorsing the officer, and before they fatally fire again, he raises his saber in a last "hero's salute to death and history." Alerted to the enemy's overwhelming number, the Union army withdraws—one cannot help but think that Bierce must have wished that General Howard had made a similar decision at Pickett's Mill. But the story is a fable, not history, a tender—or sardonic—allegory in which a Christ-like figure makes the ultimate sacrifice for his fellow men, the same sacrifice that they were making by the thousands en route to Atlanta, without the benefit of a grateful and admiring audience. Bierce is speaking for them all when he mourns: "Ah, those many, many needless dead! That great soul whose beautiful body is lying over yonder, so conspicuous against the sere hillside—could it not have been spared the bitter consciousness of a vain devotion? Would one exception have marred too much the pitiless perfection of the divine, eternal plan?"[41]

In real life, of course, there are no such exceptions, and Bierce had already had an inkling of his own predestined fate. The "divine plan," if such there was, involved continual little acts of heroism by each individual in the army, acts performed in the face of such an overwhelming awareness of death that they would later seem to Bierce like examples of unwilled—or, at any rate, will-less—self-murder. Two weeks and one day after writing to Clara Wright that "my turn will come," it came. On June 23, 1864, leading a skirmish line forward at Kennesaw Mountain, Bierce was shot in the head by a rebel sharpshooter. The bullet struck him in the left temple, fracturing the temporal bone, and burrowed around the side of his skull to a point behind the left ear. Hazen, in reporting the incident, described the wound as "very dangerous and complicated...the ball remaining within the head." (In his memoirs Hazen complained that Bierce, "a brave and gallant fellow," had been needlessly wounded, since the skirmish line was already close enough to the enemy.) Even now, Bierce's luck held—at least in part. Either the bullet that struck him was already spent or else it hit him at an odd angle, like a carom shot in pool. Or perhaps he just had an unusually hard head. At any rate, although the vast majority of head shots in the Civil War were fatal, Bierce somehow survived both the initial wound and the jolting two-day train ride back to Chattanooga in an open flatcar. Covered with a tarpaulin like so much damaged cargo, he and the other Union wounded rattled northward in steaming heat and drizzling rain. Afterward, he remembered that the bright, cold moonlight had bothered him more than the rain, penetrating his closed eyelids and making his head throb ceaselessly with the jarring rhythm of the train.[42]

From his hospital bed in Chattanooga, Bierce asked for and received a thirty-day furlough home to Warsaw, a recuperation period that subsequently was extended through August and into September. His head healed slowly, and he remained prone to splitting headaches and fainting spells at the least physical exertion. But it was his heart that pained him more. Five months after leaving Warsaw with his health intact and his girlfriend waiting, he was back home again, walking the familiar dusty streets with an enormous bandage on his head, and walking them alone—he and Bernice were no longer a couple. The break was bitter, although its genesis has been lost to time. It seems to have involved a quarrel over one or the other's letter-writing deficiencies, sharpened perhaps by Bierce's habitual suspicions regarding the ultimate fidelity of women. Hot words were exchanged, keepsakes returned, and the engagement—formal or informal—was broken. It had not lasted very long.[43]

In the long run, it was probably the best thing that could have happened to either of them, but for the moment, Bierce was inconsolable. He moped about his father's library, lying on a sofa reading, a heavy military cape thrown over his legs, and one day he rode out to the old farmstead to visit his brother Gus, who recalled later that Ambrose's head "was all tied up." (Inside as well as out, apparently—Gus told their brother Albert that Ambrose had not seemed quite right at the time, which was not surprising, given all that he had been through recently.) His parents may have consoled him with pertinent bits of Scripture, or they may have simply left him alone. At any rate, he endured Warsaw for as long as he could, then returned to the army in mid-September. He was still unwell—he would later say that his head had been "broken like a walnut"—and he had to ride in a wagon wherever he went. But at least he was away from Indiana and all its unhappy associations. And this time, he vowed, he would never go back. That part of his life was over.[44]

5

I Respectfully Decline
the Appointment

*M*uch had changed during the three months that Bierce was away from the front recovering from his wound. Most significantly, William Tecumseh Sherman had taken Atlanta, famously telegraphing back to Washington: "Atlanta is ours, and fairly won." The Confederates, under a new commander, thirty-three-year-old general John Bell Hood, had finally come out from behind their breastworks and attacked the Union army, only to meet with devastating defeat in three separate ill-conceived sorties before abruptly abandoning the city on September 1, 1864. Once inside Atlanta, Sherman began making plans for an ambitious march to the sea. He would leave Hood to his own devices (and those of Maj. Gen. George H. Thomas, who had been given command of all remaining Federal forces in Tennessee) and strike out for the eastern coast of Georgia. Along the way, freed from the inconvenient interference of any organized Confederate resistance, Sherman intended to "make Georgia howl." With the help of his sixty thousand superbly conditioned, battle-hardened veterans, he would prove his favorite dictum, "War is hell."[1]

Among those set to accompany Sherman on his march was Bierce's old commander and friend William B. Hazen. After thirty-two months of capable, even valorous service at the head of the Nineteenth Brigade, Hazen had finally been rewarded with command of a division—Sherman's own Second Division,

Fifteenth Corps, Army of the Tennessee. Hazen had already taken leave of his old brigade when Bierce returned in late September, and the two would not see each other again for the rest of the war. Bierce resumed light duties on the staff of Col. Sidney Post, a somewhat rotund former newspaper editor from Illinois who had taken Hazen's place as brigade commander. Fortunately for Bierce, there was little in the way of topographical duties requiring his personal attention just then. As he later admitted, he was still "subject to fits of fainting, sometimes without assignable immediate cause, but mostly when suffering from exposure, excitement or excessive fatigue." He carried with him a doctor's note excusing him from marching, and he generally stuck close to camp.[2]

A possible clue to Bierce's state of mind after his return to the front may be found in his brief, almost negligible short story "The Other Lodgers." In it, a Colonel Levering recounts an eerie experience he had in Atlanta "in September, 1864—shortly after the siege." Besides the place and date of the story, Levering's circumstances also mirror Bierce's in that, as the narrator notes, he "had not entirely recovered from a gunshot wound in the head, received in an altercation." Stopping for the night at a ramshackle hotel, Levering is shown to a darkened room by a spectral night clerk. "Worn out by two days and a night of hard railway travel," the colonel lies down on a mattress and quickly falls asleep. Awakened by moonlight "which seemed, somehow, a bit spooky," Levering is startled to find that he has been sharing the room with a dozen other lodgers—all of them dead and carefully laid out in rows along the wall. Going downstairs to complain, he finds the night clerk sitting motionless, "with a colorless face and the whitest, blankest eyes I ever saw. He had no more expression than the back of my hand." After the clerk suddenly disappears, a second man arrives on the scene, a night watchman who tells Levering that the hotel had been used as a hospital during the siege, and that the room he had stayed in was "the dead-room," where corpses had been stored; moreover, says the watchman, the clerk himself had been dead for several weeks. He offers to take Levering back to the room for a second look, but the colonel loudly declines and bolts out the door and into the street.[3]

Admittedly, "The Other Lodgers" is not much of a story, but its outward circumstances, echoing Bierce's wound, his train trip to the hospital (complete with intrusive, unsettling moonlight), and his childhood dreams of dead men arranged in a gruesomely symmetrical fashion, reveal a young man who is not yet at ease with his own survival. The dreamy, confused state of the narrator is also suggestive of Bierce's persistent dizziness in the aftermath of his wounding, a headachy netherworld somewhere between the daylit world of the living and the dark, uncertain world of the dead. It is not uncommon for survivors of a major trauma—and a bullet wound to the head would certainly qualify—to feel themselves living a sort of posthumous existence, not entirely convinced of their own survival. And

Bierce, who had already seen hundreds of his comrades killed in just such a way, may be permitted a bit of wonder at his own somewhat miraculous deliverance.[4]

At any rate, he did not have long to lounge about camp. In mid-October, while still awaiting final approval from Washington for his march to the sea, Sherman brought his army north to Gaylesville, Alabama, to keep an eye on Hood's Confederates, now camped thirty miles away at Gadsden. For several days, the two sides waited warily for the other to make the first move. It was, said Bierce, "an interregnum of expectancy between two regimes of activity." The waiting wore on everyone's nerves, and Bierce and a fellow lieutenant named Cobb decided one morning to put some adventure back into their lives. After splashing through a deep creek—and ruining Bierce's "resplendent new uniform" in the process—the pair dried off and rode down to the Coosa River. There they found a trio of Union soldiers hiding a small boat, which they immediately commandeered for their "madmen's enterprise." Once across the river, the quintet moved through a field of standing corn until they came to an overgrown plantation where a handful of Southern women and children were playing in the yard. Suddenly, rebel cavalry appeared ahead and behind them, opening fire. Cobb dove into the woods, while Bierce and the three privates climbed a fence and dashed across the field toward a swamp a few hundred yards away. Panting hard, Bierce concealed himself in some brambles, "the others continuing—as a defeated commander would have put it—to fall back." Behind him, he heard someone calling out the dogs.[5]

For the rest of the day, Bierce hid in a brier patch beside the road, from which place he could clearly hear "a variety of disparaging remarks upon Yankee valor and dispiriting declarations of intention conditional on my capture." He also overheard the enemy reporting that they had captured the three privates and intended to send them south to Andersonville prison camp; he never learned what became of them. At nightfall, he dodged back across the road and picked his way through the towering cornfield, making his way toward the river. Disdaining an attempt to swim the dark water, Bierce tramped along the shoreline, looking for the boat. At one point, he almost stepped on a rebel sentry guarding a small campsite. Fortunately for him, the sentry and his fellows were all asleep, and Bierce quickly and quietly retraced his steps.[6]

He was not so lucky when he came upon another enemy camp. A guard snapped off a rifle shot at him, and Bierce scampered away into the corn, climbed a tree, and "perched until dawn, a most uncomfortable bird." Then he forded the river to an island in the middle of the stream and prepared to swim back across to the Union side. By now exhausted and alarmed, he blacked out. When he woke, it was late afternoon, and he spent the rest of the daylight hours attempting to construct a raft out of some old logs from a fallen-down shed. He was just about to set out for the far shore when "I heard a sharp metallic click—the cocking of a rifle! I was a prisoner." A member of the Confederate Home Guard had heard Bierce stomping around on the island. Now he took his prize prisoner back to his home, where "there was a reception, attended by the elite of the whole vicinity. A Yankee officer in full fig—minus only the boots, which could not be got on to his swollen feet—was something worth seeing, and those who came to scoff remained to stare. They were a trifle disappointed by the absence of horns, hoof and tail, but bore their chagrin with good-natured fortitude." In the midst of the festivities, Bierce fell dead asleep, and his captors politely put him to bed.[7]

The next morning, he was escorted to the rear by two mounted guards, accompanied by another Union prisoner picked up in a raid across the river. Bierce did not think much of his fellow captive, "a most offensive brute—a foreigner of some mongrel sort, with just sufficient command of our own tongue to show that he could not control his own." Moreover, he was thoroughly alarmed by the casually ventured opinion of his guards that if they chanced to meet a local guerrilla chieftain named Jeff Gatewood along the way, "he would probably take me from them and hang me to the nearest tree." Once or twice, hearing horsemen coming down the road, the guards humanely concealed Bierce in some nearby brush to prevent just such an undertaking.[8]

That night, the four put up at a farmhouse, and Bierce pretended to sleep until his guards dozed off. Then, taking particular care not to awaken his fellow prisoner, he sprang through the door and struck out for the woods, vaulting fences and dodging dogs. Amazingly, there was no pursuit. After another long day trudging through brier patches and splashing through creeks, Bierce made it back to the river and plunged straight in. On the other side, he saw "a more heavenly vision than ever the eyes of a dying saint were blessed withal—two patriots in blue carrying a stolen pig slung upon a pole." He reeled back into camp, where he found the resourceful Cobb already returned and sharing "a pleasant story about a man cut in two by a cannon-shot," and immediately fell headfirst into the campfire. "What is it, Cobb?" asked Col. Henry McConnell, the acting brigade commander. "I don't know, Colonel," said Cobb, dragging Bierce out of the ashes by his feet, "but thank God it is dead!"[9]

Despite his close brush with death or imprisonment—and confinement in the Confederate prison at Andersonville amounted to pretty much the former—Bierce was sufficiently recovered in time to accompany his brigade on its headlong march into Tennessee in mid-November. Hood and his thirty-thousand-man Army of Tennessee had crossed into their home state from northwest Alabama with the desperate intent of interposing themselves between General Thomas, in Nashville, and the Fourth and Twenty-third corps, hastily en route thereto from Pulaski. With the help of a better road and some unseasonably bitter weather that roiled the countryside into a glutinous, wagon-stalling muck, the Federal forces managed to beat the rebels to the crossroads village of Columbia, just south of Duck River, and prepared to meet the oncoming horde. "It is one of the proudest recollections of my life," Bierce proudly recalled twenty-four years later in the San Francisco *Examiner,* "that although the movement was one of the most rapid and persistent that occurred during the war, I was strong, hardy and resolute enough to keep up with the procession." With Confederate cavalryman Nathan Bedford Forrest roaming the countryside like an avenging devil, shooting down anything that moved, he had little alternative but to keep up.[10]

On November 27, Maj. Gen. John Schofield, commanding the Union column, fell back again, this time in the direction of Spring Hill, ten miles north of the Duck River. The next morning, Bierce and the rest of Post's brigade watched from their advanced position while Hood's army marched relentlessly toward Spring Hill in a "fascinating and portentous pageant." Somehow the rebels, having finally managed to win the race, allowed Schofield's cutoff column to sneak past them that night into the pretty little town of Franklin, ten miles farther north, in the direction of Nashville. "Fools are God's peculiar care," noted Bierce, "and one of his protective methods is the stupidity of other fools." Still, it was such a close call that Bierce imagined he could feel his hair turning gray as he marched.[11]

The Union army fanned out in a semicircle south of Franklin while friendly engineers desperately began repairing the lone railroad bridge across the Harpeth River north of town. In the interim, Hood and his army drew up, like so many thousands of dragon's teeth, along the crest of Winstead Hill, two miles away. Between the two armies lay a flat, open plain, uninter-rupted by any natural cover. Union muskets and artillery had a clear shot at anyone foolish enough to attack them. Bierce, for one, did not believe any-one could be that foolish, and "in a more tranquil temper than his failure at Spring Hill had put him into Hood would probably have passed around our left and turned us out with ease"—which is exactly what Forrest was in the very act of suggesting to Hood that he do. Instead, the impetuous young commander, who had lost the use of an arm at Gettysburg and an entire leg two months later at Chickamauga, determined to make a fight. "Apparently," said Bierce, "that was not his day for saving life."[12]

The ensuing Confederate charge, undertaken an hour before sundown on November 30, 1864, was perhaps the most gallant, and certainly the most doomed, of the entire war. Not even Pickett's charge at Gettysburg had a higher casualty rate—6,252 Confederate dead, wounded, or captured, including 1,750 killed outright—more, by way of comparison, than the entire Union army had lost during the Seven Days' Battles around Richmond in 1862. Included in that funereal toll were six Southern generals: Patrick Cleburne, Otho Strahl, John Adams, John Carter, Hiram Granbury, and the provocatively named States Rights Gist. Adding to the poignancy of the moment was the near-unanimous certitude among the soldiers gathered on Winstead Hill that their attack was foredoomed to failure. Cleburne, whose blue-and-white battle flag had flown above his redoubtable division at every major battlefield in the west, and who had led the murderous repulse of Hazen's brigade at Pickett's Mill six months earlier, spoke for many when he said quietly, "If we are to die, let us die like men."[13]

Bierce's brigade had the rare good fortune, for once, of being removed from the center of the fighting, and he observed the battle from the high cliffs north of the Harpeth River. Like many that day, he was struck by the ironic contrast between the lovely fall weather and the "devil's work" about to take place. "Sleep was in the very atmosphere," he wrote. "The sun burned crimson in a gray-blue sky through a delicate Indian-summer haze, as beautiful as a daydream in paradise." When the Confederate attack came, one of Bierce's companions, a Captain Dawson of Brig. Gen. Thomas Wood's staff, could not bear to watch. "It is all up with us," Dawson told Bierce despairingly. "I am going to have a quiet smoke." Bierce, less squeamish, continued watching, spellbound by "a hand-to-hand contest of incredible fury. Two long, irregular, mutable, and tumultuous blurs of color were consuming each other's edge along the line of contact. Slowly the mobile blur moved away from the town, and presently the gray half of it dissolved into its elemental units, all in slow recession." The Union line had held. That night, the Federals pulled out of Franklin unmolested and made their way safely into Nashville. The next morning, the surviving Southerners buried their dead, numb with horror at the useless slaughter. One private on burial detail, Sam Watkins of the First Tennessee, was not far from home—he had been born and raised in Columbia. Now he looked out upon "a grand holocaust of death. Death had held high carnival there that night. The dead were piled one on another all over the ground. I was never so horrified and appalled in my life." It was a fitting epitaph for an entire army.[14]

At Nashville, the Federals waited patiently inside their fortifications while Hood and his broken army ringed the wintry hills beyond. The Union troops now were supremely confident, so much so that Bierce and his comrades had the time to play an elaborate practical joke on a fellow staff member, a young lieutenant named Haberton, who "had an intolerable weakness: he was a lady-killer, and like most of his class eager that all should know it." The self-proclaimed rake had wearied everyone with his endless tales of romantic conquest, and his staff mates devised a suitable punishment: They persuaded a seventeen-year-old orderly named Arman, who "was notably effeminate in face and figure," to trick himself out in some women's clothing they had found in the house they were using as headquarters. Haberton was prevailed upon to use his formidable powers to entertain the young "lady," who, he was told, was the former resident of the house. He was in the process of tenderly comforting the fair visitor when an enemy shell exploded in the room above them. The orderly, crying, "Jumping Jee-rusalem!" leapt up and ran out of the room, tearing off his "girl-gear" as he ran. Bierce and the others, who had been furtively eyeing the conversation, unloosed "billows of inexhaustible laughter." Thunderstruck by the abrupt turn of events, Haberton "fashioned his visage into the sickliest grin that ever libeled all smiling," then said, somewhat unconvincingly, "You can't fool me!"[15]

Bierce was now serving on the staff of Brig. Gen. Samuel Beatty, who commanded the Third Division. An earthy, jolly, hail-fellow-well-met type of officer, the Pennsylvania-born Beatty had won Bierce's heart by joking, upon receipt of a telegram from a hard-pressed colonel asking to be relieved due to "an attack of General Debility," that the aforementioned "general" was "the ablest cavalry officer in the Confederate army. I served under him in Mexico." At the Battle of Nashville, on December 15 and 16, Bierce again was exempted from the actual fighting and passed the time "just sitting in the saddle and looking on." He was particularly interested in the conduct of a brigade of black troops on the second day of the battle. At one time, he recalled in an 1898 column in the *Examiner,* he had applied for a position as a line officer with a black regiment, only to withdraw his application after he had "repented and persuaded myself that the darkies would not fight." At Nashville, he ruefully recognized "that I had made a fool of myself." Observing the repulse of a mixed command of black and white troops at Overton Hill, Bierce watched the inexperienced black soldiers attack unhesitatingly through a jungle of felled trees in front of the rebel breastworks. "Better fighting was never done," he noted. "They did not hesitate a moment: their long lines swept into that fatal obstruction in perfect order and remained there as long as those of the white veterans on their right. And as many of them in proportion remained until borne away and buried after the action. It was as pretty an example of courage and discipline as one could wish to see." Bierce's opinion was seconded by the Union commander on the scene, Maj. Gen. James B. Steedman, who reported after the battle that "I was unable to discover that color made any difference in the fighting of my troops. All, white and black, nobly did their duty as soldiers."[16]

The Battle of Nashville was a final crushing defeat for the Confederate Army of Tennessee, which to all intents and purposes ceased to function as a cohesive unit after the battle. Bierce accompanied part of Thomas's army into winter camp at Huntsville, Alabama, where he received a last official commendation from General Beatty asserting to his worth as a volunteer soldier: "Lieut. A. G. Bierce, Ninth Indiana, topographical engineer, rendered me efficient service." Still troubled by his head wound, and no doubt sensing that the war was rapidly drawing to a close, Bierce had himself examined on January 8, 1865, by Dr. C. T. Hoagland, regimental surgeon for the Seventy-first Ohio Infantry, who formally attested that his patient was "unfit for the United States Military Service" due to a serious head wound that prohibited "severe mental or physical exertion." Two days later, Bierce forwarded Hoagland's findings to headquarters, along with a personal letter tendering his resignation from the army for medical reasons. It went swiftly up the chain of command, and on January 25, General Thomas affixed his closing signature to the request. After three years, nine months, and six days in the army, Ambrose Bierce was once again a civilian. Years later, he would write, with a characteristic mixture of pride and disgust: "It was once my fortune to command a company of soldiers—real soldiers. Not professional life-long fighters, the product of European militarism—just plain, ordinary American, volunteer soldiers, who loved their country and fought for it with never a thought of grabbing it for themselves; that is a trick which the survivors were taught later by gentlemen desiring their votes."[17]

He was out of the army but not out of the service. Disdaining any notion of returning to Indiana, Bierce immediately accepted a job with the Treasury Department, helping to collect "captured and abandoned property" for a salary of $105 a month, less tax. His superior was Capt. Sherburne B. Eaton, his former associate on Hazen's staff. (Indeed, Eaton may have talked Bierce into resigning from the army in the first place, since a letter dated January 6, 1865, already speaks of Bierce as being in his employ.) The work was as dangerous as it was distasteful, involving mainly the tracking down of hidden cotton bales in swamps, on ruined plantations, in secret warehouses, or wherever else imaginative cotton planters could conceal their lucrative caches. By the close of the war, cotton was worth five hundred dollars a bale, and an often deadly game of hide-and-seek began between the Treasury agents and their prey: cotton producers who had previously sold their goods to the Confederate government but had been unable (or unwilling) to deliver their consignments due to the Union naval blockade and the sudden collapse of the Confederacy. Such "public" cotton was declared contraband and liable to seizure by the U.S. government, for whom the Treasury agents supposedly acted. In fact, the agents—and dozens of outright thieves pretending to be agents—acted mainly for themselves, freely confiscating all the cotton they could find, irrespective of its legal status. By law, the agents were allowed a one-quarter bounty on any Confederate cotton they could locate; naturally, whatever cotton they managed to find was immediately labeled Confederate cotton.[18]

An elaborate system of corruption sprang up across the state of Alabama. Besides unscrupulous Treasury agents, the chief players included so-called cotton spies, local residents who ferreted out hidden caches in return for a share of the profits; "loyal" Southerners who would duly swear that the confiscated cotton belonged to them and would then sell it on the open market and split the proceeds with the agents; corrupt railroad conductors who would somehow manage to lose whole carloads of cotton en route to Mobile and New Orleans; and shady steamboat captains who would make unscheduled nighttime stops at private docks. Planters who wanted to sell their cotton, lawfully owned or not, had no choice but to deal with the Treasury agents and their minions, usually for no better than a quarter or half share of the market value of their crop. More credulous owners were sometimes told by agents that they should simply sign over their cotton to the government, which would be only too happy to reimburse them for their troubles upon proper application to the Treasury Department. Invariably, such applications would then be rejected after the agents in question denied any knowledge of such voluntary surrenders. Fortunes were there for the making—one industrious Treasury agent in Demopolis, Alabama, skimmed off $80,000 in one month—and it was not uncommon for the heads of the various agencies to sell agency commissions for $25,000 a pop. Alabama, which had more cotton on hand at the close of the war than any other state, was a particularly desirable posting. As early as August 1865, President Andrew Johnson was warning General Thomas, now the Army's district commander, that "I have been advised that innumerable frauds are being practised by persons assuming to be Treasury agents, in various portions of Alabama, in the collection of cotton pretended to belong to the Confederate States government." Statistics later revealed that of the 150,000 bales of Alabama cotton to which the United States government had clear title, only about 20,000 bales were ever received, and even those had been reduced by as much as one-third of their weight before reaching government hands. "I am sure I sent some honest cotton agents South," Secretary of the Treasury Hugh McCulloch later lamented, "but it sometimes seems very doubtful whether any of them remained honest very long."[19]

One who did remain honest was Ambrose Bierce. Although he was always quick to disavow any connection to his Puritan forebears, a wide streak of personal rectitude remained within him, impervious to bribes and other corruption. Simply put, he could not be bought, and that admirable trait put him in some danger in postwar Alabama. Besides his crooked fellow agents, his incorruptibility also threatened the local planters, who were used to offering thousands of dollars for blank, signed shipping permits. He was also at odds with the cotton spies and perjurers whose disreputable livelihoods depended upon equally disreputable Treasury agents, to say nothing of the Southern citizens whose homeland was now swarming with hated occupation forces. Lastly, there were the returning Confederate veterans, "men trained to the use of arms," who did not necessarily consider themselves included in the formal surrender documents recently signed by Robert E. Lee and other Confederate commanders in the field. "Many, no doubt, made the easy and natural transition from soldiering to assassination by insensible degrees," said Bierce, "unconscious of the moral difference, such as it is."[20]

The central Alabama town of Selma, to which Bierce and Eaton relocated in late April, had been particularly hard hit by the war. Just hours before the end of hostilities, a Union cavalry force led by Maj. Gen. James Wilson had ravaged the town, burning down the local arsenal, niter works, prison, and shipyard. Unfortunately, little distinction was made between military targets and private property, and a number of homes and businesses also went up in smoke. Hundreds of captured horses and mules were shot down and left to rot on the city's streets, leaving a stench that hovered in the air for months like a harbinger of Southern defeat. Every Northerner on the scene was "horribly hated" as a walking embodiment of that defeat, and, said Bierce, "although my duties were now purely civil my treatment was not uniformly so, and I am not surprised that it was not." Just how uncivil such treatment could be was forcefully brought home to him a few days after his arrival by the grisly fate of two federal marshals found lying alongside a Selma roadway with their throats cut. Eaton, who had preceded Bierce into town, "had arrived just in time to act as sole mourner at the funeral of his predecessor—who had had the bad luck to interpret his instructions in a sense that was disagreeable to a gentleman whose interests were affected by the interpretation." So dangerous was Selma in the spring of 1865 that the two comrades made it a point to shake hands formally each night upon parting and "to say something memorable that was worthy to serve as 'last words,'" a precaution they had not considered necessary during the war itself. "Really," wrote Bierce, "the mortality among the unacclimated in the Selma district at that time was excessive."[21]

With Eaton in New Orleans much of the time on government—or personal—business, Bierce was left to administer the public trust however he saw fit. He found his duties "exceedingly disagreeable not only to the people of the vicinity, but to myself as well." Still, he tried to act properly, once spending several weeks attempting to locate seven hundred bales of unconfiscated cotton by dining nightly with two local gentlemen whom he suspected of knowing the cotton's whereabouts. Each side hoped to gain a practical advantage by getting the other drunk, but since both parties knew the other's plans, everyone remained "singularly abstemious" during their dinners together. Ultimately, the matter ended in a standoff, Bierce declining a one-fourth share in the profits for signing a blank shipping permit and the planters rejecting a similar offer for disclosing the cotton's hiding place. "I am sometimes disloyal enough to indulge myself in the hope that they baffled my successors as skillfully as they did me," wrote Bierce. "One cannot help feeling a certain tenderness for men who know and value a good dinner."[22]

A similar temptation came his way through a rowdy acquaintance named Jack Harris, a sometime employee of Eaton's whom Bierce would later come to see as a typical specimen of California adventurer. At the time, however, Harris seemed somewhat larger than life, "a rather large, strong fellow, swarthy, black-bearded, black-eyed, black-hearted and entertaining, no end. He drank hard, gambled high, swore like a parrot, scoffed at everything, was openly and proudly a rascal, did not know the meaning of fear, borrowed money abundantly, and squandered it with royal disregard." Harris was the sort of irresistible adventurer who once persuaded a steamboat captain to delay departure for four full days, at a cost to the captain of four hundred dollars a day, while he continued roistering and wenching ashore. Now, Harris proposed to Bierce that he collude in the theft of a thousand bales of cotton, which Harris had stored at various points along the banks of the Alabama River. Bierce could either sign some blank shipping permits or else personally accompany Harris on his trip downriver. It was, said Bierce, "a rather more sinful proposal than he had heretofore done me the honor to submit." When Bierce refused, using as an excuse the impossibility of transferring the stolen cotton to a larger ship in Mobile Bay, Harris "was astonished, and, I think, pained by my simplicity. Did I think him a fool?" Harris did not intend to unload the cotton at all; instead, he planned to slip through the bay in the dead of night and take his cargo on to Havana. The island of Cuba seemed to hold a fatal attraction for Harris. Years later, Bierce heard that he had been captured and shot on a filibustering expedition, smuggling arms to Cuban rebels, telling a priest who officiated at the execution, "I am an atheist, by God!" This time, Bierce had the good sense to decline the invitation.[23]

He formed a more useful friendship with two Selma brothers who had served as officers in the late Confederacy. Charles and Frank—he withheld their last name—were "well educated, brave, generous, sensitive to points of honor, by all respected, by many loved and by some feared." Quick to fight and addicted to dueling, they nevertheless provided Bierce with some much-needed protection. "From the time that I became generally known as their friend my safety was assured through all that region; an army with banners could not have given me the same immunity from danger, obstruction or even insult in the performance of my disagreeable duties. What glorious fellows they were." One evening, Bierce had occasion to view their fighting abilities firsthand. Returning home from a night on the town, the group was followed by a strange man who refused to identify himself or say what he wanted. The brothers were unarmed, but Frank simply lifted Bierce's pistol from his coat pocket, wheeled, and shot the man in the leg, smashing a bone above the knee. Somewhat abashed by the sudden turn of events—"the shooting was a trifle hasty and not altogether justifiable"—Bierce helped carry the man into a nearby hotel, where a surgeon amputated his leg the next morning. Bierce and the brothers paid the stranger's bills and sent him on his way to Mobile, but they never did learn why he was following them in the first place. Subsequently, the trio was acquitted of any serious wrong doing by a bogus justice of the peace, who merely fined Frank five dollars for disorderly conduct.[24]

Gunfire of a more serious nature greeted Bierce a few weeks later as he and Eaton were transporting a steamboat full of confiscated cotton down the Tombigbee River to Mobile. Just before dusk, the steamer rounded a bend in the river where the current carried it close to shore. Suddenly, a volley of gun-fire peppered the boat, splintering wood and breaking glass. Bierce, pistol in hand, saw the left bank swarming with armed desperadoes; dodging from tree to tree, the bandits continued a steady barrage. The agents had thought-fully arranged for an armed guard of a dozen soldiers to accompany the ship; unfortunately, none of the soldiers had brought along any ammunition. Returning fire, Bierce listened in vain for the soldiers to open on the hijack-ers. "Of all helpless mortals," he observed disgustedly, "a soldier without a cartridge is the most imbecile." To make matters worse, the pilot had deserted his wheel and the boat was drifting ever closer to shore. The captain was nowhere to be seen, the fireman had also abandoned his post, and dozens of bales of precious cotton—at five hundred dollars a throw—were tumbling off the deck and into the river. Capture meant a quick rope for Eaton and Bierce. In the end, the only thing that saved them was the fact that the ambushers had selected a poor spot for their attack: An impassable bayou lay just around the bend. Bierce persuaded the captain, by poking a pistol into his ear, to resume command of the vessel, and despite some fifty-odd bullet holes in the pilothouse, the steamer made it safely past. Afterward, Bierce learned that he had had an unlikely ally in the fight. A former Confederate whom they were giving a free ride to Mobile had pulled out "an old-fashioned horse-pistol" and unloosed a few rounds at the would-be robbers. When Bierce asked him why he had helped two Yankee Treasury agents escape from his fellow Alabamans, the reb replied simply that he was working off his fare.[25]

The gunfire and thievery—official or otherwise—continued apace throughout the summer and fall of 1865. One Treasury agent loaded two thousand bales of confiscated cotton onto a ship and blithely sailed away to France. Another was arrested for conspiring to buy 227 bales at well below market price; his sentence was commuted after he implicated other agents in the theft of a staggering fifty thousand bales of Alabama cotton. It was widely suspected, though never proven, that a great munitions explosion in Mobile that May, which killed dozens of people and leveled twenty city blocks, had been set by crooked agents seeking to cover up their crimes. Bierce continued to remain untouched by the fraud, although the same could not be said with any degree of certainty for his immediate superior. A surviving ledger sheet of Eaton's shows, at the very least, some creative accounting practices. Against the receipt of $27,799.48 from the sale of confiscated cotton, Eaton listed unspecified expenses totaling exactly $27,799.48. The entire system, Bierce noted, "opened up such possibilities of fraud as have seldom been accorded by any system of conducting the public business, and never without disas-trous results to official morality."[26]

It was thus with a sense of surprised relief that Bierce received an unex-pected letter from Maj. Gen. William B. Hazen that autumn inviting him to join a fact-finding tour of western forts. Hazen, now serving as acting assistant inspector general of the Department of the Platte, had been given the assignment of inspecting conditions in the newly created Mountain District, which included the Powder River territory of Montana and Wyoming. Bierce immediately accepted the offer, which carried with it the promise of a captaincy in the Regular Army, but it was several months before he was finally relieved of his Treasury duties and could scrape the red clay of Alabama from his boot heels for good. He joined Hazen in July 1866 at Omaha, Nebraska, the railhead of the Union Pacific Railroad then inching westward to link up with the Central Pacific Railroad at Promontory Point, Utah, three years hence. The traveling party, which included Hazen, Bierce, a cook, and a teamster—various cavalry escorts and guides would also accompany them part of the way—set out in late July, following the Platte River Valley for two hundred miles to Fort Kearny. A dusty wagon trail was the only permanent mark that civilization had made on the still-unsettled land. The trail was bordered by regular piles of bones, "not always those of animals," and an occasional tombstone sported such homely valedictories as "He was a good egg" or "He done his damnedest." Bierce was scarcely exaggerating when he remarked that "I left the one road a few miles out of the Nebraskan village and met the other at Dutch Flat, in California." Between those two points was the trackless area marked on existing maps as the Great American Desert.[27]

For all its isolation, however, the trip was something of a lark for the twenty-four-year-old Bierce. He had few official duties besides sketching an occasional map and "amus[ing] the general and other large game." The fresh air was good for his asthma, which oddly had not troubled him much during the war but which had returned to plague him in postwar Alabama—perhaps it was all the cotton bolls. The traveling party took in all the sights: Court House Rock, Crazy Woman Flats, Clear Fork, Tongue River, Little Bighorn, Yellowstone, the Black Hills. Along the way, they stopped to inspect the widely scattered military posts that were guarding—after a fashion—the government's interests in the Platte River Valley and along the old Bozeman Trail. These interests regularly diverged from those of the region's traditional occupants, the Sioux, the Cheyenne, the Arapaho, the Pawnee, the Shoshoni, and the Crow, who were beginning to grow increasingly restive about the massive influx of gold-seekers, sodbusters, rail-layers, and other variously accoutered white adventurers steadily traipsing across their land. One month before Hazen's party set out on its journey, government commissioners had parleyed with the Indians at Fort Laramie, the jumping-off point for the Bozeman Trail. The council had not ended happily. Sioux war chief Red Cloud, of the Oglala tribe, had stormed off in a huff after learning of government plans to build three new forts along the trail to protect white immigrants to the area. The chief negotiator, Commissioner E. B. Taylor, was either wildly optimistic or crassly cynical when he reported back to Washington: "Satisfactory treaty concluded. Most cordial feeling prevails."[28]

Red Cloud was in the process of forcefully demonstrating a second opinion when Bierce and the others arrived at Fort Reno, one of the new army posts, on August 10. Two days after their arrival, a band of Sioux attacked a civilian wagon train camped nearby, running off cattle and stealing horses. Two days later, they murdered a pair of unwary travelers a few miles from the fort. And a few days after that, the Indians stole a herd of mules from the post corral. Hazen, alarmed, urged the army to transfer two additional companies of cavalry from Fort Laramie to the Powder River region to guard against future depredations. The cold welcome undoubtedly contributed to his low estimate of the Plains Indians. "The ideal Indian of the popular mind is found only in poetry and Cooper's novels," Hazen wrote. "The Indian who now inhabits the plains is a dirty beggar and thief, who murders the weak and unprotected, but never attacks an armed foe. He keeps no promises, and makes them only the more easy to carry on his murder and pillage. He knows no sentiment but revenge and fear, and cares only to live in his vagrancy. All efforts to better his condition have and will but add to his debt of ingratitude, and prove unproductive of any good."[29]

As if to demonstrate his low opinion of the Indians, Hazen pushed on without an escort to Fort Phil Kearny, sixty-seven miles northwest of Fort Reno on the Little Piney fork of the Powder River. Bierce, for one, did not find that leg of the trip entirely pleasant. He later described a typical night on the trail. "The flame of a campfire stands up tall and straight toward the black sky," he wrote. "We feed it constantly with sagebrush. A circling wall of darkness closes us in; but turn your back to the fire and walk a little away and you shall see the serrated summitline of snow-capped mountains, ghastly cold in the moonlight. At irregular intervals we hear the distant howling of a wolf—now on this side and again on that. We check our talk to listen; we cast quick glances toward our weapons, our saddles, our picketed horses: the wolves may be of the variety known as Sioux."[30]

Despite his apprehensions, Bierce and the others arrived safely at Fort Phil Kearny on August 27. Once there, they were "hospitably entertained" by the post's officers, including the commanding officer, Col. Henry B. Carrington; Capt. Frederick H. Brown, the post quartermaster; and Lt. George Washington Grummond. Not yet present at the fort was Capt. William J. Fetterman, a thirty-three-year-old infantry officer who had seen action at many of the same Civil War battles that Bierce had fought. In less than four months, Fetterman, Brown, and Grummond would all be dead, killed along with seventy-eight other soldiers and civilians by Red Cloud's Sioux in an ambush along the Bozeman Trail not far from the fort. They were the sort of "ambitious young army officers" who, Bierce said, "passed the best years of their lives guarding livestock and teaching the mysteries of Hardee's tactics to that alien patriot, the American regular." Sometimes, of course, their lives were not very long. It may have been Fetterman's tragic example that caused Bierce to ruminate that had he stayed in the army, he might have "served long enough [that] I might have become a captain. In time, if I lived, I should naturally have become the senior captain of the Army; and then if there were another war and any of the field officers did me the favor to paunch a bullet I should become the junior major, certain of another step upward as soon as a number of my superiors equal to the whole number of majors should be killed, resign or die of old age—enchanting prospect!"[31]

After three days at Fort Phil Kearny, the party headed north to Fort C. F. Smith, this time accompanied by a twenty-six-man mounted infantry detachment commanded by Lt. James Bradley, another young Civil War veteran. Bradley, who would miss the Fetterman massacre by a scant month, after being transferred temporarily to Fort Bridger in Utah Territory, later had the horrific distinction of being the first white man to view the aftermath of Custer's Last Stand. As chief of scouts for Col. John Gibbon during the abortive campaign of 1876, Bradley was scouting ahead of the infantry column when he saw in the distance some pale lumps that he assumed to be the carcasses of butchered buffalo. It was Custer and his men. Bradley apparently did not learn a lasting lesson from his near miss at Fort Phil Kearny or his ghastly discovery of Custer and the slaughtered Seventh Cavalry—a year later, he was killed while leading a headfirst cavalry charge into a Nez Percé village on the banks of the Big Hole River in western Montana.[32]

Another companion for part of the journey was the fabled black mountain man Jim Beckwourth. A former slave from Virginia who later became an adopted chief of the Crow Nation and also discovered a long-sought pass through the Sierra Nevada to California, Beckwourth was seventy-seven in 1866, but he was still a vigorous and quick-minded scout. One night when they were sitting around the campfire listening to the wind rustle through the trees, Hazen asked Beckwourth what he would do if he discovered that they were surrounded by Indians. "I'd spit on that fire," the old man said. Such precautions, luckily, were unnecessary; the party made it to Fort C. F. Smith without incident. The fort, located on an elevated bank three hundred yards from the Bighorn River, was still in the opening phase of construction. Tents were scattered around a tall flagpole from which an outsized American flag was raised and lowered each day to a roll of drums and a salvo of cannons. Capt. Nathaniel Kenney was post commandant and the famous trailblazer Jim Bridger was camp scout.[33]

The party got its first glimpse of buffalo while staying at the fort. The shaggy titans of the prairie showed little fear of humans, despite being slain in ever-increasing numbers by white hunters and other "sportsmen." According to Bierce, the campers had to guard their campsite with blazing fires and a special antibuffalo patrol armed with swords to prevent the animals "from biting us as they grazed." Even these measures proved insufficient one night when "one of them half-scalped a teamster as he lay dreaming of home with his long hair commingled with the toothsome grass. His utterances as the well-meaning beast lifted him from the ground and tried to shake the earth from his roots were neither wise nor sweet, but they made a profound impression on the herd, which, arching its multitude of tails, absented itself to pastures new like an army with banners."[34]

From Fort Smith, the party turned northwest to inspect Fort Benton, an old American Fur Company post on the headwaters of the Missouri River above Helena, Montana. Once across the Yellowstone River, the countryside turned increasingly barren and wild game became scarce. Freshwater, too, became hard to find, and starvation, said Bierce, "was a welcome state: our hunger was so much less disagreeable than our thirst that it was a real treat." Eventually, the travelers made it safely into Benton, although by then they were admittedly "a sorry-looking lot." Years later, Bierce was still shuddering over that portion of their trip: "If in all that region there is a mountain that I have not climbed, a river that I have not swum, an alkali pool that I have not thrust my muzzle into, or an Indian that I have not shuddered to think about, I am ready to go back in a Pullman sleeper and do my duty."[35]

After a few days of rest and refitting, the party turned south through Helena and Virginia City, Montana, two gold-mining boomtowns that, according to Hazen, needed no special army protection, since "miners are better Indian fighters than soldiers, are numerous and always armed, and organized for defense." It was now getting on to October, and the party was ordered to return to Washington by way of Salt Lake City, San Francisco, and Panama—"a master stroke of military humor," as Bierce put it. At Camp Douglas, three miles east of Salt Lake City, Hazen met with Brigham Young and other Mormon leaders who a decade earlier had fought their own abbreviated civil war with the United States government. Hazen found the Mormons "loyal to the letter of our laws, but in spirit a separate and distinct nationality." They lived, he said, under "a theocratic despotism" that kept the faithful "ignorant, industrious, and obedient." Surprisingly, for one who generally loathed organized religion, Bierce formed a lifelong appreciation of Mormons, if not necessarily Mormonism. "Excepting the Jews and Chinese," he later wrote, "I know no worthier large class of people than they." He denounced the continuing persecution of the Mormons as "one of the most hateful and sneaking aggressions that ever disgraced the generally straightforward and forthright course of religious persecution." As for himself, "I have no religious convictions. I do not care a copper for the Mormons. But I do care a good deal for truth, reason and fair play; and whenever I cease to be indignant at the falsehood, stupidity and injustice that this harmless people have suffered at the hands of the brutal and harmless mob of scribblers and tonguesters who find profit in denouncing them, I shall have had a longer life than I merit." Such thunderous championing of underdogs recurs often in Bierce's writings, and it is distinctly at odds with his simplified reputation as an inveterate hater of all humanity.[36]

At Camp Douglas, Hazen received word that he had been commissioned a colonel in the newly reorganized army. He was to take command of the Thirty-eighth Infantry Regiment, one of four additional black regiments just authorized by Congress. Prior to that, however, he would be permitted to spend the winter of 1866–1867 touring Europe as a representative of the government. With his new commission in hand, Hazen hurried west toward California with Bierce and the others, the party making its last bivouac— appropriately enough, given Bierce's ghoulish bent—on the site of the Donner Party's infamous picnic in the High Sierra twenty years earlier. "In the flickering lights and dancing shadows made by our camp-fire," wrote Bierce, "I first heard the story of that awful winter, and in the fragrance of the meat upon the coals fancied I could detect something significantly uncanny. The meat which the Donner party had cooked at that spot was not quite like ours. Pardon: I mean it was not like that which we cooked."[37]

Making good time, the party followed the new roadbed of the Central Pacific Railroad into Sacramento, where they lingered just long enough to admire the colorful paintings of Fort Laramie and the Wind River Range— sights they had just seen with their own eyes—at the Plains Saloon in the California capital. Hazen was anxious to reach San Francisco and sail back east to Washington; Bierce confidently awaited his captain's commission. The pair caught a river packet from Sacramento to San Francisco, crossing the San Francisco Bay and disembarking at Clark's Landing. At the old army base known locally as the Presidio, they called for their mail. Bierce's commission, with the Fifth U.S. Infantry, was waiting. It had been sent initially to Lafayette Burr, former adjutant of the Ninth Indiana Regiment, at Elkhart. Burr returned it to Washington, where it was forwarded in care of Hazen to Omaha. By that time, the party had headed west, and the commission even-tually made its way to San Francisco. When Bierce opened it in a Presidio anteroom, he was incensed—the commission was that of a second lieutenant. Hazen, too, was disappointed, and not a little embarrassed by his inadvertent misleading of his youthful protégé. "Ingratitude, more strong than traitors' arms, quite vanquished me," said Bierce. "I resigned, parted from Hazen more in sorrow than in anger and remained in California."[38]

Actually, if the two had thought things through—or if they had been less combative personalities to begin with—they would have seen that, far from being an insult, Bierce's commission was something of a coup for a young man seeking to remain in the army after the Civil War. Under the Army Act of July 28, 1866, Congress had mandated a force of 54,000 men, three times that of the prewar army, but only a fraction of the volunteer-swelled ranks of

1861–1865. Officers who had ended the war as major generals (like Hazen) were now routinely reduced in rank to colonel, major, or even in one extreme case to sergeant. It was a tribute to Bierce's war record that, as an unknown volunteer soldier from small-town Indiana, he had been offered any commission at all. It was also entirely like him to write back, in prideful high dudgeon: "I respectfully decline the appointment." From now on, the United States Army would have to get along without Ambrose Bierce.[39]

6

The Mentor, Whip and Mirror of the Town

After nearly a decade of wandering and war, during which time he had been with varying degrees of success a printer's devil, a military school cadet, a bricklayer, a soda jerk, a saloon swabbie, a soldier, a Treasury agent, and a frontiersman, Ambrose Bierce found himself in early 1867 marooned and jobless in San Francisco. There were worse places in the world for a twenty-four-year-old bachelor to be, although Bierce may not have thought so at the time. Unlike thousands of others in the preceding twenty years, he had never intended to make San Francisco his new home; nor had he arrived on its fog-shrouded shores with a head full of get-rich-quick schemes, a miner's shovel, or a sailor's sack. It was purely a fluke that brought him to the city—or, at any rate, a superior's orders—and he could not have suspected that, except for brief interludes, it would be his home for the next three decades. Bierce and San Francisco would prove to be, if not perhaps a match made in heaven, at least a fitting pair of adversaries.

San Francisco, by the mid-1860s, had grown from a sleepy Mexican seaport into a vital, one might even say protean, city of 100,000 commercial-minded souls. The 1849 gold rush had first emptied the city, as San Franciscans joined the manic exodus to the nearby gold fields, then quickly filled it again as bankers, shippers, merchants, and saloonkeepers poured into town to help the miners alternately save, spend, lose, or waste their easy riches. During the first boom period, the city's population doubled every ten days; two years after the discovery of gold at Sutter's Mill, San Francisco's population had grown to 35,000. Not even six major fires between 1848 and 1851 could stay the city's remarkable growth, although they did understandably give rise to a long-standing civic obsession with volunteer firemen, an obsession best exemplified by the flamboyant Lillie Hitchcock, a transplanted southern belle who developed a lifelong affinity for firemen in general and Engine Company No. 5 in particular after a fireman from that company saved her life in a hotel fire when she was eight. Dressed in a red blouse, black skirt, and gold fire helmet with a large diamond inset into its No. 5 shield, the tomboyish Miss Hitchcock scrambled from debutante balls and drawing room teas into the front seat of a company fire engine whenever the alarm arose, as it often did in those days, for Company No. 5 to fight another blaze.[1]

Many of the city's fires were arson, set by organized bands of hooligans such as the infamous Sydney Ducks, a distinctly unsavory collection of former English convicts who had been transported to Australia for their myriad sins before joining the forty-niners in California and quickly discovering that it was far easier to steal gold than it was to mine it. They were preceded in crime by the Hounds, a semimilitary group comprised of former New York soldiers who had come to the state during the Mexican War. The Hounds preyed primarily on foreign immigrants in the North Beach and Telegraph Hill neighborhoods, staging nighttime raids on the Mexicans, Chileans, and Peruvians who lived in tent cities on the outskirts of town. They fueled their nocturnal diversions by pushing en masse into local eateries and helping themselves to everything on the menu—gratis, of course. Eventually, the groups' depredations grew so bad that a Committee of Vigilance was formed to deal with them. Dozens of miscreants were variously hanged, beaten, horsewhipped, and transported back to Australia by the quasi-secret peacekeepers during two separate periods of privatized justice in the mid-1850s.[2]

Harder to eradicate were the runners, crimps, and impressment gangs who waylaid unwary sailors in dockside dives like the Boar's Head, the Nymphia, the Fierce Grizzly, Cowboy Mag's, Fat Daugherty's, and the So Different. Led by such fearsome toughs as Shanghai Kelly, one-armed Johnny Devine, and the amazonian Mother Bronson, the denizens of the Barbary Coast, as the area soon became known, kept merchant ships regularly supplied with a full complement of crews by means of such persuasive recruiting tools as the billy club, the belaying pin, the bung starter, and the more subtle but equally effective Mickey Finn, a knockout drop of laudanum or chloral hydrate slipped into an unwary sailor's drink at the bar. Shanghai, a regular if distant port of call, gave its name to the local pastime, and *shanghai* quickly entered the native language as a definitively transitive verb.[3]

For the more refined visitor, San Francisco offered a variety of sights, from the narrow alleys of Chinatown to the nouveau riche mansions on Nob Hill.

Inevitably, first-time visitors were taken to the Cliff House, overlooking Seal Rocks on the oceanfront. One tourist, at least, the celebrated journalist Helen Hunt Jackson, was less than impressed with the sight. "It is," she wrote, "so much the fashion to be tender, not to say sentimental, over the seals of the Cliff House rocks that I was disappointed not to find myself falling into that line as I looked at them. If there be in the whole animal kingdom any creature of size and sound less adapted than a seal [actually sea lion] as a public pet I do not know such creature's name. Shapeless, boneless, limbless, and featureless, neither fish nor flesh; of the color and consistency of India-rubber diluted with mucilage; slipping, clinging, sticking, like gigantic leeches; flapping, wallowing with unapproachable clumsiness, lying still, lazy, inert, asleep, apparently, till they are baked browner and hotter than they like, then plunging off the rocks, turning once over in the water to wet themselves enough to bear more baking; and all the while making a noise too hideous to be described,—a mixture of bray and squeal and snuff and snort. Let them be sold, and their skins given to the poor; and let peace and quiet reign along that delicious beach and on those grand old rocks."[4]

Another unimpressed visitor, English journalist W. F. Rae, climbed the hill at the north end of Montgomery Street, the main business thoroughfare, and "was suprised to see the greater part of the lower town enveloped in a dense cloud of smoke. A large number of tall chimneys were emitting volumes of smoke such as in London would entail heavy fines on their proprietors. The darkness and dinginess of the city surprised less than did the sight of so many manufactories. I had supposed San Francisco to be a second Liverpool: I was not prepared to find it was also a second Birmingham." Rae's less than rhapsodic reaction to the city was echoed by his fellow countryman, novelist Anthony Trollope, who confided in a travel letter to the Liverpool *Weekly Mercury* that "I do not know that in all my travels I ever visited a city less interesting to the normal tourist. Strangers will generally desire to get out of San Francisco as quickly as they can."[5]

Famous and successful writers have the wherewithal for such abrupt changes of base, but Ambrose Bierce that winter of 1867 did not. Acting on a tip from helpful fellow officers at the Presidio, he parlayed his previous Treasury Department experience into a post as night watchman for the United States Mint. The job paid a nonprincely fifteen hundred dollars a year, and Bierce moved into bachelor digs with another employee of the Mint, Elisha Brooks, who, like Bierce, was a Union Civil War veteran. The two young men got along well enough, refighting old battles and discussing local politics, which in the hurly-burly of boomtown San Francisco amounted to pretty much the same thing. Using his old drawing skills, Bierce turned out for his own amusement a series of humorous sketches lampooning the various office hopefuls in either party. An enterprising fellow employee, without Bierce's knowledge, gathered up a handful of the sketches and sold them to the rival political camps, netting a quick eight-hundred-dollar profit that he split with the unwitting editorial cartoonist.[6]

The boys at the U.S. Mint, like most people who encountered Bierce throughout his life, found him an odd mixture of physical grace and emotional reticence, of undoubted animal magnetism undercut by a lacerating wit and a crabbed disinclination to entertain conflicting opinions. On one subject, in particular, he was unbending to the point of obsession: organized religion. He loathed it, then and later, and was not shy about making his impiety known. "Bierce," recalled his roommate Brooks, "was a very genial and pleasant man to associate with if you could tolerate his denunciation of all religions and his habit of using the most offensive language in speaking of matters that people usually regard as sacred. He would never allow you to differ with him in his views of religious or sacred matters. Otherwise people liked him very much." The baffled, conventional young men he worked beside could not have known—and probably he did not tell them—how far back and how close to home his irreverence went, but they knew enough to avoid the topic after a few late-night harangues from the frosty newcomer.[7]

Sometime that spring—the exact date is unknown—Bierce told another worker, Emory Long, that he intended to become a writer. Since San Francisco, with an inordinate ratio of college graduates, harbored any number of amateur and professional scribblers, Long did not find the announcement particularly noteworthy—why should he have? It sometimes seemed as though everyone in town was either reading or writing, sometimes simultaneously, in a citywide rush to explain and extol. An astonishing 132 publications had appeared in San Francisco in the 1850s, giving the city more published newspapers than London and providing those papers with a higher per capita circulation than media-mad New York City. A decade later, 87 of the original 132 were still publishing, including 6 daily newspapers, 9 ethnic-language journals, 8 religious and political party organs, various medical and law reviews, business and commercial publications, literary magazines, a *Police Gazette,* and even a fashion flyer detailing the latest Paris modes. Bayard Taylor, the California correspondent for the New York *Tribune,* caught something of the local atmosphere when he wrote: "The very air is pregnant with the magnetism of bold, spirited, unwearied action, and he who but ventures into the outer circle of the whirlpool, is spinning, ere he has time for thought, in its dizzy vortex."[8]

At the center of that urban vortex were some decidedly zany citizens. On any given day, the native San Franciscan might find promenading the downtown streets such daffy individualists as the Great Unknown, a mysterious, elegantly dressed old gentleman who paraded down Montgomery Street in silence every afternoon; Old Rosie, who wore a trademark fresh flower in the lapel of his threadbare suit; Money King, who lived up to his name by doing a booming curbside money-lending business in the well-chosen vicinity of the city stock exchange; and Professor Frederick Coombs, the reigning local expert on phrenology, who capitalized on a vague physical resemblance to George Washington by cavorting about town in a powdered wig and Colonial costume, carrying a banner that boldly proclaimed himself Washington the Second. These solitaries might find themselves eclipsed momentarily by a parade of the Ancient and Honorable Order of E Clampus Vitus, a tongue-in-cheek social club that mocked the pretentious titles and jargon-heavy mumbo jumbo of such established organizations as the Masons and the Elks. In keeping with its motto, *Credo Quia Absurdum,* members of the club met at the Hall of Comparative Ovations to hear the directives of their chosen leader, the Noble Grand Humbug, and to serve as unanimous cochairmen of the Most Important Committee. In the midst of such japery, the club even found time to raise money for widows and orphans and to compile learned treatises on such esoteric topics as the alleged discovery and colonization of California by the Chinese and the complete history of the venerable "plate of brasse" that Sir Francis Drake had nailed to a post at Point Reyes, twenty-five miles north of San Francisco, in 1579, claiming the land for Queen Elizabeth I and announcing, in the usual style of swashbuckling empire-builders everywhere, that the previous owners of the choice West Coast real estate, the Miwok Indians, had "freely resigne[d] their right and title in the whole land unto herr majesties keepeng."[9]

Without a doubt, the preeminent local character was Joshua Abraham Norton, the self-proclaimed Emperor Norton I, who ruled his people with a firm but fond hand for the twenty-one years following his initial appearance at the city desk of the San Francisco *Bulletin* in 1859, at which time he announced with unflappable equability, "Good morning, I am the Emperor of the United States." Norton, the London-born son of a humble ship's chandler, had come to San Francisco during the gold rush and made a small fortune operating a general store. After losing his entire wealth in an ill-considered scheme to corner the rice market (he and his partners bought up all the rice in California, only to find that they had forgotten one small detail: San Francisco Bay was teeming with ships loaded to the gunwales with still more rice), Norton lost his mind as well, disappearing for several years before making his dramatic reemergence as Norton I. Dressed in a blue-and-gold colonel's uniform that he had somehow wangled from the garrison commander of the Presidio, Emperor Norton held court daily at his rooming house—the imperial residence—issuing well-reasoned and well-received proclamations abolishing Congress and the presidency "because of corruption in high places" and ordering the army to "clear the halls of Congress." He levied taxes—twenty to twenty-five cents for business and three dollars for banks—and printed his own imperial bonds in denominations of ten, twenty-five, and fifty cents. It was a mark of his noble puissance that shops and restaurants throughout the city unhesitatingly accepted his money at face value.[10]

Each day, the emperor made a royal progress down Montgomery Street—his subjects duly bowed and scraped as he passed—accompanied by his two imperial mastiffs (actually mongrels), Bummer and Lazarus. The dogs, like Norton, ate for free, attended the theater in their own reserved seats, and were once formally introduced to Brazilian emperor Dom Pedro II during that worthy's state visit to the city. When Bummer passed away, no less a writer than Mark Twain composed his epitaph, noting that the deceased had "died full of years and honors and disease and fleas." And when Norton himself passed away in 1880, thirty thousand mourners filed past his coffin, flags all over the city were flown at half-mast, and the San Francisco *Chronicle* headlined, LE ROI EST MORT! The rival *Bulletin* observed, with some justice, that "the Emperor killed nobody, robbed nobody and deprived nobody of his country, which is more than can be said for most of the fellows in his trade."[11]

Keeping tabs on such hothouse flowerings was an equally colorful contingent of writers. First among equals was Francis Brett Harte, a New York native who had come to California as a teenager and stayed to immortalize the already-mythical exploits of the forty-niners. Bret Harte was a frequent contributor to the *Golden Era*, a weekly publication that served as a training ground for such future literary lights as Samuel Clemens, Charles Warren Stoddard, and Alonzo Delano, who wrote under the respective noms de plume Mark Twain, Pip Pepperpod, and Old Block. Other journalists on the scene included John Rollin Ridge, a part-Cherokee Indian who went by the moniker Yellow Bird; West Point graduate George H. Derby, better known as John P. Squibob or John Phoenix; and the somewhat unfortunately named Louise A. K. S. Clappe, who wisely improved her byline to Dame Shirley.[12]

The use of such pen names was a long-standing frontier practice dictated in part by the occupational hazards faced by journalists of the era. The ad hominem nature of news reporting then, coupled with the western tradition of violent self-defense and the ready availability of guns, made the newspaper business a decidedly chancy occupation. The founding editor of the *Bulletin*, James King, was shot dead on the street by the rival editor of the *Sunday Times*, James P. Casey, whom he had accused (accurately) of being a former resident of the New York State correctional facility at Sing Sing. Casey was subsequently lynched by the Committee of Vigilance alongside a local gambler named Charles Cora, who had killed a United States marshal. Edward C. Gilbert, editor of the *Alta*, was killed in a rifle duel with state senator James W. Denver, who narrowly avoided similar punishment for his act and later became a U.S. congressman, governor, and founder of the Mile High City. Yet another San Francisco editor, Charles De Young of the *Chronicle*, was shot and killed by the son of newly elected Mayor Isaac Kalloch after De Young previously had wounded the mayor with a gunshot of his own. And the editor of the *Mazeppa* was publicly horsewhipped by a local woman who felt her maidenly virtue had been compromised by the paper. Given such a working climate, it was understandable that a city editor for another newspaper, applying for a permit to carry a gun, noted—somewhat tortuously—that "the position which the journal with which I am connected has assumed in the present political campaign, and the character of the aspirants for office, render it necessary for me to provide myself with a weapon of defense."[13]

To be sure, the journalistic standards of the era frequently encouraged a violent response. There was no such thing as professional courtesy. Prentice Mulford once opened an editorial on his fellow journalists at the *Bulletin* by observing: "Hear the corrupt and ulcerated tongue which with its stench renders almost impassable the mouth of Market Street." Elbert P. Jones, founding editor of San Francisco's first newspaper, the *California Star*, adjudged his alter egos on the Monterey *Californian* to be "a lying sycophant and an overgrown lickspittle." And transplanted Cornishman Tremenhere Lanyon Johns, writing in the theater journal *Figaro*, complained that "the *Alta* had rabies badly on Monday. Yesterday one of the *Call* pack was similarly afflicted. If the *Alta* and *Call* proprietors would muzzle their mad dog editors, they would do the public a service. If they don't, *Figaro* will feel it a duty to strew strychnined cigars in the passage leading to the editorial rooms, and thus abate the nuisance."[14]

For the most part, however, working journalists were willing to set aside personal differences when they met for drinks at the Montgomery Block, a four-story building that boasted of being the largest structure west of the Mississippi. The Monkey Block, as it was affectionately known, was one block north of the U.S. Mint, and it is likely that Bierce made his first embryonic literary connections there. Another popular meeting place was at the offices of the *Golden Era*, located another block north on Montgomery. The March 31, 1867, edition of the paper contained a tantalizing, if inconclusive, note in its correspondence column: "B. Brains are at a discount here. Your only chance is to edit a country paper." If, indeed, Bierce had applied for a job with the newspaper, or at any rate had made discreet inquiries concerning such a possibility, the printed rejection might have been the catalyst that spurred him on to the next step of his journey, an ambitious course of self-education that involved the reading of great stacks of books borrowed from the local library. Brooks and Long, his colleagues at the U.S. Mint, recalled that Bierce read his way through Edward Gibbon's sonorously cadenced six-volume work, *The History of the Decline and Fall of the Roman Empire*, that summer, and his later work shows unmistakable traces of Gibbon's heavily Latinate influence. Other stylists he may have read at the time, judging from his later bibliographical recommendations to aspiring young writers, included Edmund Burke, Herbert Spencer, Walter Savage Landor, and Alexander Pope. "Precision," he would note in his handbook on proper English usage, *Write It Right*, "is the point of capital concern" of all good writing. And good writing is "essentially clear thinking made visible." It was a style he would strive for all his life.[15]

Sometime that summer, Bierce gave up housekeeping with the rather prissy Brooks and moved into a room of his own at the Russ House, located four blocks south of the U.S. Mint on Pine Street, just around the corner from the Mercantile Library on Bush Street and a mere stone's throw from the Mechanic's Library at the corner of Post and Market streets. Besides its convenience to the lending libraries and the U.S. Mint, the Russ House featured an ever-changing clientele of ranchers, cattlemen, gamblers, and other colorful characters. It was centrally located to the theaters, restaurants, and bars where much of the city's social life—then and now—was arbitrated. Chinatown was a few blocks farther north, with its dark, mysterious shops selling exotic teas, silks, lacquerware, porcelain, cigars, and, for the more discriminating tastes, opium and prostitutes, all under the dubious protection of the shadowy tongs, gangs of hatchet-wielding toughs who camouflaged their true extortionate purposes behind such misleadingly peaceful names as the Chamber of Tranquil Conscientiousness and the Chamber of Far-Reaching Virtue. Chinese herb doctors, who one observer noted dryly were "not afflicted with modesty as to the nature of their powers," stretched banners across the narrow alleyways, boldly proclaiming that "Dr. Hung Ly cures all diseases upstairs," or "The most obstinate and painful chronic diseases treated with entire success . . . cures guaranteed." One particularly confident practitioner styled himself, with true Oriental simplicity, "The King of Pain."[16]

Bright and observant, Bierce took in everything, including the public hanging of local bad man Juan Salazar, whose final send-off was skillfully stage-managed by the town sheriff. "The sheriff," Bierce wrote, "performed his peculiar duties with a skill and dignity that made one rather covet the distinction of being hanged by him. Salazar assisted with intelligent composure, and the spectators, who had repented of his crime, endured his death with Christian fortitude and resignation." This was written a decade later, but its characteristic note of flippant scorn was apparently struck first during Bierce's stay at the U.S. Mint. There, like Shelley at Oxford, Bierce began his writing career with a spirited defense of atheism that he handed out to fellow employees for their bemused enlightenment. His first published work, however, was a rather hysterical poem, "Basilica," printed in the September 21, 1867, edition of the *Californian*. It ran on for sixty-six lines, detailing the poet's discovery at the beach of an evil basilisk, a mythological lizard that could kill with a glance or a poisonous breath. A few phrases are sufficient to catch the poem's strident tone: "An opal chalice brimming gold"; "From bloody death of stricken day/And ocean's leprous agony"; "With ivory throat of pallid white/And snaky folds concealed from sight"; "With jeweled teeth, alas! and breath/Whose touch to passion ministreth." A second poem, published by the *Californian* two months later, was something of an improvement. "A Mystery" defined life as "The weight of the Past with its burden of sin,/A shadow thrown from the Future within,/And the weight unfelt and the shadow unseen,/With the cry of the Present unheard between." Life itself is a disappointment, "the secret of Pain . . . the payment in blood for each wish we obtain." Derivative, mawkish, and overwrought, the poems did not make much of an impression on the local literary scene, except perhaps to get Bierce's name before the public for the first time. He sensed as much, recalling later that "when I was in my twenties, I concluded one day that I was not a poet. It was the bitterest moment of my life."[17]

Freed from his poetic pretensions, Bierce turned his energies toward essay writing. Curiously, in light of his future reputation as a woman-hater and political reactionary—both simplifications, it should be said, of his true positions—his first signed essay, in the December 1867 issue of the *Californian*, was a mild-mannered defense of women's suffrage. In it, he deplored women's lack of educational opportunities, observed that their entrance into politics would make the profession more decent and respectable, and even excused the more egregious excesses of the suffragettes, noting that such fanaticism was "essentially progressive, and progress was truth." He realized, he said, the unpopularity of the issue. "For a considerable period," he wrote, "it seemed to number among its advocates only the philosophers and the fools; and as the latter of course made the most noise, it came to be regarded as a matter germane to them alone. It is even now associated in the popular mind with spiritualism, free-love, and other crazy heresies: and the phrase 'Women's Rights,' the very mention of which ought to call into our cheeks the blush of shame that it should ever have been necessary to invent it, has acquired by association a signification little short of contemptible." Bierce being Bierce, he felt constrained to add a backhanded observation about modern women's supposed dearth of outside interests: "Her babies and her visitors are about her only society; and though the former are usually a source of delight and the latter of annoyance, neither are particularly well-calculated to give her broad views or mental culture."[18]

During his first summer in San Francisco, Bierce's literary efforts were pleasantly interrupted by an unexpected message from the War Department. By order of Congress, the adjutant general had been directed to promote some 6,200 selected Civil War veterans to the next rank above their last wartime position. For some reason, never explained, Bierce was promoted not to captain, as would have been the correct rank, but to major. The official citation read: "Captain Ambrose Bierce for distinguished service during the war to be Brevet Major from March 13, 1865." Bierce had never been a captain, but no matter. He seldom used his new title, and he was as aware as anyone of its slightly bogus inception, but he was also understandably proud of his war record, and he never joked about it, publicly or privately.[19]

Meanwhile, he continued to write and publish short articles in the *Californian* and the *New Era,* contributing an uninspired anthropological piece on "The Pi-Ute Indians of Utah" and a slight bit of frippery on "The Tresses of the Fair Ladies." But his most important contact during the first part of 1868 was with a third publication, the *San Francisco News Letter and Commercial Advertiser,* known familiarly as the *News Letter.* Founded in 1856 by English journalist Frederick A. Marriott, the weekly was modeled after Marriott's earlier London publications, the *Illustrated News* and the *Morning Chronicle.* Within a decade, it had grown from a hand-folded one-page sheet of advertisements, letters, and spot news into a sixteen-page weekly of literary criticism, theater reviews, and broad-brush satire, with a decided taste for the macabre, which it indulged through its regular column on births, deaths, and marriages entitled "The Cradle, the Altar, and the Tomb." Marriott himself, a white-haired, pink-cheeked, Dickensian sort of character, had narrowly escaped lynching in the wake of Abraham Lincoln's assassination, when an enraged mob of mourners broke into his office, wrecked his press, and scattered his news type into the street in response to the *News Letter's* long-held pro-Southern sentiments. He recovered quickly enough to make the *News Letter,* by 1868, the city's most profitable advertising organ. Much of his profits Marriott immediately plowed back into his true obsession, a thirty-seven-foot-long steam-driven airship named the *Avitor* that he successfully test-flew twice in the summer of 1869. Unfortunately, the second flight took place on the star-crossed date—for a Briton—of the Fourth of July, and a curious onlooker got just close enough to the machine to ignite the *Avitor's* hydrogen-filled balloon accidentally and effectively put an end to Marriott's now-shipless Aerial Steam Navigation Company, but not before Bierce had sketched the machine being blown into stormy weather by a moneybags-toting Marriott, while editor James W. Watkins attempted to keep it afloat with a gust of hot air and a jackal-faced devil—Bierce?—sat grinning at the helm.[20]

Bierce began his professional association with the *News Letter* by contributing unsigned "Interior Items" in the spring or summer of 1868. The exact date of his first contribution is unknown, but his personal connection with the weekly can be dated fairly precisely. In later accounts of his first face-to-face meeting with Mark Twain, Bierce placed the event in the offices of the *News Letter;* Twain had dropped by, he said, to repay a loan from Marriott. Twain left San Francisco on December 15, 1866, for the rollicking sea voyage to Europe and the Holy Land that would shortly make him famous as the author of *The Innocents Abroad;* he did not return to the city until April 2, 1868, when he commenced a three-month speaking tour of California and Nevada. And since he left the West for good on July 6 of that same year (his farewell lecture was given at the Mercantile Library on Bush Street), he would have had to encounter Bierce sometime during those three months. Whenever he started, by midyear 1868, Bierce was hard at work turning out drolleries for the *News Letter* under the benevolent eye of editor Watkins, an experienced and well-traveled journalist who had worked on newspapers in London and on both American coasts. Watkins was kind enough to take Bierce in hand and redirect his reading to such masters of the epigram as Swift, Voltaire, and Thackeray, a service that earned him the exceedingly rare privilege of remaining Bierce's friend for life. As late as 1889, when Watkins departed San Francisco for New York, Bierce was still praising "the incomparable charm of his enchanted pen" and vouchsafing the rather inflated opinion "that in variety of language, definition of thought and charm of style he is among Americans incomparable and supreme."[21]

Bierce's touches were quickly evident, as the *News Letter* began running incidental items from such unlikely sources as the *Hangtown Gibbett,* the *Weekly Howl,* and the *Siskiyou Knockdown.* The paper had long featured a regular column called "The Town Crier," which traditionally was written by the editor. In December 1868, the column became the province and property of Ambrose Bierce, after Watkins either resigned or was amicably moved aside for his young protégé. Whatever the case, it was the beginning of Bierce's career and the making of his reputation. The man and the moment were met.[22]

The first issue of the *News Letter* under Bierce's direct supervision, on December 5, 1868, contained an editorial promise to "chaff" the city's parsons for "the immense difference between the religious ideal which the minister of religion is held to represent, and the lives human beings in general really lead." This was a favorite topic of Marriott's but one that Watkins had more or less eschewed as lacking good taste. Bierce, of course, had no such qualms; he allowed that he, as "theological editor," intended to "resume and continue our gentle ministrations, seeking not the applause of men, but the commendation of the faithful." It has been suggested that Bierce's savaging of organized religion in general and assorted San Francisco parsons in particular was a simple editorial ploy to help the *News Letter* compete for readers with the newly founded *Overland Monthly,* Bret Harte's more cosmopolitan literary magazine. This explanation, however, ignores Bierce's long-held and often-stated antipathy to organized religion at every level. If, indeed, that was Marriott's main reason for elevating him to the editor's post in the first place, it may be said to have been an inspired—if not perhaps a divinely inspired— choice.[23]

With the unconcealed glee of a Sunday school student let loose from a particularly boring sermon, Bierce set about flaying various men of the cloth. "The Rev. Mr. Fitch, Professor of Divinity in Yale college," he reported, "is gone to glory. It affords us a cheerful satisfaction to reflect that the Doctor has been accorded an opportunity to test the correctness of his theological theories by actual examination of the records at Headquarters. After explaining the New Life for a series of years, it is proper that he should go and learn what it is like. We beg for all his co-workers a similar privilege." He passed along the news that "the Rev. Dr. Hallelujah Cox has played his farewell engagement, and will appear no more before a California audience. In parting with the Rev. Doctor we cannot withhold the present slight tribute to his equally slight talent. We know of no public performer who has had to contend against equal natural disadvantages of personal ignorance and professional incapacity, and the fact that with such heavy odds against him he has succeeded in getting away without incurring actual disgrace is evidence of indomitable energy upon his part and criminal neglect upon our own." Later he told readers: "Dr. Scudder, it seems, is really going away. [He] has had an offer of a lucrative sinecure in Brooklyn. Upon receiving this grateful proposition, the Reverend Doctor speedily became aware that he was intensely sick, and had been so for some months, and his life depended upon a change of climate. It is very nice to have him go, upon any pretext, but we are touched with grief that he had not sufficient originality to reject one so flimsy in itself and so hackneyed with the profession; he might at least have claimed that a poverty-stricken mother in the congregation to which he had been called demanded his filial care."[24]

As expected, outraged letters poured into the *News Letter* office denouncing Bierce's irreverent attitude. "The clergy, poor devils, cannot divest themselves of the hallucination that we bear malice to the church," he airily responded to one such complaint. "Not a Sunday passes but some of them project from the pulpit a blinding beam of Gospel calcium light in the direction of our humble lair, lest at any time some benighted lamb should stray hitherward and fall a prey to our jaws dripping with the blood of masticated innocents. And we blink placidly in the cheerful ray, gape good-naturedly and stretch our claws in this artificial sunshine, with a dreamy sense of ineffable repose." To a second correspondent he replied: "We have received from a prominent clergyman a long letter of earnest remonstrance against what he is pleased to term our 'unprovoked attacks upon God's elect.' We emphatically deny that we have ever made any unprovoked attacks upon them. 'God's elect' are always irritating us. We have nothing against the parsons," he added magisterially; "we regard them with the same sort of interest that an entomologist feels in the habits of some singular insect."[25]

Not all Bierce's observations were so (comparatively) mild-mannered. In a city where anti-Chinese sentiment was growing daily—within a decade a new political party would arise in San Francisco with the unsubtle slogan "The Chinese Must Go!"—crimes against Chinese residents were all too common. For a supposed elitist, Bierce demonstrated a consistent and career-long concern for such abused minorities as the Chinese and the Mormons. As Town Crier, he duly noted the depressing regularity of assaults on the heathen Chinese by white Christians, in effect killing two birds with one stone. "The dead body of a Chinese woman was found last Tuesday morning lying across the sidewalk in a very uncomfortable position," he wrote in 1870. "The cause of her death could not be accurately ascertained, but as her head was caved in it is thought by some physicians that she died of galloping Christianity of the malignant California type." Another notice read: "On last Sunday afternoon a Chinaman passing guilelessly along Dupont Street was assailed with a tempest of bricks and stones from the steps of the First Congregational Church. At the completion of this devotional exercise the Sunday-scholars retired within the hallowed portals of the sanctuary, to hear about Christ Jesus, and Him crucified." A third column observed: "On last Monday two little Christians (with a big C) were up before his Honor (with a big H) for pelting a Chinaman with rocks. On account of their youth, good character, color, nationality, religion and the politics of their fathers, they were let off with a reprimand." And finally: "The other day the dead body of a Chinaman was found in an alley of this city, and taken to the morgue for identification. The body was found partially concealed under a paving-stone which was imbedded in the head like a precious jewel in the pate of a toad. A crowbar was driven through the abdomen and one arm was riven from its socket by some great convulsion of nature. As the deceased was seen enjoying his opium pipe and his usual health just previously to the discovery of his melancholy remains, it is supposed he came to his death by heart disease."[26]

Crimes of all sorts elicited regular editorial comment, with Bierce remarking happily that "our Criminal Market Review exhibits considerable activity. Since our last similar reference, moderate transactions have taken place in Burglaries; Robberies are looking up; Assaults active; Forgeries dull; in Confidence-games there has been no movement since the late operation by the Young Men's Christian Association; Embezzlements are quiet; Murders, neglected; Juvenile delinquencies are lively; Election frauds, out of season; Perjuries, brisk; Abortions are kept strictly private; a few transactions in Black Mail are reported; Drunks continue depressed; Gambling tends downward; Arson is firm; Brokers, without improvement." He found the local constabulary to be sorely lacking in both style and effect, the typical policeman being a slum-bred blackguard who "shall eye you insultingly as you pass, and make himself a nuisance to modest women and young girls. He shall rejoice in all beastliness. When you pay him his monthly dues for protecting your property, you shall have the soothing consciousness that you are encouraging vice by rewarding idleness—that you are promoting burglary, and arson, and midnight theft, and all naughtiness, by sustaining a system upon which they fatten and grow bold." As an alternative, he recommended a return to vigilante justice: "It is the duty of the people to take the assassins out of the hands of the law and beat their brains out with such articles as may be readily snatched up. Ten years of security would be cheaply purchased by a month of pretty general hanging."[27]

Two particular forms of homicide—wife-murder and suicide—attracted Bierce's somewhat obsessive attention. One of his first items, in December 1868, observed that "Charles O'Neil was, it seems, temporarily insane when he threw his wife off the balcony, and broke her precious neck. Charles O'Neil, would that we had but the sentencing of thee—there would have been another neck broken. We yearn for a law making temporary insanity a capital offense." He considered it a murder in bad taste that "Mr. John Beever, of St. Cloud, Minn., went to call upon his wife, from whom he had been some time separated, and before leaving took occasion to inveigle her into a back kitchen by the chignon, and then threw off the disguise and revealed himself in his true colors with a sharp hatchet. He chopped away at the lady's head until he had made of it a basket of unsightly chips, hanging confusedly together by tangled skeins of hair, clogged with warm brain and smoking with blood—altogether a very discouraging spectacle for the hired girl who had to clean up after him. It doesn't seem right to treat a woman in this way after having left her. When one frees himself from the obligations of matrimony he should be held to have renounced its privileges. The privilege to hack and mangle the conjugal head should be very sparingly exercised anyhow." This is strong stuff, and not particularly amusing, even if one grants the earlier era a less enlightened view of spousal abuse than our own. The regularity with which Bierce took note of spousal murder in his column suggests either that the crime was more common in the Victorian era than it is today, which seems doubtful, or else that it held an unhealthy and enduring fascination for the columnist himself, which seems all too apparent.[28]

Suicide, too, fascinated Bierce, even at the peak of his young manhood. Indeed, given the regularity of its appearance in his writings, then and later, self-murder would seem to have come in a close second to his favorite sport of religion bashing. (Is it too easy, where Bierce is concerned, to find a psychological congruence between the two?) In an 1870 column, he observed: "Men appear to believe, says the *Bulletin,* that they have their lives in their own hands, and are entitled to decide at what particular time they will go out of the world. To this we have only to add that we appear to believe exactly the same thing." He congratulated a German baker for swiftly following through on a sudden notion to blow off the top of his head. "By this example," wrote Bierce, "we may be taught that when a man gets an idea in his head he may accomplish great results by nailing it, and acting on it at once. There is no use fooling about such things. Be sure you're right, then go ahead. Many a brilliant scheme has perished ingloriously at its birth for want of the prompt decision of this poor German baker. Statesmen may profit by his example." Less efficient was "a poor devil named Linton [who] cut his wind-pipe entirely off with a very dull chisel because he could not get work. He immediately obtained all the work he wanted: he had to work very hard to breathe. There was a loaded pistol in the room, with which he might just as easily have taken himself off. There are some men who will play the fool even in fulfilling their most sacred obligations to society."[29]

As a public service for depressed readers, Bierce expounded at length on the art of suicide. "Razors," he wrote, "are good in their own way, but some knowledge of the location of the jugular vein must precede their use. Don't attempt to use more than one at a time, and go about it deliberately. Give yourself at least half an hour after business hours. Saw from left to right. A pistol is objectionable; it makes too much noise and wakes baby. If you must do it in this way, take a revolver, put the muzzle in your mouth (having previously removed the teeth), close the lips to deaden the sound, and fire five barrels. Wait two minutes by the watch, and if you don't feel sick, pull off the other barrel and hold your head in a tub of water. Shotguns are vulgar. Besides, they must be fired with the toe, which is liable to slip off the trigger and hurt one's corns. Hanging will do on a stretch, and arsenic may be taken at a pinch. Asphyxiation by blowing out the gas should not be thought of; it makes the corpse smell bad. We tender this advice gratis, in the interest of art."[30]

One Michael Brannan of Los Angeles earned Bierce's "unmixed admiration" for his self-annihilating determination, if not necessarily his aim. "Mr. Brannan had tired of life's fitful fever," observed Bierce, "and sought to effect a cure with a pistol—a vulgar, hackneyed expedient justly deserving of emphatic disapproval. But mark the high qualities of this man! He emptied five barrels of that weapon at his head, each leaden pellet plowing its crimson groove through the Brannan scalp, but not ducking beneath the bone to the heroic brain within. The man who could look upon this marvelous attempt unmoved with admiration—nay, who could himself withhold a friendly shot, or deny the succor of the exterminating axe, is not to be lightly classed with Christian gentlemen."[31]

More amusing, and considerably lighter in tone, were some of Bierce's observations concerning less lethal forms of civic wrongdoing. "Somebody has attempted to rob the safe in the office of the City and County Treasurer," he noted. "This is rushing matters; the impatient scoundrel ought to try his hand at being a Supervisor first. From Supervisor to Thief the transition is natural and easy." When an insurance company was robbed, he exulted, "Tit for tat." He was the soul of sympathy for "a gentleman who is suspected of insanity [and] has been committed to the Asylum. His idea is that the devil is in him, and he wishes to find the Virgin to cure him. It is just as well that he is gone to the Asylum; it is not likely that in San Francisco he would find any virgin of sufficient age to undertake his restoration to health."[32]

Bierce also took a lively interest in the local board of education, finding in that body of worthies a number of diverting incidents. On one occasion, when it was reported that the board had been given a list of two hundred books to approve or disapprove for purchase by the local high school, he observed that the task of winnowing down the list "will require the first intellectual labor they have ever done in their lives," and he expressed the hope that "the works are printed in large, clear type, with the syllables properly estranged." Noting that a group of right-thinking citizens had opened a new school for Chinese children, he wondered aloud whether "some of our public-spirited Chinese [will] open a school for American children . . . either as a reciprocatory measure or a retaliatory measure." And when it was being debated whether or not to educate boys and girls together, he strongly recommended that the two sexes "be kept out of one another's way while preparing for matrimony. They gather more strength in that way, and, as it were, secrete more moisture to sustain them in their sweltering travel across conjugal sands. It is a refinement of cruelty to subject the youth of either sex to the society of the other until they are themselves willing to submit to the infliction and take to it naturally." When an unlucky—or, at any rate, uncautious—candidate for the school board came under fire for consorting with a prostitute, Bierce urged the man's election on the grounds that it would inevitably lead him to reform, since "no respectable harlot who cares for her reputation would continue her acquaintance with a man who had been elected to the Board of Education."[33]

On the subject of school prayer—still a controversial topic today—Bierce came down in favor of the law that prohibited "the chanting of the Lord's Prayer in the public schools. The Lord's Prayer has been brought into disrepute long enough by being snarled through the dirty noses of a hundred bad boys and preposterous girls. The Town Crier attributes every wicked action of his next-door neighbor's children directly to this barbarous practice. Down with the Lord's Prayer!—in schools." In partial restitution for this attitude, he offered his own self-written prayer, one that he liked so well that he later reprinted it in his second book-length collection of essays, *Nuggets and Dust:* "O, Lord, who for the purposes of this supplication we assume to have created the heavens and the earth before man created Thee; and who, let us say, art from everlasting to everlasting; we beseech Thee to turn Thy attention to this way and behold a set of the most abandoned scalawags Thou hast ever had the pleasure of setting eyes on. But in consideration of the fact that Thou sentest Thy only-begotten Son among us, and afforded us the felicity of murdering him, we would respectfully suggest the propriety of taking into heaven such of us as pay our church dues, and giving us an eternity of exalted laziness and absolutely inconceivable fun. We ask this in the name of Thy Son whom we strung up as above stated. Amen."[34]

In a remarkably short time, Bierce became a household name in San Francisco, his sweepingly confident editorial pronouncements read with individual admixtures of anger, shock, amusement, and delight everywhere from the artistic salons on Russian Hill to the lowest rumpots on the Barbary Coast. It was his first brush with fame, and he enjoyed himself greatly and dressed the part. The Town Crier, he announced proudly, was forever being interrupted by "lady admirers [who] are always bothering him with notes asking for his photograph." And well they might, for Bierce in his late twenties had grown into a strikingly handsome young man, an inch or so under six feet in height, with sandy blond hair, a tawny, full mustache, piercing blue eyes, and a smooth pink complexion that was almost feminine in its flawlessness. As ever, he was scrupulously clean—a friend said that he looked as though "he shaved all over every day"—and with the possible exception of Bret Harte, he was the best-known—and certainly the best-dressed—journalist in San Francisco. His fame and his confidence were soaring. In a note to his somewhat unlikely friend Charles Warren Stoddard, a slender, effeminate poet with a pronounced taste in prepubescent Polynesian boys, Bierce advised him to "tell anybody anything that is not complimentary, and attribute the same to me." Newspapers as far away as New York and London quoted his best lines, praising the "Rabelaisian audacity of his homicidal paragraphs," and the *California Mail Bag* called his column "the Mentor, whip and Mirror of the town . . . wise, witty, grave, gay, lively and severe." The competing *Bulletin* paid him the sincerest form of flattery, reporting on the discovery of a baby's body in a garbage can: "It seems impossible for a man to dig potatoes in a garden, or excavate a post hole in a front yard, without turning up some little innocent thing that has been dumped there without either coffin or shroud. Yesterday the body of a baby was found lying at one of the wharves, in a tin-can. When it comes to canning babies, putting them up, so to speak, 'for exportation,' as though they were oysters, shrimps, green turtle, or jellies, it becomes time to speak and remonstrate."[35]

Soon Bierce began acquiring some sharp-edged and not entirely fond nicknames: the Rascal with the Sorrel Hair, the Diabolical Bierce, the Laughing Devil, and one that he was particularly proud of, the Wickedest Man in San Francisco. This last nickname had become so well known by 1871 that a reporter on the San Francisco *Call,* interviewing Bierce at an exhibition bullfight in San Rafael, informed his readers that "the Wickedest Man" had found the proceedings "a dreadful fraud; not a single corpse to embalm, not even of a bullock." Judging from that quote, it would seem that Bierce was already playing the role of local bad boy to the hilt. Certainly, he tried to find something to offend everyone. Besides religion, crime, and politics, other targets of his editorial lash included such proven crowd-pleasers as babies, mothers, Christmas, the Fourth of July ("the annual exhibition of national idiocy"), the Society of California Pioneers, senior citizens, baseball, dogs, and the painter Albert Bierstadt's much-loved rendering of the Yosemite Valley, which Bierce was glad to report had been destroyed by fire. "That picture," he complained, "has incited more unpleasant people to visit California than all our conspiring hotel-keepers could compel to return. We are glad that a blow has finally been struck at the root of immigration." Even suffragettes like Susan B. Anthony, whom he had praised in his early column for the *Californian,* now suffered a heated blast. "That hatchet-faced old angularity, Miss Susan B. Anthony," he wrote rather unchivalrously, "said in her lecture the other evening that in Boston ten thousand women earn a living by working as shoemakers. Then Boston may justly boast that it contains at least ten thousand better and more useful women than this he-hearted old termagant. And it isn't much of a boast."[36]

Nor were fellow journalists exempt. "We wish it distinctly understood," he thundered, "that we hold the Press of this State in profound contempt, and that the Press of this State hates us with a holy hatred. We feel no delicacy about viciously assailing the newspapers and their editors, and no resentment at being meanly defamed in return." On another occasion, he called for "the unspeakable extirpation of the noxious brood of sycophants and toadies," adding, "We are proud to confess that we have more in common with the average San Francisco jackass than with the average San Francisco journalist. You have never seen a jackass lick the feet of his master. You have never seen him wear his owner's collar, knowing it to be a badge of disgrace. These things a jackass has never done; and these many a San Francisco journalist has done, and does." Even the unoffending Mark Twain, whom Bierce scarcely knew at the time, came in for a share of Town Crier abuse. "Mark Twain, who, whenever he has been long enough sober to permit an estimate, has been uniformly found to bear a spotless character, has got married," Bierce noted in 1870. "It was not the act of a desperate man—it was not committed while laboring under temporary insanity; his insanity is not of that type, nor does he ever labor—it was the cool, methodical, cumulative culmination of human nature, working in the breast of an orphan hankering for some one with a fortune to love—some one with a bank account to caress." A little later, Bierce followed up on the Twain nuptials. "It is announced that Mark Twain, being above want, will lecture no more," he reported. "We didn't think that of Mark; we supposed that after marrying a rich girl he would have decency enough to make a show of working for a year or two anyhow. But it seems his native laziness has wrecked his finer feelings, and he has abandoned himself to his natural vice with the stolid indifference of a pig at his ablutions." And still later: "Mark Twain's father-in-law is dead, and has left that youth's wife a quarter of a million dollars. At the time of Mark's marriage, a few months since, we expressed some doubt as to the propriety of the transaction. That doubt has been removed by death."[37]

Amazingly, given all his vituperation, Bierce was involved in only one libel suit, undertaken in 1871 by San Francisco printer and editor George T. Russell. Russell ran afoul of Bierce by criticizing the *News Letter* in the pages of *Figaro,* a drama publication that Russell owned for a time. He compounded his error by rejoining the Typographical Union and going to work for the *Morning Call* one day before that paper's printers had gone out on strike, an unlikely coincidence that Bierce considered a professional betrayal. For his apostasy, Russell earned a Biercian blast that, even by the rough-and-tumble standards of the day, set something of a precedent for character assassination, or, as Bierce considered it, self-defense. The offending passage, from the April 23, 1870, issue of the *News Letter*, needs to be savored whole for its full effect: "The vacant-headed simpleton who has for some months misconducted a dramatic paper in this city has been so persistently kicked by gentlemen into whose path he has had the temerity to crawl, that he has finally been compelled to purchase the luxury of sitting down without pain, by disposing of his interest. This ridiculous incarnation of inspissated idiocy, who, by a miraculous manifestation of morbid meanness in Mother Nature, was thrust upon a protesting world as a faultless specimen of the human hog, was a decent printer until his mirror suggested the aspiring monkey, which he straightway attempted to emulate in ambition as in face. His brief but brilliant career affords another illustration of the folly of attempting the role of a gentleman with the brain of a jackass. If it be not already clear that we allude to George T. Russell, we despair of describing a dunce by any ordinary method of delicate insinuation."[38]

In subsequent columns, Bierce variously described the overmatched Russell as "whilom proprietor of the *Figaro* smut-machine"; "peripatetic liar for a horse opera"; "a consistent sneak"; "this Judas"; "a most disreputable character"; "the laboring tumble-bug"; "a lame pullet"; and—most damning of all, in Bierce's eyes—"a George T. Russell." This last characterization brought the brutal addendum that "if any gentleman will kindly furnish us with a more odious epithet, or one more richly deserved, we shall be happy to stain our page with that, too." After Russell made the mistake of bragging to acquaintances that he had personally visited Bierce's office and intimidated the editor into promising not to continue his attacks, Bierce fired back with his own defiant version of events. "The facts are about these," he wrote. "Mr. Russell came to this office and said something about libels and his singular distaste for them. The editor happened at the moment to be deeply absorbed in the act of crucifying a blue-bottle fly in attendance upon Mr. Russell, and neglected to get the drift of the latter's remarks. Mr. Russell was then blandly requested to betake himself to the street, and assured that in the forthcoming issue of the paper he would be roasted to a delicate nut brown. As he passed out of the office his bearing so forcibly suggested to the editorial mind the dignified demeanor of a chastened spaniel, that it became merely consistent to wallop our dog Jack, in which pleasing duty the flagellation due to the other puppy was wholly forgotten. It is hoped this paragraph may be accepted as sufficient reparation for an unintentional neglect."[39]

Russell sued Marriott, as proprietor of the *News Letter*, for fifteen thousand dollars and sought a similar amount from the San Francisco *Chronicle*, which reprinted Bierce's original column. The grand jury failed to return a criminal indictment, and a subsequent trial in civil court also decided against the plaintiff. Ultimately, Russell withdrew his suit, though not before Bierce had the satisfaction of observing in print that "several of his choicest modes of speech [had] become household words." For his money, claimed Bierce, he "would have been as content to see Mr. Russell go forth from the Courtroom vindicated as a gentleman, as he was to see him slink out branded as a 'peripatetic liar' and a 'consistent sneak'; but it is worth something to have enriched the vituperative vocabulary of mankind with these sweet, pungent and expressive terms."[40]

In January 1871, Bierce took time away from his self-appointed task of enriching the language to write a series of five loosely organized essays for Bret Harte's *Overland Monthly.* By then, the *Overland* was widely considered the best magazine in the West, if not the entire country. Harte, availing himself of an editor's ageless prerogative, had already published—at four times the journal's usual rate of twenty-five dollars per submission—a number of his own short stories, including such instant classics as "The Luck of Roaring Camp," "The Outcasts of Poker Flat," and "Tennessee's Partner," as well as the comic poem "Plain Language from Truthful James," which under its alternative title, "The Heathen Chinee," made him world-famous. For this latter accomplishment, Bierce claimed some credit. According to his version of events, Harte had not wanted to publish the poem in the *Overland;* instead, he sent it to the *News Letter.* It was only after Bierce's repeated urging that he agreed to publish it in his own magazine, where it was quickly picked up and reprinted throughout the world. Bierce had first met Harte at the U.S. Mint, where Harte enjoyed what amounted to a well-paid sinecure as secretary to the director. In stubborn contradiction to the prevailing sentiment of San Francisco's literary community, to say nothing of the legion of tailors whom Harte had personally ruined with unpaid debts, Bierce actually liked the *Overland* editor. A year earlier, he had defended him against the rival editors of the *Call* and the *Examiner* when they complained about a plan by the University of California to name Harte an honorary professor of recent literature.[41]

Now, Harte returned the favor by accepting Bierce's atypically solemn and ruminative essays on self-reliance and conformity, faith and reason, art and altruism, war and peace. In the articles, which Bierce signed "Ursus" and Harte christened the "Grizzly Papers," Bierce did a little thinking and a lot of showing off, variously citing as authorities for his opinions such weighty thinkers as John Stuart Mill, Samuel Taylor Coleridge, Francis Bacon, John Ruskin, Empedocles, Voltaire, and Plato. A more polished cynicism showed through the *Overland* pieces than in the sledgehammer ironies of the *News Letter,* partly because the subjects of the essays were more elevated than the usual gutter reportage that Bierce, as *Town Crier,* was accustomed to writing. Such a rarefied topic as didacticism in art, for instance, is more conducive to fine thinking than the latest braining, say, of a San Francisco guttersnipe.

Still, despite the high seriousness of the essays, a characteristic antihumanism leaked in. Altruistic acts were scorned by Bierce as empty gestures performed by self-interested individuals to make themselves feel better, without regard to the particularized wants of the needy. "When you find a man starving, the least you can do is to loan him your umbrella," Bierce mocked. "That is the proper course." Nor should one expect to be repaid for his kindness. "There is not a more erroneous belief than that one good turn deserves another," he wrote. "In repaying a kindness you degrade it to the level of barter." In all matters, one must choose for oneself. "If a man have a broad foot, a staunch leg, a strong spine, and a talent for equilibrium, there is no good reason why he should not stand alone," said Bierce. "A mind that is right side up does not need to lean upon others: it is sufficient unto itself. The curse of our civilization is that the 'association' is become the unit, and the individual is merged in the mass."[42]

This rather existential philosophy carried over to the realm of warfare, which Bierce found an all-too-popular human pastime. Although war was typically "ascribed to the ambition of the few, and the credulity of the many . . . the bald fact is that the average man takes a diabolical delight— or, what is very nearly allied to it, a human satisfaction—in fighting his neighbor to death." Indeed, war is perhaps "the one thing capable of igniting in the bosom of the average man a perfectly satisfactory enthusiasm." The previous two decades, Bierce noted with grim satisfaction, "have been marked by an unwonted activity of slaughter, as if on purpose to give the lie to the Bible-commentators who have fixed the birth of the Millennium hereabout." As for "the amiable maniac who believes in a tolerably rapid rate of human progress toward a tolerably stupid state of human imperfection through cumulative accretions of brotherly love, the events of the past few years must seem singularly perverse, if not wildly wayward. This worthy party has been steadily assuring us that the lion and the lamb were just upon the point of lying down together, without the latter observing the customary formality of getting himself inside the former."[43]

The Grizzly Papers lacked the low-life fizz of the Town Crier column, but they succeeded in bringing Bierce's name before a wider and more sophisticated audience. They also prepared the ground for the appearance of his first work of fiction, the short story "The Haunted Valley," which appeared in the July 1871 issue of the *Overland Monthly*. Contrary to a popular misconception, the story was not published by Harte, but by his successor, William C. Bartlett, who took over as editor after Harte left California in February 1871 to write for the *Atlantic Monthly*—a fatal decision artistically, since it removed Harte from his most loyal and long-lived audience. (Mark Twain, for one, always believed that the train carrying Harte eastward that winter might just as well have carried his casket, since "he had lived all of his life that was worth living.") Despite Harte's absence, "The Haunted Valley" clearly shows a deep indebtedness to his vivid tales of the mining frontier. In it, a "young Easterner" pays a visit to the "hermaphrodite habitation, half residence and half groggery," of an unsavory saloonkeeper named Whiskey Jo Dunfer. There he hears the odd tale of Dunfer's apparent murder of his Chinese servant Ah Wee, whom Dunfer hints he killed for the rather weak motive that Ah Wee did not know how to cut down trees properly. After Dunfer is frightened by his hired hand, Gopher, who is staring at him through a knothole in his cabin, the Easterner rides away, coming at length to the haunted valley, where he finds Ah Wee's lonely tombstone lying in some grass. The tombstone has an odd inscription: "AH WEE—CHINAMAN./Age unknown. Worked for Jo. Dunfer./This monument is erected by him to keep the Chink's/memory green. Likewise as a warning to Celestials/not to take on airs. Devil take 'em!/She Was a Good Egg." The Easterner, perplexed, observes that the headstone was "the work of one who must have been at least as much demented as bereaved."[44]

Four years later, the Easterner returns to the valley, where he hitches a ride with "a queer little man" who turns out to be Dunfer's man Gopher. Gopher tells him that Dunfer is now dead and "lies aside of Ah Wee up the gulch." According to Gopher, Dunfer killed Ah Wee with an ax after he caught the two workers lying down beside each other while Gopher sought to pull a tarantula out of Ah Wee's sleeve. "W'en 'e saw the spider fastened on my finger; then 'e knew he'd made a jack ass of 'imself," Gopher recalls. "He threw away the axe and got down on 'is knees alongside of Ah Wee, who gave a last little kick and opened 'is eyes—he had eyes like mine." Gopher says that Dunfer died soon after he saw Gopher peering at him through the knothole during the Easterner's first visit. He even accuses the visitor of poisoning Dunfer, an accusation that causes the Easterner to realize that Gopher is insane. "When did you go luny?" he asks. Gopher says he lost his mind "w'en that big brute killed the woman who loved him better than she did me!—me who had followed 'er from San Francisco, where 'e won 'er at draw poker!—me who had watched over 'er for years w'en the scoundrel she belonged to was ashamed to acknowledge 'er and treat 'er white!—me who for her sake kept 'is cussed secret till it ate 'im up!"[45]

"The Haunted Valley" is a decidedly odd story. The structure is a common one for western stories: the innocent young tenderfoot coming into contact with colorful and dangerous frontiersmen, in whose company he learns something about real life out west. But the story seems, on another level, to be about something else: homosexuality (or the fear of homosexuality). Sexual inversion was not uncommon in the mining camps, where there was a decided shortage of women, and Bierce had undoubtedly heard stories about such forbidden practices. The stereotypical Chinaman of the day—slightly built, obsessively clean and polite, dressed in pajamas and slippers and wearing pigtails—was a sexually ambiguous figure, and the story deliberately confuses Ah Wee's sexual identity, calling him first man, then woman, and linking him to the equally ambiguous Gopher—"he had eyes like mine." Other hints are strewn throughout the story: Dunfer's "hermaphrodite habitation"; Gopher's description, repeated three times, as "a queer little man"; Ah Wee's characterization as a "pagan" and "the perversest scoundrel outside San Francisco," with "the damn'dest eyes in this neck o' woods." The murder itself seems like the act of a jealous lover—Gopher says explicitly that "W'isky was jealous o' me," then adds that Dunfer "thought a lot o' that Chink; nobody but me knew how 'e doted on 'im."[46]

Nor is the Easterner immune to the perversity of the haunted valley. When he meets Gopher, the man is poking his oxen with a long pole, "which neither blossomed nor turned into a serpent, as I half expected." At times, Gopher seems to be flirting with the young man: "The little wretch actually swelled out like a turkeycock and made a pretense of adjusting an imaginary neck-tie, noting the effect in the palm of his hand, held up before him to represent a mirror. He assumed a mocking attitude of studied grace, and twitched the wrinkles out of his threadbare waistcoat." Significantly, the Easterner has a conflicted response to Gopher and his story. "I fancied that I could detect beneath his whimsical manner something of manliness, almost of dignity. But while I looked at him his former aspect, so subtly unhuman, so tantalizingly familiar, crept back into his big eyes, repellant and attractive." When the young man finally leaves the valley and its crazed inhabitants, it is with a distinct sense of relief, of having escaped something uncanny, like the ghost of Dunfer that Gopher is mortally afraid he will meet.[47]

Years later, Bierce defined *ghost* in *The Devil's Dictionary* as "the outward and visible sign of an inward fear." Without suggesting that Bierce was anything other than heterosexual, it nevertheless seems obvious that his first published short story contains several outward signs of an inner unease. Certainly, Bierce, himself an easterner, had come to be living in a city that, like the haunted valley, had few taboos, sexual or otherwise. Moreover, with his fastidious personal habits, his sartorial elegance, and his almost feminine handsomeness, Bierce was a somewhat sexually ambiguous figure himself. One of his closest friends, Charles Warren Stoddard, was a well-known homosexual—"Such a nice girl," Mark Twain once sneered—and in "The Haunted Valley," Bierce seems to be protesting, if not too much, then at least enough, that he has escaped a similar fate.[48]

A reputed incident late in Bierce's life would seem to underscore his uneasiness about his perceived sexual orientation. According to Bierce's friend and publisher, Walter Neale, he once grabbed a revolver and headed straight for the home of a man who had accused him of being homosexual, only to be stopped at the last moment by a mutual acquaintance, who told him that the man was a bedridden cripple. Neale, who knew Bierce well and considered the charge "a preposterous lie," probably came closest to the truth of the matter when he observed that "no doubt the subject of sex depravity fascinated him, as did all pathology." But, he observed, "Nobody who knew Bierce could possibly believe him guilty of an unnatural sex act."[49]

Whatever the case, in the summer of 1871, Bierce chose a more obvious way of asserting his masculinity. To the surprise of his friends and the consternation of his enemies, the notorious misogynist and curmudgeon the Town Crier fell in love with a Bay Area beauty, and, equally amazing, she fell in love with him. The lady in question was Mary Ellen "Mollie" Day, the attractive, vivacious, dark-haired daughter of a wealthy mining engineer and his socially ambitious wife. For a time, at least, their utterly conventional courtship, complete with sailboat rides, band concerts, society balls, card parties, book readings, and picnics, seemed to presage a new life of great happiness for them both. But this was, after all, the same man who had written in a newspaper column earlier that year: "The T.C. does not hope to ever understand the sublime mysteries of the feminine sex. He knows that the female of the species is comely, and vivacious, and innocent, and pure, and holy; and that she will be like Satan when provoked thereto by opportunity. But she is very nice to kiss when you have nothing else to do." Their own first kiss, whenever it took place, would prove to be, in its way, no less fatal to their happiness than that other first kiss in the long-ago garden.[50]

7

A Better Country

By an almost literary coincidence, the only two significant American writers to serve in the Civil War and live to tell about it, Ambrose Bierce and Sidney Lanier, both married women named Mary Day. Neither woman went by her given name: Macon, Georgia–born Mary Day was called, in proper southern-belle concatenation, "May-day"; Mary Ellen Day of San Francisco was called "Mollie." Both were slight, attractive, dark-haired young women who played the piano (New York–trained May-day was the more accomplished); both had pleasant, open personalities; and both were considered quite the catch in their respective circles. Both married, to their divergent sorrows, talented but difficult ex-soldiers who carried with them for the rest of their lives the ineradicable scars of the great national catastrophe and who later wrote bravely—and often unfashionably—about it. (There is no evidence that Bierce ever read Lanier's early novel, *Tiger-Lilies,* but he would have appreciated the graphic battle scenes in it, even if he would likely have hooted in derision at the hero's anguished question: "How does God have the heart to allow it?") But here the comparison begins to break down. By all accounts, the Laniers were a passionate, loving couple whose one great tragedy was the tuberculosis Sidney contracted in a Northern prison camp, which necessitated his living apart from his wife and children for long periods of time in a futile attempt to recover his health. The Bierces' marital troubles were altogether less obvious, just as Ambrose's psychic and physical wounds were less apparent to the casual viewer, but in the end they were no less heartbreaking for being kept better hidden.[1]

Mollie Day, in the first blush of young womanhood, was lovely, as dark as her new suitor was fair. Whether or not she was "very beautiful," as biographer Carey McWilliams alleges, or simply "more attractive than the average," as fellow biographer Richard J. O'Connor believes, depends as always on the individual. Her best-known photograph shows a young lady with limpid black eyes, strong, straight eyebrows, a great mass of curly dark hair, a rather long nose, and an ironic half smile. In her nautical blouse, ruffled neckerchief, and billowing skirt, she looks no different than any other mid-Victorian debutante, except perhaps around the eyes. There is a frankness in her level gaze and hint of good humor behind it, qualities she would have need to call upon in the years to come. She seems, on balance, to have taken after her father, which was all to the good, if contemporary opinion can be believed. Capt. Holland Hines Day (the rank, like Bierce's brevet majority, was honorary) had gone west from Illinois in the early 1850s to ply his trade as a mining engineer. He worked as a superintendent for a number of mines in California and Nevada before striking it rich with the Tintic mine near Salt Lake City. He had one son, James, as well as a daughter, and their care and feeding he left to their mother while he spent most of his time in Mormon country, overseeing his bonanza. On at least one occasion, his name was bandied about for United States senator, but nothing ever came of it. Probably the captain did not care enough about it, or perhaps he declined to ante up the seed money needed to purchase the cherished position. At any rate, he stayed in mining, and Ambrose Bierce, who was notably frugal with compliments, always called him "the Grand Old Man."[2]

Mrs. Day was another matter. A native New Yorker who could trace her bloodlines back to the early Dutch founders, Mollie's mother was as socially ambitious as her husband was indifferent. She saw to it that her children were properly schooled in snobbery, a lesson the priggish James learned all too well but one that Mollie, despite her music lessons, her dance classes, and her carefully cultivated "eligibility," more or less disregarded. When the family (minus, as usual, the ever-working captain) went in 1871 for their annual summer visit to the resort community of San Rafael—in Marin County, across the bay—Mollie was ready for something more than the wispy young men in straw hats and white flannels hanging around the Lotus Club yachting slips. She found it, in spades, in the bristling personage of the Wickedest Man in San Francisco.[3]

From the start, her mother opposed the pairing. A notice in one of Bierce's "Town Crier" columns makes this manifest: "Mollie—tell your mother not to relax her efforts to keep you from writing to us. The chances are that the old lady is right." The old lady was right, in the end, but no one could see it yet, least of all the privileged young belle who increasingly had her sights set on the good-looking Civil War veteran turned newspaper columnist. The fact that he was socially nondescript meant nothing to Mollie or her egalitarian father. And Bierce, for his part, played the role of the conventional suitor to the hilt, escorting Mollie to such then-notable social events as the Sharon Reception and the Calico Ball and squiring her about on weekend boat rides, long walks by the bay, daylong picnics, and visits to Woodward's Gardens to look at the seashells. For the time being, he even set aside his lifelong aversion to parlor games, organizing four-handed card games with Mollie, Charles Warren Stoddard, and the reigning doyenne of San Francisco literature, Ina Coolbrith, whom he had recently gotten to know. Somehow, he managed to sit through Mollie's impromptu piano recitals, forgetting for a time his hatred of the instrument, which he would later define as "a parlor utensil for subduing the impenitent visitor." If there is any truth to the after-the-fact claim by Bierce protégé Adolph Danziger that Bierce "was not so madly in love with her as she was with him"—and given what we know of Bierce's essential character, this seems entirely plausible—the alleged discrepancy between the respective ardor of the two was not apparent at the time. They seemed, and no doubt were, in love—whatever that meant to the interested parties. It would be some years before Bierce wrote his own definition of the word, one that reflected something other than beaches and picnics: "LOVE, n. A temporary insanity curable by marriage."[4]

They took the cure on Christmas Day, 1871, an odd choice in itself, given Bierce's lifelong loathing for the holiday. Odd, too, was the fact that it was a private ceremony held at the Day home in San Francisco; one would have thought that the marriage of such a socially prominent couple would have merited a more public laying on of hands. Perhaps Bierce simply refused to have the wedding inside a church, although he did accede to the formal ministrations of a local man of the cloth, the Reverend Horatio Stebbins of the First Unitarian Church, "a better preacher, a more liberal man, a profounder theologian and altogether a more desirable person to have around," in the groom's rare favorable opinion, than any other Bible-thumper of his acquaintance. Captain Day came down from Utah to give away his daughter's hand, and Mrs. Day no doubt smiled grimly through the ceremony. A reception was held at the home of the captain's old mining buddy, Sandy Bowers, an Irish-born laborer who had struck it even richer than Day, although he had never learned how to read and so kept pictures of famous authors taped over their selections of books in his library, in the unlikely event he ever had the need to reference them. He also kept nude Italian statuary in his house, but for the wedding reception he had the pieces modestly draped in pink cloth to avoid any hint of impropriety. The next day, the *Daily Evening Bulletin* noted: "In this city, married, December 25th, by Rev. Horatio Stebbins, Ambrose G. Bierce and Mary E. Day." Years later, Bierce supplied his own poetic version of the ceremony: "They stood before the altar and supplied/The fire themselves in which their fat was fried./In vain the sacrifice!—no god will claim/An offering burnt with an unholy flame."[5]

The couple settled into a honeymoon cottage in out-of-the-way San Rafael, and Bierce reported to Stoddard that they were "living cosily." It was a temporary arrangement, anyway: Captain Day had promised the newly-weds an all-expenses-paid trip to England, which they intended to undertake in the spring. Meanwhile, Bierce refocused his attention on the *News Letter*, authoring a purported response to his nuptials by a committee of "Female Suffragers" sporting the Dickensian names of Almira Faircheek, Miss Turn-toes, Eliza Straitlace, Jane Squinteye, and Medora Sawnose. In it, the good women noted that the "implacable reviler of women and scoffer of the marriage relation, the Town Crier" had been "caught in the pit which he himself digged." They extended their sisterly sympathy to "the victim of the altar" who had inherited the "dreadful task" of raising to the level of ordinary men the "one eternal soul that had been playing all his life hide-and-seek with the devil, and had been caught every time." They further resolved "that the sympathies of this society and of the world are bestowed upon the heroic woman who has offered herself a victim upon the altar of that dreadful being's desire to be received into decent society" and expressed hope that "she ought to be relieved at an early date from the purgatory of such a marital existence, into the haven of widowhood."[6]

In later years, Bierce took a decidedly less amused view of marriage. To his Washington friend and editor Walter Neale, he held forth at some length on the rite's religious and historical significance. Bierce believed, wrote Neale, that the whole institution of marriage, "an institution contrary to human nature as man has been revealed through seven thousand years," was doomed. The root of the problem, as Bierce explained it, was that marriage was an artificial construct designed to do two related but not mutually beneficial things: to trap the naturally polygamous man in a lifelong monogamous relationship and to give moral and religious sanction to what Bierce rather revealingly termed "the sinfulness of sex love." The Old Testament, he told Neale, "is crammed full of references to marriage in which the writers of those Scriptures showed their disgust with the whole process. But since the relationship seemed inevitable, there grew up a terminology that became matrimony's own,—words and phrases that are now used as a coating of sugar to make palatable a bitter pill. After long usage, this terminology conveys but little or no 'indelicate' meaning these days. The words *love-making, marriage, honeymoon, birth,* are shamelessly uttered in the most polite society. Copulation, to be sure, still remains in the dictionary, but is not uttered in drawing-rooms. Synonyms of the word— synonyms known to the most modest of little misses in their teens—have been ignored by the lexicographer. Perfectly innocent in themselves, these words describe a 'shameful act,' just as *marriage* does; but unlike the word *marriage,* the edge has not been worn off and the meaning obscured by frequent use."[7]

This is a heavy load to place on even such a sturdy social contract as marriage, and one inevitably hears in Bierce's words the Calvinist echoes of his
founding father, Augustin Bierce, and of the Reverend Mr. Stone of Cornwall, Connecticut, who shaped the childish personalities—and thus the
future marriage—of Bierce's own parents, Marcus and Laura, and, by extension, their youngest son's. What exactly the new Mrs. Bierce may have
thought of her husband's surprisingly prudish sexual views is unknown.
Given Bierce's low opinion of women's intellectual accomplishments in general, it is unlikely that he shared with Mollie his choicest philosophical tid-
bits—certainly not in the first days of their marriage, anyway. As a woman,
however, she presumably exhibited all her sex's unreasonable postmatrimo-
nial demands. The typical bride, said Bierce, "demands of her mate, to the
end, the same ardor in word and deed that animated him in the amorous
hours of the honeymoon. She places emphasis on words, too, and on caresses,
and on all the boyish inanities that were consistent with betrothal. There is
nothing of the sort with which to supply her demands. Her lover died on the
bridal night. The next morning he could not be brought to life. He was forever dead. He did not pass on to his successor, the husband, even the memory of the follies of courtship. In sooth, the male mate could not be brought
even to surmise what he the lover had done, since he was reluctant to speculate on situations so absurd as those into which his predecessor, the wooer,
had been inveigled."[8]

Granted, these were the words of an older, sadder, and presumably wiser
man, not those of a twenty-nine-year-old newlywed, but as a rule, Bierce did
not change his position on any subject. In a review of Tolstoy's *The Kreutzer
Sonata* in 1890, he wrote of marriage: "For my part, I know of no remedy,
nor do I believe that one can be formulated. It is of the nature of the more
gigantic evils to be irremediable—a truth against which poor humanity
instinctively revolts, entailing the additional afflictions of augmented nonsense and wasted endeavor. The marriage relation that we have we shall probably continue to have, and its Dead Sea fruits will grow no riper and sweeter
with time. But the lie that describes them as luscious and satisfying is needless. Let the young be taught, not celibacy, but fortitude. Point out to them
the exact nature of the fool's paradise in which they will pretty certainly enter.
Teach them that the purpose of marriage is whatever the teacher may conceive it to be, but *not* happiness."[9]

On March 9, 1872, Bierce bade a rather wistful farewell to his readers.
"With this number of the *News Letter*," he wrote, "the present writer's connection with it ceases for at least a brief season. That he has always been
entertaining he does not claim; that he has been uniformly good-natured is
no further true than that he has refrained from actually killing anybody; that
he has been 'genial' is not true at all. It must be pretty evident that in penning
some six or eight thousand paragraphs with the avowed design of being

clever, he must have told a great number of harmless lies, and perpetrated divers cruel slanders. For the former he is responsible to his Maker, and shall offer no apologies; for the latter no apologies would avail, even if he were in the humor of making them—which he is not." It was not true, said Bierce, that he was seeking a wider field for his talents. The only talents he possessed were "a knack of hating hypocrisy, cant, and all sham, and a trick of expressing his hatred. What wider field than San Francisco does God's green earth present?" The valediction urged his readers to "be as decent as you can. Don't believe without evidence. Treat things divine with marked respect—don't have anything to do with them. Do not trust humanity without collateral security; it will play you some scurvy trick. Remember that it hurts no one to be treated as an enemy entitled to respect until he shall prove himself a friend worthy of affection. Cultivate a taste for distasteful truths. And, finally, most important of all, endeavor to see things as they are, not as they ought to be." It was, on balance, the gentlest description of his own particular worldview that Bierce would ever write.[10]

With Mollie in hand, Bierce caught the Southern Pacific Railroad to Salt Lake City, then switched to the Union Pacific for the trip back east across the plains. He carried with him a packet of letters from Frederick Marriott formally introducing him to Marriott's old London associates. If he reflected on the distance he had come, not just in miles, since he first rode west with General Hazen half a dozen years earlier, he did not comment on it. Despite his promise in his last *News Letter* column that California would "be his abiding place for some years," it is unlikely that Bierce intended to return to San Francisco, whatever his San Franciscan wife may privately have believed. He was by nature a wanderer, and he put little stock in his journalistic career. In turning his sights toward London, he was signaling his desire to transcend mere paragraph writing for a more comprehensive literary achievement. He had ample exemplars for the move. Mark Twain had quit San Francisco about the time Bierce arrived and had gone on to find worldwide fame—and English lionization—as the author of *The Innocents Abroad.* Bret Harte had left town in glory a year earlier, his precipitate plunge in reputation and ability not yet realized. Even Joaquin Miller, the self-styled "Poet of the Sierras," whom everyone in San Francisco considered something of a joke, had taken his one-man Wild West show to England and been received with great applause, if only in the nature of children tossing peanuts to a monkey on a stick. As a literary gold mine, San Francisco was pretty much played out; London was a never-ending vein of ore.[11]

En route to New York, Bierce stopped over in Elkhart, Indiana, for a brief reunion with his family. What those stern moralists, his parents, must have made of their youngest son's beautiful socialite wife—to say nothing of her father's apparently limitless money—is anyone's guess. As for Bierce's reaction to his homecoming, an indirect hint may be found in one of his later stories, "My Favorite Murder," in which the narrator's father is described as "a reticent, saturnine man . . . though his increasing years have now somewhat relaxed the austerity of his disposition." There is no similar description of the mother, although in the story Bierce makes her out to be a dance hall girl in "The Saints' Rest Hurdy-Gurdy" saloon, a performer known to the regulars as "The Bucking Walrus." It was, at any rate, a short visit. Brother Andrew, still living at home and working as a baggage man on the railroad, merited a passing glance from Bierce, who went down to the station one morning to watch his train go by. He caught sight of Andrew standing beside a black man in the door of the baggage car. "H'm," said Bierce in a stage whisper, "he'd make a good nigger himself."[12]

The couple sailed from New York for Liverpool in late April; Mollie had her picture taken bravely waving farewell from the deck of their ship. Liverpool itself, nine decades before the Beatles and the British Invasion, was "wildly uninteresting commercial soil, a sordid earth, in which nothing but trade will flourish." But London, when they got there, was wonderful, "the cleanest of cities," although overrun just then by Americans. Everything about England enchanted Bierce, and he never changed his happy first impression. The countryside was greener, the trains were faster, the food was cheaper, and the people were nicer. The typical Englishman, he said, was "a warm-hearted chap—a sentimentalist a little ashamed of sentiment." To the extent that this described Bierce himself, one may infer a personal reason for his Anglophilia. A few weeks after landing in England, the erstwhile Town Crier—late scourge of mothers, babies, preachers, politicians, baseball, Christmas, and the Fourth of July—was virtually supine before the glories of the ancestral homeland. In a "Letter from London" published in the *Weekly Alta California,* he explained the reasons for his newfound mildness. "This is a better country, has nicer people, and is in every way superior," he wrote. "You will infer from this that I like England. I do—rather—ubette!" It was a note of radiant happiness that he would seldom, if ever, strike again.[13]

The honeymooners spent their first days in London taking in the standard tourist attractions: Westminster Abbey, Trafalgar Square, St. Paul's Cathedral, and the Tower of London. They went to the horse races at Ascot, to restaurants, theaters, and concert halls, and to a boat race on the Thames—in which, Bierce reported somewhat unpatriotically, the American team had been thoroughly trounced by the British. Everywhere they looked, there were other Americans similarly taking advantage of the favorable exchange rate to bask in the glories of London's unparalleled culture. One familiar face was that of the old San Francisco journalist Prentice Mulford, whose muckraking articles on London's slum dwellers painted a decidedly less sunny picture of the English capital. Perhaps taking a cue from his former associate, Bierce sent back to California a more characteristic missive. "I know of no more wretched class than the English farm laborers," he wrote in the *Alta Califor-*

nia; "and their existence in their present degraded state would be a lasting reproach to the Government, if only that had ever aided and abetted their existence in any state. When a man can ride all day in a direct line across his estates, and in so doing pass a thousand doors behind which Want crouches with hollow eyes, there is something radically wrong in the system under which that man lives."[14]

But Bierce hadn't come to England to criticize; he wanted to amaze and amuse his charming hosts. Armed with Marriott's letters of introduction, he intended to storm the journalistic bastions of Fleet Street and add his name to the storied roll of great English essayists—Addison and Steele, Samuel Johnson, Lamb, Hazlitt, Carlyle, De Quincey, and the rest. His first professional contact, and in short order his first English friend and employer, was Thomas Hood the Younger, son of the much-beloved author of "The Song of the Shirt" and other popular Victorian poems. Tom Hood, of whom it was said that he was christened in a punch bowl and for the rest of his life was never far from one, was the editor of *Fun,* a weekly humor magazine that was something of a poor cousin to the better-known *Punch.* Hood was a warm, friendly man with a pronounced soft spot for Americans. It was he who convinced Joaquin Miller to grow his hair long and affect an outlandish and theatrical Wild West costume in the streets and salons of Pre-Raphaelite London—a brilliant public-relations move that made the modestly talented Miller an overnight sensation.[15]

Hood was familiar with Bierce's work at the *News Letter,* and he quickly signed him up to write for *Fun.* The first in a series of humorous "Fables of Zambri the Parsee" appeared in Hood's magazine on July 13, 1872, under the somewhat puzzling byline "Dod Grile." Bierce biographer Paul Fatout has claimed that the nom de plume was an anagram for Douglas Jerrold, or "Dg Ierold," the author of the play *Ambrose Gwinett; or A Sea-Side Story,* after which Bierce was named. However, the true source of the anagram was less torturous and more appropriate. Hood, in a letter to Bierce in December 1872, addressed him as "Dear God Rile (which is of course an anagram)." Dod Grile was simply God Riled rearranged. Why Bierce decided to use a pseudonym at all is unknown; perhaps he hoped to create a monosyllabled alter ego similar to Sam Clemens's Mark Twain. If so, he failed; Dod Grile never caught on, even in England, and in America he was always Ambrose Bierce.[16]

The Zambri fables were commissioned by Hood to accompany a series of woodcut engravings that *Fun's* proprietors, the Dalziel brothers, already had on hand. Perhaps because they necessarily had to illustrate a preexisting situation, the fables are not Bierce's best work. One example may suffice to demonstrate their flavor: "'I should like to climb up you, if you don't mind,' cried an ivy to a young oak. 'Oh, certainly, come along,' was the cheerful assent. So she started up, and finding she could grow faster than he, she wound round and round him until she had passed up all the line she had. The oak, however, continued to grow, and as she could not disengage her coils, she was just lifted out by the root. So that ends the oak-and-ivy business, and removes a powerful temptation from the path of the young writer." This is fairly loose writing for someone as experienced as Bierce, but it apparently served the purpose, and it did give him—or, at any rate, Dod Grile—a foothold in a leading London magazine.[17]

Through Hood, Bierce also gained entrée to a varied group of London journalists who gathered regularly in the bar of the Ludgate Hill railway station. Chief among them was George Augustus Sala, the flamboyant columnist for the *Daily Telegraph,* who had previously written for Charles Dickens's weekly, *Household Words,* and served as a war correspondent in the Crimea, the American Civil War, and the Franco-Prussian War, once being held by the Germans as a spy before narrowly escaping to Switzerland. Sala, a personal friend of William Makepeace Thackeray, had written a number of novels himself, as well as a popular biography of the illustrator William Hogarth, in addition to his voluminous journalism. So recognizable and pervasive was his style that undergraduates at Oxford were urged, "Try not to write like Sala." A gifted linguist and raconteur, he was also a much-sought-after public speaker. "It was said," wrote Bierce, "that he could make an after-dinner speech in eighteen languages. I can testify that he could eat the dinner in any language known to man." When Sala was on a roll, Bierce had the "comfortable sense of having got into the show without paying at the door."[18]

Other members of the Ludgate Hill group included Henry Sampson, the gimpy-legged thirty-two-year-old contributing editor of *Fun;* Walter Thornbury, a poet, novelist, biographer, and fellow contributor of Sala's to Dickens's *Household Words* who shared Bierce's interest in the macabre and the criminal (Dickens eventually fired him for spending too much time on such distinctly nonhousehold subjects as "The Resurrection Men—Burke and Hare," and "The Two Great Murders in the Radcliffe Highway in 1811"); and Capt. Mayne Reid, the adventurer and the author of such boy-pleasing novels as *The Rifle Rangers, The Scalp-Hunters, The Forest Exiles, The Wild Huntress,* and *The Ocean Waifs,* works that Bierce had read as a youth in Indiana. An occasional visitor to the revels was W. S. Gilbert, Arthur Sullivan's collaborator. It was, all in all, a hard-drinking set of fellows, and Bierce, the budding Anglophile, fit in nicely. Years later, he still recalled the Ludgate Hill mob fondly: "I am told that the English are heavy thinkers and dull talkers. My recollection is different. I should say they are no end clever with their tongues. Certainly I have not elsewhere heard such brilliant talk as among the artists and writers of London. I found these men agreeable, hospitable, intelligent, amusing. We worked too hard, dined too well, frequented too many clubs, and went to bed too late in the forenoon. We were overmuch addicted to shedding the blood of the grape. In short, we diligently, conscientiously, and with a perverse satisfaction burned the candle of life at both ends and in the middle."[19]

The only other American member of the circle—and he scarcely qualified, having been an expatriate for over twenty years—was James Mortimer, the editor and publisher of *Figaro,* another weekly humor magazine. Mortimer was an intimate friend of the deposed French emperor Napoléon III and Empress Eugénie; after their fall, he had found them a place to live in the English countryside and later had the dubious distinction of being the last living person to speak to the emperor before that worthy's fatal gallbladder operation in the summer of 1873. Mortimer was a thoroughgoing cynic, libeler, and roué, and he eagerly secured Bierce's services for *Figaro.* Under the title "The Passing Showman," Bierce wrote items similar to his old "Town Crier" column, posing as a not-so-innocent abroad. Mortimer, sensing a kindred spirit, egged him on, urging Bierce to "be as cynical and disagreeable as you like, which is saying much." He routinely teased Bierce about his hated first name, calling him by such elaborate variations as Abner, Abdelkader, Adolphus, and Abednego Goliath Bierce. It was probably Mortimer who tagged the writer with his most enduring and alliterative English nickname: Bitter Bierce.[20]

Ambrose and Mollie moved into quarters near Tottenham Court Road, and in early July 1872, Bierce went outside the Ludgate Hill circle to contact one of the most notorious figures in literary London, pirating publisher John Camden Hotten. The thirty-nine-year-old Hotten had made his reputation—and a small fortune besides—as the local English champion of American humorists, including James Russell Lowell, Artemus Ward, Oliver Wendell Holmes, and, most recently, Mark Twain. Owing to the lack of an effective international copyright law (which he himself rather disingenuously championed), Hotten was able to publish at no cost to himself in inconvenient royalties the works of any American writers he chose. Just then he had chosen Mark Twain, whose book *The Innocents Abroad* he broke into two separate volumes, *The Innocents Abroad: The Voyage Out* and *The New Pilgrim's Progress: The Voyage Home.* The subsequent success of the two-volume set helped popularize Twain in London, but the author did not particularly appreciate the help. Not only had Hotten failed to pay any royalties to Twain but he had also had the effrontery to piece together two more publications, with the somewhat lurid titles *Eye-Openers* and *Screamers,* that purported to be Twain's work but that Hotten himself had augmented with a little creative writing of his own. Twain was so incensed by the publisher's actions that he hopped a transatlantic steamer and headed for London himself, after first writing an open letter to the London *Spectator* denouncing Hotten's "foul invention" and admitting a certain lingering temptation "to take a broomstraw and go and knock that man's brains out. Not in anger, for I feel none . . . but only to see, that is all.

Mere idle curiosity." A better name for him, Twain said, would be John Camden Hottentot.[21]

Bierce doubtless knew of Hotten's literary buccaneering, and he may have hoped to forestall a similar fate for his own work by personally approaching the publisher about collaborating on a book. What the prudish Bierce is unlikely to have known—certainly he makes no mention of it later—was Hotten's other, sub rosa reputation as the leading London publisher of pornography. The eccentric millionaire book collector Henry S. Ashbee, a contemporary of Hotten's (and a satisfied customer), considered him "almost the only reputable English publisher of tabooed literature." Items in the Hotten catalog included such rarefied titles as *A Discourse on the Worship of Priapus, Aphrodisiacs and Anti-Aphrodisiacs,* and *Flagellation and the Flagellants: A History of the Rod in all Countries, from the Earliest Period to the Present Time,* with "numerous illustrations."[22]

At first, Bierce and Hotten got along together quite nicely. Hotten professed to share a personal connection with Bierce. Learning that Mollie had been born in Galena, Illinois, Hotten claimed that during a youthful visit to the United States he had once lived in Galena himself. Not only that; he had lived in a room directly above the tannery belonging to Ulysses S. Grant's father. "I knew him quite well," Hotten said of the then President, "and certainly never supposed from his quiet manner that he would reach his present position." Grant must have been very quiet indeed during Hotten's stay in Galena: He did not move there until the summer of 1860, four years after Hotten had returned to England. Inconvenient chronologies aside, Bierce and Hotten quickly came to terms—seventy-five pounds—for a collection of Bierce's California journalism, including the Grizzly Papers and a number of old "Town Crier" columns. The proposed book was to be called *The Fiend's Delight.* Hotten closed the deal by sending Bierce a copy of his newest publication, *Practical Jokes,* by "Mark Twain and other Humourists." He also invited the Bierces to take tea with "Mr. and Mrs. Pirate" at their Hampstead "cave," an invitation the couple had to decline, since they were on their way to Stratford-upon-Avon to visit Shakespeare's home.[23]

The visit to Stratford, duly reported in a letter to the *Alta California* in October 1872, was to be the couple's last holiday jaunt for a while. Bierce was finding that London's clammy weather aggravated his chronic asthma, and he made plans to move his wife, who was then seven months pregnant, to the southern port city of Bristol, in hopes that the salt breezes would give him some relief. First, however, he attended a gala dinner with Mark Twain and Joaquin Miller at the exclusive Whitefriars Club in Mitre Court. Surprisingly, given Twain's recent well-publicized arrival on English shores, Bierce was the guest of honor at the banquet. The *South London Express* reported the next day: "Last night a personage of worldwide celebrity dined at the White Friar's Club—as honorary guest. I refer to the Town Crier, one of the most original and daring humorists this age has produced." Nettled, perhaps, by Bierce's top billing, Twain proceeded to one-up him with a skillful bit of audience stealing. Asked to say a few words, Bierce began a humorous account of his first meeting with Twain in the office of the *News Letter* five years earlier. Twain, much more practiced at public speaking than Bierce, mischievously contrived to undercut him with some judicious deadpanning, looking off into the middle distance with an affected air of patient boredom. The audience, taking their cue from Twain, maintained a deathly silence throughout Bierce's now-faltering speech. When it was over, Bierce sank back into his seat, white-faced and embarrassed. For the rest of his life, he never again spoke before a crowd.[24]

Not to be outdone, the irrepressible Miller put on a show of his own later that evening. Clad in his usual drawing room costume of knee-high cowboy boots and spurs, white buckskin shirt, and Mexican sombrero, a brace of Bowie knives hanging from his belt in case Charles Algernon Swinburne or some other dangerous desperado happened to menace the Duchess of Kent, Miller arrived late for the dinner and was met with studied indifference by his fellow Californians. Desperate for attention, he suddenly rose to his feet, plunged his hand into a nearby fishbowl, and pulled out a goldfish, which he proceeded to swallow whole. "A wonderful appetizer!" he boomed. Bierce and Twain blandly ignored the theatrics, continuing their dinner as though nothing untoward had happened, and Miller left the gathering in a huff.[25]

Before Bierce departed London in late September, Hotten purchased the rights to another manuscript, this one with the provisional title *Nuggets and Dust*. On October 12, he placed an ad in the London *Spectator*, announcing—somewhat prematurely—the incipient appearance of "NUGGETS AND DUST./Panned out by DOD GRILE. A new style of Humour and Satire. If Artemus Ward may be considered the Douglas Jerrold, and Mark Twain the Sydney Smith of America, Dod Grile will rank as their Dean Swift. There is a grimness and force in him which places his humour far above anything of the kind ever attempted. The New York *Nation*—a literary authority of marvellous ability—is struck with Dod Grile's wit and delightful badinage, every line in the most forcible English." The editors of the *Nation*, for their part, professed complete ignorance of Dod Grile, noting that "we have not been struck by Dod Grile; that his wit and his delightful badinage, and his forcible English are all entirely unknown to us; that we never heard of him or them till we saw Mr. Hotten's advertisement, and that we should like to know why we are quoted as having been struck with the powers of Mr. Grile." They did, however, congratulate Hotten for making "a certain covenant and agreement with that serpent, that hardy blasphemer, that foe of all the gentler feelings adorning our nature, that prodigious and frontless contemner of virtue and morality, the San Francisco *News Letter*'s 'Town Crier.'" The paper predicted that Bierce's first book would expose the reading public to "a specimen of 'American humor' as unlike that of any of the other American humorists as the play of young human merry-andrews is unlike that of a young and energetic demon whose horns are well-budded."[26]

By advertising a second Bierce book before he had even published the first, Hotten may have thought he was preparing the field, so to speak, for a fertile critical harvest. But Bierce, stuck in Bristol during Mollie's confinement, was becoming increasingly disenchanted with his would-be publisher. The two could not decide on a proper mix of writing; Bierce wanted the book to be all new stories, while Hotten still wanted to include clippings from Bierce's *Overland Monthly* and *News Letter* days. An impasse developed, carrying over into the new year. Meanwhile, Mollie gave birth in early December to their first child, a son, whom they named Day after Mollie's father. Bierce reported later that Mollie had really wanted a daughter and had expressed her disappointment to the crusty old Bristol doctor in attendance. The doctor responded dryly, "Well, madam, at his age it really doesn't make much difference." What he himself felt about becoming a father, Bierce did not say, although he joked in writing that "it is sweet to have a baby in the house; when clean and fresh, and sweet as new-mown hay, they are nice to have about . . . excellent to soothe one's ruffled temper, for you may readily relieve your feelings by pinching them, and they can't tell!" This W. C. Fields–like attitude toward children was considerably lighter in tone than his later musings to Walter Neale. "We hear a great deal about children being sufficient compensation for the woe entailed by copulation," said Bierce, "and by persons, too, who would not speak of death by murder as rewarding the bereaved. Of all the evils that flow from matrimony, the child is the greatest—except children. Both parents spend their entire adult lives in unrelieved slavery, quarreling with each other about their children the while, and unaware that the little miscreants will soon come to hold them in contempt, flout them, and probably never give them a thought after the final separation brought about by death." It was sadly typical of this conflicted man that Bierce could never permit himself any feelings of pride or happiness in fatherhood. "I don't believe," he later wrote, "that outside the heart of an insulate fool it ever existed. Why should it?—what is there to be proud of? It is a tradition of grannies and mid-wives, promoted by the vanity of girls and adopted by cackling bachelors as a cat-call of derision."[27]

As if to underline his point, Bierce was back in London within the month, leaving Mollie and the baby in the care of strangers while he and Hotten thrashed out a mutually agreeable table of contents for *The Fiend's Delight*. Too busy to write any new stories anyway, Bierce gave up the notion of a book of short stories. Instead, he settled for a catchall collection of uninspired pieces culled from old "Town Crier" paragraphs, "current journalings," and off-the-cuff aphorisms that he labeled "laughorisms." As usual in Bierce's work, there is a fair amount of mayhem, including the obligatory wife-killing (by poker and mallet), assorted murder (by bootblack, pick handle, and shot-gun), and accidental death (by mowing machine and, for one child, the family dog). Hotten attempted to get Bierce to tone down the "knife business" in favor of more "delightful conceits," but Bierce was unapologetic. "One of the rarest amusements in life is to go about with an icicle suspended by a string, letting it down the necks of the unwary," he observed. "The sudden shrug, the quick, frightened shudder, the yelp of apprehension are sources of pure, because diabolical, delight." This element of demonism was made manifest in his introduction to the book. "The atrocities constituting this 'cold collation' of diabolism are taken mainly from various California journals," he confessed. "I think I have killed a good many people in one way or another; but the reader will please to observe that they were not people worth the trouble of leaving alive. Besides I had the interests of my collaborator to consult. In writing, as in compiling, I have been ably assisted by my scholarly friend, Mr. Satan; and to this worthy gentleman must be attributed most of the views herein set forth." The title page featured a drawing of a jolly English gentleman casually roasting a baby over an open fire.[28]

Bierce later told Charles Warren Stoddard that *The Fiend's Delight* was "a foolish book," a judgment he reiterated publicly if pseudonymously in the pages of *Figaro,* where he called the work "a piece of exasperating blackguardism, begot of comprehensive ignorance and profound conceit." Despite the sudden outbreak of modesty, Bierce still wanted to be paid for his work; Hotten owed him one hundred pounds on the balance of the first book and *Nuggets and Dust.* By this time he, Mollie, and the baby had moved twice more, to Bath for two months and then to Keats's old stamping grounds near Hampstead Heath. He continued to badger Hotten about the money, even while affecting a certain aristocratic disdain for such petty matters. "I am doing just work enough over here to pay my current expenses," he wrote to Stoddard. "Have not attempted to get any permanent work, and don't suppose I shall, as my object in coming was to loaf and see something of the country—as Walt Whitman expressed it, when the paralysis had, as yet, invaded only his brain, 'to loaf and invite my soul.'"[29]

Things came to a head later that spring when Hotten suddenly became gravely ill. His business manager, Andrew Chatto, called on Bierce, and after an acrimonious two-hour debate, he handed over a signed check for the full amount owed him. Chatto asked Bierce, however, not to cash the check for another week, adding, "I hope you will go out to Hotten's house and have a friendly talk. It is his wish." The next Saturday, Bierce duly turned up at Hotten's residence, only to discover that "in pursuance, doubtless, of his design when he ante-dated the check he had died of a pork pie promptly on the stroke of twelve o'clock the night before." Bierce raced to the bank, hoping to cash the check before word of Hotten's death—from brain fever, not pork pies—reached the bankers. En route, he stopped off at

Ludgate Hill to tell the other "gentlemen of wit and pleasure" about the publisher's passing. Hood, Sala, Sampson, and Reid were there, among others, and "I am sorry to say my somber news affected these sinners in a way that was shocking. Their levity was a thing to shudder at." The wits, Bierce included, set about devising appropriate epitaphs for Hotten, whose death was not so amusing for the wife and three young daughters he left behind. Sala, by acclamation, won the competition with a pithy if heartless summation of Hotten's career: "Hotten/Rotten/Forgotten." The dead man—his estate, at least—got the last laugh, however: When Bierce finally arrived at the bank, he and his check were turned away. "We can't pay this," he was told. "Mr. Hotten is dead." It was, said Bierce, "the old, old story of the hare and the tortoise."[30]

Worse luck, of a sort, befell Bierce later that summer when his mother-in-law unexpectedly arrived for a lengthy visit. Mrs. Day had not revised her earlier estimations of Bierce as husband material, and she cannot have been much amused by his frequent absences and tipsy late-night returns. "My mother-in-law is here," Bierce gloomily told Stoddard before taking off for a month-long visit to Paris with his wife, her mother, and the new baby somewhat inconveniently in tow. The City of Lights did not enchant Bierce as London had—his chief memory of it was dining on horse-meat steak—but he later told Neale that in the course of a private side trip to the south of France he met and romanced an unidentified young woman. This may, of course, have been sheer invention, but it is also possible that it was the rebellious act of a man too much beset by relatives. True or not, Bierce later blamed the affair for all his subsequent marital difficulties.[31]

Prior to leaving for the continent, Bierce wrote a rather condescending, if well-intentioned, letter to Stoddard, who was coming to London to serve as Mark Twain's designated personal secretary-cum-drinking companion. The letter, which Bierce left for Stoddard taped to his front door, revealed a different attitude toward his Ludgate Hill associates than his steady socializing may have suggested. "I have told Tom Hood to look after you," Bierce wrote. "Now mark this: Tom is one of the very dearest fellows in the world, and an awful good friend to me. But he has the worst lot of associates I ever saw—men who are not worthy to untie his shoe latchet. He will introduce you to them all. Treat them well, of course, but (1) don't gush over them; (2) don't let them gush over you; (3) don't accept invitations from them; (4) don't get drunk with them; (5) don't let them in any way monopolize you; (6) don't let them shine by your reflected light. I have done all these things, and it is not a good plan." Sounding a little like Ernest Hemingway, who also liked to dispense advice that was remarkable chiefly for the creative ways in which he chose to ignore it himself, Bierce assured Stoddard, "You just 'bet your boots' I know these fellows and their ways. They think they know me, but they don't. I am hand-in-glove with some hundreds of them, and they think they are my intimate friends. If any man says he is, or acts as if he were, avoid him, he is an impostor. This letter is strictly confidential, and when I come back I shall ask you to hand it to me."[32]

Bierce was still in Paris when his second book, *Nuggets and Dust,* was published by the firm of Chatto and Windus, which had purchased the rights from Hotten's widow. ("Successors to John Camden Hotten," the firm announced on the title page, evidence perhaps that not everyone in London thought as little of Hotten as the Ludgate Hill crowd did.) Like *The Fiend's Delight,* the book was a hodgepodge of earlier columns dredged from Bierce's California days, coupled with a few new short stories and a series of English travel pieces collectively titled "Notes Written with Invisible Ink by a Phantom American," which are somewhat reminiscent of Twain's earlier travel writing, but without his inimitable humor. If, as some Bierce scholars have maintained, such articles as "Stratford-on-Avon," "St. Paul's," and "Kenilworth" are indicative of the direction Bierce's writing might have taken had he stayed in England indefinitely, it is fortunate for everyone that he did not; they are blandly proficient journalism, at best. More successful, although still not up to the standards he would later set for himself, are the stories "D.T." and "A Working Girl's Story." The first, a Poe-like tale of a drinker confronted by an all-seeing eye while in the throes of delirium tremens, contains an interesting hint of Bierce's own domestic situation: "I am quite certain I had not been drinking too much, for I make it a rule never to do so, though there is an irreconcilable difference between myself and my wife as to the exact amount which one may take without having too much." The story ends with a curiously Hemingwayesque attempt at understatement. "I never told anyone before about the Eye, and should not do so now, but that I feel myself going and think such a jolly experience ought not to be lost. It's all so very funny, you know, about the tavern, and Dan Budd, and the old haunted house, and the Eye." Isn't it pretty to think so, as Lady Brett once told Jake Barnes in the back of a Madrid taxi.[33]

"A Working Girl's Story" is, until its ill-conceived last paragraph, an affecting little fable about a starving young girl, her pet canaries, and two guardian angels who either do or do not visit her (they may be mere hallucinations) on the last night of her life. "I don't think this one will need our services much longer," one angel tells the other. "I looked in the register the last time I was up there at the office, and her term is nearly expired." The story is probably the most sentimental that Bierce ever wrote—until the last paragraph, anyway, when he somehow felt the need to undercut his effects by interjecting an Amos and Andy–type darkie who tells the girl, "Hi, missy! You luff dem fings be, will yer: dey b'longs to number seben on de fust flo'!" It is almost as if Bierce could not bear to finish the story in an emotionally satisfying way: He has to make a joke of it—which is, of course, more revealing of the author's peculiar psychology than a more polished ending would have been.[34]

Also revealing are the paragraphs he chose to reprint from his California writings. Besides the obligatory parade of murders, suicides, fatal accidents, abortions, frauds, larceny, and "numberless other occurrences of the kind inseparable from, and essential to, the existence of man," Bierce chose to preserve an apparently random cross section of musings on women and marriage that must have given pause to Mollie Bierce when she read them. "A young man while skating on Lake Champlain broke through the ice and came near drowning," Bierce wrote. "He was finally rescued by a young woman, who made a rope by tearing up her clothes, and with it snaked him out. Of course he afterwards married her. Had he not lost his presence of mind he might have saved himself by drowning." In another piece, he offered to box the ears of a bride who had sought to publish a "little joke on hubby" concerning his less than ideal physique. "We don't believe in encouraging brides to go after their 'hubbies' in this remorseless way," Bierce thundered, "at least not within a week after marriage." As for a despondent young man who threw himself down a mine shaft after being tossed aside by his sweetheart, Bierce said he "would be glad to learn the name and address of some young woman worth an abraded head, a shattered shin, and a brace of legs that won't work. This battered corpse is of the impression that a girl of that character does not exist." He advised another young man, who was worried about his girlfriend taking advantage of the leap year to propose to him, to "set your dog at her." A squib about the alleged cancer-causing effects of pinching someone brought the pointed advice, "If you have a wife or sweetheart, you must no longer nip with playful nail her pearly skin. Bite her."[35]

One woman, in particular, whom Bierce would have been happy to bite that autumn was freelance journalist Helen Burrell, who wrote under the pseudonym "Olive Harper." After unsuccessfully attempting to interview Bierce, Burrell wrote a mean-spirited column for the New York *Daily Graphic* portraying him as an air-sniffing "snobocrat" who, having once labored in a humble brickyard, had now come to Europe on his wife's (actually his father-in-law's) money. There was an uncomfortable amount of truth in Burrell's account, which is probably why it hit home so painfully. Burrell was a close friend of Joaquin Miller's, and Bierce strongly suspected that Miller had been the source of Burrell's most telling anecdotes. On November 16, 1873, he wrote an open letter to Miller that appeared in several leading London journals. "Dear Mr. Miller," it read. "It would be a favor to Mrs. Harper if you would kindly indicate to her, in any way you like, that I hope she will not do me the doubtful honor of calling. Perhaps when she shall have associated long enough with the nobility and tradespeople, her manners will improve, and her conversation acquire a touch of decency; at present she is rather vulgar. I trust this will not offend you; if it does I shall be sorry. Anyhow, it is better you should keep her from calling than to have my servant shut the door in her face." Bierce had no way of knowing, but Miller was not in London just then; having managed to get himself involved with both a baronet's daughter and a Cockney flower girl who was the perfect spiritual forerunner of Eliza Doolittle, the poet had decamped for Rome, where he immediately began a torrid romance with an Italian countess. He and Bierce remained on cordial, if distant, terms, however, and the Burrell article was soon forgotten, if not forgiven.[36]

By the spring of 1874, Bierce was back in England, living at Leamington, in Warwickshire. On April 29, Mollie gave birth to their second son, Leigh, who had an unspecifiably difficult time of it for the first six weeks of his life. Once he turned the corner, Mrs. Day finally departed for the States, having stayed—Bierce would have said overstayed—with the family for ten long months. Meanwhile, Bierce was hard at work turning out copy for *Fun* and *Figaro* and complaining to Stoddard that he never heard from any of his old London friends, with the occasional exception of Hood. Besides his regular columns for the weekly humor magazines, he had taken on a new job for James Mortimer, writing and editing what amounted to a vanity publication for the exiled French empress Eugénie, Napoléon III's recent widow. The empress had become alarmed at the news that an old political enemy, Henri Rochefort, Marquis de Rochefort-Luçay, had escaped his forced exile in a New Caledonia penal colony and was on his way to England to resume publishing his anti-imperial broadside, *La Lanterne*. Rochefort, whom one contemporary aptly characterized as "Baudelaire turned politician," was a pale, horse-faced, sallow-complexioned adventurer with a harsh guttural voice and long, pointed fingernails. During the course of his extraordinary journalistic career, which lasted from the Second Empire until the outbreak of World War I, Rochefort quarreled with everyone, from Napoléon III to Georges Clemenceau, whom he labeled with typical restraint "a loathsome leper." But he reserved his deepest enmity for the emperor and his family, noting in one of his frequent calls to revolution: "I have had the weakness to believe that a Bonaparte could be something other than an assassin! For eighteen years now France has been held in the bloodied hands of these cutthroats, who, not content to shoot down Republicans in the streets, draw them into filthy traps in order to slit their throats in private!" With rhetoric like that, it is no wonder that Eugénie considered him, in Bierce's words, "a menace and a terror."[37]

To forestall Rochefort's much-dreaded return to form, Mortimer contracted with Bierce to produce a sort of prophylactic publication of his own. *The Lantern* (a name the empress insisted upon to block any sudden reappearance of an anglicized *Lanterne*) had no regular publishing schedule and no overriding editorial stance, except a rather vague injunction from Mortimer that it should resemble Rochefort's original and "be irritatingly disrespectful of existing institutions and exalted personages." Despite some unresolved professional reservations, Bierce agreed to take the job. He seems to have entertained some hope of making *The Lantern* a regular forum for his own distinctive weltanschauung, which he announced in the first issue of the magazine that May. "My future program," he declared, "will be calm disapproval of human institutions in general, including all forms of government, most laws and customs, and all contemporary literature; enthusiastic belief in the Darwinian theory . . . intolerance of intolerance, and war upon every man with a mission . . . human suffering and human injustice in all their forms to be contemplated with a merely curious interest, as one looks into an anthill."[38]

In keeping with his new role as "the champion growlist of Leamington," Bierce fired off an opening barrage aimed not at Rochefort but at the unoffending general Sir Garnet Wolseley, who had just been showered with monies and honors for his punitive expedition against the rebellious Ashanti tribesmen of West Africa. Overlooking the fact that the Ashantis had started the war themselves by raiding other Gold Coast tribes and British garrisons, Bierce assumed an outsider's contrarian stance. "When the great heart of England is stirred by quick cupidity to profitable crime, far be it from us to lift our palms in deprecation," he wrote. "When by whatever of [*sic*] outrage we have pushed a feeble competitor to the wall, in Heaven's name let us pin him fast and relieve his pockets of the material good to which, in bestowing it upon him, the bountiful Lord has invited our thieving hand. But these Ashantee women were not worth garroting . . . the entire loot fetched only £11,000—of which sum the man who brought home the trinkets took a little more than four halves. We submit that with practiced agents in every corner of the world and a watchful government at home this great commercial nation might dispose of its honor to better advantage."[39]

Mortimer, realizing (as Bierce apparently did not) that *The Lantern* existed for only one real purpose, suggested to his editor that he give the villain Rochefort "a little wholesome admonition here and there." Bierce cheerfully complied in the next—and ultimately the last—issue of the magazine on July 16. "M. Rochefort is a gentleman who has lost his standing," he mocked. "There have been greater falls than his. Kings before now have become servitors, honest men bandits, thieves communists. Insignificant in his fortunes as in his abilities, M. Rochefort, who was never very high, is not now very low—he has avoided the falsehoods of extremes: never quite a count, he is now but half a convict. He is not even a *misérable;* he is a person. M. Rochefort, we believe, is already suffering from an unhealed wound. It is his mouth." For someone as practiced as Bierce, this was easy work, and it paid well. The empress even had a special edition translated into French for her reading pleasure. Unfortunately for Bierce, the magazine did its work too quickly and too well. After only two issues, the newly arrived Rochefort found himself being trailed through the London streets by jeering mobs of *Lantern* readers whose comfortable Victorian values presumably were outraged by the Frenchman's communist-inspired republicanism. When he left for Geneva, Rochefort effectively took Bierce's job with him. Deprived of both its chief target and its raison d'être, *The Lantern* folded that summer, and a disappointed Bierce had to settle for a carved ivory card case from the empress as a token of her imperial esteem.[40]

The demise of *The Lantern* was a serious blow to Bierce's long-term employment prospects. With a wife and two small children to support, he was more and more beginning to feel the press of finances. His asthma, which was always worse in times of stress, returned to plague him, and on one of his infrequent trips to London he quarreled bitterly with George Augustus Sala after Sala had chided him, half in jest, for "conduct unbecoming a colonial." His isolated existence in Leamington left him feeling out of touch, a sentiment the increasingly homesick Mollie no doubt shared. Occasional visitors such as Prentice Mulford (who lately had taken up with Joaquin Miller's erstwhile flower girl) did little to relieve the couple's mood of anxious boredom. It is an indication of Mollie's sadly neglected state that, years later, she would remember "toasting crumpets with Prentice Mulford" as being the happiest times she spent in England. Her husband, who considered Mulford "a growler by constitution," did not share her affection for "Dismal Jimmy." Not even the appearance of a third book of fables, *Cobwebs from an Empty Skull*, brightened Bierce's mood. He now took little pride in the books, telling Stoddard, "I have the supremest contempt for my books—as books. As a journalist I believe I am unapproachable in my line; as an author, a slouch!" The fact of the matter was that virtually everything he published in England, whether in book form or in the various humor magazines, was second-rate. Like other self-exiled American writers, before and after, he had cut himself off in some essential way from the vital heart of his inspiration. For all his lord-of-the-manor posturing, he was still in many ways a tourist. As Sala had said, more woundingly perhaps than he had intended, Bierce was a colonial, and all the eminent tankard raising in the world could not change that essential fact of life.[41]

In late November 1874, the only real friend Bierce had made in England, Tom Hood, died at the age of thirty-nine at his cottage in Surrey. Hood had gone out of his way to make Bierce feel welcome, both personally and professionally, in the insular world of English journalism, and his death left a void that no one else could, or would, fill. At their last meeting, the two friends had made a boyish pact that whoever died first would attempt to come back and contact the other. One night soon after Hood's death, Bierce was returning home to Leamington when he suddenly felt the uncanny spirit of Hood rush past him in the dark. "That I had met the spirit of my dead friend," he wrote, "that it had given me recognition, yet not in the old way; that it had then vanished—of these things I had the evidence of my own senses. How strongly this impressed me the beating of my heart attested whenever, for many months afterwards, that strange meeting came into my memory." Years later, in his somewhat Jamesian ghost story, "The Damned Thing," Bierce described the sensation: "Looking at the stars last night as they rose above the crest of the ridge east of the house, I observed them successively disappear— from left to right. Each was eclipsed but an instant, and only a few at the same time, but along the entire length of the ridge all that were within a degree or two of the crest were blotted out. I could not see it, and the stars were not thick enough to define its outline. Ugh! I don't like this." For weeks after the encounter, Bierce was unable to write a word.[42]

Hood's death, in a way, marked the beginning of the end of Bierce's stay in England, although it would be another ten months before he left for good. Mollie, however, did not wait that long. In May 1875, she and the boys sailed home to San Francisco, intending to visit her mother for an indefinite period of time. Bierce, lonely and distracted, fell ill again with "a cursed sort of semi-lunacy . . . from lack of sleep, hard work, and unchristian cooking." That summer he moved back to London, where he continued writing for *Fun,* now under the editorship of Henry Sampson. In September, he received the shocking and unwelcome news that Mollie was six months pregnant with their third child; worse yet, she intended to remain in San Francisco for the birth. Immediately booking passage on the steamer *Adriatic,* Bierce left London in mid-September. He would never see it—or the rest of Europe—again. "For nearly all that is good in our American civilization, we are indebted to England," he would later write; "the errors and mischiefs are our own creation. In learning and letters, in art and the science of government, America is but a faint and stammering echo of England." Speaking of himself in the polite, anglicized third person, he observed: "A certain friend of mine, who writes things, is commonly accused by those of whom he writes them of thinking himself a Titan among pigmies. It can hardly be from vanity, for he frankly confesses that the happiest and most prosperous period of his life was passed where he felt himself a pigmy among the Titans. My friend used to write things in London."[43]

8

Prattle

*W*hen Bierce returned to San Francisco in late September 1875, he found the city much changed—and not necessarily for the better. Like the rest of the country, San Francisco was locked in the throes of a bone-crushing depression occasioned by the failure of Jay Cooke & Company, the nation's premier banking house, and the subsequent panic the failure had created among Wall Street's jittery financiers. While Bierce was in London trading bons mots with Tom Hood, G. A. Sala, and the other resident wits of Ludgate Hill railway station, millions of his fellow countrymen were struggling desperately to make ends meet during the worst economic crisis in fifty years. Not even California, a continent away from Black Friday, was immune to the numbing aftereffects of the crash. A few weeks before Bierce returned to San Francisco, Bank of California president William A. Ralston resigned his post in the wake of the bank's sudden, unexpected closing and went for his daily swim off North Beach. A few minutes later, passing fishermen pulled his lifeless body from the afternoon surf. Whether accident or suicide—or a little of both—Ralston's death cast a pall across the entire city. Ironically, the bank reopened six weeks later, with scarcely a pause in operation, gleaming piles of twenty-dollar gold pieces ostentatiously displayed at each teller's window to affirm physically the bank's renewed solidity.[1]

Despite the reopening of the Bank of California, San Franciscans remained understandably nervous about the state of the economy. This was caused to a great extent by the widespread speculation in mining stocks that had long since become something of a civic obsession. From the first days of the gold rush, San Francisco had been dominated by the search for, and the spending of, precious metals; new discoveries of silver in 1874 had driven up the value of the market shares in the Comstock mines by a phenomenal $1 million a day for nearly two months. A quartet of Irish shopkeepers turned stockbrokers—James Flood, John Mackay, James Fair, and William O'Brien—almost overnight gained control of the Comstock Lode through canny investments and stock manipulation, becoming in the process the city's first and greatest "silver kings." Thousands of other San Franciscans, eager to duplicate the Irishmen's bonanza, speculated heavily in the market, only to learn to their regret that such Croesus-like riches do not normally descend to the lower masses. Subsequent word of a decline in the Lode's production caused stocks to tumble $42 million in one week. By the time the decline was halted, the value of stocks in the silver kings' Consolidated Virginia and California holdings had lost a staggering $140 million. Historian John S. Hittell later estimated that the sum represented "an average of $1,000 for every white adult in the city, and though a large majority had never owned any of these shares, all were affected indirectly, if not directly, by the decline." The silver kings themselves were too rich—and too smart—to lose their own vast fortunes, but thousands of smaller investors lost everything, and thousands of other regular citizens were thrown out of work by the stricken market's domino effect on the local economy. Others kept their jobs, but only after taking "voluntary" wage cuts of 40 to 60 percent.[2]

Such rarefied financial dealings had a direct effect on Ambrose Bierce's immediate job prospects in the autumn of 1875. Although Frederick Marriott had assured Bierce when he left San Francisco that he could always return to his old job at the *News Letter,* when the time came for Marriott to keep his word, he was forced to concede that he no longer had an opening for the erstwhile Town Crier. Nor were the city's other newspapers hiring just then. Bierce, for all his expensive Savile Row tailoring and wealth of amusing anecdotes about the London literary scene, had to settle for a nonwriting job in the assay office of the U.S. Mint. The birth of his third child, a red-haired daughter named Helen, in October 1875 coincided with his new, reduced position, and Bierce lapsed into another of the black depressions that periodically dot his life. His chronic asthma kicked in as well, and he moved his growing family back across San Francisco Bay to San Rafael, where he and Mollie had first set up housekeeping four years earlier. The move had as much to do with attempting to escape his mother-in-law's renewed intrusive presence as it did with seeking a cure for his respiratory troubles—and had about as much success with the one as it did with the other. Mother Day was frequently in the Bierce home, helping Mollie with the children, and Bierce was just as frequently absent, spending much of his free time in the smoky haunts of the Bohemian Club, which he uncharacteristically served as secretary in 1876–1877. At the club, Bierce renewed his friendship with the *Chronicle's* Jimmy Bowman and other local journalists, trading gibes and gossip and tossing down drams of mood-altering brandy, which he defined only half-jokingly as "a cordial composed of one part thunder and lightning, one part remorse, two parts bloody murder, one part death-hell-and-the-grave and four parts clarified Satan." After one particularly hard night of drinking, Bierce came near to drowning when he fell off the ferry into San Francisco Bay during a collision between the ferry and another boat. Fished out of the water by some passing trawlers, he was vastly amused to read, in a newspaper account of the mishap, that "an unknown man crazed by terror jumped overboard and was drowned."[3]

This Micawber-like round of squalling babies, irksome in-laws, boring jobs, and heavy drinking came to a close in early 1877 when Bierce was hired as associate editor of a new San Francisco publication, the *Argonaut*. Like most of the city, Bierce owed his position—at least indirectly—to the silver kings' residual effect on the economy. The continuing vagaries of personal employment had created a dangerous two-headed beast of a workplace: a heavily unionized labor force and an equally large and discontented mass of unemployed. Each group, from its different vantage point, looked dyspeptically at the steady rise of Chinese immigrants through the city's social and financial strata. From an initial influx of 787 Chinese who arrived in San Francisco in 1849–1850 to work as houseboys in the gold rushers' swanky estates, the number had grown to 75,000 by 1876, thanks largely to the importation of coolie labor on the Central Pacific Railroad. The coolies brought to private industry an Asian willingness to work long hours for short pay, a trait universally contemned by their white counterparts. Ten years earlier, in 1866, a mob of displaced white workers who had been fired by a local contractor to make way for lower-salaried Chinese had taught their replacements a lesson in union solidarity by means of those always-persuasive bargaining tools, the ax handle and the rock. The erring Chinese had learned their lesson well, so well, in fact, that they generally stuck to their own businesses after that, gaining in the interim a near-total monopoly of San Francisco's laundry, cigar-making, and garment industries by the early 1870s and thereby displacing another five thousand or so white workers and bringing down on their own industrious heads a predictable spate of anti-Chinese ordinances, statutes, and special taxes.[4]

With the city in the grip of a worsening depression, every job became sacrosanct, and every out-of-work laborer blamed the Chinese for his specific woes. In the fall of 1875, just as Bierce was returning to San Francisco, a new Workingmen's party comprised mostly of Irish blue-collar workers succeeded in electing to office a handpicked slate of municipal candidates, including the mayor. New, ever more restrictive ordinances against the Chinese ensued. They were prohibited from walking the city's streets after 2:00 A.M., from peddling goods on city sidewalks, from operating laundries in nonfireproof buildings, from gambling and smoking opium, from using their ubiquitous shoulder poles—even from entering local hospitals. Only the air was free, and that was filled with the furious cries of the Workingmen's party and its minions. The increasingly radicalized party held open meetings on a sandlot next to city hall, where union agitators alternately denounced the heathen Chinese and the homegrown capitalists who employed them. As long as the members confined themselves to the Chinese, city fathers looked the other way; but when the party began targeting the silver kings and railroad tycoons as being equally responsible for the workers' plight, the fabulous nabobs on Nob Hill began to grow uncomfortable. One of their acolytes, a former United States district attorney turned Republican party stalwart named Frank Pixley, decided to do something about it. In the spring of 1877, he launched a new weekly newspaper, the *Argonaut,* to counteract the growing political muscle of the Workingmen's party. Local journalist Fred Somers was chosen to serve as editor of the newspaper, and Bierce quickly and no doubt eagerly signed on as associate editor.[5]

From the start, Bierce clashed with the *Argonaut* publisher. Pixley saw the newspaper as a political weapon in a looming class war; Bierce (who did most of the actual editing work) wanted to develop it into a literary journal similar to Bret Harte's old *Overland Monthly* or Tom Hood's *Fun*. The memory of James Mortimer's cynical misuse of his talents on *The Lantern* still rankled; indeed, the title Bierce took for his regular new column, "The Prattler," harkened back to Henri Rochefort's *Lanterne,* where Rochefort had a similarly named column. In his first column, in the *Argonaut*'s debut issue of March 25, 1877, Bierce set forth a defiantly literary creed. "It is my intention," he wrote, "to purify journalism in this town by instructing such writers as it is worthwhile to instruct, and assassinating those that it is not." The latter category made up a large pool of prospective victims, and Bierce, despite having been absent from the scene for over five years, was not shy about diving in. One of his first victims was a local poet named Sam Davis. "Mr. Davis says I make war on the verse-makers who contribute to this paper," Bierce noted in the June 9, 1877, issue. "Of course I cannot prevent the verse-makers upon whom I make war from contributing to the *Argonaut;* that is the editor's duty— which, I am sorry to say, he basely neglects. Mr. Davis' remark, however, affords me an opportunity to make, seriously, an explanation which I have long felt was due to the gentlemen whose rhymes have received the distinction of notice at my hands. To verse-makers, as verse-makers, I have no objection. It is only when the verse-maker fancies himself a poetry-maker that he becomes offensive to the cultivated and discriminating—my taste. It is important that the broad and sharp distinction between verse and poetry be as clearly perceived and sacredly respected by my brother rhymesters as it is by myself; and, God willing, I'll hold their noses to the mark until they see it."[6]

Another would-be poet, Hector Stuart, compounded the sin of having no talent by striking back at Bierce in verse: "When he lived long enough/He belched his last puff,/And burst like a wad of gun-cotton;/Now here he doth lie,/Turned to a dirt pie,/Like all that he scribbled—forgotten." Bierce immediately responded in kind. "Concerning my epitaph by Hector S. Stuart," he wrote, "it is perhaps sufficient to say that I ought to be willing to have my name at the top of it if he is willing to have his at the bottom. As to Mr. Stuart's opinion that my work will be soon forgotten, I can assure him that that view of the matter is less gloomy to me than it ought to be to him. I do not care for fame, and he does; and his only earthly chance of being remembered is through his humble connection with what I write." It was prediction as heartless as it was true. A fellow member of the *Argonaut* staff, Jerome Hart, later gave a fair assessment of Bierce's one-sided war with outgunned local scribblers. "Bierce certainly knew the technique of verse," he observed, "and knowing it was a savage critic of poets—or let us say, poetasters. There were then many writers of verse who felt the urge for print. Most of their work was mediocre, much of it was bad, and some of it was ludicrous. Upon these 'poets' Bierce was wont to pounce like a hawk on a hen. Similarly their squawks resounded throughout the poetic barnyard as the feathers flew. Most of the poor creatures did not deserve such savage treatment." Deserving or not, many felt the sting of Bierce's impenitent lash. "Every time my editor accepts and prints literary matter of a worthless kind from an amateur writer he does its author an irreparable injury," Bierce fumed. "In weak and intractable minds the rage for writing once kindled is inextinguishable; each gratification is a new incitement, and the luckless fool's ambition, which like the Lord's Prayer might once have been inscribed upon a nut-shell, grows by indulgence until the wall of a mad-house is too narrow for its display."[7]

Bierce's column, whose title he soon shortened to the more economical "Prattle," was virtually identical to his old "Town Crier" paragraphs. Between fulminations at hack writers, rival journalists, and other assorted literary offenders, he returned to his lifelong obsession with the macabre. Suicide, as always, enchanted him. "A well-known San Franciscan has blown out his brains in the streets of St. Louis," he noted in May 1877. "And yet no city in the world presents greater advantages to the suicide than San Francisco. We have an efficient and accommodating coroner, and a comfortable, though rather badly lighted, dead-house. Our undertakers have engaging manners, and their hearses easy springs. There is a charming view from every cemetery. In addition to these advantages, San Francisco itself is a very good motive." When an eastern journal commented that hanging seemed to be the preferred method of suicide for both the criminal and the respectable class, Bierce retorted, "This is most fortunate; for the persons whom it is commonly deemed desirable to hang by judicial process always belong to the one or the other of these classes—under our system of administering judgement it is not always easy to say which." And after the rival *Bulletin* reported that a man who had thrown himself down a two-hundred-fathom-deep mine shaft had "enjoyed poor health," he mocked: "What a crested idiot to go kill himself, with consumption wooing him in every breeze, and dyspepsia beckoning him from the summit of every pudding! Why a man who can really enjoy poor health should wish to part with his body transcends conjecture."[8]

Wife-murder, too, regularly caught his discerning eye: "I am sorry to observe that Mr. Lynch, of this city, a gentleman aged sixty-three, has committed the happily not very common error of killing his wife, with whom he had lived for forty years, but whom he must, of course, henceforth live without. Mrs. Lynch's offense consisted in declining to drink a glass of beer when requested; perhaps it would be more accurate to say refusing when commanded. For this the husband deemed it expedient to cut her fatally in the abdomen, though few will agree with him that such a course was either necessary or humane. On the other hand, if the beer was good there is no obvious reason why the lady should have refused it." A murder-suicide in New York also found its way into his column. "It was a religion with Johnson— the late James Johnson of New York—what was worth doing was worth doing well. It accordingly happened that the lady of whose society Mr. Johnson was fatigued was found, the other day, with her throat cut, her forehead broken in, and her body penetrated by sixteen knife wounds, eight of which—an impartial half—seem to have been intended for her unborn babe. Near the ruin thus wrought lay a revolver, a razor, a shoemaker's knife and a heavy iron stove-hook—an exposure of mechanical devices that proves Mr. Johnson to belong to the Eastlake school of Art, which scorns concealment of methods and as frankly discloses its means as its end. In simple justice to the tragedian it ought to be added that at the end of his dark performance he bowed himself off the stage with a graceful flourish of the razor that laid his head at his feet." Bierce sympathized with "Senor Felipe Carillo, of Monterey county, [who] is meanly designed by a contemporary as 'the vilest wretch that walks unhanged,' because he poisoned his mother with a strychniated pumpkin pie in the tenth decade of that lady's life. Some journalists appear to think a woman has the right to live forever. We do not share that opinion. Even Ninon de l'Enclos, the most beautiful, admired and elegant woman of her century—of accommodating morals withal—had the delicacy to die at ninety. If her son had had the spirit of Senor Carillo she would have perished earlier. Unfortunately he became enamored of her, and instead of performing the filial duty of assassination selfishly seized the lover's privilege of suicide. So passed from earth the sole suitor to whom this amiable lady denied the favor of her preference."[9]

Bierce was saved from having to perform a similar duty by the unassisted deaths of his father and mother in February 1876 and May 1878, respectively. Marcus, who died in Elkhart at the age of seventy-seven, in his declining years had inexplicably taken to calling himself "Colonel" Bierce and claiming that he had once served as private secretary to President Martin Van Buren. The Elkhart *Review* noted at his passing that the colonel had been "a man of no ordinary abilities, of quiet disposition and no great pretensions"— his new military rank and years of phantom presidential service notwithstanding. Bierce did not make it home for the funeral. Nor did he swell the ranks of mourners when his mother, Laura, died two years later. In a sense, they had already been dead to him for years. This was, after all, a man who was capable of beginning a short story: "My father was a deodorizer of dead dogs, my mother kept the only shop for the sale of cats' meat in my native city." An orphan now himself, he would shortly afterward define the term as denoting "a living person whom death has deprived of the power of filial ingratitude—a privation appealing with a particular eloquence to all that is sympathetic in human nature."[10]

While Bierce was busy lambasting poets and losing his parents, Pixley was urging him to step up his attacks on the shanty Irish holding sway in the sandlot beside city hall. At first, Bierce was slow to do so, whether from a residual sympathy for minorities—Irish as well as Chinese—or merely from a perverse disinclination to oblige his boss, it is impossible to say. The more Pixley exhorted him to slam the Irish, the more Bierce busied himself with such ephemeral targets as fatuous art critics ("this prodigious dolt—this goose in letters and ass in art"), Masonic rituals ("glorify a page of your humdrum life with the blazonry of meaningless mystery, attain to the dignity of Most Worshipful Blue Ring-Tailed Turtledover and Past Arch Grand Lunatic"), and popular dances ("amongst these the 'Glide' is in dominant favor, the grossness of its character commending it alike to the lecherous intelligence of the fading rake and the prying mind of the she simpleton"). A persistent and just criticism of Bierce's journalistic career has been that he spent altogether too much time straining at gnats and, in the words of his one time protégé George Sterling, "breaking butterflies on a wheel." Years later, *Argonaut* editor Fred Somers alluded to this bullying tendency in Bierce's work when he complained to him: "Now if you had not drummed and hunted these literary pismires out of their holes, and bruited them into public sympathy and recognition we should have been free of them. Yet you still continue poling at Windmills, setting them up often yourself—and for a wage—sneering at the industry. Sycophant or blackguard there is little choice."[11]

Still, while the disaffected dock workers and unemployed hod carriers in the Workingmen's party were forming themselves into "Pickhandle Brigades" and muttering ominously about "bread or blood," Bierce was content to join his friends Thomas A. Harcourt and William Rulofson in concocting a wildly successful literary hoax based on the current local rage for ballroom dancing. In June 1877, the three wrote and published a little pamphlet entitled *The Dance of Death,* ostensibly condemning the waltz as being "an open and shameless gratification of sexual desire." Using the joint pseudonym William Herman, the trio devised a tongue-in-cheek style that superficially damned the waltz for being lascivious and libidinous, while at the same time detailing its supposed sinfulness in prose as lush and sinuous as the dance itself. One passage may serve to stand for the whole: "Let us take this couple for a sample. He is stalwart, agile, mighty; she is tall, supple, lithe, and how beautiful in form and feature! Her head rests upon his shoulder, her face is upturned to his; her naked arm is almost around his neck; her swelling breast heaves tumultuously against his; face to face they whirl, his limbs interwoven with her limbs; with strong right arm about her yielding waist, he presses her to him till every curve in the contour of her lovely body thrills with amorous contact . . . his eyes, gleaming with a fierce intolerable lust, satyr-like over her, yet she does not quail; she is filled with a rapture divine in its intensity—she is in the maelstrom of burning desire—her spirit with the gods."[12]

Continuing the joke, Bierce reviewed the book in the *Argonaut,* denouncing it as "a high-handed outrage, a criminal assault upon public modesty, an indecent exposure of the author's mind! From cover to cover it is one long sustained orgasm of a fevered imagination—a long revel of intoxicated propensities." He ended with the hope that William Herman might be tempted to come forward to acknowledge his authorship. "Then," said Bierce, "he can be shot." The book, endorsed by a Methodist Church conference, sold eighteen thousand copies and inspired a rebuttal, *The Dance of Life,* which Bierce may also have had a hand in writing, although he always denied it. Ironically, both his collaborators later committed suicide over what he ruefully termed "domestic infelicities." Rulofson, he wrote, "executed a dance of death off the roof of a building"; and Harcourt drank himself to death after his wife ran off with another man. Rulofson's wife, it was said, was inordinately fond of the waltz.[13]

Such larks effectively diverted Bierce's energies from the political warfare that Pixley had initially hired him to fight. But in late July 1877, the Workingmen's party got his reluctant attention by means of a brutal two-day riot that began as an expression of solidarity for striking railroad workers in the East. In Baltimore, Pittsburgh, and Martinsburg, West Virginia, federal troopers firing Gatling guns had killed or wounded dozens of strikers—and not a few innocent people, as well—after President Rutherford B. Hayes caved in to demands by officials of the Baltimore & Ohio Railroad that U.S. soldiers be dispatched to serve as glorified strikebreakers for the embattled capitalists. It was the first time since the presidency of Andrew Jackson that army guns had been turned on other Americans (Confederates and Indians, who were not citizens, anyway, notably excepted), and it infuriated both the strikers and the not-inconsiderable segment of the thinking public, who rightly wondered when such guns might possibly be turned on them. Bierce did not think much of fellow Union veteran Hayes, who had entered office four months earlier behind a similar phalanx of flourished weapons after a blatantly partisan electoral commission had formalized his highly suspect victory over Democratic nominee Samuel J. Tilden. "There was enough of Lincoln to kill and enough of Grant to kick," observed Bierce; "but Hayes is only a magic-lantern image without even a surface to be displayed upon. You cannot see him, you cannot feel him; but you know that he extends in lessening opacity all the way from the dark side of [Ohio senator] John Sherman to the confines of space."[14]

In San Francisco, the rage over the eastern shootings turned all too predictably on the Chinese. Following a mass rally by the Workingmen's party on July 24, which was highlighted by an incendiary speech from party leader James D'Arcy, hundreds of so-called Sand-lotters set off toward Chinatown, where they proceeded to frolic away the remainder of the night, smashing windows in Chinese businesses, kicking down doors, and setting fire to assorted laundries, garment shops, cigar factories, and other Asian-owned enterprises. Then, when squads of firemen rushed to the scene—the city was still decidedly pyrophobic—the rioters cut the firemen's hoses to prevent them from dousing the flames. The next night, a mob of five thousand jobless workers assembled at the corner of Fifth and Mission streets for another night of summer revels. And while the largest group headed back to Chinatown to resume their trashing of stores and their pummeling of pedestrians, other groups fanned out for devilment in the white sections of town. This was too much for the city fathers to bear—even Mayor Bryant, a complete creation of the Workingmen's party, was forced to issue a proclamation warning that the police would use drastic measures to suppress further violence. In the meantime, former Committee of Vigilance chairman William T. Coleman organized a new crime-fighting detail and led it down to the waterfront, where the mob had set fire to a large warehouse containing imported Chinese goods. After an hour-long battle on the bluff overlooking San Francisco Bay, the vigilantes managed to chase off the rioters, and the federal government pitched in by dispatching two warships to anchor just offshore, with detachments of sailors and marines ready to disembark at a moment's notice.[15]

The July riots left a void at the top of the party ranks, and leadership somewhat inexplicably devolved into the hands of a newly naturalized citizen named Denis Kearney, a former Irish merchant seaman turned Teamsters union negotiator who ironically had carried an ax handle for the Committee of Vigilance during the late unpleasantness. Kearney, a native of County Cork, had set to sea at the age of eleven, arriving in San Francisco in 1868 and starting a draying business that prospered for a time before going under in the harsh economic climate of the mid-1870s. An active, nervous, intense individual, Kearney began attending the Lyceum for Self-Culture, where he overcame his natural shyness and soon developed into a riveting stump speaker. When the Workingmen's party reorganized itself after the riots, Kearney took a leading role. While no friend of the Chinese—"The Chinese must go!" was his trademark motto—he expanded his circle of animus to include San Francisco's mining and railroad magnates. "The monopolists who make their money by employing cheap labor have built themselves fine mansions on Nob Hill and erected flagpoles from their roofs," he thundered. "Let them take care they have not erected their own gallows." Kearney offered to provide each of his followers with a musket and a hundred rounds of ammunition and lead them on a march to Sacramento to encourage legislators to pass the Chinese Exclusion bill or else "string them up to the nearest lamppost." Also threatened with hanging were "the thieving millionaires, the hell-born, the hell-bound villains, the bloated bondholders" who had run him and so many other small shop owners out of business.[16]

One day Kearney led three thousand workers to the top of Nob Hill to protest railroad tycoon Charles Crocker's infamous "spite fence," a thirty-foot-high board fence that Crocker had erected completely around the cottage of an inconvenient Chinese neighbor who refused to sell his property to him. "If I give an order to hang Crocker, it will be done!" Kearney announced from the steps of Crocker's own mansion. No such order was given, but Crocker understandably began keeping a brace of Springfield rifles in his study, just in case. Bierce, for his part, treated the incident with studied impartiality. "Mr. Charles Crocker, who has the misfortune to live in a nice house, opposite which some hundreds of lawless miscreants are accustomed to meet and threaten to demolish it, naturally wishes to know of the police what measure, if any, it is proposed to take to preserve his property," Bierce wrote. "Seriously, Mr. Crocker, it is not easy to see what is to be done for you. Perhaps you will have the worthiness to consider whether you really need so fine a house when Mr. Lunglusty Sunbummer is haybunking along the wharves, and the Hon. Mr. Gory O'Ruffian and his pig have but wan mane parlor to the pair o' them."[17]

"Kearneyism," as the movement soon became known, presented something of a moral dilemma for Bierce. He had scant use for the robber barons, whose increasingly rococo mansions threatened to block the sun from many more city dwellers than merely Crocker's fenced-in neighbor. Neither did he respect the political process that cravenly caved in to the leather-lunged demands of cynical demagogues like Kearney or sold its votes to the highest bidder. When a prominent Oakland industrialist died, Bierce observed dryly: "The personal property of the late Anthony Chabot, of Oakland, has been ordered sold. This is a noble opportunity to obtain Senator Vrooman." But like many self-made men from struggling backgrounds, Bierce had an absolute horror of anarchy, which threatened to cancel in a moment's cataclysm the patient work of a lifetime. The great strikes of that smoke-darkened summer had terrified middle-class America. The ongoing depression had already revealed the social and financial fragility of a nation in which millions of hardworking, God-fearing folk found themselves a mere mortgage payment away from the streets. Many agreed with *Nation* columnist E. L. Godkin, who wrote, "We have had what appears a widespread uprising, not against political oppression or unpopular government, but against society itself."[18]

Bierce's response, conditioned by a lifetime of steadily eroded faith in religious, political, and military institutions, was to condemn the messenger Kearney (an "odious blackguard"), while accepting, at least in part, his central message: that the system itself was corrupt. But Bierce, unlike Kearney, did not believe in either a political or a revolutionary solution to the problem. He believed, in fact, that no real solution was possible, at least within culturally accepted democratic norms. It is hard to say whether he was more disgusted by the anarchistic threat the Sand-lotters represented to law and order or by the political threat their organized voting power presented to the existing body politic. Somewhat hysterically, he warned: "The Kearneyism 'episode' is not an episode; it is part of the general movement. Thousands of armed men are drilling all over the United States to overthrow the government. I tell you the good God, Majority, means mischief." But to Bierce the threat was equally grave whether the weapon was the bullet or the ballot. Unlimited suffrage, he warned in February 1878, had created a system in which "the tyranny of public opinion" had brought about a government that was both unstable and unprincipled. "Majorities, embracing as they do the most ignorant, seldom think rightly," he complained; "public opinion being the opinion of mediocrity is commonly a mistake and a mischief. The result is that public writer and public speaker alike find their account in confirming the masses in their brainless errors and brutish prejudices—in glutting their omnivorous vanity and in inflaming their implacable race and national hatreds."[19]

This sounds a bit like the snobby elitism associated, then and now, with the Republican party, but Bierce was no Republican. He may have hated Denis Kearney and all that he represented, but he had no great truck with what he termed the "Rights of the Rich Against the Poor," either. Despotism, he said, was the best form of government, since "the despot is powerful for evil, but equally powerful for good." This was not exactly a message of unalloyed reassurance to Frank Pixley and the political constituency he coveted, and Bierce increasingly found himself at odds with the *Argonaut* publisher. Nor were their differences confined strictly to politics. Pixley (and to a lesser extent Somers) annoyed Bierce by leaving him to do all the editing work while they concentrated on outside projects. Somers, a well-bred, well-educated young man of twenty-seven who later married the daughter of a former Missouri governor and founded the critically acclaimed journal *Current Literature,* was occupied just then with his work on two other literary magazines, *Figaro* and the *Californian.* Pixley had aspirations of running for governor of the state—something Bierce's plague-on-all-their-houses moralizing did little to advance—and was busy running errands for railroad magnate and political kingmaker Leland Stanford. Bierce found himself increasingly spread thin editing the newspaper, writing his columns, dealing with contributors, and overseeing production. There was some justice to his later complaint that "when Fred Somers died the world was copiously informed that he 'made' the *Argonaut.* Now that Fred Pixley is dead we are told that it was he who 'made' the *Argonaut.* In light of these statements I seem to see myself standing in the literary Pantheon, before the statues of the two great founders, scratching my poor dazed head and vaguely wondering if I am anybody in particular, whither I have strayed and why I am not put out by the janitor."[20]

Somers, at least, escaped with that mild rebuke. Pixley, who like Bierce's father affected the unearned title of colonel, was not so lucky. Bierce scorned the publisher's rather limited Civil War career, which he said consisted of "travel[ing] all the way from San Francisco, following the sound of the heaviest firing, until he arrived upon the field just as the battle of Cold Harbor was going against his side." Having missed the battle, he joked, Pixley somehow managed to get himself shipwrecked off the coast of Labrador and then "was rescued by the crew of a passing iceberg and returned forthwith to the extreme western verge of the continent. Having in mind his gallant ride from Cold Harbor to Labrador, the Humane Society soon afterward presented him with its gold medal for saving life. And the Peace Society says that nothing ever so advanced its cause as this editor's sight of a battlefield." Bierce also grumbled about Pixley's well-known shortcomings as a paymaster. "While an excellent debtor," he said, Pixley "was an abominable creditor. He did not mind owing, because he was sure to pay, sooner or later, but he positively hated anyone who owed him." Years later, when their relationship had irretrievably soured, Bierce finished off his former publisher with one of the shortest and most lethal obituaries on record: "Here lies Frank Pixley—as usual."[21]

On one occasion, at least, Bierce was happy to have Pixley close at hand. In early October 1878, Bierce printed a pair of breezy, slangy letters written by an actress named Kate Mayhew, who was then appearing onstage at the Baldwin Theater in San Francisco. The letters were nothing remarkable; Miss Mayhew, like numberless actresses before and since, complained that a local talent agent was an "old blow-hard" who put on "heaps of airs." She also groused that she was not making the sort of money she deserved. Bierce, who had obtained the letters from an unknown source, observed mildly that "letter-writing is *not* a lost art," and described the correspondent as "a charming blackguard, this Mayhew girl." Miss Mayhew's husband, Henry Widmer, who conducted the house orchestra at the Baldwin Theater, read the remarks and decided to be unamused. Accompanied by a friend, he stormed into Bierce's office at the *Argonaut* and demanded to know if Bierce was the author of the piece. "On being promptly assured that such was the case," Bierce told his readers, "he as promptly struck at me with his fist or open hand—as the blow failed of its intent I cannot say which. I do not enter contests of that kind, and drew my pistol, when Mr. Widmer's friend, who had entered unperceived by me, and whose name I have not taken the trouble to ascertain, sprang upon me and seized the cocked weapon, Mr. Widmer closing with me at the same time. At this stage of a struggle rather dangerous for all concerned and all within pistol shot, Mr. Pixley, knowing nothing of the cause of the conflict nor who was the aggressor, emerged from his private office, seized Mr. Widmer and forced him into the corner. The 'subsequent proceedings' consisted in a struggle between Mr. Widmer's friend and myself for the weapon, which eventually remained in possession of its owner."[22]

There the matter might have died, had Widmer not given the rival San Francisco *Chronicle* a conflicting account of the incident, describing himself as the injured party and accusing Bierce of being a coward. Bierce fired back in the *Argonaut,* damning Widmer for "devot[ing] the life which I mercifully spared to systematic defamation of my character and conduct. I, therefore, take this opportunity to remind those who have the misfortune to know him, and inform those who have not, that he has the distinguished honor to be, not a man of principle, but a ruffian; not a man of truth, but a liar; not a man of courage, but a coward. In order that there may be no mistake as to what member of the *canaille* I mean, I will state that I refer to Fiddler Widmer, the charming blackguard." The war of words died out after that, but Bierce took to carrying his loaded Colt revolver with him whenever he went out. That such a precaution was not simply paranoid was proven beyond a doubt when Charles De Young, the prominent and influential publisher of the *Chronicle,* was shot and killed a year later by newly elected mayor Isaac Kalloch's son after the younger Kalloch took similar exception to a De Young editorial.[23]

When life became too interesting in the city, Bierce could always take the ferryboat home to San Rafael. There, life was all too quiet. Mollie, accustomed by then to taking care of the children alone, left her erratically returning husband pretty much to his own devices, which consisted chiefly of sleeping half the day, writing half the night, and drinking and talking the other half with such roughneck friends as Marin County sheriff Jake Tunstead, who usually announced his presence by sticking his head through an open window and bellowing, "Where's Bierce?" When Mollie wondered aloud how Ambrose could tolerate such an ill-mannered lout, he merely shrugged, saying, "You should see him shoot." As for Tunstead's professional accomplishments, Bierce wrote in the *Argonaut:* "Mr. Tunstead is hanging people so neatly and pleasantly that the fellows who wish to die in that way are flocking into Marin to commit their murders."[24]

Ruffian or not, Tunstead was infinitely better company than Bierce's ubiquitous mother-in-law, who was still frequently on hand, helping with the children, or his social-climbing brother-in-law, James. Bierce had taken to calling Mollie and her relatives "the Holy Trinity," and he usually contrived to spend as little of his waking hours as was humanly possible around the house. By now, it had become painfully obvious to all concerned that he and Mollie were woefully ill-matched. When the couple was listed, a little charitably perhaps, in the *Argonaut's* sister publication, the *Elite Directory of San Francisco,* Mollie and her mother were overjoyed. Bierce, by contrast, lashed into a local society editor who had innocently noted that a recently born two-legged calf could "go backward and forward with equal facility." "Attach a cork right-hand to this creature, operated by strings connected with its tail," groused Bierce, "and it would write excellent society personals for the daily newspapers." About the same time, he observed: "Two male skeletons of the mound builders have been dug up in Kentucky, one lying across the other, and the fingers of each clutching the throat of the other. The skeleton of the woman has not yet been discovered, but it is probably somewhere thereabout, reposing with tender trust on the breast of a third male." To Bierce, hearth and home offered increasingly few consolations.[25]

Between political brawls, family squabbles, and office dustups with irate husbands, Bierce turned his hand to fiction writing for the first time in several years, publishing two new stories, "The Night Doings at 'Deadman's'" and "The Famous Gilson Bequest," in the *Argonaut* on December 29, 1877, and October 26, 1878, respectively. The stories, both set in California mining camps, are obviously derivative of Bret Harte's already-dated gold rush tales, and they reveal an author still struggling to find his own voice. Both are ghost stories, although neither is particularly scary. "The Night Doings at 'Deadman's'" concerns a lone, possibly crazed, miner named Beeson who is visited one night at his isolated cabin by a spectral stranger. The stranger remains mute as Beeson spills out his story: Two years earlier, his Chinese servant had died of natural causes, and since the ground was frozen solid for the winter, Beeson had buried him beneath the floorboards of his cabin. Before burying him, however, Beeson had snipped off the dead man's pigtail and nailed it to the wall above his grave. "According to the Chinese faith," Beeson explains, "a man is like a kite: he cannot go to heaven without a tail." Each night, the ghost of the servant returns for the pigtail, which Beeson somewhat unaccountably refuses to give him. That night, the ghost comes again, accompanied by the devil ("from San Francisco, apparently," Beeson observes). In the ensuing confusion, the ghost grabs the pigtail in his teeth, the devil disappears up the chimney, and the speechless visitor fires a pistol shot that ricochets off an overhead beam and strikes Beeson in the heart. The following spring, some wandering miners find Beeson's body and a set of moldy clothes worn by the visitor. They recognize the clothes "as those in which certain deceased citizens of Deadman's had been buried years before." Death, it seems, had come for Beeson in disguise.[26]

"The Famous Gilson Bequest" is a better story—Bierce scholar M. E. Grenander rather charitably compares it to Mark Twain's infinitely superior "The Man That Corrupted Hadleyburg"—and, like Twain's story, it concerns the corrupting power of seemingly easy money. Here, the principal victim is an upright resident of the Mammon Hill mining community, Henry Brentshaw, who has taken the lead role in capturing and hanging a gambler and suspected horse thief named Gilson. Before his execution, Gilson writes a will leaving all his surprisingly considerable fortune to Brentshaw—with one codicil: If anyone can convincingly prove, within the next five years, that Gilson had robbed their sluice boxes (another crime of which he was widely suspected but never caught), he is to receive the bequest instead. Brentshaw, who had caught Gilson red-handed with a stolen horse tied to his wrist, now contrives to prove, by means of bribery, chicanery, and the best legal experts money can buy, that Gilson was falsely convicted and executed. Brentshaw's increasingly desperate efforts to prove Gilson innocent have the ironic side effect of corrupting the entire community. Judges, jurors, witnesses, even the local press, which now prints "a most complimentary obituary notice of the deceased," rush to outdo themselves in proclaiming their love for Gilson. Brentshaw successfully changes public opinion, but at the cost of the entire estate he has stood to inherit. Moreover, his bribery leaves Mammon Hill "a region in which the moral sense was dead, the social conscience callous, the intellectual capacity dwarfed, enfeebled, and confused." Brentshaw himself changes from a vigorous, good-humored man into a brooding melancholic who has convinced himself of Gilson's "entire blamelessness." When he finally catches sight of Gilson's ghost stealing the ashes of other dead men from their caskets, the shock of his foolish credulity kills him.[27]

Most critics have treated "The Famous Gilson Bequest" as simply another genre ghost story with an ironic twist at the end. But a closer reading reveals a surprisingly subversive and sacrilegious text. As a passage late in the story indicates, Brentshaw has made Gilson into his own private religion, one that Bierce implies could stand for all religions, not least of which is Christianity: "The firm, vigorous intellect had overripened into the mental mellowness of second childhood. His broad understanding had narrowed to the accommodation of a single idea; and in place of the quiet, cynical incredulity of former days there was in him a haunting faith in the supernatural, that flitted and fluttered about his soul, shady, batlike, ominous of insanity. Unsettled in all else, his understanding clung to one conviction with the tenacity of a wrecked intellect. That was an unshaken belief in the entire blamelessness of the dead Gilson. It had become to him a sort of religious faith. It seemed to him the one great central and basic truth of life—the sole serene verity in a world of lies." Such unexamined belief, Bierce implies, is a product of the kind of narrow-mindedness that wrecks a man's intellect and leaves him trapped in a kind of second childhood, a shady, ominous place that reeks of insanity.[28]

The very name of Brentshaw's newfound idol, Milton Gilson, is an amalgam of sorts for Jesus Christ: the name Milton recalls John Milton and *Paradise Lost;* Gilson is a conjoining of *gill,* for the early Christian fish sign, and *son,* for the Son of God. Indeed, Gilson's extraordinary apotheosis from common horse thief to spotless avatar virtually replicates Christ's passion. Exiled from one mining camp, New Jerusalem, Gilson moves to Mammon Hill, where he is falsely condemned by a ravening crowd and hanged—literally— from The Tree. There his body is reclaimed by his new apostle, Brentshaw, who has "repaired to The Tree to pluck the fruit thereof." A great monument is erected over Gilson's grave, noting that he, like Christ, was "a victim to the unjust aspersions of Slander's viper blood." Finally, again like Christ, Gilson is released from his tomb by an act of God—this time a flood—and walks for a brief time among the living. That he spends his time ghoulishly robbing the graves of his neighbors and adding their dust to his own symbolizes, in an impious way, the Christian doctrine of the Rapture, when Christ is expected to descend and judge the dead, whose graves, like those on Mammon Hill, will have broken open. The lingering image of Christ as a grave robber is a particularly virulent one, even for Bierce.[29]

Besides his own literary productions, Bierce used the *Argonaut* as a ready forum for his friends' work. Along with his *Dance of Death* coauthor, T. A. Harcourt, other regular (and now mostly forgotten) contributors included Ina Coolbrith, Emma Dawson, William Morrow, Annie Townsend, Madge Morris, Richard Realf, and Charles Warren Stoddard, who was newly returned from the Continent. Bierce and Stoddard, who had been friends since the old *Overland Monthly* days a decade before, were now growing increasingly estranged. Stoddard's fawning account of a tea party at George Eliot's London home irritated Bierce as a particularly egregious example of American toadyism, and he lashed out in "Prattle" at his old friend. Another reason for their estrangement, as Bierce implied years later to George Sterling, was Stoddard's late-blooming homosexuality. He was not content, Bierce said, with the way God had made him.[30]

Another acquaintance—they were never friends—who attracted a whiff of the Biercian grape across his bow was Mark Twain. In December 1877, Twain had mortified New England's leading literary lights with an antic appearance at a dinner party celebrating John Greenleaf Whittier's seventieth birthday. For reasons known only to himself, Twain inexplicably chose the occasion to poke fun at the trebly named Augustans, Ralph Waldo Emerson, Henry Wadsworth Longfellow, and Oliver Wendell Holmes. In a long—it quickly became interminable—after-dinner speech, Twain regaled the astonished listeners with a typical western "stretcher" about three drunken tramps who had impersonated the famous writers during a visit to a miner's remote cabin in the Sierra Nevada foothills. The three tramps, he said, had taken over the cabin, eaten up the miner's food, drunk his whiskey, cheated brazenly at cards, and stolen their host's last pair of boots. Twain's good friend William Dean Howells was in attendance that night, and he looked up once from his dinner plate to see Twain frozen with embarrassment before an appalled and unlaughing audience. Twain's performance, Howells said later, "was like an effect of demoniacal possession."[31]

Bierce, when he heard of the incident a few weeks later, found the whole thing hilarious. Remembering his own infamous performance at London's Whitefriar's Club five years earlier, and not forgetting Twain's scene-stealing role in his subsequent embarrassment, Bierce could not let the opportunity pass for a gratifying, if long-deferred, last laugh. "Mark Twain's Boston speech," he noted in the January 5, 1878, issue of the *Argonaut*, "in which the great humorist's coltish imagination represented Longfellow, Emerson, and Whittier engaged at a game of cards in the cabin of a California miner, is said to have so wrought upon the feelings of 'the best literary society' in that city that the daring joker is in danger of lynching. I hope they won't lynch him; it would be irregular and illegal, however roughly just and publicly beneficial. Besides, it would rob many a worthy sheriff of an honorable ambition by dispelling the most bright and beautiful hope of his life."[32]

For Howells, who would later call Bierce one of America's three finest writers, the columnist nursed a lifelong antipathy. In part, this stemmed from his strong disagreement with the literary tenets of realism, which Howells famously championed and which Bierce defined in *The Devil's Dictionary* as "the art of depicting nature as it is seen by a toad." Denouncing what he termed "the reporter school of writing," Bierce grumbled that "the master of this school of literature is Mr. Howells. Destitute of that supreme and almost sufficient literary endowment, imagination, he does, not what he would, but what he can—takes notes with his eyes and ears and 'writes them up' as does any other reporter. He can tell nothing but something like what he has seen or heard, and in his personal progress through the rectangular streets and between the twin hedges of Philisitia he has seen and heard nothing worth telling." Such writers, he said, "hold that what is not interesting in life becomes interesting in letters—the acts, thoughts, feelings of commonplace people, the lives and loves of noodles, nobodies, ignoramuses and millionaires."[33]

That was bad enough, but Bierce also seemed to despise Howells for his lack of manliness and his avoidance of service in the Civil War. He consistently lumped him together with Henry James, another delicate contemporary who had escaped the war, calling them "Miss Nancy Howells and Miss Nancy James"—*nancy* being slang for homosexual. That Howells was a kind and generous man who went out of his way to help other writers whenever he could (and was, for that matter, a married heterosexual) mattered less to Bierce than the fact that he had sat out the war in an Italian consulate while Bierce and the other Boys of '61 were being shot to pieces at Shiloh and Chickamauga. "The lousy cat of our letters," he sneered at Howells, dismissing him and James as "two eminent triflers and cameo-cutters-in-chief to Her Littleness the Bostonese small virgin." Not for Bierce "the more smiling aspects of life" that Howells, in his favored and comfortable existence, had championed. The war, among other things, had soured him forever on that worldview.[34]

By the summer of 1879, Bierce was growing tired of both the literary and political wars. Increasingly, he distanced himself from Pixley and the *Argonaut,* spending more and more time in San Rafael in a vain attempt to combat a new onslaught of asthma. Bored with his job, his family, and himself, Bierce desperately needed a new challenge. He found one soon enough when a voice from his past, Sherburne B. Eaton, contacted him about an opening with the newly organized Black Hills Placer Mining Company, which was planning to open operations in Rockerville, South Dakota, in early 1880. Eaton, who had served with Bierce on General Hazen's staff during the war and then had been his superior in the Treasury Department during the postwar carnival of greed in Alabama, was general counsel for the company. In the fall of 1879, the Hayes administration had announced that the Black Hills were being reopened to miners and settlers following a decade-long struggle with the Sioux and their allies over the rightful ownership of the sacred Paha Sapa, as the tribe called the mineral-rich region. The BHPMC was one of several giant corporations rushing to join the new bonanza. By now, George Armstrong Custer and the 261 troopers who had followed him to their doom down the grassy slopes above the Little Bighorn River in the centennial summer of 1876 were so many powdery bones and rusted buttons, as were the mortal remains of the fabled shootist James Butler "Wild Bill" Hickok, who had been gunned down in a Deadwood, South Dakota, saloon not far from where Bierce was planning to set up for business. Without bothering to consult his father-in-law or other experienced miners about the new venture (one wonders how much he consulted Mollie, for that matter), Bierce hastily severed ties with the *Argonaut* and set out for Deadwood in July 1880, intending, he wrote to his old London drinking companion Henry Sampson, to free himself forever from journalism's tainted inks. If he was bothered by Sampson's reply—something about dogs returning to their vomit—he resolutely kept it to himself.[35]

From the start, the venture was a risible failure. While investors in the East were depositing hundreds of thousands of dollars into the company on the basis of nothing more substantial than a spit and a promise, the man Bierce was supposed to replace as general agent on the ground, the improbably named Capt. Ichabone M. West, was managing to make a comparable sum of money evanesce, with nothing to show for it but an uncompleted seventeen-mile-long box flume from Spring Creek to Rockerville and a stack of bad paper at the Deadwood First National Bank. In retrospect, Bierce's ill-conceived entry into the world of big-time gold mining looks suspiciously like the standard midlife crisis of a discontented thirty-eight-year-old writer. Aside from a few short stories about miners and ghosts and a grudging year spent behind a desk in the assay office of the U.S. Mint, the sum total of Bierce's gold mining experience was his trip across the plains with Hazen a decade earlier and a map he had drawn along the way of the Black Hills region. It was not much on which to base a new career.[36]

Nevertheless, Bierce manfully gave it his all. Somehow, in the face of resistance from both Captain West, who adamantly refused to hand over his duties, and the now-wary officers of the Deadwood Bank, who just as adamantly refused to advance Bierce any more money, he managed to complete the Sisyphean task of bringing water down from the creek to the mine. In this, he was assisted by an unlikely ally, a hulking gunslinger named Boone May whom he had hired to guard the company's depleted assets. The regular stage line from Deadwood to Rockerville was infested with robbers, and hard-pressed mine owners imported half a dozen "shotgun messengers" from Wells, Fargo & Company in California to safeguard their payroll runs. The hired guns, said Bierce, were "fearless and trusty fellows with an instinct for killing, a readiness of resource that was an intuition, and a sense of direction that put a shot where it would do the most good." One Sunday morning, he saw two of them dispatch half a dozen desperadoes on a Deadwood street while out for a leisurely after-breakfast stroll. May, for his part, was already something of a local legend. Said to be the fastest gun in the Dakotas—at least now that Wild Bill had cashed in his chips—he had once tracked down a well-known bandit named Frank Towle at a place called Robber's Roost. In the course of bringing Towle back to Deadwood for justice, May had been forced to kill him and bury his body beside the road. When he subsequently learned that there was a two-thousand-dollar reward on Towle's head, May, taking the letter of the law seriously, went back and dug up the bandit's body, cut off his head, and carried it back to town, in much the same way that a faithful dog will bring its master a stick. That was too much even for Deadwood, and May was indicted (though later acquitted) for murder.[37]

To Bierce's way of thinking, this was just the sort of man he needed to protect the BHPMC's interests, and he quickly put May on the payroll. The investment paid an immediate dividend. One day, Bierce and May left Deadwood for Rockerville, carrying with them thirty thousand dollars in company funds. They were riding in an open wagon through a thin drizzle of rain when, as Bierce later reported, "suddenly we heard the clinking of a horse's shoes behind, and simultaneously the short sharp words of authority: 'Throw up your hands.' With an involuntary jerk at the reins I brought my team to its haunches and reached for my revolver. Quite needless: with the quickest movement that I had ever seen in anything but a cat—almost before the words were out of the horseman's mouth—May had thrown himself backward across the back of the seat, face upward, and the muzzle of his rifle was within a yard of the fellow's breast!" What occurred then, Bierce deadpanned, "has never been accurately related." At any rate, they were not molested again. When company officials in New York got word of Bierce's newest employee, they complained a little about his hiring methods. Bierce responded that he did not have time to risk his own life on such dangerous missions, and so was risking May's instead. As a sop to proper business practices, however, he took to formally listing May on company payrolls as "Boone May, Murderer."[38]

Despite Bierce's best efforts, the mining venture was doomed to fail. New investors shied away from putting up any more money without tangible proof of a fair return on their investment, and Bierce and his workers went unpaid for weeks at a time. In desperation, Bierce went to New York in the fall of 1880 to remonstrate personally with Eaton and the board of directors, but it soon became apparent that neither he nor anyone else associated with the company was going to get rich in the Black Hills of Dakota. (No gold was ever struck at the Rockerville site, then or later, although various independent miners continued working the ground well into the 1890s.) At last, admitting defeat, Bierce left New York and returned to San Francisco in December 1880. The only legacy of his brief fling at gold mining was a niggling lawsuit, *Ambrose G. Bierce* v. *First National Bank of Deadwood,* which company officials filed in his name to recover three thousand dollars of outstanding funds that the bank refused to release to the now-bankrupt company. The suit dragged on well into the next decade, and not only was Bierce forced to give lengthy depositions from time to time but the legal fees came out of his own pocket. Infinitely worse, to someone as proud as Bierce, was the necessity of admitting to his wife and her family that he had been wrong to take the gamble in the first place. He returned to San Francisco broke and exhausted, with nothing to show for his one adult venture into Gilded Age capitalism but a few western anecdotes that he was too dispirited to recount and yet another friendship, with Sherburne Eaton, lying in ruins at his feet. All in all, the new decade had not gotten off to a very auspicious start.[39]

9

The Devil and the *Wasp*

or the second time in five years, Bierce found himself back in wintry San Francisco, adrift, jobless, and deeply depressed. Any hopes he may have had of returning to the *Argonaut* were quickly dashed when he was visited in his remote new hillside home at Fort Mason, overlooking the San Francisco Bay, by his former colleague Jerome Hart. It was Hart's unpleasant duty to inform Bierce that his services on the *Argonaut* were no longer needed. Frank Pixley and Fred Somers had discovered, to their relief, if not indeed their delight, that the paper could get along quite well without Bierce, and so could they. Hart, the innocent bearer of evil tidings, earned a glancing cuff from Bierce for his troubles; "he had learned," said Bierce, "to recite poetry, paint on velvet and smile, and became known as the Magnetic Clam." But his hardest punches he reserved for Pixley, "Mr. Pigsley of the *Hogonaut*," he called him, a little juvenilely. From now on, it would be open warfare between the two—as soon as Bierce could find a new dreadnought for his guns.[1]

This time, at least, he did not have long to wait. An opening had arisen on the established satirical journal *Wasp*, and Bierce was offered the job of editor in January 1881. Like the rest of San Francisco, he was unaware that the ostensible owner of the publication, Harry Dam, was merely the front man for a gifted schemer named Charles Webb Howard, the president of the Spring Valley Water Company. The company was a public utility doing business with San Francisco and other Bay Area communities, and Howard deftly funneled the company's large advertising outlays into his own pocket by buying up space in the *Wasp* each week. This amounted to a double or even a triple conflict of interest, but it did not seem to unduly trouble Howard. Bierce, kept in the dark about the *Wasp's* finances, happily set up office downtown and went about reviving "Prattle" as a weekly column.[2]

The columnist who began appearing weekly in the pages of the *Wasp* was, if anything, even more bitter than the one who had written for the *News Letter* and the *Argonaut.* For one thing, he was older, saddled with an unhappy wife, three young children, and an ever-present mother-in-law he could not seem to shake, no matter how often he moved. Then, too, the unseemly shambles of the Black Hills Placer Mining Company, although not his fault, was deeply demoralizing. Bierce returned to journalism as a last resort, not a first love, and he immediately began making people pay for his misfortunes, self-inflicted or not. As usual, he did not lack for targets. The open political warfare of the previous decade was largely over, due in part to personal abuses of power by Workingmen's party leader Denis Kearney and in part to the cynical political realignment his party's earlier successes had forced upon the behind-the-scenes power brokers in Sacramento. A two-headed calf calling itself the Democratic-Republican party had seized control of the state legislature with the generous help of deep-pocketed lobbyists employed by the so-called Big Four of the California railroad monopoly—Leland Stanford, Collis Huntington, Mark Hopkins, and Charles Crocker—and the brief outburst of participatory democracy (both for and against the Workingmen's party) had faded. Bierce took one look at the new alignment and spat: "If nonsense were black, Sacramento would need gas lamps at noonday; if selfishness were audible, the most leathern-lunged orator of the lot would appear a deaf mute flinging silly ideas from his finger tips amid the thunder of innumerable drums. So scurvy a crew I do not remember to have discovered in vermiculose conspiracy outside the carcass of a dead horse—since they adjourned."[3]

The *Wasp* had long been a Democratic organ and, as such, reflexively anti-railroad. Bierce fit right in. Repeatedly, he ridiculed the performance of the Central Pacific, listing various methods "devised by the railroad company to punish the Demon Passenger." He roared with laughter when some of the trains were designated "flyers," noting that in truth the special trains were among the slowest in the country, invariably arriving so late that the passengers were "exposed to the perils of senility" before reaching their destinations. "The Overland arrived at midnight last night, more than nine hours late, and twenty passengers descended from the snow-covered cars," he reported. "All were frozen and half-starved, but thankful they had escaped with their lives." The savage "Ode to the Central Pacific Spade," occasioned by a report that the spade used to turn the first shovelful of soil on the railroad was about to be featured at an exhibition, apostrophized "the maculating stains/Of passengers' commingled blood and brains;/In this red rust a widow's curse appears,/And here an orphan tarnished thee with tears;/Upon thy handle sanguinary bands/Reveal the clutching of thine owner's hands/When first he wielded thee with vigor brave/To cut a sod and dig a people's grave." An 1882 cartoon showed a woman labeled "California" tied up with tapes marked "selfishness" and "railroad power," while three Indian chiefs—Stanford, Huntington, and Crocker—prepared to scalp a child labeled "progress." Another showed a pigsty inhabited by three hugely fat hogs bearing the trio's faces; beneath them the caption read: "Fat enough to kill."[4]

When some readers complained—perhaps for pay—that the *Wasp* was focusing too much on the tycoons and not enough on issues, Bierce replied that "swindling corporations are not objects of our animosity; they are facts of our observation. The real facts of the Central Pacific Railroad Company, for example, are Stanford, Crocker and Huntington. If the corporation is a thief, it is because Stanford, Crocker and Huntington have stolen. Three knaves cannot by combining their rascality make themselves honest men." Besides, he noted, the paper was simply following the current of public opinion in denouncing abuses "whose causes are so obvious, simple and constant as the greed of Stanford, Crocker and Huntington." It was up to the public to apprehend "the moral difference between an honest man with a printing press and a rogue with a railroad."[5]

Bierce's attacks on the railroad were unprecedented, and not a little brave. He took over as editor only a few months after railroad goons had perpetrated one of the worst outrages of the Gilded Age, the swindling and murder of half a dozen wheat farmers during what became known as the Mussel Slough Massacre. In the late 1870s, railroad executives had induced a number of farmers to settle on railroad land in the San Joaquin Valley of California. In return for developing and populating the region, the farmers were given a gentleman's agreement to buy the land for no more than five dollars an acre. However, when the time came for the railroad to sell the land— which until then it had been leasing to the farmers—the price shot up to thirty-five dollars an acre. The settlers challenged the sale in court, but the Big Four simply began moving new settlers onto the disputed land. Predictably, bad blood festered between the groups. In May 1880, at the crossroads settlement of Mussel Slough, a group of farmers clashed with hired gunslingers, a U.S. marshal, and a company agent sent by the railroad to evict them from their land. Five settlers and two gunmen were killed, and five other settlers were arrested and later convicted of resisting a federal officer. The heartless cynicism of the railroad magnates shocked the nation, and the embattled farmers became a symbol—later repeated by the Okies who immigrated to the state during the Great Depression—of the poor but hardworking little man ground underfoot by the combined powers of rich landowners, corrupt courts, and an all-too-accommodating police force. Twenty years later, another San Francisco writer, Frank Norris, fictionalized the incident in his 1901 novel *The Octopus*.[6]

Emotions over the incident still ran high when Bierce took over as editor of the *Wasp*. He immediately dubbed Leland Stanford "$tealand Landford" and, writing from the settlers' point of view, poeticized: "Our fallen brave sleep well; each keeps/This ground, where none besets him./And well the fallen Stanford sleeps—/When conscience lets him." As for Crocker, Bierce was criticized for being too hard on a man who had "constructed many works of great and permanent value to the State." Scoffed Bierce: "As he has done this with other people's money, it is easier to concede the value of the works than the merit of their author. I do not discern anything praiseworthy in following the bent of one's nature without expense. His tendency to make improvements is merely a natural instinct inherited from his public-spirited ancestor, the man who dug the postholes on Mount Calvary." When Crocker threatened to move to New York, in part to escape Bierce's continued calumny, the columnist expressed the fervent hope that Crocker would devote to the task of leaving the same "energy and activity as two laborious decades of public and private sinning have left him." He wished Crocker godspeed "from a people whose generous encouragement he has punished by plunder—from a state whose industries he has impoverished, whose legislation he has sophisticated and perverted, whose courts of justice he has corrupted, of whose servants he has made thieves, and in the debauchery of whose politics he has experienced a coarse delight irrelative to the selfish advantage that was its purpose—from a city whose social tone he has done his best to lower to the level of his own brutal graces, and for whose moral standards he has tried to substitute the fatty degeneration of his own heart."[7]

If that wasn't plain enough, Bierce simplified matters even further for his readers. Denouncing "the freebooters of the Railroad," he thundered: "We believe these men to be public enemies and indictable criminals. We believe that their wealth, illegally acquired, is sinfully enjoyed and will be dishonestly transmitted." In the state where the Big Four had gotten their start, many agreed with Bierce's sentiments, but few had the courage to speak their convictions openly. Just how courageous his opposition was, in the social and political climate of the time, may be inferred from the reminiscences of another San Francisco journalist of the era, Fremont Older, editor of the San Francisco *Bulletin*. "In the early eighties the political power of the railroad became absolute," Older wrote. "It controlled both political parties in California. Its power had superceded all law, all government and all authority. The real capital of the state was moved from Sacramento into the railroad building at Fourth and Townsend streets. There, in a magnificent office, sat the big railroad boss [Huntington] who dictated public politics and appointments not only in this state, but throughout the entire West. This stupendous organization became an overshadowing influence in all walks of life. Here and there, a feeble note of criticism broke loose occasionally, but whoever had the audacity to make it was soon silenced by the big boss." For whatever reason, Bierce was not silenced, then or later. Perhaps there were limits to power, even for the Big Four. Or, more likely, they were so powerful that no amount of criticism could penetrate their thick skins. Nevertheless, Bierce kept firing away at their elephantine profiles, and the failure to deflect or discredit him would come back to haunt Huntington, in particular, a few years down the road.[8]

The railroad barons, in a way, were merely the most obvious symbols of an entire nation gone badly astray. Bierce's disaffection for the country as a whole had been growing—or festering—for several years now, probably since that long-ago morning at Shiloh when the ultimate logic of war was spelled out for him in crimson letters. It had been underlined by the subsequent human disasters (on all but a narrow military scale) at Stones River, Chickamauga, Missionary Ridge, Franklin, Resaca, and Pickett's Mill and painfully punctuated by a bullet to the head at Kennesaw Mountain. In subsequent years, his vision had darkened even further as he observed firsthand the widening gap between the haves and the have-nots, the native-born and the immigrants, the workers and the bosses. His own sporadic attempts at replicating the American dream—complete with wife, family, and get-rich-quick mining scheme—had all proven unsatisfactory, to say the least. Now, out of a deep personal sense of disappointment and disillusion, he began to articulate an alternative vision of his native land, a vision that for sheer caustic cynicism was probably unrivaled in the Victorian age.

In what amounted to an understatement, he announced in the December 23, 1882, issue of the *Wasp:* "We are not enamored of the world as it is. We find it peopled with a thousand-and-odd millions of inhabitants, who are mostly fools, and it is our custom to set forth and illustrate this unsatisfactory state of affairs by instancing conspicuous examples." He intended to be both witness and judge, roles to which he brought all the self-righteous fervor of his Calvinist forebears. "Now mark you, rogues of all degrees and lettered fools with phosphortized teeth in mouths full of moonshine, I am among you to remain," he warned. "While the public buys my rebuking at twice the price your sycophancy earns—while I keep a conscience uncorrupted by religion, a judgment undimmed by politics and patriotism, a heart untainted by friendships and sentiments unsoured by animosities—while it pleases me to write, there will be personalities in journalism, personalities of condemnation as well as commendation."[9]

In practice, of course, there were far more of the first category than of the second. Whenever Bierce tired of the railroad tycoons, he could always find diversion at the expense of another favorite target—religion. As ever, the city was overrun with ministers of all stripes and denominations. "What a procession of holy idiots we have had in San Francisco," he groused in October 1881. "Hot gospellers and devil-pelters of all degrees! Thick-necked Moody with Sanky of the nasal name; Hallenbeck, Earle, Knops and all their heharlotry of horribles. And now this grease-eating and salt-encrusted Harrison from the pork regions of the northeast, thinking holy hog-and-hominy and talking his teeth loose for the dissuasion of sinners from their natural diet of sin." When a former colleague from the old *Overland Monthly* days, Sarah Cooper, was tried for heresy by her minister, Bierce waded in with both barrels: "Dim-pinnacled in the intense shame of his theological environment, he [Rev. J. B. Roberts] sits astride his evil eminence of personal malignity, breaking the seals that close that pestilence, his mind, and its insupportable rain of red ruin falls alike upon the just and the unjust, the while he cackles with holy glee. Look at him—the hideous apparition perched between the world and the light, flinging his ugly shadow athwart the scene to fray the souls of babes and sucklings." He amused himself by inventing ever more elaborate names for the preachers: Rev. Dr. Dobrane, Rev. Mr. Twackbible Shrique, and—a personal favorite—Brother Mortificationoftheflesh J. Mucker. With ecumenical glee, he smote them heel and thigh.[10]

But if Bierce could still enjoy a certain amount of profane fun skewering local evangelists, the political scene in the early 1880s sickened and disgusted him. After moneymaking, politics was the great national pastime of the Gilded Age—at least for white middle- and upper-class males. In millions of gaslit American homes, a practiced ritual was reenacted nightly after dinner: Well-brought-up ladies lingered at table while their ruddy-faced husbands, bewhiskered and big-bellied, retired to the parlor to smoke cigars, swirl brandy, and bemoan the impending ruination of the republic if ever—God forbid—so-and-so were elected to public office. Bierce, a congenital outsider, did not participate in such diversions; he lacked the requisite faith in the system. A September 1882 cartoon in the *Wasp* showed Republicans and Democrats "as they pretend to be," warring savagely with each other, while a second panel showed them "as they really are," drinking collegiately in a bar. "For years," he wrote, "in the heated combats of the two parties there has not been one important principle at stake: the offices have been the only prize." The drab succession of bearded war heroes who moved through Congress and the White House during the era did not elicit much respect from Bierce, a war hero himself, though without the beard. Sounding very much like a modern voter, he observed: "The public officials of this favored country are, as a rule, so bad that calumniation is a compliment. Our best men, with here and there an exception, have been driven out of public life, or made afraid to enter it. Unless attracted by the salary, why should a gentleman 'aspire' to the presidency of the United States? During his canvas he will have from his own party a support that should make him blush, and from all others an opposition that will stick at nothing to accomplish his satisfactory defamation. After his election his partition and allotment of the loaves and fishes will estrange an important and thenceforth implacable faction of his following without appeasing anyone else. At the finish of his term the utmost that he can expect in the way of reward is that not much more than one-half of his countrymen will believe him a scoundrel to the end of their days."[11]

It was just such a division of loaves and fishes that brought newly elected President James A. Garfield to grief in the summer of 1881. Garfield, like Bierce, had been a Union soldier. As chief of staff to commanding general William S. Rosecrans at Chickamauga, he had ridden back to the battlefield while his stricken superior had ridden away from it, a spur-of-the-moment decision that made Garfield's career, even as it wrecked Rosecrans's. He had come out of the House of Representatives to win the presidency (the last man to do so, as a matter of fact); but a disappointed office-seeker named Charles J. Guiteau, who was actually something of a lunatic, shot Garfield in the back as the new President was strolling through Pennsylvania Station on July 2, 1881. The wound itself was not fatal, but a procession of blunt-fingered doctors alternately pushed, prodded, poked, and probed the stricken President until they managed to give him a fatal infection. He died on September 19, 1881— the eighteenth anniversary of Chickamauga—after having sweltered all summer in a state of semidelirium. (In an effort to give their patient some relief from the heat, the doctors had rigged up a rudimentary cooling system by blowing moist air over a block of ice, the prototype of the modern air conditioner; in a way, James A. Garfield died for air-conditioning.)[12]

At first, Bierce seemed suitably affected by Garfield's suffering. "Since man began his awful career upon the earth nothing has occurred more detestable than this assassination," he wrote. "A man of brain and character; a man with a past and a future; a great-hearted, clear-eyed gentleman, standing worthily upon his honors—such a man as that is suddenly brushed aside and effaced by the caprice of a smirking hoodlum." Just how firmly Bierce's tongue was in his cheek may be gathered from his subsequent musings on the assassination. Reading that a convention of black newspaper editors had "gravely resolved never to mention in their papers the name of the aspiring youth who shot President Garfield," Bierce joked: "Things have come to a pretty pass when a man can't keep his name out of the newspapers without shooting the chief magistrate of his beloved country." After Garfield died, Bierce fumed over the press's reporting of the news. "I should like to know," he wrote, "what purpose is furthered by the downright lying of our daily newspapers about the way in which the public was affected by the news of the President's death. What public interest did it serve, whose private pocket did it fill, to talk of strong men weeping in the streets; of women fainting with emotion; of vast crowds, pale with grief, discussing the sad event under their breath; of prominent politicians shocked into speechless silence by the tidings of the interviewer, who considerately waited for them to recover? Every man gifted with eyes and the faculty of observation knows there was nothing of all this, and could have been nothing. It is not even picturesque lying. It is open and forthright vilification."[13]

The main problem, to Bierce, was not the character of the nation's politicians, but the overweening stupidity of the electorate, exemplified by the paradigmatic figure he dubbed, with supreme scorn, "that immortal ass, the average man." "Surely 'the average man,' as everyone knows him, is not very wise, not very learned, not very good," he railed. "It seems to me that the average man is very much a fool, and something of a rogue as well. He has only a smattering of education, knows virtually nothing of political history, nor history of any kind, is incapable of logical, that is to say clear, thinking, is subject to the suasion of base and silly prejudices, and selfish beyond expression." When such men interrupted their leisure to vote, it was usually with predictable results. "Do you know, Johnny Voter, that you are a dupe? Does it penetrate your poor understanding that every time you throw off the top of your head to give tongue for the man of another man's choice the worthy persons who keep the table in the little game of politics are affected with merriment? Have you ever a dawnlight of suspicion that in the service of their purpose your wage is their derision, your pension their silent contempt? O, you will uphold principle. You will stand in to avert the quadrennial peril to the country. You will assist in repelling the treasonable attempt of one half its inhabitants whose interest (obviously) lies in its destruction. You will be a 'Republican'—or a 'Democrat'; you will be it diligently, loudly and like the devil. Pray do; and when you have processioned your feet sore and your teeth loose, and been a spectacular extravaganza to the filling of your ambition's belly, may it comfort you to know that you have been a Tool." He suggested an 1884 presidential dream ticket of the American Hog for president and the Nicaraguan Canal for vice president. "Murder," he advised, "but do not vote."[14]

The months-long hubbub over Garfield's wounding and death did have one unexpected effect on Bierce: It got him to thinking again about the Civil War. In the December 25, 1881, issue of the *Wasp,* he published his great reminiscence, "What I Saw of Shiloh," his first written account of the war and an article whose revolutionary treatment of warfare as a hallucinatory and absurd experience prefigures much of modern literature's attitude toward the subject. The essay and its effects have already been discussed, but it is still worthwhile to put the work into proper historical context. By December 1881, the Civil War had been over for sixteen years. The two regions were once again at peace, and not even the disputed election of 1876 had brought about a new outbreak of violence between the two regions, however much political zealots on both sides had tried to provoke just such a fight. Even the practice of waving the "bloody shirt," which had proven so successful for Republican presidential candidates throughout the era, was becoming passé. The 1880 election, after all, had been between two former Union generals, and one of them, Winfield Scott Hancock, the universally certified hero of Gettysburg, had enjoyed solid southern support. Veterans of both sides had entered a period that modern historian Gerald F. Linderman has aptly termed "the Hibernation," a period in which the vast majority of ex-soldiers consciously sought to heal themselves of war's hellish memories by studiously avoiding all talk of such matters. In the decade preceding Bierce's ground-breaking essay, the nation's most prestigious history publication, *The North American Review,* had published a grand total of one article on the Civil War; *Harper's,* the leading popular magazine, had published two. It would be another three years, in late 1884, before *Century Magazine* began running its well-received "Battles and Leaders of the Civil War" series. As for the handful of published novels set during the war, all were uniformly sentimental and pedantic, thinly disguised allegories in which manly northern veterans wooed and won coquettish southern belles, thus symbolically completing the reunion—or was it the ravishment?—of the regions.[15]

Bierce, like most veterans, had been too busy getting on with his life to spend much time refighting the war. But Garfield's death made him look back, if not in anger, then at least in regret, to the "fine far memories" of that long-ago time "when there was something new under the sun." The contrast between the high drama of the Civil War years and "the harsher figures of this later world, the drear and somber scenes of today," made him yearn for the seemingly simpler days of his youth. At thirty-nine, he was entirely typical of his idealistic generation, which now felt increasingly out of touch with the fast-paced and often brutal acquisitiveness of the new age. He cared nothing for the larger issues of the war, believing them to have been politically moti-vated and hopelessly muddled. He did not hate Confederates, nor did he idolize his former Union comrades. (Four years later, when U. S. Grant lay dying of cancer, Bierce would worry mainly about "the advancing tide of bosh that will submerge the land" after the general's death.) What he cared about was setting down, as accurately as possible, the physical sense of how it had felt to be nineteen years old and going into your first and possibly your last real battle. And in this, he succeeded admirably. "What I Saw of Shiloh" may well be Bierce's finest piece of writing; certainly it is his most heartfelt.[16]

In contrast to that "blood-stained period" when, ironically, "all was gra-cious and picturesque," the nation now seemed merely "a great, broad blackness with two or three small points of light struggling and flickering in the universal blank of ignorance, bigotry, crudity, conceit, tobacco-chewing, ill-dressing, unmannerly manners and general barbarity." Again sounding like his Protestant forebears, Bierce moralized: "If our sins, which are scarlet, are to be washed as white as wool it must be in the tears of a genuine contri-tion: our crocodile deliverances will profit us nothing. We must stop chasing dollars, stop lying, stop cheating, stop ignoring art, literature and all the refining agencies and instrumentalities of civilization. We must subdue our detestable habit of shaking hands with prosperous rascals and fawning upon the merely rich. It is not permitted to our employers to plead in justification

of low wages the law of supply and demand when it is giving them high profits. It is not permitted to discontented employees to break the bones of contented ones and destroy the foundations of social order. It is dishonest to look
upon public order with the lust of possession. Until we amend our personal
characters we shall amend our laws in vain." In the meantime, Election Day
would bring only the circuslike spectacle of "millions of voters who mostly
are fools,/Demagogues' dupes and candidates' tools—/Armies of uniformed
mountebanks,/And braying disciples of brainless cranks." Before such
paraded ignorance, one could only shrug: "Walk up, gentlemen—nothing to
pay—/The Devil goes back to Hell today."[17]

The devil was much on Bierce's mind just then. Beginning with his first
issue of the *Wasp,* he had inaugurated a new column entitled "The Devil's
Dictionary," featuring ironic definitions of common words. A few earlier
installments, under the title, "The Demon's Dictionary," had appeared in
the pages of the *News Letter* and *Fun.* For some reason—perhaps because of
the number of political words beginning that way—Bierce started his list
with the letter *P.* A few of his first offerings included such characteristic definitions as: "PEACE, n. In international affairs, a period of cheating
between two periods of fighting"; "POLITICS, n. A strife of interests mas-
querading as a contest of principles"; and "PRESIDENT, n. The leading figure in a small group of men of whom—and of whom only—it is positively
known that immense numbers of their countrymen did not want any of
them for President." Nonpolitical definitions included "PIANO, n. A parlor
utensil for subduing the impenitent visitor"; "PIETY, n. Reverence for the
Supreme Being, based upon His supposed resemblance to man"; "PRAY, v.
To ask that the laws of the universe be annulled in behalf of a single peti-
tioner confessedly unworthy"; "PLEASURE, n. The least hateful form of
dejection"; and "POSITIVE, adj. Mistaken at the top of one's voice." In all,
there would be eighty-eight installments of the dictionary, numbering over
one thousand definitions and representing Bierce's wit at its most mordant
and corrosive.[18]

The dictionary allowed Bierce, who had always been something of a
pedant where the English language was concerned, to range widely over all
aspects of human endeavor: love, war, politics, religion, business, law, and
philosophy. The work was addressed, he said later, to those "enlightened souls
who prefer dry wines to sweet, sense to sentiment, wit to humor and clean
English to slang." The distinction between wit and humor is an important
one, and one that Bierce made more overtly in his essay "Wit and Humor."
"Humor is tolerant, tender," he wrote; "its ridicule caresses. Wit stabs, begs
pardon—and turns the weapon in the wound." Americans, he observed, had
always been humorous, but "if any are born witty heaven help them to emi-
grate." The true witticist needed, along with an acquaintance with rhetoric
and a passable knowledge of classical literature, "an ever-present conscious-

ness that this is a world of fools and rogues, blind with superstition, tormented with envy, consumed with vanity, selfish, false, cruel, cursed with illusions—frothing mad! He must be a sinner and in turn a saint, a hero, a wretch." That job description has more in common with Baudelaire's *poète maudit* than with the outwardly genial lecture-hall personae of such home-grown American humorists as Mark Twain, Artemus Ward, or, a generation later, Will Rogers. Fittingly, a modern French critic, Jules Sternberg, has labeled Bierce's preferred writing style *humour noir.* Unlike Twain and Rogers (both of whom were, in fact, more deeply subversive to the national fabric than their folksy images suggested), Bierce stood outside the society he was satirizing. Not only was he not laughing with the targets of his abuse; he was frequently not laughing at all. His distance was not simply the Augustan distance of the true wit from his intended victim but also that of the disenfranchised outsider from the hated object of his rage and scorn.[19]

All of which should not suggest that the definitions in "The Devil's Dictionary" are somehow tendentious or unamusing. They are, in their way, deadly serious, but they are also howlingly funny. Delve in anywhere and there are aphorisms worthy of Bierce's revered master, Alexander Pope (who was known, coincidentally, as "the Wasp of Twickenham"). One comes across "BRIDE, n. A woman with a fine prospect of happiness behind her"; "VOTE, n. The instrument and symbol of a freeman's power to make a fool of himself and a wreck of his country"; "SENATE, n. A body of elderly gentlemen charged with high duties and misdemeanors"; "LAWYER, n. One skilled in circumvention of the law"; "LITIGATION, n. A machine which you go into as a pig and come out of as a sausage"; "DOG, n. A kind of additional or subsidiary Diety designed to catch the overflow and surplus of the world's worship"; "CHRISTIAN, n. One who follows the teachings of Christ in so far as they are not inconsistent with a life of sin"; "EPITAPH, n. An inscription on a tomb, showing that virtues acquired by death have a retroactive effect"; "CABBAGE, n. A familiar kitchen vegetable about as large and wise as a man's head"; "IDIOT, n. A member of a large and powerful tribe whose influence in human affairs has always been dominant and controlling"; "DANCE, v. To leap about to the sound of tittering music, preferably with arms about your neighbor's wife or daughter"; "SAINT, n. A dead sinner revised and edited"; "PEDESTRIAN, n. The variable (and audible) part of the roadway for an automobile"; "GALLOWS, n. A stage for the performance of miracle plays, in which the leading actor is translated to heaven"; and "REVERENCE, n. The spiritual attitude of a man to a god and a dog to a man." Then there are the shorter but equally devastating definitions: "HERS, pro. His"; "WHITE, adj. Black"; "ONCE, adv. Enough"; "TWICE, adv. Once too often"; "BRUTE, n. See Husband"; "ALONE, adj. In bad company"; "FAMOUS, adj. Conspicuously miserable"; and "CAPITAL, n. The seat of misgovernment."[20]

The critic Robert F. Richards has rightly observed that "each of these definitions, to some degree, may be said to define Bierce." They constitute, in a way, a hidden autobiography, an indirect self-portrait of a profoundly lonely and estranged individual at odds with his country, his family, his past, and himself. Nowhere is this more pointed than in the series of definitions concerning love and marriage. One wonders what Mollie Bierce must have made of such definitions as "HELPMATE, n. A wife, or bitter half"; "HUSBAND, n. One who, having dined, is charged with the care of the plate"; "INTIMACY, n. A relationship into which fools are providentially drawn for their mutual destruction"; "INCOMPATIBILITY, n. In matrimony a similarity of tastes, particularly the taste for domination"; "AFFIANCED, n. Fitted with an ankle-ring for the ball-and-chain"; "YOKE, n. A word that defines the matrimonial situation with precision, point and poignancy"; "WEDDING, n. A ceremony at which two persons undertake to become one, one undertakes to become nothing, and nothing undertakes to become supportable"; and "MARRIAGE, n. The state or condition of a community consisting of a master, a mistress and two slaves, making in all, two." By 1881, Ambrose and Mollie had been married a full ten years, but judging from his contemporaneous definitions, it was anything but a gala anniversary. Time after time, Bierce reveals a deep—and deeply personal—disgust with marriage as an institution, and with the female sex as the chief instruments of masculine unhappiness. Consider these definitions: "WITCH, n. An ugly and repulsive old woman, in a wicked league with the devil. A beautiful and attractive young woman, in wickedness a league beyond the devil"; "WOMAN, n. An animal usually living in the vicinity of Man, and having a rudimentary susceptibility to domestication. The species is the most widely distributed of all beasts of prey"; or, perhaps cruelest of all, "SATIETY, n. The feeling that one has for the plate after he has eaten its contents, madam."[21]

That Bierce was unhappy in his marriage is indisputable. But all his unhappiness cannot be blamed solely on Mollie or her mother. The various definitions in "The Devil's Dictionary" also reveal a person who has been intensely at odds with his life from the very beginning. With a little hindsight, one can almost chart Bierce's autobiography chronologically: "BIRTH, n. The first and direst of all disasters"; "CHILDHOOD, n. The period of human life intermediate between the idiocy of infancy and the folly of youth"; "PAST, n. That part of Eternity with some small fraction of which we have a slight and regrettable acquaintance"; "RELIGION, n. A daughter of Hope and Fear, explaining to Ignorance the nature of the Unknowable"; "FAITH, n. Belief without evidence in what is told by one who speaks without knowledge, of things without parallel"; "CEMETERY, n. An isolated suburban spot where mourners match lies, poets write at a target and stonecutters spell for a wager"; "HISTORY, n. An account mostly false, of events mostly unimportant, which are brought about by rulers mostly knaves, and soldiers mostly fools"; "CYNIC, n. A blackguard whose faulty vision sees things as they are, not as they ought to be"; "DEFAME, v. To lie about another. To tell the truth about another"; "FRIENDLESS, adj. Having no favors to bestow. Destitute of fortune. Addicted to utterance of truth and common sense"; "DAY, n. A period of twenty-four hours, mostly misspent"; "NOVEMBER, n. The eleventh twelfth of a weariness"; "YEAR, n. A period of 365 disappointments"; "MISFORTUNE, n. The kind of fortune that never misses." Given such a liverish worldview, there was probably little that Mollie or anyone else could have done to improve Bierce's basic disposition.[22]

So long as he confined himself to such deserving targets as the California railroad tycoons, Bierce's savage ill humor was well founded and even meritorious. But the smug and bullying strain of his criticism, particularly when directed at minor offenders, was often simply cruel. Increasingly, he saw himself as the final arbiter of artistic good taste. In March 1882, he gave due notice to would-be contributors. "Persons who wish to contribute to the *Wasp*," he advised, "will find it advantageous to their interests, as insuring acceptance, to write logically, brilliantly and with marked impressiveness, in a style that is without fault, and with a taste that is perfect. That is about all that we demand. Articles requiring a higher order of literary merit are written in the office." A few weeks later, he blasted Bay Area writers: "Get out, you gruesome ingrates! Cease to afflict with circulars, pester with prospectuses and torment with your presence in the flesh. For, by the black right hand of the sovereign Satan, I will no longer spare!" A *Wasp* cartoon of the period depicts "Ambrose Bierce, literary dissector" in the act of plunging an oversized quill pen into the left eye of an "aspiring bard," while behind him are displayed drawings of previous victims, variously hanged, crucified, roasted over an open fire, or dejectedly hurling themselves off the nearest pier.[23]

Bierce's dissections were sometimes brief and to the point, as when he wrote of local drama critic Peter Robertson: "How better is a grave-worm in the head/Than brains like yours." Others were more elaborate. W. C. Bartlett, art critic for the San Francisco *Bulletin* and an irrepressible booster of all things western, suffered a public pillorying. Said Bierce: "The old he-hen who makes the *Bulletin's* art criticism has been in full cackle ever since the opening of the Spring exhibition. He has executed this identical prostration of his spirit every spring since California art began to defy the law against indecent exposure. Doubtless the senile and unhaired wretch can now show as many little notes of gratitude from the ladies, as he has mentioned names which will visibly enhance the superiority of his smile and endow him with fat sleep and free dreams." Not even old friends were immune from dissection. Prentice Mulford, who had done so much to brighten Mollie Bierce's lonely days in England while Bierce was off drinking with the boys, had begun writing a Sunday travelogue for the *Chronicle.* Mulford's articles, said Bierce, were "the cold collations of his Paris notebook, raw records of a mind incapable of observing and wotless how to write. They say that journalism is an ill-paid profession, yet for twelve years it has kept this literary lout out of the alms houses that were racking their foundations to enclose and digest him." As usual, he made no allowances for the gentler sex. Nearly fifty years later, San Francisco writer Charlotte Perkins Gilman still remembered Bierce's lash. "He was the Public Executioner and Tormentor, daily exhibiting his skill in grilling helpless victims for the entertainment of the public," she wrote. "He was an early master in the art of blackening long-established reputations of the great dead, of such living persons as were unable to hit back effectively, and at his best in scurrilous abuse of hard-working women writers. He never lost an opportunity to refer to the cotton-stuffed bosoms of the women writers."[24]

Not all Bierce's targets were so obscure. In the spring of 1882, the ineffable Oscar Wilde wafted into San Francisco in the midst of a 105-city tour of the colonies. Wilde, who certainly was qualified to speak on the subject, had earlier disparaged satirists as a breed, and Bierce apparently took umbrage at the remark. He savaged Wilde as an "intellectual jellyfish," and lambasted his fellow San Franciscans for spreading a welcome mat before Wilde's custom-made patent leather shoes. Then, disputing all the way, he declined in verse to "Dispute with such a thing as you—/Twin show to the two-headed calf." He flayed the Irish-born playwright for "limpid and spiritless vacuity," and termed his well-attended lectures "mere verbal ditch-water." It scarcely improved Bierce's mood that the rest of the city gave Wilde a rapturous welcome—or that Wilde himself took absolutely no notice of Bierce's rant.[25]

Increasingly, as he fought his literary battles, Bierce had taken to living apart from his family. At first, he kept a small apartment in the city at 1428 Broadway, near the offices of the *Wasp*. But San Francisco's notorious fogs, like those of London a decade earlier, aggravated his asthma, and he began venturing into the countryside in search of relief. Nicasio, a Marin County resort near his old stamping grounds at San Rafael, came first, followed by Auburn, in Placer County. Auburn advertised itself as "the healthiest town in California," and Bierce moved into the ramshackle Putnam House there. To him, Auburn was "The Perverted Village," an insular little community "where Health and Slander welcome every train" and "smiling innocence, its tribute paid,/Retires in terror, wounded and dismayed." There was more to Bierce's wanderings, of course, than mere health concerns. To outsiders, at least, he and Mollie had seemed to be effectively separated since his days on the *Argonaut*, when his coworkers were surprised to hear that he had a wife and family at home. For years, he had been in the habit of coming and going as the mood struck him; now his homecomings became fewer and further between. Just prior to leaving for Auburn, Bierce and Mollie quarreled violently over her brother James, one-third of the "Holy Trinity" that Bierce railed against whenever the spirit moved him. This time, for a change, the offending party was not Ambrose but James, who had scandalized the family by romancing the virginal daughter of an old clergyman they all knew. The minister—never named in accounts of the incident—later committed suicide. Bierce refused to have anything more to do with his brother-in-law and angrily moved out of the house. Despite the somewhat tortured claims of Carey McWilliams and other biographers that the couple had not yet separated at the time, there seems little reason to doubt that by early 1883 the marriage was deeply troubled, if not, in fact, irretrievably broken.[26]

When Bierce did make it into the city, he joined his old newspaper cronies Arthur McEwen and Petey Bigelow along the famed San Francisco "cocktail route," which ran from the Baldwin Theater bar at the corner of Kearny and Market to Hacquette's and Hageman's Crystal Palace at Market and Powell. The three were longtime drinking companions, and Bierce excepted his friends from his generalized antipathy toward journalism as a profession. As for the rest of his associates, Bierce flatly declared, "I will say this for my own profession, horribly I hate it." It was a calling, he said, that was "almost a disgrace to belong to." But Arthur and Petey were different. McEwen, in particular, was in awe of Bierce's capacity for alcohol. Anyone who could drink as much as Bierce did the night before and then get up and write so brilliantly the next morning more than lived up to his reputation as "an eminent tankard-man." As for Bigelow, he was one of the most popular figures on the local scene, an anglicized dandy (like Bierce) who strolled the streets with a flower in his buttonhole and a cane in his hand. He was famous in his circle for announcing one day at the *Examiner* office, "There are two things I'm going to do right now: have a glass of beer and go to France." He did both. A year later, he returned to his desk at the newspaper as though nothing unusual had happened. "Thank God, Petey has no virtues," Bierce said admiringly.[27]

Whatever his own virtues, they did not extend to parenting. Bierce was a tolerant but largely absent father, one who would occasionally take the time to write to his children individually, enclosing some little gift or keepsake, and then sign the letter formally, "Your father, A. G. Bierce." When he was home, usually on weekends, he typically slept most of the day, then sequestered himself in his library, writing. The children simply did not interest him. As long as they were clean—he was always a fanatic about personal hygiene—and reasonably quiet, he was content to go his way and let them go theirs. For their part, the children worshiped their father and did their best to imitate him. The boys, particularly Day, mimicked Bierce's military walk and martial bearing, and tried on a little of his salty language, as well. Once, when a minister happened to be visiting Mollie (Ambrose sat wordless and glaring in a corner), Leigh came running in to report, "Daddy, Day just said 'Damn God.'" Bierce relished his reply. "Go and tell Day," he instructed the younger boy, "that I have repeatedly told him not to say 'Damn God' when he means

'God Damn.'" The minister took his leave a few minutes later. When his daughter, Helen, later wrote that her father was "a home-loving man, fonder of his own hearthside than of anything else in the world," it was more in the spirit of wishful thinking than actual experience.[28]

In truth, Bierce was alone much of the time, hotel-hopping in the drab hillside communities around San Francisco. From the Putnam House at Auburn, he went to Cranes Hotel at Sunol, Angwin's on Howell Mountain, the El Monte at Los Gatos, Wright's near Santa Cruz, and Jeffreys Place at Wrights. They were all unlavish establishments, catering to an anonymous and interchangeable clientele of traveling salesmen, graying spinsters, and the variously mad, lonely, or unattached. Their charms were minimal at best. His fellow boarders, Bierce remembered, included "the elocution chap, the mimic and the funny dog, the social sponge, the adiposing dame, the kitten-playful virgin of half-a-hundred years, the widow all too gracious." Dinners were particularly gruesome. "I would rather dine in a receiving vault of a cemetery than in an American dining-room," he wrote. "The awful hush, the peculiar ghastly chill, the visible determination to be proper and avert the slow stroke of the rebuking eye that awaits the miscreant who laughs or speaks above his breath—these things overcome me. I can't breathe in that atmosphere of solemn stupidity. I choke my food and strangle on my drink. The waiter carries me out."[29]

His homelessness brought a return of the terrible dreams that had racked him as a youth. One presented "a singularly dismal picture, long, dim vistas ending in a bank, buildings appallingly high and threateningly top-heavy. The ghost of a city is at the bottom of the ghost of an ocean. I do not perceive any sounds, nor any living beings. I am the only fish that swims this dismal sea. I glide on aimless, hopeless, emotionless, yet with a half-expectant sense of an enchantress somewhere with pallid eyes and hair of seaweed." He summed up his depressive spirits in a fine Hardyesque poem, "A Study in Gray," in which he looks back at "the years that are dead," when he was "lured and beckoned" by those twin betrayers, Hope and Fame:

> *Believe me, I've held my own, mostly*
> *Through all of this wild masquerade;*
> *But somehow the fog is more ghostly*
> *To-night, and the skies are more grayed,*
> *Like the locks of the restaurant maid.*
>
> *If ever I'd fainted and faltered*
> *I'd fancy this did but appear;*
> *But the climate, I'm certain, has altered—*
> *Grown colder and more austere*
> *Than it was in that earlier year.*

> *The lights, too, are strangely unsteady*
> *That lead from the street to the quay.*
> *I think they'll go out—and I'm ready*
> *To follow. Out there in the sea*
> *The fog-bell is calling to me.*[30]

Bierce's isolate wanderings made it difficult for him to continue full duties on the *Wasp,* and in early 1883 he began limiting himself to his weekly column. There was more to his decision than mere logistics; he had finally discovered Charles Webb Howard's hidden ownership of the newspaper. Angrily, he threatened to expose the whole mess unless Howard sold his interest in the paper to Ned Macfarlane, the managing editor. Without too much prodding Howard did what Bierce wanted. But Macfarlane was not an inspired choice. He had obtained the money to buy the journal from his brother George, who had vast holdings in the Hawaiian Islands. The Macfarlanes intended to champion gradual annexation of the islands by the United States and, in the meantime, push hard for continued sweetheart terms for sugar exports. Bierce, in effect, had traded one compromising position for another, although, true to form, he did not cater to the new owners, either. He vented undisguised contempt for American colonists on the islands. "Not a man jack of them but if he were a saint in Heaven would strip the bark from the Tree of Life and smuggle it into Hades for fuel," he wrote. As for the native islanders, he brusquely declined an invitation to attend the coronation of a new Hawaiian queen in February 1883 with the dismissive question, "Why should I bother to see a negress crowned queen of the Fly-Speck Islands?"[31]

White women, too, felt the Biercian lash. "The Opposing Sex," he called them, or "the women folks." "For study of the good and bad in woman," he noted, "two women are a needless expense." He held that he did not favor equal rights for women, since there were unequal biological differences between the sexes. "There is one service of incomparable utility and dignity," he conceded, for which women were "eminently fit—to be mothers of men." Some were not even fit for that. Two of the more egregious examples of the latter were the Italian opera singer Adelina Patti and the English actress Lillie Langtry. Both included San Francisco on their performing itineraries, a decision that Bierce took as a direct slap in the face. The raven-haired Patti had traveled across the plains in a specially appointed railroad car, complete with pink bedroom trimmed in ebony, gold, and amaranth. She was married to a French marquis, but she was traveling with an Italian tenor. When she rode her carriage through town, San Franciscans mobbed her. Local women took to sporting Patti fashions and serving Patti menus; scalpers paid a special hundred-dollar tax to sell her tickets in front of the opera house; and an enterprising merchant advertised that he was the sole shopowner to carry her special brand of corset. Bierce, as usual, tacked away from the crowd. Patti's singing he compared to "the squalling of a singed cat." But it was her conti-nental notions of morality that angered him most. "Second only to this woman's fame as a singer is her fame as an adulteress," he wrote in the spring of 1884. "This glorification of the world's whole harlotage marks a civiliza-tion that is ripe and rotten."[32]

Lillie Langtry, the "Jersey Lily," fared no better. She numbered among her admirers the Prince of Wales, the colorful Judge Roy Bean (the self-proclaimed "law west of the Pecos"), and even—somewhat bemusingly—Oscar Wilde. She arrived in San Francisco with thirty-two trunks of clothes, twenty-eight valises, and a Colt revolver presented to her by Bean at his west Texas saloon. She also arrived with a wealthy gambler and playboy named Freddie Gebhardt, who had already offered to fight a duel with a St. Louis newspaper editor who published a salacious diagram of their adjoining hotel rooms. Bierce was even harder on Langtry than he was on Patti, denouncing "the posings of a prostitute recommended by a prince." The famous Langtry face, said to be the most beautiful in the world, was nothing more than "a brow still reeking of a drunken lecher's royal kisses and the later salutes of a dirty little gambler." Somehow, he managed to avoid having to fight a duel of his own.[33]

During his time on the *Wasp,* Bierce wrote five new short stories: "Mr. Swiddler's Flip-Flap," "Cargo of Cat," "An Imperfect Conflagration," "George Thurston," and "A Tough Tussle." The first two are insignificant examples of the western tale, which Bierce never handled as well as Twain or Harte. The third, "An Imperfect Conflagration," was the initial entry in the notorious quartet of stories that Bierce later entitled *The Parenticide Club.* It begins with one of the writer's classic lines: "Early one June morning in 1872 I murdered my father—an act which made a deep impression on me at the time." Patricide, of course, was a favorite theme of Bierce's, rooted in his life-long internal conflict with his parents, and he has fun—of a sort—with the story of a young burglar who kills his father, his partner in crime, for trying to keep back a music box during the late-night division of their most recent theft. The instrument in question could "not only play a great variety of tunes, but would whistle like a quail, bark like a dog, crow every morning at daylight and break the Ten Commandments. It was this last mentioned accomplishment that won my father's heart and caused him to commit the only dishonorable act of his life, though possibly he would have committed more if he had been spared."[34]

The narrator kills his father and—almost an afterthought—his mother and hides them in a bookcase in the library. He freely confesses his crime to the chief of police, "himself an assassin of wide experience." The chief advises him to take out a large insurance policy and set fire to his house. He does so, but the bookcase remains standing, "bolt upright and uninjured," when the narrator returns home. The bodies of his murdered parents are clearly visible through the glass, but typically in Bierce's fiction, the killer still manages to get off scot-free. Three years later, "when the events herein related had nearly faded from my memory," he goes to New York to pass some counterfeit Treasury bonds and finds an exact duplicate of the bookcase in a furniture store. From the storeowner, he learns that the bookcase was specially designed by a mad inventor to withstand fire. He declines to buy the companion piece, however, since "it revived memories that were exceedingly disagreeable."[35]

At the time "An Imperfect Conflagration" was written—March 1886—Bierce's father had been dead for nearly ten years, but reading the story one gets the sense that Bierce was writing more to amuse himself than to impart any moral, however indirect, to the reader. It is a decidedly odd form of amusement, nevertheless, and it says as much about Bierce's own feelings toward fatherhood as it does about his conflict with his father. Bierce's oldest son, Day, was then approaching the age of fourteen, and it may be that an underlying sense of guilt at his virtual abandonment of his children—something Marcus Bierce, for all his faults, never did—inadvertently found its way into the story. The critic Stuart C. Woodruff is wrong to suggest that "An Imperfect Conflagration" and the other stories that comprise *The Parenticide Club* are the worst that Bierce ever wrote—he wrote several that are worse than these—but while they are not particularly good from a literary standpoint, they are invaluable from a biographical one. They contradict the popular assumption that Bierce was somehow warped by the Civil War. A man driven to kill his parents over and over again in his stories, years after their actual deaths, is a man who was a casualty long before the first cannon fire at Fort Sumter.[36]

The two Civil War stories Bierce wrote in the early 1880s, "George Thurston" and "A Tough Tussle," are also psychologically interesting, if somewhat below the quality of his later war stories. Both deal with another of his obsessions: suicide. So many of his war stories end in suicide that one is tempted to extrapolate from this that Bierce simply considered war itself to be suicidal. In a way, of course, it is, but such a reading misses a crucial point: For Bierce, if not perhaps for others, there were good and bad types of suicide. Throughout his career, he insisted that men had the right to "take themselves off" whenever life became insupportable. Like the French existentialists half a century later, he believed that under the right circumstances suicide could be a profoundly moral act. "The smug, self-righteous modern way of looking upon the act as that of a craven or a lunatic is the creation of priests, philistines and women," he wrote. "No principle is involved in this matter; suicide is justifiable or not, according to circumstances; each case is to be considered on its merits, and he having the act under advisement is sole judge. To his decision, made with whatever light he may chance to have, all honest men must bow." As for the morality or immorality of the act, Bierce conceded that "the ethics

of suicide is not a simple matter; one cannot lay down laws of universal application, but each case is to be judged, if judged at all, with a full knowledge of
all the circumstances." He put down a list of six possible justifications for
moral suicide: painful or incurable disease; unrelieved burdening of friends;
the threat of permanent insanity; drunkenness or other destructive habits; the
loss of friends, property, employment, or hope; and personal disgrace. Under
such circumstances, "suicide is always courageous," since "the suicide does
more than face death; he incurs it, and with a certainty not of glory, but of
reproach. If that is not courage we must reform our vocabulary."[37]

Bierce's list was intended for peacetime applications. During wartime, a
seventh type of moral suicide is acceptable: disinterested self-sacrifice. A good
example of the latter may be found in the story "A Son of the Gods," in
which an unnamed young officer on a snow-white horse purposefully rides to
his death to disclose the enemy's presence behind a distant hill. "Killed at
Resaca," "The Mocking-Bird," "The Story of a Conscience," and "An Affair
of Outposts" also instance morally acceptable suicides. The officers in "Killed
at Resaca" and "An Affair of Outposts" sacrifice themselves to redeem their
honor after being betrayed by faithless lovers. Private Grayrock in "The
Mocking-Bird" shoots himself after discovering that he has unwittingly killed
his own brother. And Captain Hartroy in "The Story of a Conscience" dies
by his own hand after being forced to execute a Southern spy who earlier in
the war had saved his life.

By contrast, the protagonists in "George Thurston" and "A Tough Tussle,"
like the panicky Captain Graffenreid in "One Officer, One Man," are examples of bad suicide. All three die because they cannot control their emotions.
The title character in "George Thurston" is so afraid of doing something
cowardly that he repeatedly exposes himself to danger, only to die absurdly in
a banal accident (caused by suicidal recklessness) in camp. Lieutenant
Byring's "tough tussle" is with his own excessive squeamishness; a nearby
corpse so unmans him that despite increasingly desperate attempts to take his
mind off his predicament, he ultimately loses control and hacks the corpse to
pieces before falling on his own sword. Captain Graffenreid kills himself
because he can no longer stand the suspense of waiting for an attack that,
ironically, never comes. In all three cases, suicide is a cowardly response to
fear, not a brave reaction to a moral quandary. To Bierce, cowardice means "a
shrinking from danger, not a shirking of duty." And war is nothing if not a
dangerous duty.

By mid-1885, Ned Macfarlane's mismanagement of the *Wasp* had become
increasingly obvious, even to its absentee editor. He sold out to Col. J. P. Jackson of the *Evening Post,* and Bierce wrote his farewell panegyric: "We retire
with an unweakened conviction of the rascality of the Railroad Gang, the
Water Company, the *Chronicle* newspaper, and the whole saint's-calendar of
disreputables, detestables, insupportables, and moral *canaille.* As for the mere

fools and blockheads—thrifty sky-pilots, sons o' light, literary imposters, aspiring vulgarians hanging on to society by the teeth, inflated patriots, offensive partisans, sentimentalists, quack philanthropers, talking teetotalers and other vine-pests, cobble-trotting whisky soldiers and peacocking gregarians generally, muckers and the unlovely lot of potential rogues in the stony soil of whose natures the seeds of crime lie ungerminated by the sun of opportunity, we trust that the *Wasp* will now extend to them a general amnesty." He did not promise as much from himself.[38]

Jobless again at forty-three, Bierce retreated to higher ground, in this case St. Helena at the northern end of Napa Valley. Mollie and the children took a home in town, while Bierce withdrew still farther, to Angwin's, an erstwhile mining camp turned health resort at the base of Howell Mountain. There, according to his daughter, he bicycled, hiked, hunted pinecones and arrowheads, and literally charmed the birds out of the sky—"they gathered in clouds upon his outstretched arms and head." Perhaps they did; there is an existing photo of a squirrel eating directly out of Bierce's hand. His neo-Franciscan lifestyle was occasionally interrupted by visits from an old acquaintance, Lillie Hitchcock Coit, the madcap fire engine chaser, who had separated from her husband and was living at nearby Larkmead. In fine defiance of local gossip, the unlikely pair began spending time together, hiking mountain trails and picnicking in the glens. "Lil Coit," he said later, "is a real woman." Mollie Bierce, as usual, kept her own counsel.[39]

Bierce had been told by a friend that a year's stay among the pine trees on Howell Mountain would cure him forever of his dreaded asthma. He was determined to stick it out, although his fellow convalescents at Angwin's— which he immediately dubbed "the place of last resort"—were the usual crowd of pasty-faced social climbers he had long despised. When the St. Helena *Star* reported in January 1886 that "Mr. Bierce, known as the *Wasp* stinger has been sojourning at Angwin's on Howell Mountain for some time," Bierce bitterly complained to the editor of what he termed the St. Helena *Liver-Complaint*. He produced his own mincing column of social frippery: "Old Sightdraft and his wife are split again. Mrs. Chairman of the United States Committee on Oyster Statistics Jones is registered at the Occidental. Mrs. Major Rampage has returned from Boneville, where she has been sponging on her brother's family all summer. Mrs. Colonel Pompinuppy's Wednesday evenings will henceforth eventuate on Thursday afternoons. Mr. Chris Buckley is preparing to go west and grope with the country." Repose was hard to come by, even on a mountaintop.[40]

Gradually, Bierce began going back into the city, at least as far as Oakland, where he rented a small apartment near his brother Albert's home. He was staying there in March 1887 when a blond young man of twenty-three turned up on his doorstep one afternoon. It was William Randolph Hearst. Bierce recounted the meeting years later in a well-known passage from his

Collected Works: "I found a young man, the youngest man, it seemed to me, that I had ever confronted. His appearance, his attitude, his manner, his entire personality suggested extreme diffidence. I did not ask him in, install him in my better chair (I had two) and inquire how we could serve each other. If my memory is not at fault I merely said, 'Well' and awaited the result.

"'I am from the San Francisco *Examiner*,' he explained in a voice like the fragrance of violets made audible, and backed a little away.

"'Oh,' I said, 'you come from Mr. Hearst.' Then that unearthly child lifted its blue eyes and cooed: 'I am Mr. Hearst.'"[41]

The soon-to-become-legendary Hearst explained to Bierce that he had crossed San Francisco Bay to secure his writing services for the *Examiner.* He was in the process of assembling the finest stable of journalists in the West— Bierce's old friends Petey Bigelow and Arthur McEwen had already signed on—and he wanted Bierce to contribute a column or two of "Prattle" a week to the newspaper. Bierce, who by then had breathed enough pine-scented air to last him a lifetime, was instantly amenable, provided that Hearst agree to publish "Prattle," without inconvenient revisions, on the editorial page. That done, the two men shook hands on a deal that would pay handsome dividends to them both for the next twenty years. Bierce was about to embark on the period of his greatest professional accomplishments—and his deepest personal tragedies.[42]

10

The Friction
That We Name Grief

espite his often-stated contempt for journalism as a profession, by the spring of 1887 Ambrose Bierce had been a working journalist for nearly two decades. Beginning with his apprentice work for the *Californian,* the *New Era,* and the *Overland Monthly* in the late 1860s, he had progressed to the "Town Crier" columns of the *News Letter,* an expatriate stint on the London journals *Figaro, Fun,* and *The Lantern,* and an increasingly high-profile position as the fearsome Prattler of the *Argonaut* and the *Wasp.* In the fratricidal, hothouse milieu of West Coast journalism, he was famous or infamous, depending on one's point of view. At any rate, he was unavoidable. But nothing in Bierce's long career had quite prepared him for the antic experience of working for William Randolph Hearst on the San Francisco *Examiner.* Unwittingly, he had hitched a ride on the newest, wildest, most recklessly extravagant carnival wagon of a newspaper in American history. And like the rest of Hearst's writers, editors, artists, and readers, Bierce would find his ensuing twenty-year ride alternately exhausting, exciting, and exhilarating.

The unlikely wagon master, at the time he showed up on Bierce's doorstep, was two years out of Harvard, where he had contrived to get himself thrown out of school by the simple expedient of sending each of his instructors an ornate chamber pot with the recipients' names hand-lettered on the bottom. No one, including Bierce, could have guessed that William Randolph Hearst was destined to become the most influential newspaperman of modern times. Tall, slender, and soft-spoken, with pale gray eyes and a wispy blond mustache that seemed to fade away if anyone looked too closely at it, Hearst was shy and retiring, almost a photographic negative of himself. But beneath that washed-out exterior lay the crowd-pleasing instincts of a born showman. All his life, Hearst was fascinated by professional entertainers, a proclivity that culminated in his notorious decades-long affair with showgirl turned actress Marion Davies. This was not as improbable as it seemed, since Hearst was something of an entertainer himself; the front page, not the soundstage, was his proscenium. As a young man, he liked to wear flamboyantly colored neckties and flourish his large collection of walking sticks, one of which whistled as he walked. He was polite, if not friendly; articulate, if not wordy; and he had only one idea in his head: to make the *Examiner* the most popular newspaper in the West—the most popular, not necessarily the best, although Hearst never made a distinction between the two.[1]

Like many men with a single large idea, Hearst worked indefatigably at it. Unlike most, he had the singular advantage of starting at the top. His father, George Hearst, was another Nob Hill millionaire, a transplanted Missourian whose sheer genius at sniffing out gold and silver strikes had won him the admiring Indian nickname "Boy-That-Earth-Talked-To." Comparatively late in life, the elder Hearst developed a passion for politics, contributing lavishly to Democratic candidates and loaning piles of money to the party's California house organ, the *Examiner*. In October 1880, he took sole possession of the newspaper, having invested himself with the quaint notion that somehow he should be governor of the state. He lost that election, but six years later he was rewarded for his generosity by being appointed to serve out the unexpired term of the late Senator John T. Miller. In the meantime his son, whom he affectionately called "Billy Buster," was serving a year-long apprenticeship on Joseph Pulitzer's pacesetting newspaper, the New York *World*. At the *World*, Hearst learned firsthand the precepts of the new journalism, a frothy blend of sensationalism and idealism that placed the stress on vividly written and illustrated stories concerning crime, scandal, corruption, and vice— ingredients that any major city, on either side of the country, could furnish in virtually inexhaustible degree. Critics derided Pulitzer's "yellow journalism," but in three years' time he raised the *World*'s circulation from 15,000 to 150,000. Young Hearst took notice, and when his father was elected to his own Senate term in 1886, he immediately wrote to him, requesting that he be allowed to take over the *Examiner*. "We must be alarmingly enterprising, and we must be startlingly original," he advised his father. "We must be honest and fearless. We must have greater variety than we ever had." He had thought it all out, and his father, who seldom denied him anything, did not deny him this. In February 1887, Billy Buster took over the newspaper, and two weeks later he hired Ambrose Bierce as his chief editorial columnist.[2]

As a weekly columnist, Bierce was not required to sit behind a desk in the *Examiner* newsroom; his office, as usual, was wherever he lay his head. But he occasionally dropped by the newspaper's Montgomery Street headquarters for the sheer diversion of being entertained. Under the singularly unflappable Hearst, the *Examiner* was a never-ending welter of sound and fury—part pirate ship, part three-ring circus, someone said. Reporters were constantly dashing in or out, in headlong pursuit of stories that would produce the newspaper's coveted benchmark, the "gee-whiz emotion." Readers were expected to exclaim "Gee Whiz!" when they saw the front page, "Holy Moses!" when they read the second, and "God Almighty!" when they turned to the third. Anything less was accounted a failure. A reporter who was there at the time, George P. West, later recalled: "The *Examiner* office was a madhouse inhabited by talented and erratic young men, drunk with life in a city that never existed before or since. They had a mad boss, one who flung away money, lived like a ruler of the late Empire and cheered them on as they made newspaper history."[3]

Frequently, they made news as well as reporting it. One staff writer got himself committed to an insane asylum by jumping off a steamer in the middle of San Francisco Bay and raving like a lunatic when rescuers fished him out. After a month inside the asylum, he emerged, perfectly sane, to write a bloodcurdling account of his experience. Red-haired reporter Winifred Sweet, an ex-chorus girl who is credited with inventing the "sob sister" style of pathetic journalism, dressed herself up as a homeless woman, faked a collapse, and was taken to the city receiving hospital for the poor, where she was successively insulted, pawed, given a hot mustard emetic, and turned back onto the street. Her subsequent front-page exposé resulted in a staff shake-up at the hospital and a visit to the newsroom by the facility's indignant chief physician, who was summarily knocked to the floor by a burly colleague of Miss Sweet's for physically threatening the delighted reporter. Other reporters rescued marooned fishermen, tested the lifesaving techniques of Bay Area ferryboat crews, and personally escorted visiting actress Sarah Bernhardt on a late-night tour of Chinatown's sinister opium dens to see firsthand the human misery there on display.[4]

While his eager young staff was off pursuing the news, Hearst was back at the office beefing up circulation through an incessant campaign of self-promotion. The "Monarch of the Dailies," as Hearst grandly described his publication, was "the largest, brightest and best newspaper on the Pacific Coast." It promised readers "the most elaborate local news, the freshest social news, the latest and most original sensations." To keep his promise, Hearst spared no expense. When other papers scooped the *Examiner* on a major hotel fire in Monterey, the chagrined publisher immediately chartered a train and sped to the scene with a carload of writers and sketch artists, turning out an unheard-of fourteen-page special edition, topped by a two-column headline written by the boss himself in patented gee-whiz style: HUNGRY, FRANTIC FLAMES/"Leaping Higher, Higher, Higher,/With Desperate Desire"/Running Madly Riotous Through Cornice,/Archway and Facade,/Rushing in Upon the Trembling/Guests with Savage Fury. On a slow news day, Hearst was apt to send up a young couple high above the city to be married in a balloon emblazoned EXAMINER, or to sponsor free boat rides aboard the chartered paddle wheeler *James M. Donohue* for the first one thousand subscribers who clipped the required coupon from the back of the paper. Whatever he did, it worked. Within a few months, Hearst had doubled the *Examiner's* circulation, and by 1890 the previously debt-ridden newspaper was showing a profit.[5]

Success, however, was not without its trials, most of them self-inflicted. Even in a profession notorious for its drinking, the staff of the *Examiner* set new standards of insobriety. Bierce, who was no slouch himself when it came to holding down a bar rail, was practically an amateur compared with his colleagues. Managing editor Sam Chamberlain, known citywide as "Sam the Drunken," was given to suddenly hopping a transatlantic steamer and heading for his favorite bar in Antwerp, Belgium, where he would hole up, elegantly sporting spats and a monocle, until one of Hearst's European representatives could track him down and ship him home. ("If he is sober one day in thirty, that is all I require," Hearst said forgivingly.) Bierce's old drinking mates Arthur McEwen and Petey Bigelow were also prodigious tipplers, if not perhaps as continental in their tastes. Hearst once searched all over San Francisco for McEwen, only to find him drunkenly curled up beneath his rolltop desk in the *Examiner* newsroom. On another occasion, the sepulchrally thin Bigelow, in the midst of a bender, shaved off his characteristic beard and weaved his way into a Market Street tavern, where a fellow drinker reared back in horror at his ashen appearance and exclaimed, "Good God, the Holy Grail!"[6]

The staff standard for drinking was set by reporter Robert Duncan Milne, whom Hearst finally induced to take a well-publicized cure at the paper's expense. Milne dutifully obliged, undergoing a grueling two-week treatment at a sanitorium and writing a sensational firsthand account of the mental and physical pangs of alcohol withdrawal. As soon as the article was completed, Milne headed straight back to the barroom, leading Hearst to write an exculpatory editorial declaring that Milne "took the bichloride treatment merely as an experiment. No desire for sobriety prompted him to seek relief from alcoholic craving." An accompanying letter from the director of the clinic noted, a little unnecessarily, that "Milne seems to have had no wish to be cured, thinking that all the pleasure he had in life was gotten while under the influence of liquor and believing that he could have more pleasure in the future drunk than sober." Not even Bierce could improve on that description.[7]

Hearst as an employer was notably forgiving, a trait that Bierce, for one, neither exhibited nor understood. "Never just, Mr. Hearst is always generous," Bierce recalled. "He is not swift to redress a grievance of one of his employees against another, but he is likely to give the complainant a cottage, a steam launch, or a roll of bank notes. As to discharging anybody for inefficiency or dishonesty—no, indeed, not so long as there is a higher place for him. His notion of removal is promotion." Bierce once looked on in wonder as Hearst retained an editor who had been caught with his hand in the till. "Oh, that's all right," Hearst airily explained. "I have a new understanding with him. He is to steal only small sums hereafter; the larger ones are to come to me." It was not unusual for one Hearst employee to fire another, only to have the dismissed party storm into the publisher's office and adamantly refuse to be fired, in which case Hearst would simply shrug, lose interest, and keep both men on the payroll. It was not so much that Hearst was a weakling—he had an iron will about things that mattered to him—but, rather, that he knew he had an excellent staff and was willing to overlook personal foibles in the furtherance of his larger design.[8]

Hearst and Bierce had a complex relationship—where Bierce was concerned, who did not? The publisher seems to have genuinely liked Bierce; certainly he respected his writing ability. On more than one occasion, Hearst personally lured him back into the fold after the columnist had angrily resigned over some real or imagined slight. He wound up paying Bierce one hundred dollars a week, not a bad salary for one column of work, and the *Examiner* also published a number of Bierce's groundbreaking short stories. Bierce, for his part, heatedly defended Hearst against charges that the publisher told him what to write or in any way interfered with the subject or contents of Bierce's columns, even when those columns were diametrically opposed to an *Examiner* position. Still, Bierce never warmed to his oddly distant employer, whose somewhat radical political views he considered those of "a mischievous demagogue." Under Hearst, the *Examiner* was consistently prolabor, to the point of running a regular workingman's column and defending rioting strikers in the various labor troubles of the 1890s. Such views, of course, were anathema to Bierce; he worked one side of the street and Hearst worked the other. "If asked to justify my long service to journals with whose policies I was not in agreement and whose character I loathed," Bierce wrote many years later, "I should confess that possibly the easy nature of the service had something to do with it. As to the point of honor . . . I, O well, I persuaded myself that I could do more good by addressing those who had greatest need of me—the millions of readers to whom Mr. Hearst was a misleading light."[9]

A congenital outsider himself, Bierce could see a similar trait in Hearst's character. "With many amiable and alluring qualities, among which is or used to be a personal modesty amounting to bashfulness, the man has not a friend in the world," wrote Bierce. "Nor does he merit one, for either con-genitally or by induced perversity, he is inaccessible to the conception of an unselfish attachment or a disinterested motive. Silent and smiling, he moves among men, the loneliest man. Nobody but God loves him and he knows it; and God's love he values only in so far as he fancies that it may promote his amusing ambition to darken the doors of the White House. As to that, I think that he would be about the kind of President that the country—daft with democracy and sick with sin—is beginning to deserve." Take away the modesty and the political ambition, and that is not a bad description of Bierce himself.[10]

In the *Examiner,* Bierce's column was largely unchanged from its previous incarnations in the *Argonaut* and the *Wasp.* A typical column, appearing reg-ularly in the Sunday edition of the newspaper, contained about eight hun-dred words divided into a dozen paragraphs on a similar number of topics. The essential targets remained the same: politicians, ministers, journalists, feminists ("Them Loud," he called them), bureaucrats, businessmen, and amateur writers. "Have you tried hanging?" he asked one would-be poet who approached him for advice. "If so, and if nobody will shoot you, or if you have no wish to be dead, you may try sending your poetry to me for review in these columns. That will not stop the poetry but it will cure you—of the reluctance to be dead." Another Bay Area poet, writing under the nom de plume Berenice, earned a backhanded compliment for her "singular fluency," which Bierce likened to "the ripple of a rill of bedroom furniture flowing down a staircase." A third poet's verse was as "rhythmic as the throb and gur-gle of a roadside pump replenishing a horse-trough." Bierce almost got the newspaper slapped with a libel suit by California vintner Arpad Haraszthy when he reported: "The wine of Arpad Haraszthy has a bouquet all its own. It tickles and titillates the palate. It gurgles as it slips down the alimentary canal. It warms the cockles of the heart, and it burns the sensitive lining of the stomach." When the outraged winemaker threatened to sue unless the *Examiner* printed a retraction, Bierce obligingly responded: "The wine of Arpad Haraszthy does not have a bouquet all its own. It does not tickle and titillate the palate. It does not gurgle as it slips down the alimentary canal. It does not warm the cockles of the heart, and it does not burn the sensitive lin-ing of the stomach."[11]

Politicians, great and small, fared little better. When President Benjamin Harrison—yet another former Union general—toured the West in May 1891, Bierce complained that the tour had all the earmarks of a "royal progress," with the public evincing "the same abasement of the Many before the One." Harrison, he said, was "going about the country in gorgeous state, shining and dining and swining—unsouling himself of clotted nonsense in pickled platitudes calculated for the meridian of Coon Hollow, Indiana." He marveled at the country's continued faith in the political system. "You can effect a change of robbers every four years," he wrote. "Inestimable privilege to pull off the glutted leech and attach the lean one! And you cannot even choose among the lean leeches, but must accept those designated by the programmers and showmen who have the reptiles on tap." As for himself, "My allegiance to republican institutions is slack through lack of faith in them as a practical system of governing men." He had retained his political hopes, he said, until he was thirty-five—"True, Benjamin Harrison had not in that time been elected to the Presidency." Even George Washington, the "Father of Our Country," came in for a drubbing. Washington, said Bierce, "was a fairly honest man of third-rate ability, a tolerably efficient soldier, a better politician, intelligently appreciative of the opposite sex, diligent and painstaking in profanity, a high-stepping aristocrat" who had now been transformed into a mythic national figure and "an unspeakable bore." Christopher Columbus, putative discoverer of the country, was an unlearned pirate and adventurer whose accidental discovery of America was the unexpected result of pure greed. "Had the Italian failed to cross the Atlantic," wrote Bierce, "the gods would have missed the elevating spectacle of an entire people prostrate before the blood-beslubbered image of a litany of lies." Closer to home, California senator James Frye was "that incarnate lachrymosity and slavering sentimentaler," while a San Francisco police official was "this hardy and impenitent malefactor—this money-changer in the temple of justice—this infinite rogue and unthinkable villain of whose service Satan is ashamed and, blushing blackly, deepens the gloom of hell."[12]

The entire country, for that matter, was going to hell, and Bierce for one was not sorry to see it go. "The fruits of the people's rule have been Dead Sea fruits," he observed, "turning to ashes and bitterness upon the lips of our political hope. Our country is the home of political heresy, the paradise of robbers and the hell of true men." The American people—"this assorted and unsifted rubbish dump—carted upon what was once a sufferable vacant lot"—had become "a nation of blockheads and scoundrels. I favor war, famine, pestilence—anything that will stop the people from cheating and confine that practice to contractors and statesmen." Bierce himself "once had the indiscretion—pardonable in youth—to fight four years and incur a smashed head in an attempt to preserve this country's institutions. Today—the smashed head cooled a trifle by the snows of age—I am of the conviction that the country's institutions ought not to be preserved, and that the slaves were not fit to be freed."[13]

Given Bierce's well-known political views, it came as a surprise when a delegation of San Francisco worthies visited him at Auburn in the spring of 1888 and asked him to write a special poem commemorating the Fourth of July. Perhaps equally surprising, he agreed. Bierce worked hard on the poem, writing and rewriting its twenty-eight stanzas and reading them aloud to the publisher of the Auburn newspaper for discussion. The 112-line poem was declaimed by local actor George Osbourne at a mass gathering on the night of July 4 at the San Francisco Opera House and was republished in the *Examiner* the next day with an introductory note probably furnished by Bierce himself: "The poem is not one of the made to order kind. It is not perfunctorily written up to the occasion. It is appropriate, but not with the ephemeral appropriateness that loses its flavor when immediate occasion is past." In fact, its flavor was altogether more acrid than the typical Fourth of July outpouring, which was not surprising, coming as it did from a writer who would observe of the same holiday two years later: "It is not desirable that political independence should be celebrated, world without end, by showing that its most conspicuous product is a national conceit invulnerable to derision and invincible to sense." A characteristic passage reads:

> *But when (O distant be the time!)*
> *Majorities in passion draw*
> *Insurgent swords to murder Law,*
> *And all the land is red with crime;*
>
> *Or—nearer menace!—when the band*
> *Of feeble spirits cringe and plead*
> *To the gigantic strength of Greed,*
> *And fawn upon his iron hand;—*
>
> *Nay, when the steps to state are worn*
> *In hollows by the feet of thieves,*
> *And Mammon sits among the sheaves*
> *And chuckles while the reapers mourn:*
>
> *Then stay thy miracle!—replace*
> *The broken throne, repair the chain,*
> *Restore the interrupted reign*
> *And veil again thy patient face.*

Despite its somewhat grudging patriotism, the poem was considered a great success, and Bierce, ever the frustrated poet, basked in his seasonal acclaim.[14]

Less successful, in fact disastrous, was his family life. On one visit home in the spring of that year, Bierce and his son Day argued bitterly about the young man's desire to quit school and become, like his father, a newspaperman. Most men would have been flattered by their son's obvious desire to imitate them, a desire given added poignancy by the fact that Bierce was so seldom home to notice or encourage his children in anything they did. But in light of Bierce's jaundiced view of the journalistic profession and his lifelong sensitivity to his own lack of schooling, it was inevitable that he would disapprove of the scheme. At fifteen, he said, Day was too young to strike out on his own. Voices were raised, Mollie burst into tears, and the intensely proud young man—his father's son if there ever was one—stormed out of the room. A few weeks later—by now Bierce was gone again—Day ran away from home and found work on the Red Bluff *Sentinel,* a hundred miles north of St. Helena. Mollie urged her husband to go to Red Bluff and bring him back, but Bierce refused, apparently thinking that a few weeks on his own might do the boy some good. (Perhaps, too, he was more gratified by Day's prideful act of emulation than he would openly admit.) The weeks turned into months, and still Bierce declined to contact his son. Concerned, Mollie sent Day some money, but the youth disdainfully returned it with a bitter letter.[15]

Bierce, back at his haunt on Howell Mountain, did not let Day's absence affect his work. He was, in fact, on fire creatively. After a quarter of a century as a professional journalist, during which time, with the notable exception of his 1881 reminiscence "What I Saw of Shiloh," he had written very little about the Civil War, Bierce now found himself obsessed with the subject. A trio of events in 1887 may have reawakened his slumbering interest in the war. The first, in mid-January, was the sudden, unexpected death of his wartime friend and mentor William Hazen. Only fifty-six, Hazen had contracted a cold while attending a reception hosted by President Grover Cleveland at the White House. Three days later, he was dead. Despite time and distance, Bierce and Hazen had kept in touch in the two decades since their parting at the Presidio in 1867. Bierce had been particularly moved by Hazen's mention of him in his *Narrative of Military Service* in 1885: "Bierce, a brave and gallant fellow . . . is now well known in California for rare literary abilities." The second Civil War–related event was an invitation that August to attend the Ninth Indiana's regimental reunion at Delphi, Indiana. He declined, but sent a gracious note to former sergeant Abe Dils declaring that "it would give me great pleasure to meet the members of the Old Ninth, for some of whom I entertain the tenderest regard, and I hope to be able to do so some day." He noted with pleasure a complimentary mention in the regimental history of his brave, if unsuccessful, attempt to rescue Cpl. Dyson Boothroyd during the 1861 Battle of Laurel Hill, adding that he hoped Dils would correct the erroneous spelling of his name—"Bruce"—in subsequent editions. "I recollect you with special kindness as a good soldier and a good fellow," he wrote.[16]

Later that autumn, Bierce weighed in with an opinion concerning the controversial proposal by Secretary of War William Endicott to return captured Confederate battle flags to the individual southern states. The seemingly innocuous suggestion touched off a firestorm of protest from northern veterans and newspapers. The New York *Tribune* headlined one editorial "The Old Slave Whip Cracking Again." Lucius Fairchild, national commander of the Grand Army of the Republic, vented a public malediction: "May God palsy the hand that wrote that order, the brain that conceived it, and the tongue that dictated it." Bierce, who was never vindictive toward former Confederates, advised in verse: "Give back the foolish flags whose bearers fell,/Too valiant to forsake them./Is it presumptuous, this counsel? Well,/I helped to take them."[17]

With the war again fresh in his mind, Bierce imaginatively reenlisted. Writing by candlelight from midnight to dawn at his camp on Howell Mountain, the skull of a dead friend—William Rulofson? Thomas Harcourt? the English poet Richard Realf?—at his elbow, Bierce began a remarkable three-year stretch of creative endeavor, one that, within the limits of its author's narrow but not inconsiderable talents, has seldom been surpassed in American literature. From the first story he wrote during this spurt, "One of the Missing," in March 1888, to the last, "The Death of Halpin Frayser," in December 1891, Bierce skillfully switched back and forth between rigidly controlled war stories and macabre, otherworldly ghost stories. The regular venue for his work, the Sunday supplement section of the *Examiner*, encouraged the outré and the shocking; nonfiction accounts of lurid murders, premature burials, unexplained disappearances, and sensational executions competed for space with eerie short stories by Arthur Conan Doyle, Guy de Maupassant, and other masters of the mystery writer's art. But Bierce was not writing merely formulaic stories for a particular market or readership. Like all good writers, he was looking inside himself for a compelling—and compulsive—theme. And what he found as his prevailing subject, one to which he returned again and again in both his war stories and his supernatural tales, was fear. The soldier's rational fear of violent death (and the scarcely less dominating fear of cowardice and disgrace) alternates in the stories with the civilian's irrational fear of the uncanny and the inexplicable. Often, in both worlds, the fear is self-created and self-fulfilling. The young lieutenant in "A Tough Tussle" who kills himself after a long night's struggle against the obsessional fear of a nearby corpse is echoed by the worldly intellectual in "The Man and the Snake" who dies of fright after catching sight of a stuffed snake under his bed. Both are victims of themselves. Their failure to master their fears (which both ironically are quite aware of having) undoes them as surely as an enemy bullet or a rattlesnake's fangs.[18]

Bierce himself was not afraid of death; he had faced it many times on Civil War battlefields without shirking his duty or shying away from a fight. It was not so much death he feared as it was—*pace*, FDR—fear itself. Like his spiritual descendant Ernest Hemingway a generation later, Bierce was a naturally brave man whose hypersensitive intelligence and morbid self-preoccupation consistently led him to question his own perfectly normal response to danger. For both men, the fear of cowardice seems to have been rooted in a less-than-satisfying relationship with their fathers, men who rightly or wrongly were perceived by their sons as being weak and cowardly. Hemingway's father, of course, is ruthlessly depicted in his son's fiction as a wife-dominated ditherer;

Bierce's father, to the extent that he is depicted at all, is usually seen as a distant authoritarian whose more forceful wife seems to have the upper hand in their relationship. Not incidentally, both Hemingway and Bierce detested their mothers, and the homophobic tone (explicit in Hemingway, less obvious in Bierce) may perhaps be traced to a lingering fear of female—that is, maternal—domination.

Implicit also in both men's work is a sense of impending doom. In *A Farewell to Arms,* Hemingway famously writes of an indifferent world that kills first the good, the gentle, and the brave, while getting around eventually to the rest of us. For Bierce, there is the sense of being "sentenced to life" in a world where "'Nature red in tooth and claw' has made an ambuscade for him." In December 1888, while in the midst of his creative spurt, Bierce referred back in an *Examiner* column to the spectacular explosion on the island of Krakatau five years earlier, which had killed an estimated 36,000 islanders. Noting "the fury and despair of a race hanging on to life by the tips of its fingers; doomed from birth all: in the tick of clock all gone, slaughtered to the last man," he ruefully concluded: "Let us be grateful that we live upon such an earth, hold our lives by so precarious a tenure, and have the good luck to pull through until picked off singly or in paltry thousands by the neighborly ministrations of malevolences less picturesque than the wreck of matter and the crush of worlds." It was all a function, he noted in another column, of "Chance itself . . . a malign and soulless Intelligence bestirring himself in earthly affairs with the brute unrest of Enceladus under his mountain." Such chance, akin to Hardy's "crass casualty," is not always actively hostile to mankind, but it never operates with goodwill toward men. It is, instead, "a brutal, blind design, like the unconscious malevolence of an idiot."[19]

By the time these words were written (August 31, 1890), Bierce had good reason to believe that there was indeed a malevolent spirit ruling his world. Twin tragedies, one of his doing and the other not, had struck his precariously maintained equilibrium. The first, in the winter of 1888–1889, was the breakup of his marriage to Mollie. The two had been on increasingly poor terms for some time, at least since the failure of Bierce's gold-mining scheme a decade earlier, and his erratic comings and goings had further widened the gap between them. Mollie was still comparatively young and attractive, and if her husband did not value her charms, others apparently did. The cause of the final break, according to their daughter, Helen, who was thirteen at the time, was Bierce's accidental discovery of some love letters written to Mollie by a mysterious "Danish gentleman" who was summering at St. Helena. Bierce later alluded to the incident in his poem "Oneiromancy":

> *I fell asleep and dreamed that I*
> *Was flung, like Vulcan, from the sky;*

> *Like him, was lamed—another part:*
> *His leg was crippled, and my heart.*
> *I woke in time to see my love*
> *Conceal a letter in her glove.*[20]

According to Helen, "There was a big scene when he found the Dane's letter and after that he packed his things and left, never to return. Mother was broken-hearted. She did not see the other man again, and she swore to me that it had not been a real romance, but Father would not listen—it was enough that she had permitted some love-letters to be written to her." Infuriated by the deception, Bierce left Howell Mountain and moved to Sunol, where he adamantly refused to communicate with Mollie. "I don't take part in competitions—not even in love," he told a mutual friend. The flirtation apparently was innocent enough, although even Helen had to admit that "Mother was really rather charmed by this stranger. It was a decorous and discreet fascination, but—she had certainly not sent him back to Denmark up to the time Father found the letter." Still, it is difficult, at this remove, to be too hard on Mollie for her actions. Bierce's continued absences, to say nothing of his running comments on the unsatisfactory nature of marriage— "Marriage is like an electric thrilling-machine: it makes you dance, but you can't let go" was one characteristic observation at the time—would have driven away most women years ago. Instead, it was Bierce who left. His cold, inflexible dismissal of his loyal wife of seventeen years was typical of his judgmental streak. Yet the suspicion lingers that he was looking for a convenient excuse to kill his marriage, which had never brought him much satisfaction in the best of times. Mollie's hidden letters gave him that option.[21]

Still worse was to come a few months later. Day Bierce, not yet seventeen, had gotten himself into a jam over a girl. Neither of his parents knew anything about it; indeed, they may not have known where he was living at the time. In April 1889, Day met a girl his own age named Eva Atkins at a lodge picnic in neighboring Chico and impulsively quit his job with the Red Bluff *Sentinel* to be close to her. Day, like his father, was proud and touchy; he also carried a gun on his hip. The object of his affections, the voluptuous Miss Atkins, was an uneducated cannery worker whose twice-married mother ran a boardinghouse in Chico. Day moved into the house and began keeping such close tabs on Eva that when she took a job as a maid at a local hotel, he hung around the premises to make sure she was not speaking to the guests. As it turned out, his suspicions were well founded. In a story so banal his father would have laughed it off the page, Day's girl, Eva, ran off with his best friend, Neil Hubbs. Not only that, but the pair eloped two days before Day and Eva were due to be married. The local press had a field day with the story. The Chico *Enterprise* headlined its account: WITH A HANDSOMER MAN! COURSE OF TRUE LOVE RUNS AMUCK, and added insult to injury by identifying Day as "the son of the famous satirical writer on the San Francisco *Examiner.*"[22]

Four days later, the newlyweds returned to Chico and immediately called on Eva's mother. Day, described after the fact as "a hot headed young man, quick to resent an insult or a fancied wrong," was upstairs lying down when the couple arrived. He quickly went downstairs and, according to the new Mrs. Hobbs, greeted them with, "You are a damn fine pair, ain't you?" This sounds more like a cannery girl speaking than the son of a fanatically precise writer who hated slang and improper diction, but whatever his actual words, Day went back to his room and returned a moment later with his pistol. Hubbs, who was probably expecting a less-than-cordial welcome from his erstwhile friend, had in the meantime drawn his own gun, and the two young men opened fire on each other across the living room. Day, unhit, struck Hubbs in the stomach with his first shot, then wheeled and fired at Eva, crying, "Now I'll finish you!" His next bullet passed through the girl's ear and grazed her skull. Hubbs, although mortally wounded, managed to wrestle the gun away from Day and bash him on the head with it. "My God, Neil, what have I done?" Day is supposed to have cried, apparently returned to reason instantaneously by the blow to his head. "Just put a cartridge in your revolver and kill me—I'm not fit to live." Again, the wording sounds wrong. Unless Hubbs normally went around with only one bullet in his gun, he should have had plenty of ammunition left to oblige his suddenly conscience-stricken friend. At any rate, Hubbs was preoccupied just then with getting his wife to a doctor. Day, according to the *Examiner,* "crawled into the bedroom, got on the bed, put another cartridge into his pistol, laid a cloth saturated with chloroform over his face, then placing the pistol to his right temple, fired it, blowing his brains out over the counterpane."[23]

The two young men lingered through the night before dying a few hours apart on July 27, 1889. Bierce, reached at Sunol with the awful news, wired back, "I will come tomorrow." He arrived in Chico "sadly broken by his son's terrible actions," the ubiquitous *Enterprise* noted, and arranged to take his son's body back to St. Helena for burial. At the local undertaker's, he looked down at the boy's lifeless form and supposedly murmured, "You are a noble soul, Day. You did just right." This was an odd thing for a father to say, if indeed he said it. So much of the sordid little story is second- or third-hand (Bierce never spoke of it to anyone) that through the years the particulars have gotten hopelessly scrambled. The only inarguable facts are that two young men, formerly the best of friends, died in a gunfight over a teenage girl, and one of them was Ambrose Bierce's elder son, a youth of such promise that great things were universally expected of him, and not just by his father. As for the widow Mrs. Hubbs, she reportedly went down to the train station to watch the caskets of her husband and her ex-fiancé depart on separate trains, in opposite directions. "Now ain't that queer?" she is said to have told a local reporter. "One goes one way and one goes another, but here I am!"[24]

Bierce, of course, was devastated. Yet even in the depths of his grief he could not bring himself to reconcile with his wife. The two had a brief private conversation at Mollie's home immediately following Day's funeral, and Mollie later told friends that she realized then that no further reconciliation was possible. Except for a momentary chance meeting a few years later, it was the last time the couple would ever see each other. Alone, Bierce retreated to the Sunol Glen Hotel, where he had another recurrence, undoubtedly stress-related, of asthma. For several weeks, he was virtually speechless with grief, stoically answering all expressions of sympathy with the same curt phrase: "Nothing matters." He carried around Day's ivory-handled revolver, and probably gave some thought to putting it to similar use himself, before finally giving it to a friend, Amy Cecil, to toss overboard on her voyage to Japan. He could no more throw it away than he could forget about it, he said. It took a brutal low blow from his archenemy Fred Pixley to rouse him, at least partly, from his paralyzing grief.[25]

On August 5, in the *Argonaut,* Pixley seized the opportunity to give Bierce a swift, hard kick while he was down. Even by Pixley's standards, it was astonishingly mean. "If it be true, as alleged, that the jibes and jeers of the local press so worked upon the *weak* mind of a young man, maddened by passion and crazed by jealousy over an *unworthy* woman, that he should have resorted to murder and suicide to terminate his unpleasant and ridiculous predicament, may not the incident teach a *moral lesson* to those writers who indulge in such cruel and inhuman satire?" wrote Pixley. "May not the death of the younger Bierce teach the older man, his father, how sinister have been the bitter, heartless, and unprovoked assaults which he has spent his life in cultivating that he might the more cruelly wound his fellow-men? Might not a life, now growing nearly to its close, have been passed more profitably to humanity, more happily to himself, than in indulgence in the practiced use of a pen more cruel than the most destructive and death-dealing of swords? Does there not rest upon his father the shadow of a haunting fear lest inheritance have resulted in *crime* and death, while he was cultivating the gift of wounding natures just as sensitive and tender, who had not the courage to end them in murder and self-destruction, but were driven to hide their sorrows in secret? Perhaps this man with the burning pen will recall the names of those he has held up to ridicule and shame; the men and women whom he has tortured and humiliated; perhaps he will analyze the *moral code* which has governed him, and review the relations he has held toward men of whom he might at least have remembered that gratitude was something other than merchandise and payable as a debt."[26]

There was more, including Pixley's unctuous protestation that he was a "sincere admirer" of Bierce, but that gives the gist of the attack. It took Bierce three weeks to work up the energy to respond, and then it was a comparatively lukewarm retort. "You disclosed considerable forethought, Mr. Pixley, in improving the occasion to ask for lenity, but I see nothing in the situation to encourage your hope," Bierce wrote. "You and your kind will have to cultivate fortitude in the future, as in the past; for assuredly I love you as little as ever. Perhaps it is because I am a trifle dazed that I can discern no connection between my mischance and your solemn 'Why persecutest thou me?' You must permit me to think the question incompetent and immaterial—the mere trick of a passing rascal swift to steal advantage from opportunity. Your *ex post facto* impersonification of *The Great Light* is an ineffective performance: it is only in your own undisguised character of sycophant and slanderer for hire that you shine above."[27]

Admitting that he was "a trifle dazed" was as far as Bierce would go in revealing his grief. He probably did wonder, as Pixley suggests, whether he had contributed to the death of the son he now spoke of as "another Chatterton." He had been no better a father to his own children than his father had been to him; if he spared them both the rod and the religion, he also deprived them of a parent's greatest gift: his time. What consolation he could find for his sorrows came, as he later advised another grieving parent to do, from reading Epictetus. "Never say of anything, 'I lost it,' but say, 'I gave it back,'" the philosopher instructs. "Has your child died? It was given back. Has your wife died? She was given back. Has your estate been taken from you? Was not this also given back? But you say, 'He who took it from me is wicked.' What does it matter to you through whom the Giver asked it back? As long as He gives it to you, take care of it, but not as your own; treat it as passers-by treat an inn." In time, Bierce would devise his own epigram: "To parents only, death brings an inconsolable sorrow. When the young die and the old live, nature's machinery is working with the friction that we name grief."[28]

Slowly, Bierce went back to work. He was still, he advised *Examiner* readers in September 1889, "a chap whose trade is censure; fools are his theme and satire is his song." Not surprisingly, given the events of the past few months, the perfidy of women was a favorite topic. "You shall not know a girl well enough to remember the color of her hair but she will one day flaunt upon her lodge-pole a deftly executed facsimile of your scalp," he warned in his October 13 column. "Never have I known a female antagonist who did not lie and cheat with as little concern as a pig with a mouthful of young larks." One week later, he published his first short story since the Chico tragedy, "The Affair at Coulter's Notch." It is a curiously ambiguous story, containing echoes of several other Bierce stories. The plot concerns a Union artillery officer, Captain Coulter, who has left his native South to fight for the North. Returning to the region of his home, apparently western Virginia, Coulter is ordered one day by his new commanding general to engage in a seemingly suicidal artillery duel with a dozen enemy cannons that have been left behind to guard the mountain pass through which the Confederates are retreating. The rebel guns are within clear range of Union infantry marksmen, but for some reason the general refuses to let the infantry fire on them; he wants Coulter to set up a cannon in the "notch" between the passes and fight the enemy by himself. The colonel who transmits the puzzling order objects, pointing out that there is only room for one Union gun in the notch. "That is true—for only one at a time," says the general. "But then, your brave Coulter—a whole battery in himself." The colonel is also puzzled by Coulter's seeming reluctance to obey the order: He had always thought the young man an exceptionally brave officer.[29]

At length, Coulter does obey, and the resulting artillery duel leaves several Union gunners killed, as well as a similar number of Confederates who had placed their guns in the vicinity of a large mansion. The colonel eventually learns from his adjutant the reason for the general's baffling order. The year before, the general had commanded a division that camped for several weeks near Coulter's home. Some sort of trouble between the general and Coulter's wife—"a good wife and a high-bred lady"—had resulted in a complaint to headquarters and the general being transferred to a different division. Unbeknownst to the colonel, Coulter had been ordered to fire on his own home. That night, the colonel finds Coulter, now "a fiend seven times damned," sitting dazedly in the ruined basement of his mansion, clutching the bodies of his dead wife and child, who had been killed by his own shells.[30]

The story, while not one of Bierce's best, has great psychological resonance. By writing, especially now, a tale in which a man kills his own wife and child, Bierce is echoing his own recent losses. Coulter's wife, like Mollie, has apparently been the recipient of another man's advances; the story pointedly fails to say whether they were welcomed or rebuffed. The word *Affair* in the title would seem to give a clue to the wife's actions, at least in the husband's (and Bierce's) mind; in a similar story, "An Affair of Outposts," the officer's wife had an extramarital affair with the governor. At the same time, the general's vengefulness seems to suggest either that he had been rebuffed by Mrs. Coulter or else that their affair had ended badly. Either way, the incident results in the literal destruction of Coulter's home and family, in much the same way that Mollie Bierce's innocent flirtation, and her husband's reaction to it, ruined their marriage. The death of the child can also be read, in a way, as a slant comment on Day Bierce's death. Since the father is demonstrably the cause of the infant's death in the story, it would seem to indicate a certain unresolved sense of guilt on Bierce's part over the tragedy. In such stories as "The Mocking-Bird" and "A Horseman in the Sky," soldiers kill their brothers or fathers, and in "One Kind of Officer" a callous Union artillery commander kills his own men, but "The Affair at Coulter's Notch" is the first time that Bierce depicts a soldier killing his wife and children. When the desolate young captain admits at the end of the story, "I am Captain Coulter," he might almost be speaking for Bierce himself.

The publication of Leo Tolstoy's controversial novel, *The Kreutzer Sonata,* that same year gave Bierce another opportunity to comment obliquely on his failed marriage. The book, which was briefly banned in the United States, concerns a Russian nobleman who marries a younger woman at the age of thirty after having led "the well-regulated and reasonable life of a bachelor." He soon grows tired of his wife, a weariness that coalesces into hatred, and finally kills her after she falls in love with a dashing musician. The parallels to Bierce's own marriage are obvious, and it is undoubtedly for that reason that he was so taken with the book. For all his literary fulminations, Bierce did very little book reviewing, and his review of the Tolstoy novel is almost embarrassingly naked in its ill-disguised rage. He begins by noting that "criticism is an erring guide. Its pronouncements are more interesting than valuable, and interesting chiefly from the insight that they give into the mind, not of the writer criticized, but of the writer criticizing." His capsule plot description is particularly revealing: "A man marries a woman. They quarrel of course; their life is of course wretched beyond the power of words to express. Jealousy naturally ensuing, the man murders the woman." He praises Tolstoy for having "had the courage to utter a truth of so supreme importance that one-half the civilized world has for centuries been engaged in a successful conspiracy to conceal it from the other half—the truth that the modern experiment of monogamic marriage by the dominant tribes of Europe and America is a dismal failure."[31]

The Kreutzer Sonata, says Bierce, should be read most urgently by young girls, who would learn from it the bitter truth "that marriage, like wealth, offers no hope of lasting happiness. Despite the implication that 'they lived happily ever after,' it is not for nothing that the conventional love story ends with the chime of wedding bells." As for married couples, "They are all members of a dishonest conspiracy. They conceal their wounds and swear that all is right and well with them. They give their Hell a good character, but in their secret souls they chafe and groan under the weight and heat of their chains. They come out from among their corruption and dead men's bones only to give the sepulchre another coating of whitewash and call attention to its manifold advantages as a dwelling." Marriage, he concludes, is an institution which has become "most monstrously wrenched awry to the service of evil."[32]

A man who sees marriage as a living hell inhabited by stinking zombies is not necessarily someone who has come to terms with his own newly altered condition. A vivid picture of Bierce at the time comes down to us from the novelist Gertrude Atherton, who made a memorable visit to Sunol to see him in January 1891. Atherton, a much-traveled thirty-four-year-old widow, had taken it upon herself to contact Bierce after she returned to San Francisco the previous fall. He agreed to see her after she praised his short story "A Watcher by the Dead," saying it had kept her awake for a week and made her afraid to sleep alone. The story, one of Bierce's better ventures into the macabre, concerns a practical joke gone disastrously awry. Three friends, two of them doctors, wager among themselves whether or not someone can successfully spend a full night alone with a corpse in a locked room "without going altogether mad." The test is arranged, and one of the men agrees to impersonate the corpse—without the knowledge of the man being locked in the room. The "corpse" decides to play a trick on the watcher by sneaking up on the man in the dark. The joke works too well—the man dies of fright, and the prankster, his hair turned white with shock, goes mad. He exchanges places with the dead man and escapes in the confusion, but both his life and those of the two doctors (who become itinerant gamblers after the incident) are ruined. Once more fear plays a major role. Without pressing the point, it might be said that the story is yet another echo of Day Bierce's death. The man locked inside a darkened room with a corpse may serve to stand for Bierce himself, who told an acquaintance after his son's death, "I am just beginning to forget for a moment, and then the memory rushes back worse than ever." Like the man in the story, he, too, has sat up with the dead, but in the real world the dead do not come back to life, even for a joke.[33]

Atherton arrived, as planned, at 8:30 in the morning and was met at the station by Bierce. He was, she said, "a tall man, very thin and closely knit, with curly iron gray hair, a bristling moustache, beetling brows over frowning eyes, good features and beautiful hands." Wearing "a very becoming blue frock," the attractive, somewhat plump-faced widow joined Bierce for lunch in his hotel room. Making a third was Sam Chamberlain, "Sam the Drunken," managing editor of the *Examiner*. After lunch, Chamberlain— "an easy and brilliant talker"—suavely withdrew, and Bierce rather unsubtly led Atherton into his bedroom. Noting that he had been ill again with asthma, Bierce reclined on the bed while Atherton took the only chair in the room. What followed was not what Bierce apparently had planned, a smooth seduction of a willing victim, but a battle of wits with a sharp-tongued, self-confident, and decidedly self-centered young woman who did not take a step back when Bierce told her bluntly that she had done nothing worthy of serious consideration. His own stories, she retorted, "might be models of craftsmanship and style," but they were "so devoid of humanity that they fell short of true art, and would never make any but a limited appeal." Bierce answered back that novels such as hers were a waste of time anyway, since "the only form in which the perfection of art could be achieved as well as the effect of totality, was that of the short story." This was a view he had expressed many times in his column, but Atherton, who had been away from San Francisco for several years, apparently took it as a personal slam—which perhaps it was. She flared, saying that the only reason Bierce disliked novels was that he was incapable of writing one himself. "All short-story writers are jealous of novelists," she insisted grandly. "They all try to write novels and few of them succeed. Any clever cultivated mind, with a modicum of talent, can manage the short story, even with no authentic gift for fiction—as you yourself have proved."[34]

This last riposte struck deep, and Atherton sought to lessen the hurt by praising Bierce as a great man. The change of tactics did not work. "He almost flew at me," she recalled. "He was not great. He wouldn't be called great. He was a failure, a mere hack. He got so red I feared he would have an attack of asthma. He gave me some twenty reasons why he wasn't great, but I have forgotten all of them." The pair continued sniping at each other until it was time for Atherton to catch the train home. Then (according to her), Bierce walked her down to the station and "in the shadows between the station and the malodorous grunting pigsty . . . he suddenly seized me in his arms and tried to kiss me. In a flash I knew how to hurt him. Not by struggling and calling him names. I threw back my head—well out of his reach—and laughed gayly. 'The great Bierce!' I cried. 'Master of style! The god on Olympus at whose feet pilgrims come to worship—trying to kiss a woman by a pigsty.'" Bierce immediately desisted and helped her onto the train. "I never want to see you again!" he told her. "You're the most detestable little vixen I ever met in my life, and I've had a horrible day."[35]

Atherton frequently repeated the story of Bierce's clumsy seduction attempt, always putting herself in the best light, and never bothered to explain why Bierce had not lifted a finger to molest her when he had her alone in his hotel room, only clutched at her like a bumptious schoolboy as soon as they were back in public. By her own admission, and the evidence of her now largely unread books, she was a flirtatious, adventuresome young woman who was used to treating men dismissively. Perhaps Bierce misread her signals, which were certainly mixed; or perhaps he was simply leaning forward to give her a fond, somewhat fatherly kiss. Or perhaps it never happened at all. Such a brutal rejection would have mortally wounded men far less sensitive than Bierce, particularly in his current vulnerable state. Yet Bierce kept in touch with Atherton for nearly two decades after that inauspicious parting, loyally praising her work and regularly offering professional advice. He also helped her get a job on the *Examiner*, where her column, "Woman in Her Variety," ran briefly in the fall of 1891. In it, she slavishly imitated the Bierce style, attacking marriage, plumping for divorce, and recommending that women trapped in a loveless union consider murder as a practical alternative—ground-up glass in hubby's wine, boiling lead, and a knitting needle thrust into his ear were highly recommended means of removal. As for the gentler sentiments, "May the devil fly away with charity," she wrote. "People incapable of taking care of themselves should out of pure Christian charity have their heads stuck in a barrel of chloroform." She was, it may be said, out-Heroding Herod, and William Randolph Hearst rapidly came to the judgment that he could stand one Ambrose Bierce on his newspaper, but not two. Mrs. Atherton soon left San Francisco for good.[36]

Other young writers, more worshipful in their attentions than Atherton, regularly visited Bierce at Sunol and Howell Mountain, to which he relocated in November 1891. Many were women, despite Bierce's continued hammering at their sex. It was one of his greatest inconsistencies that Bierce could write, with perfect aplomb, "Intellectually woman is as inferior to man as she is physically . . . [she] hasn't any thinker" and yet spend hours patiently reading and editing manuscripts brought to him by women. No doubt he was flattered by their attention, as they were by his, even when he observed that "women who write are destitute, not only of common sense, but of the sense of right and wrong—they are moral idiots." The list of his female disciples was long, if not particularly distinguished, beginning with the poet Ina Coolbrith's adopted niece, Ina Peterson, who saluted Bierce in unlikely celestial terms as "crowned with a halo radiant with stars." Bierce liked to intersperse his literary lectures with long walks in the woods, where, as he somewhat wolfishly remarked to another disciple, the poet George Sterling, "Sometimes I use up the scenery and sometimes I use up the girl." Given Sterling's own obsession with sexual conquest, this may have been merely a bit of locker room braggadocio, although another Bierce intimate, Adolph Danziger, later spoke of Bierce's "fenceless harem of feminine worshippers" who "adored him and came to bestow their affections upon him. When I looked at him with 'brown envious eyes,' as he phrased it, he grinned, as the fox did when the raven dropped the baby rabbit." The worshipers, said Danziger, included "grass widows and women married to poets—who, Bierce said, were sexless and their wives therefore free as air. There were gushing girls who had come to see the great man; there were women who wrote like men, and sometimes men who could not write at all but came with their pretty wives. When Bierce got bored he would lecture them so impressively that the poor creatures sobbed hysterically and blindly stumbled down the road to the omnibus."[37]

Bierce's ministrations—literary, at least—were not confined to women. Besides Sterling and Danziger, he advised and assisted such other neophyte writers as William C. Morrow, Herman Scheffauer, Edwin Markham, Carroll Carrington, Herman Whittaker, and Charles William Doyle. Of that list, only Markham achieved any real prominence as a writer, due mainly to his much-praised poem, "The Man with the Hoe," which became a national sensation after it appeared in the *Examiner* a few years later. The poem, based on the famous painting of the same title by Jean-François Millet, was once a staple of high school English classes, as much for its declamatory properties as its vaguely anarchistic message. Bierce despised the poem, and he said as much in a series of columns that effectively ended his friendship with

Markham. As poetry, Bierce charged, Markham's work was "stiff, inelastic, monotonous"; its politics were merely "the workworn threat of rising against the wicked well-to-do and taking it out of their hides. It has not the vitality of a sick fish." Those claiming that jealousy of Markham was Bierce's overriding motive in attacking the poem have missed the obvious: Bierce was right. "The Man with the Hoe" is prairie-populist cant, and no amount of Bierce bashing can change that fact. Nevertheless, one is forced to agree with another erstwhile protégé, Joseph Lewis French, who observed that Bierce "did not know when to stop and soothe with humanity the wounds his biting sarcasm made." Markham, a gentle sort of anarchist, never responded to Bierce's attacks, and he always spoke well of his former friend in public.[38]

But if Bierce could frequently be cruel to aspiring young writers—"You must have written that when you were a schoolgirl," he told one young man—he could also be surprisingly kind, as evidenced by his short-lived association with a deaf young woman named Lily Walsh. The twenty-three-year-old Walsh, a maid at a Santa Cruz hotel, was an informal charge of his friend Louise Hirshberg, whose husband ran a home for incorrigible boys (Bierce once advised Mr. Hirshberg that since none of the youths at the center would ever be cured of their criminal propensities, they should all be shipped off to a war somewhere and shot). Prompted no doubt by Mrs. Hirshberg, Walsh sent Bierce one of her poems. Something about the childish young woman touched his heart—she was the same age Day would have been—and he gently advised her to complete her education before attempting to become a poet. He then took the lead in getting her admitted to the Berkeley Institute for the Deaf, Dumb and Blind. Cruelly, Walsh had been there only one day when she was struck down by a fatal fever; she died two months later. Her family refused her last request to be buried near Bierce in the California foothills, but he paid for her headstone at St. Mary's Cemetery in Oakland and visited it regularly until the day he left California for good. "Not shock of Quaking Earth," Walsh had written of Bierce, "can move this friend of mine."[39]

Between visits from admirers and columns for the *Examiner,* Bierce continued working on his growing pile of stories. The great Civil War stories— "Chickamauga," "A Son of the Gods," "Killed at Resaca," "A Horseman in the Sky," "An Affair of Outposts," "One of the Missing"—alternated with such skin-crawling tales of the supernatural as "A Watcher by the Dead," "The Man and the Snake," "The Eyes of the Panther," and "The Suitable Surroundings." In mid-July 1890, he hit his peak with a story that masterfully combined the two genres, "An Occurrence at Owl Creek Bridge." More than any other work, this is the story for which Bierce is most remembered— and with good reason. "An Occurrence at Owl Creek Bridge" is, within its brilliantly controlled parameters, a perfect work of art. ("That story has everything. Nothing better exists," a young Stephen Crane gushed to a friend a few years later.) It is Bierce's most widely anthologized piece, appearing in virtually every college-level survey of American literature and numerous collections of great short stories. In 1963, a French screen version of the story won an Academy Award for best short film, and the film was later shown to millions of American viewers on the popular television series *The Twilight Zone*. Bierce may have surpassed the story in a few random passages here and there—the procession of wounded soldiers in "Chickamauga," the nighttime river crossing and the ravine of death in "What I Saw of Shiloh," the concluding paragraphs of "A Son of the Gods," the Faulkner-like drolleries of "Jupiter Doke, Brigadier-General"—but taken as a whole, "An Occurrence at Owl Creek Bridge" is Bierce at his best.[40]

The plot of the story is deceptively simple: a pro-Confederate civilian named Peyton Farquhar is about to be hanged from the railroad trestle over Owl Creek Bridge for attempted sabotage. Waiting wordlessly for the execution to take place, the condemned man feels his senses heighten preternaturally; the ticking of his pocket watch sounds like a blacksmith's thunderous anvil strokes. As the Union sergeant steps off the wooden plank on which Farquhar is standing, a flashback shows us how the "well-to-do planter" was tricked into attempting to burn the bridge by a disguised Union scout. (Farquhar's own highly romantic and unrealistic views of war contribute as well to his fatal decision.) The hanging takes place as planned, but the rope breaks, and Farquhar plunges to the bottom of Owl Creek, where he frees himself from his bonds and resurfaces with a shout. Desperately, he swims away as Union marksmen pepper the stream with rifle fire. He makes good his escape, emerging downstream into the thick woods alongside the creek, and eventually finds his way home, where his wife stands waiting for him on the steps of their veranda. He springs forward to embrace her, but then "he feels a stunning blow upon the back of the neck; a blinding white light blazes all about him with a sound like the shock of a cannon—then all is darkness and silence." The story concludes with one of the most famous sentences in American literature: "Peyton Farquhar was dead; his body, with a broken neck, swung gently from side to side beneath the timbers of the Owl Creek bridge." The escape had been an illusive dream.[41]

Careless readers (including, surprisingly, Cleanth Brooks and Robert Penn Warren, who no doubt disliked Bierce for being a former Union soldier) have misinterpreted the story as a bit of reverse O. Henry legerdemain. The so-called trick ending throws them off. A more careful reading of this most carefully written story reveals that the ending is no trick—except on the unfortunate and dull-witted Farquhar. Everywhere along the way, Bierce prepares the reader for the story's only possible conclusion. It is, after all, an *occurrence*—something that occurs—*at* Owl Creek Bridge—on or near the bridge, not downstream, miles away, at Farquhar's home. Given the circumstances, carefully spelled out in the precise militaristic language of the story's opening passage, the only event that could possibly have occurred that morn-ing at Owl Creek Bridge is a hanging. Moreover, in the frequently misread second section of the story, Farquhar is revealed to be just the sort of self-deluding fool who would most likely imagine such a preposterous escape. As a wealthy civilian who somehow had managed to avoid military service, probably through the "Twenty Negro Law" that exempted from active duty any slave owners with more than twenty slaves on their property, Farquhar had "chafed under the inglorious restraint, longing for the release of his ener-gies, the larger life of the soldier, the opportunity for distinction [t]hat he felt would come, as it comes to all in war time." It would come all right, but it would be the *it* of e. e. cummings's "Plato Told Him," the "nipponized bit of the old sixth avenue el in the top of his head," that teaches another obtuse war-lover the ultimate price of his naïve flirtation with war. The story, and Farquhar's story within a story, end with a jolt but not a surprise.[42]

Actually, "An Occurrence at Owl Creek Bridge" ends twice, and both times the same way. The third and final section of the story opens with a remarkably graphic and convincing account of Farquhar's death by hanging. "A sharp pressure upon his throat, followed by a sense of suffocation," is accompanied by "keen poignant agonies [that] seemed to shoot from his neck downward through every fibre of his body and limbs." These, in turn, are followed by "a feeling of fulness—of congestion" in his head, and a sense of motion as "he swung through unthinkable arcs of oscillation, like a vast pendulum." Finally, he feels himself shoot upward—the rope has reached its limit and he is being jerked upward again in reverse—with "a frightful roar-ing in his ears," until "all was cold and dark." At this point, Farquhar is dead and the story is over, but it is Bierce's brilliant achievement to show how a dying man might, in the split second of life remaining to him, mistake the sensation of falling, being strangled, and being yanked skyward again for a saving plunge into deep water. No one knows if death by hanging really mimics death by drowning (probably it does not), but the similarity of the two is beside the point: It is Farquhar's dream we are experiencing, and since he is being hanged from a bridge over water, it is only natural that he would imagine himself falling into the water to escape and that he would confuse the congestion of suffocation with the sensation of drowning.[43]

The rest of the story occurs not in real time but in the instant that Farquhar is dropping through space to the literal end of his rope. He is conscious of try-ing to free his hands, which anyone in his position would attempt to do, and his puzzling cry, "Put it back, put it back!" may indicate that he has freed one of his hands and that the Union captain is shouting at the guard to put the hand back behind him; or it might be his last, despairing wish that his execu-tioners put back the board they have just yanked out from under him. Again he experiences the sensation of hanging: "His neck ached horribly; his brain was on fire; his heart, which had been fluttering faintly, gave a great leap, trying to force itself out of his mouth. His whole body was racked and wrenched by insupportable anguish." His senses, however, are unnaturally sharp (one thinks inevitably of Dr. Johnson's remark about how the knowledge that one is about to be hanged wonderfully concentrates the mind). Impossible feats of hearing and seeing are combined with equally marvelous physical feats—"What magnificent, what superhuman strength"—as he frees himself and effects his escape. Several critics have pointed out that Farquhar's emergence from the water—first head, then shoulders, then chest, and finally an astonished cry as he gulps the air—mimics the act of being born (defined by Bierce as "the first and direst of all disasters"). One critic goes so far as to suggest that the cry "Put it back!" is simply the baby's Freudian wish to have its mother's umbilical cord reattached, in which case the hangman's rope is an ironic substitute, bringing death, not life, in its wake.[44]

Ongoing studies of near-death experiences have revealed a consistent pattern of similar sensations, of falling (or rising) through corridors of darkness toward a distant, finally all-encompassing light, which some have suggested are simply repressed memories of birth. And while Bierce could not have been exposed to such studies in his lifetime, it is significant that a "blinding white light" does blaze around Farquhar at the moment he hears "a sound like the shock of a cannon"—his own neck breaking. Since Bierce never described his own near-death experience at Kennesaw Mountain in 1864, it is impossible to say whether he was relying on personal knowledge in describing Farquhar's fate or was simply using the artist's creative prerogative. Certainly he used other personal experiences in writing the story: the real Owl Creek, which borders the battlefield at Shiloh; his regiment's railroad-guarding service in northern Alabama, which exactly corresponds to the time of the story; the hangings he witnessed as a soldier in the army and a reporter in San Francisco; even the miraculous "escape" from hanging that is the basic plot contrivance of the play *Ambrose Gwinett; or A Sea-Side Story.* The accretion of realistic details gives added weight to the unreal instant at the heart of the story. We believe it because, like Farquhar, we want to believe it.

In January 1892, Bierce published his first collection of short stories, under the title *Tales of Soldiers and Civilians* (an English edition was retitled *In the Midst of Life*). His friend E. L. G. Steele underwrote the publication, which Bierce for some reason said had been "denied existence by the chief publishing houses of this country." There is no evidence that he had ever attempted to place his book with an eastern publisher, and the puzzling prefatory note may simply have been the author's way of preempting questions about its self-publication. Whatever its provenance, the book enjoyed generally good reviews, with reviewers noting the power of the stories and the clean force of the writing. An exception was the British publication *Literature,* which called Bierce "the unfortunate victim of extravagant and uncritical laudation" and characterized the stories as "clever, violent, vigorous battle-notes heaped together between book covers." The New York *Sun,* a mortal enemy of Hearst's newspaper, carped that Bierce was "a scoffer and scorner [who] writes his tales of horror with a sort of fiendish delight." Bierce denied any fiendishness, replying, "I wrote my tales of horror without reference to the nerves, or even the existence, of the innocent, and in the belief that they are good and true art—a belief in which I have the obstinacy to remain." His old friend and colleague Arthur McEwen offered a bit of cogent marketing advice. Warning that the book might "fall as dead as a landed salmon," McEwen reasoned that "you haven't, in all you write, a trace of what we call sympathy. The pretty girl never arrives." "Darn the pretty girl," Bierce replied. "That's what is the matter with you," said McEwen. One might quibble with the charge that Bierce's stories lack sympathy; they are, in their way, enormously sympathetic, but it is the understated and unspoken sympathy of the modern stylist, not the breathy sentimentality of the Victorian. Besides, Bierce might have answered, such sentimental bosh is what got the soldiers in his stories into their deadly predicaments in the first place. It is not sympathy that Bierce is after, but clarity.[45]

Bierce followed *Tales of Soldiers and Civilians* a year later with a second collection of stories, *Can Such Things Be?* The new book, weighted more heavily toward the eerie and the supernatural, does not pack the punch that the first collection did, but there are still such minor masterpieces as "The Death of Halpin Frayser," "Moxon's Master," "A Jug of Sirup," "The Realm of the Unreal," "The Moonlit Road," "The Damned Thing," and "The Middle Toe of the Right Foot." This time, Bierce and Steele attempted to crack the New York market by arranging for Cassell and Company to publish the book, but the firm's manager absconded with the company's operating funds, and the book got off to a stumbling start. Compounding matters, Steele died that summer, leaving Bierce without a publisher on either coast. In the meantime, he had become embroiled in a public controversy with his friend and pupil Adolph Danziger over the rights to their joint production of *The Monk and the Hangman's Daughter,* a gothic tale that Danziger had translated from the original German story, "Der Monch von Berchtesgaden," by Richard Voss. Danziger, a Jewish jack-of-all-trades, had been a dentist, a lawyer, and a rabbi before deciding to become a writer. Somehow he convinced Bierce to rewrite *The Monk and the Hangman's Daughter* for serialization in the *Examiner.* The result was a curious, if not ridiculous, mixture of religio-sexual melodrama in which a Franciscan monk named Ambrosius (!) conceives an illicit passion for Benedicta, the hangman's beautiful daughter. After a crushingly tedious struggle for his soul, Ambrosius murders Benedicta to keep her from the sinful clutches of her noble suitor, Rochus. Ironically, it is revealed that the girl is really Rochus's half sister, as well as the fact that Benedicta actually had "cherished a secret and forbidden love" for Ambrosius. Like Captain Coulter, the monk has killed the one he loved.[46]

Bierce cannot be blamed for the absurd and overwrought plot, but why he consented to put his name on the work in the first place is a mystery. Perhaps it was simply an act of friendship; Danziger had assiduously courted Bierce's favor, shamelessly flattering him as "der master." Furthermore, he had convinced Bierce to loan him five hundred dollars for his fledgling Western Authors Publishing Company, which Danziger had conceived as a vanity press to publish the very sort of mediocre writers that Bierce had flayed unmercifully for two decades in his columns. In a bit of irony worthy of its victim, the only author ever published by the Western Authors Publishing Company was Bierce himself. In 1892, the company brought out *Black Beetles in Amber,* a collection of eminently forgettable satirical verse devoted almost entirely to such familiar targets as Frank Pixley, Leland Stanford, Denis Kearney, and dozens of other lesser-known San Franciscans whose myriad transgressions, despite Bierce's protestations to the contrary, have been lost to time. The book had a brief local success, mainly negative, with several of the unfortunate beetles buying up copies to keep them out of the public eye, or else skulking into lending libraries to tear out the pages on which Bierce had skewered them. On the whole, the book was a decided step backward for the author of *Tales of Soldiers and Civilians,* and there was a certain amount of rough justice to Arthur McEwen's published complaint that "he who had been for half a lifetime knocking over sparrows with an elephant rifle, when admitted to the elephant country appeared there with no better weapon than a paragraphic pop-gun." Another critic suggested the book be retitled *Red Peppers in Vinegar.* Meanwhile, a Chicago publisher, F. J. Schulte, brought out a six-thousand-book edition of *The Monk and the Hangman's Daughter,* but true to form where Bierce's publishers were concerned, it quickly went under without paying either Bierce or Danziger a cent. For the next two years, the erstwhile collaborators argued publicly over the literary and monetary rights to *The Monk and the Hangman's Daughter,* as well as the rights to *Black Beetles in Amber.* At length, tiring of the debate, Bierce broke a walking stick over Danziger's head and kept the pieces on his desk to remind him, he said, "of the nature of friendship."[47]

The public controversy with Danziger may have left Bierce open to the ringing charges of anti-Semitism that buffeted him following the suicide of the young Jewish poet David Lesser Lezinsky in early 1894. Like many of his ilk, Lezinsky had invited the columnist's lofty scorn with such inept verses as "Your greatness is a growing star/That shoots with comet's flame./Amid the crash of falling worlds/Will still be seen your name." This was no worse than many of the poems Bierce castigated in his column, and he was no more severe than usual in dealing with Lezinsky. Invoking a favorite fictitious poet, the pedestrian Mrs. Plunkett, Bierce accused the poet of plagiarizing her "famous 'Ode to a Dead Cow,'" adding, "I fancy he will write verses if he can catch another dead man to damn with his poetic fire. Well, it will make the poor fellow appreciative of Hades." Lezinsky partisans complained to Bierce about "the brutal attack which you made recently upon David Lezinsky . . . a rising young man of great genius," and they threatened him with a beating from the aforementioned genius. "I shall continue to deride until I experience the Lezinsky heavy hand," Bierce responded. It was all a typical Biercian controversy until Lezinsky abruptly committed suicide in the middle of the proceedings. According to Danziger, whose testimony must be taken with a large grain of salt, Bierce claimed he had expected as much, calling Lezinsky's suicide "the only decent thing he ever did."[48]

The not-inconsiderable ranks of Bierce haters, led by the poet Ina Coolbrith, who still bore a grudge against Bierce for supposedly attempting to lead her thirty-year-old niece astray, accused the columnist of moral complicity in Lezinsky's death. Edwin Markham, still a few years away from his own critical thrashing by Bierce, began a transparent fable about a cruel wasp who tormented frogs in a little pond. Bierce, he said, had shaken the emotionally fragile Lezinsky like "a quivering and helpless rat." Charges of anti-Semitism were in the air. Bierce denied it, but in his essay "The Jew," written about the same time, he bluntly gave his critics additional ammunition. Declaring the Jews "a peculiar people, peculiarly disliked," Bierce advised them to follow "a larger life than is comprised in rites and rituals, the ceremonies and symbolisms of a long-dead past," and to recognize that "the world is wider than Judea and God more than a private tutor to the children of Israel." Sounding like a cross between Brother Ambrosius and another, later resident of Berchtesgaden, Bierce advised the Jew to "learn why he is subject to hate and persecution by the Gentile." It is because, said Bierce, "in a thousand ways, all having for purpose the safeguarding of his racial isolation in a ghetto of his own invention, the orthodox Jew shouts aloud his conviction of his superior holiness and peculiar worth." And, he warned, "if a certain presumptuous self-righteousness is bad its natural and inevitable punishment is not entirely undeserved." From the evidence of the Bible, he continued, the Jew "was once a very bad neighbor. Every contiguous tribe which did not accept their God incurred their savage hatred, expressed in incredible cruelties. They ruled their little world with an iron hand, dealing damnation round and forcing upon their neighbors a currency of bloody noses and cracked crowns. Even now they have not renounced their irritating claim to primacy in the scale of being, though no longer able to assert it with fire and sword."[49]

All this had little to do with the suicide of one obscure young Jewish poet, except to sour Bierce further on San Francisco, "the paradise of ignorance, anarchy and general yellowness." "It is perfect rot to say that I am responsible for Lezinsky's death," he protested. "I have never met him and would have refused to do so had the occasion arisen. I never once attacked him personally but only his verse. When he elected to become a poet, he impliedly consented to public criticisms of that which he made public." Explanations aside, the controversy encouraged other aggrieved poets to rise against their tormenter. William Greer Garrison, whose verse Bierce had likened to "a roadside pump replenishing a horse-trough," now declared his nemesis to be "the most complete literary failure of the century," his work merely "a signpost marking the wreck of an utterly wasted life, and the grave of a literary bully." John Bonner of the *Wave* agreed. Bierce, he said, "is like the Irishman who never saw a head without wanting to hit it. He seems imbued with the delusion that he is the guardian of letters on this coast. To writers who may not be his equals in literary force, he denies the right not only to use the pen, but to exist."[50]

Bierce postured defiance—"I am assisting a worthy young woman to make a collection of canceled postage stamps," he remarked in his column, "now is the time to insult me through the mails"—but his reserves of combative energy were running low. The long run of bad luck that had begun with the breakup of his marriage seven years earlier at last had worn him down. In the ensuing years, he had lost his gifted elder son to suicide, his young protégé Lily Walsh to cruelly timed illness, and a number of other friends to death or desertion. His second son, Leigh, was well on the way to drinking himself to death; his daughter, Helen, was living apart from him with her mother. He had published two books of extraordinary short stories, only to see them sink from view after a brief flourish, due largely to the lack of an eastern publisher. His once-dreaded column, although still widely read, now drew an increasingly emboldened counterfire. His asthma, always worse in times of stress, plagued him regularly; a bicycle accident broke one of his ribs and bruised his hands so badly that he could not hold a pen for several weeks. He was now, in January 1896, three years past fifty, and the creative torrent that had driven him to write an equal number of short stories had slowed to a trickle. When Leigh Bierce, in the midst of an epic bender, told Adolph Danziger, "I want to go to hell," his father, with some justice, could truthfully say that in the last few years he had preceded him there.[51]

11

What a Thing It Is to
Be a Ghost

*J*ust as he had done in 1887 when Bierce was holed up in Oakland alone and depressed, William Randolph Hearst again came to his rescue in early 1896, giving him a new (actually an old) target on which to focus his flagging energies. Collis P. Huntington, the ruthless old crocodile who ran the Southern Pacific Railroad—and much of California—as a private fiefdom, had bestirred himself from his San Francisco headquarters to descend on the nation's capital with an army of lobbyists, lawyers, and all-around fixers to try to ram through Congress a so-called funding bill that would, in effect, postpone indefinitely the railroad's $75 million public indebtedness. Hearst, sensing an opportunity to launch another circulation-boosting popular crusade, mobilized the opposition forces. From New York, where he had gone to buy the *Morning Journal,* he sent a wire to Bierce, somewhere in the California foothills: "Railroad combination so strong in Washington that seems almost impossible to break them up, yet it is certainly the duty of all having interests of coast at heart to make most strenuous efforts. Will you please go to Washington for the *Examiner?*" That was as close to a direct order as Hearst was likely to give, and Bierce, bored with the same old round of local controversies and fawning students that made up his present unsatisfactory existence, immediately responded: "I shall be glad to do whatever I can toward defeating Mr. Huntington's Funding Bill and shall start for Washington on Monday evening next."[1]

With his son Leigh as a traveling companion, Bierce headed east for the first time since his own unhappy lobbying efforts with the board of directors of the Black Hills Placer Mining Company fifteen years earlier. He stopped off in Chicago for a brief visit with the young literary critic Percival Pollard, who had won his heart by denouncing Stephen Crane's remarkable new Civil War novel, *The Red Badge of Courage,* as "an imitation of Bierce," adding that "Mr. Crane had merely done crudely what Bierce had done admirably." Bierce, who dismissed the extravagantly gifted young writer as "the Crane freak," was gratified by the comparison. When Pollard mentioned two other young writers, H. W. Phillips and Rupert Hughes, as being even worse writers than Crane, Bierce responded, "I had thought that there could be only two worse writers than Stephen Crane, namely, two Stephen Cranes." The gratuitous slam reflected Bierce's frustration both at the failure of his own Civil War fiction to win a wide audience and at what he felt was Crane's appropriation of his style and themes. Pollard touched on this when he defied anyone to "show a passage in *The Red Badge of Courage* so vividly and truly descriptive of the wounded crawling over a battlefield as that in Bierce's 'Chickamauga.'" Bierce was also annoyed that a young man who had not even been born until six years after the war was over had achieved best-selling status with a book on a subject that he considered, with some justice, to be his own private bailiwick. For his part, Crane made no secret of his admiration for Bierce, but while his work does show traces of the Biercian style, Crane was inarguably the better writer, which may have provoked the older man's spleen, as well.[2]

Bierce arrived in Washington on the last week in January and immediately set up headquarters at the Page Hotel, near the Capitol. Once there, he took charge of a small battalion of Hearst writers, photographers, and cartoonists on loan from the New York *Morning Journal* and planned out a strategy of unremitting ad hominem assaults on Huntington's less-than-lovable character. The railroad tycoon, who for years had shrugged off Bierce's verbal darts like a grizzly bear languidly swatting at a bee, now began to take notice of his surprisingly formidable foe. Bierce set the terms of the contest in his first dispatch on February 1, which was headlined BIERCE ON THE FUNDING BILL/"He Tells How Huntington in Washington Is Fighting Fiercely,/Like a Cornered Rat, With His Old Familiar Weapons,/A Paid Press and a Sorry Pack of Sleek and Conscienceless Rogues." Huntington, said Bierce, had a head like a dromedary camel, "its tandem bumps of cupidity and self-esteem overshadowing like twin peaks the organ he is good with, in the valley between." He laughed off the mogul's lugubrious warning that the railroad should be forgiven most, if not all, of its indebtedness, lest it be bankrupted by the sheer weight of its burden, wondering aloud how anyone could seriously expect "that a corporation which for thirty years has defaulted in the payment of interest and is about to default in payment of principal because it has chosen to steal both principal and interest can henceforth be trusted to pay both." As the congressional hearings were set to begin, the *Examiner* gloated: "Huntington Lying in His Last Ditch."[3]

The issue had its start in the Lincoln administration's Civil War–motivated decision to promote the building of a transcontinental railroad through generous loans and outright gifts of land to anyone willing to take up the challenge. "This conscienceless gang," Bierce charged, referring to the Big Four of Huntington, Stanford, Crocker, and Hopkins, "had entered upon the work of railroad construction and operation as poor men and had somehow or other—the details read like the report of a grand larceny trial—acquired fifteen to twenty million each." As the last surviving member of the fabled quartet of "railrogues," Huntington grudgingly offered to give back some of the land to the government, in return for a seventy-five-year postponement of the debt. The transparent ploy might have worked—the fix was nearly in—had not Hearst rallied public sentiment against it in California and dispatched Bierce to Washington to turn up the heat on the legislators. Huntington did not help matters any by testifying before congressional committees in an alternately truculent or wheedling manner, professing an improbable lack of knowledge concerning the exact amount of the railroad's building costs, which he variously estimated at between $36 million and $122 million—this from a man who once caught a hotel clerk making a twenty-five-cent error in his bill and chastised him by boasting, "Young man, you can't track me through life by the number of quarters I have dropped."[4]

Bierce, who had despised Huntington for years, was in his element. Each day brought a new jab at the old grizzly's hide. Describing Huntington's convenient loss of memory concerning his capital outlays, Bierce jeered: "Mr. Huntington's ignorance is chronic and incurable. The number of things that he does not know is undiminished by time; the accuracy with which he does not know them is unaffected by reflection." Of a February 14 appearance by Huntington before the Senate Committee on Pacific Railroads, he reported: "Today he not only appeared, but took his hand out of all manner of pockets long enough to hold it up and be sworn. He was not asked if he knew the nature of an oath; it was assumed that he did." Charging that Huntington was pretending to "the infirmities of age" in a naked bid for sympathy, Bierce declared flatly that he was "merely seeking to promote plunder by perjury. The spectacle of this old man standing on the brink of eternity, his pockets loaded with dishonest gold which he knows neither how to enjoy nor to whom to bequeath was one of the most pitiable it has been my lot to observe. He knows himself an outmate of every penal institution in the world; he deserves to hang from every branch of every tree of every State and Territory penetrated by his railroads, with the sole exception of Nevada, which has no trees." Accompanying headlines read: MR. HUNTINGTON ON THE GRILL, UNPLEASANT TIME BEFORE THE SENATE RAILROAD COMMITTEE, and COLLIS'

FRAUDS FIND HIM OUT. Bierce contrived to rub salt in the wound by having extra copies of the *Examiner* specially delivered to Huntington's suite at the La Normandie Hotel, where, he noted with satisfaction, they "were contumeliously cast as rubbish to the void."[5]

At last, faced with the likely defeat of his bill, Huntington tried a characteristic ploy. Confronting Bierce on the steps of the Capitol one afternoon, he publicly invited the columnist to name his price. Bierce contemptuously shook his head. "Every man has his price," said Huntington, who surely knew that as well as any man alive. "My price," said Bierce, in a quote that would make newspaper headlines across the country, "is seventy-five million dollars. If, when you are ready to pay, I happen to be out of town, you may hand it over to my friend, the Treasurer of the United States." The next day, the *Examiner* printed a cartoon showing a combative Bierce, shirtsleeves rolled up, holding a fistful of Huntington's hair, while the fallen railroad man sprawled ingloriously at the bottom of the Capitol steps, his soles flapping in the breeze like a bum's.[6]

Bierce kept up a remorseless barrage on the now-reeling Huntington, calling him, among other things, an "inflated old pigskin," a "veteran calumniator," a "promoted peasant," and "the swine of the century." "Of our modern Forty Thieves," he trumpeted, "Mr. Huntington is the surviving thirty-six." Sensing an ominous shift in political support, Huntington tried an eleventh-hour public-relations ploy. The Southern Pacific, he reported proudly, was taking the lead in opening up job opportunities for women. Yes, said Bierce, the railroad had recently hired thirty or forty female "spotters" to ride the trains and catch dishonest conductors in the act. "A noble mission, truly," he jeered, "that of sewing up the holes in Mr. Huntington's pocket to keep other persons' money from flowing down his leg." Still, said the columnist, "Mr. Huntington is not altogether bad. Though severe, he is merciful. He says ugly things of the enemy, but he has the tenderness to be careful that they are mostly lies." When Huntington charged that the *Examiner* itself was on his private payroll, Bierce publicly promised to shake his archenemy's hand if the allegations proved correct. "I exact only one condition," he added; "Mr. Huntington is not to object to my glove." Needless to say, the handshake never took place.[7]

At length, Congress finessed the funding bill, postponing a final vote until Congressman H. Henry Powers—Bierce called him the "Chairman of the Committee on Visible Virtues"—sponsored an amendment to the bill that would replace Huntington's original plea for total debt forgiveness with a sliding schedule of long-term repayments over an eighty-year period. Neither side was pleased with the compromise, but Hearst played it as a total victory. HUNTINGTON'S RULE AT AN END, the newspaper headlined in late May, over a classic Biercian lead: "Today Mr. Huntington saw the dishonest work of years come suddenly to naught." As for the future, Bierce offered a wry prediction.

"Before this good man shall long be in the New Jersualem," he said of Huntington, "he will undoubtedly find an opportunity to pull a pack-load of blocks from the golden pavement and retire to Hades to enjoy them like a gentleman."[8]

The months of hard work—the hardest he had done in years—began to tell on Bierce. In June, he was stricken with a recurrence of asthma so severe that he had to leave miasmal Washington and spend several weeks recuperating in—of all places—Gettysburg, Pennsylvania. He passed the remainder of the summer and fall in New York, where Leigh had gone to take a job with Hearst's *Morning Journal.* He was increasingly worried about his younger son, who was developing into a full-blown womanizer. "He needs discipline, control, and work," Bierce told a family friend. "He needs to learn by experience that life is not all beer and skittles." Still, there was little Bierce could, or would, do for his son, other than help him get work in what had become the family profession. Leigh's penchant for messy romantic affairs particularly offended his father, who had always made something of an art of the discreet seduction. When—shades of Day—the young man fell in love with the daughter of his landlady, he kept the affair secret from his father, who thereafter maintained a cool distance from his son—and an icy chasm between himself and his new daughter-in-law.[9]

For a time, Bierce considered settling down in New York and working for the *Morning Journal* as well, but a series of clashes with the paper's editors—whom he characterized as "fools, fakers and freaks"—soon caused him to change his mind. The chief offender was Willis J. Abbot, whom Hearst had hired away from the Chicago *Record* and made editor in chief of the editorial page. (The joke around the copydesk was that he had really been hired as editor in charge of Bierce.) Abbot was under no illusions about his task. After his first day at work, he advised friends that he had "secured very remunerative employment in a lunatic asylum." Perhaps he was unaware of Hearst's decade-old promise to Bierce that nothing in his columns would be edited; at any rate, he soon butted heads with the infamous Prattler. Observing that a well-known actress had recently died, Bierce felt constrained to add: "Always famous for her composed manner, she is now quite decomposed." Abbot struck the offending sentence, Bierce resigned in a huff, Hearst rehired him at a higher wage, and Bierce decided to return to more congenial haunts. In December 1896, he went back to California, spending several weeks in Los Angeles at the home of his old U.S. Mint superior, Gen. O. H. LaGrange. There he met several times with his daughter, Helen, telling her at one point, "There is only one woman in my life that I have loved, and that woman happens to be your mother." If true, his actions certainly belied his words. Mollie was living in Los Angeles as well, taking care of her now-senile mother, but Bierce made no effort to contact her and pointedly declined LaGrange's offer to help effect a reconciliation between the two. The general, apparently laboring under the not-unreasonable assumption that Bierce had deserted his wife, made the mistake of lecturing him on the proper role of a husband in society, thus quickly joining the ranks of other former friends to whom Bierce had officially "disintroduced" himself.[10]

Arriving in San Francisco, Bierce was greeted as a returning hero, the crusading journalist who had successfully battled the "railrogues" to a standoff. Newspaper cartoons pictured him bestrewn with flowers like a noble centurion who has just fought off the barbarians at the gates of Rome. With the recent election of liberal candidate James D. Phelan as mayor of the city, a new age of political reform seemed imminent, and many credited Bierce with being the catalyst. Muckraking journalist Charles Edward Russell spoke for many when he praised the writer's antirailroad articles as "extraordinary examples of invective and bitter sarcasm." When Bierce began his campaign, said Russell, few imagined that the Funding Bill could be stopped, but "with six months of incessant firing, Mr. Bierce had the railroad forces frightened and wavering; and before the end of the year he had them whipped." This was getting a little ahead of the game, as Bierce himself noted in January 1897. "The battle is on in Washington," he pointed out, "where Representative Powers is pushing his infamous Funding Bill and attesting the virtues of Mr. Huntington. I feel rather like a fool sitting here three thousand miles away while my co-workers of last session set their breasts against this giant iniquity. Faith! it were good to be there again in the thick of it."[11]

As if to underline Bierce's prediction, California congressman Grove L. Johnson, firmly fixed in Huntington's pocket, savagely attacked Hearst on the floor of the House, damning "our Willie" as a debauched dude who was "licentious in his tastes, regal in his dissipations, unfit to associate with pure women or decent men." He even accused the publisher of having "sought on the banks of the Nile relief from loathsome disease contracted only by contagion in the haunts of vice"—surely the first time that anyone had ever gone to Egypt to get rid of a social disease. When Hearst supporters countered that Johnson had once been indicted for forgery in Syracuse, New York, the outraged congressman complained that it was patently unfair to "bring out the follies and crimes of his youth"—he was thirty-two at the time of his arrest. Despite Powers's and Johnson's best efforts, the House defeated the amended funding bill, 168 to 102, and substituted a new bill, whereby the railroad was required to fully repay its debt, with interest, in ten years' time. Bierce, who had recommended that the government simply "foreclose the mortgage" and run the railroad itself, was less than thrilled by the victory. "I exult with difficulty," he observed. In one of life's many ironies, Congressman Johnson's son Hiram later became governor of California and created a state railway commission whose sweeping regulatory controls effectively put an end to the railroad's last vestiges of political power.[12]

Still plagued by asthma, Bierce left San Francisco and took up residence at the El Monte Hotel in Los Gatos, at the foot of the Santa Cruz Mountains. Here he resumed his role of literary godfather to a succession of young writers, male and female. Among the former was a high-strung young Bavarian immigrant named Herman Scheffauer. Scheffauer had chucked away a promising architectural career to become a poet. Like George Sterling, he affected a free-living bohemianism that Bierce personally rejected, and Scheffauer's poetry was even worse than Sterling's. Nevertheless, Bierce loyally offered advice and assistance to both, and he even talked Scheffauer into joining him in a literary hoax in which the young man's poem "The Sea of Serenity" was passed off as a newly discovered poem of Edgar Allan Poe's that a distant relative of the great man had supposedly sent to Bierce at the *Examiner.* The hoax fell flat, and so eventually did Bierce's friendship with Scheffauer. In 1927, the architect turned poet joined the long list of Bierce associates who met macabre ends—in this instance, by fatally stabbing his wife and leaping to his death from a hotel window. Other young writers also clustered around Bierce, including a teenage poet named Lella Cotton; she literally ran into him one morning while he was staying at the Jeffreys Hotel in the mountaintop community of Wrights, above Los Gatos. Older friends included two middle-aged widows, Josephine McCrackin and Una Hume, whose well-appointed ranches, Monte Paraiso and Glen Una, functioned as much-needed sanctuaries from the long round of alcoholic picnics, nature-hike seductions, and al fresco literary seminars that filled much of Bierce's time after his return from Washington.[13]

Comfortably ensconced in the California hills, Bierce drifted through the rest of 1897, as the nation itself drifted toward war. One of the catalysts was William Randolph Hearst. Locked in a brutal circulation war with Joseph Pulitzer's New York *World,* Hearst had embraced the cause of supposedly freedom-loving Cuba, which had been in a state of near-constant rebellion with Spain for over half a century. For the past two years, while Bierce was off fighting "railrogues" in Washington, Hearst was in New York conducting a three-front war against rival newspapers, an apathetic American public, and the administrations of Presidents Grover Cleveland and William McKinley, both of whom had declined to take up arms against a largely imaginary monster of Hearst's own creation. A man for whom the term *jingo* was invented, Hearst was undeterred by the forces allied against him. With an energy that was as remarkable as it was venal, the *Journal* publisher single-handedly laid the groundwork for war. Each new issue carried a sensational story of fiendish Spanish cruelties against Cuban revolutionaries, whom the newspaper shamelessly portrayed as being "animated by the same fearless spirit that inspired the patriot fathers who sat in Philadelphia on the 4th of July, 1776." The Spanish were regularly accused of feeding their imprisoned minutemen to the sharks and of poisoning wells, wrecking hospitals, raping virgins, bul-

lying nuns, and roasting Catholic priests over barbecue pits. The more Spanish officials denied the stories, the more the *Journal* ran headlines such as
SPANISH AUCTION OFF CUBAN GIRLS. When famed illustrator Frederic Rem-
ington, in Cuba at Hearst's behest, complained in a telegram that "Everything is quiet. There is no trouble here. There will be no war," Hearst
famously replied, "You furnish the pictures and I'll furnish the war."[14]

In time, he did just that. Regiments of *Journal* writers and artists
descended on Cuba, where they reported imaginary Spanish atrocities from
the veranda of the Inglaterra Hotel in downtown Havana. A naturalized
Cuban dentist named Ricardo Ruiz, who had sneaked back into Cuba to join
the revolution and later committed suicide in a Spanish jail, was routinely
described as "the murdered American." A young woman named Evangelina
Cisneros, arrested for trying to break her revolutionary father out of jail, was
hailed as the "Cuban Joan of Arc." Her real crime, the *Journal* claimed, was
fighting off the lecherous advances of an evil Spanish colonel. Eventually,
Cisneros was "liberated" from prison by *Journal* reporter Karl Decker, who
wrote a highly romanticized account of the rescue that neglected to mention
that he had simply bribed her jailers to look the other way while they climbed
out a window. Brought to New York for a giant victory banquet at Del-
monico's restaurant, Cisneros was squired around town by Decker, "a modern
d'Artagnan," while Hearst pounded the drums for American intervention and
increased *Journal* circulation. All Hearst's efforts might have gone for
naught—Spain was desperately attempting to meet each new American
demand—had not the U.S. battleship *Maine* mysteriously exploded in
Havana harbor on the night of February 15, 1898. "This means war," Hearst
exulted when he heard the news. He immediately offered a fifty-thousand-
dollar reward (never collected) for information leading to the arrest of those
responsible, and he smeared the front page of his newspaper with six-inch
headlines declaring, a little prematurely, THE WHOLE COUNTRY THRILLS WITH
WAR FEVER. Two months later, after President McKinley bowed to pressure
and reluctantly asked Congress to declare war on Spain, Hearst hailed the
news by running a self-congratulatory blurb on either side of his masthead:
HOW DO YOU LIKE THE JOURNAL'S WAR?[15]

It was indeed the *Journal*'s war—Pulitzer's *World* was a distant second in
both the number of correspondents streaming into Cuba and in the sheer
volume of journalistic drumbeats leading up to the war—but for months on
end its most famous columnist was conspicuously silent on the subject. As
early as 1895, Bierce had ridiculed the warmongering press, noting that
"War—Horrid War!—between the United States and Spain has already broken out like a red rash in the newspapers, whose managing commodores are
shivering their timbers and blasting their toplights with a truly pelagic volu-
bility and no little vraisemblance." But this was before Hearst acquired the
Journal. Thereafter, Bierce wrote little on the subject, and for the final ten

months leading up to the start of the war in April 1898, he wrote nothing at all about the most pressing issue of the day. In light of his later admission that Hearst had "two or three times suggested that I refrain for a season from expressing an opinion that I did hold, when they were antagonistic to the policy of the paper," it is reasonable to assume that the publisher had asked him to lay off the subject.[16]

Even if this was the case, there were also other factors involved in Bierce's seemingly suspicious silence. To begin with, he did not share his country-men's faddish glorification of war in general and the Spanish-American War in particular. "Patriotism's altar-fires, newly kindled and splendoring in the Land of the Comparatively Free," did not warm him with a comparable heat. "Patriotism," he said, "is fierce as a fever, pitiless as the grave, blind as a stone and irrational as a headless hen." Nor did he accept the high-flown declara-tions of a humane larger purpose behind the national rush to war. "We are at war with Spain today merely in obedience to a suasion that has been gather-ing force from the beginning of our national existence," he observed. "The passion for territory once roused rages like a lion; successive conquests only strengthen it. That is the fever that is now burning in the American blood." As for any underlying religious motivations (McKinley had reported that he fell to his knees and asked God to show him the right thing to do with regard to Cuba), he tartly observed that "wholesale slaughter of our fellow men in this or any war should, I think, be regarded rather as a political than a reli-gious duty." He had difficulty, he said, "conceiving Jesus Christ in command of a battleship; and it might be as well not to represent God the Father as a rear-admiral in the American navy."[17]

Another factor in Bierce's nonembrace of the war may have been racism. To him, if not perhaps to Hearst, the Cuban rebels were a decidedly inferior lot, "mostly Negroes and Negroids, ignorant, superstitious almost beyond belief and brutal exceedingly." Three years earlier, when war had briefly threatened between the United States and Great Britain over Central Ameri-can boundary disputes, Bierce, the committed Anglophile, had shuddered at the thought of losing "a hundred thousand human lives in vindication of the right of a nasty little Sambo 'republic' to break with impunity the decalogue of international comity. A great war to save a swamp full of anthropoid mongrels in mad reliance on the power of our Jingoes to make the crime our own." As for Cuba, he warned that "no nation under Negro dominance has ever known commercial prosperity. Annexation could hardly help matters; the entire adult male population could not long be denied the franchise, and we should have a choice between Negro misrule and shotgun politics." In making this argument, he was in good, or at least distinguished, company. Winston Churchill, then a young subaltern in the British army, had visited Cuba in 1896 and come away with a sense of "grave danger." Noting that "two-fifths of the insurgents in the field are Negroes," Churchill worried that the rebels, if successful, would logically demand a prominent role in the government, "the result being, after years of fighting, another black republic."[18]

At least Bierce and Churchill were looking at the issue from a primarily political standpoint; compared with the public statements of other prominent public figures, they were practically moderates. Kansas newspaper editor William Allen White said flatly that the Cubans were "mongrels with no capacity for self government, a yellow-legged, knife-sticking, treacherous outfit." Speaker of the House Thomas B. Reed, an opponent of the war, called them "yellow-bellies," scoffing that "the noble Army of Cuban martyrs" was "an armed rabble as unchivalrous as it was unsanitary." Even some of the leading officers in the war had contempt for their Cuban allies. Army colonel Leonard Wood complained fastidiously that the Cuban army was "made up very considerably of black people, only partially civilized, in whom the old spirit of savagery has been more or less aroused by years of warfare." His able assistant, Lt. Col. Theodore Roosevelt, was disappointed to find that the fabled *insurrectos* were "almost all blacks and mulattoes." A widely quoted letter from a young Spanish soldier favorably contrasted the courage and gallantry of the American troops to the sneaking guerrilla tactics of the Cuban rebels, "a people without religion, without morals, without conscience and of doubtful origin." Even Bierce's young nemesis Stephen Crane, who was personally as free of racism as it was possible for a middle-class white man of the late nineteenth century to be, reported that the Cubans had accepted American assistance "with the impenetrable indifference or ignorance of people in an ordinary slum."[19]

Once the war was under way, Bierce approached the matter from the practical viewpoint of the experienced soldier. He had no doubt whatsoever about the outcome of the war. "We can conquer these people without half trying," he wrote, "for we belong to a race of gluttons and drunkards to whom dominion is given over the abstemious. We can thrash them consummately and every day of the week." But the bumbling, snafu-ridden conduct of the war made him throw up his hands in disgust at "such an exposure of rascality and incompetence as will call blushes to the cheek of apathy and tears to the eyes of hope." From the top down, Bierce searched the American leadership and found it lacking. McKinley, he said, had "probably done the best he knew how; the mistake lay in letting him do so much." Secretary of State John Sherman (William Tecumseh's brother) was "a victim of senile dementia, pitchforked into place in order to make a vacancy in the Senate for Mark Hanna." Secretary of War Russell A. Alger, a fellow Union army veteran, was "not only an all-round crank . . . but during the Civil War he was in serious trouble for abandoning his command." Both men, he said, could have been advantageously replaced by "two members in good standing of the Society of Friends." As for the accompanying army of war correspondents busily swarming across the island in pursuit—and sometimes in advance—of the army, Bierce groused that they lacked "that first, second and third qualification for [their] work, a military education."[20]

Why he did not go to Cuba himself is a question that has never fully been answered (or asked, for that matter). True, he was fifty-six, but he was a vigorous and fit fifty-six, his recurrent asthma excepted. Most likely Hearst, who did go to Cuba for a brief but action-filled stint as his own chief correspondent, purposely refrained from asking him to go, probably from the well-founded belief that an ex-soldier as experienced and questioning as Bierce could do a world of damage to the *Journal*'s cause at the front. Whether Bierce would have gone, if asked, is another question. He was comfortable in California, surrounded by admiring students, complaisant young women, and a brace of rich widows; he *was* fifty-six; and, most important, he did not believe in the war, either as a necessary extension of American foreign policy or as a grand adventure for the boys in blue. In four years of civil war, he had seen what war could do, had "been to touch the great death," as the upstart Crane described it, and unlike such jingoistic *Journal* correspondents as Richard Harding Davis, who viewed the war as a sort of glorified Harvard-Yale football game, he harbored no illusions about the patriotic glories of a Spanish Mauser bullet to the heart. But the avidity with which, once engaged, he followed the war's prosecution suggests that Bierce would at least have entertained the notion of going. As it was, Hearst never asked. Given Bierce's abundant journalistic gifts—a clear eye, a tight style, and, most of all, a hard-won appreciation of the gritty, nonheroic details of an infantryman's war—it was literature's loss that he did not. What Bierce could have done fictionally with the Spanish-American War, in all its comic-opera variations, is a tantalizing, if ultimately unknowable, speculation.

Instead, he followed the war from a distance, renaming his column "War Topics" for the duration of the 113-day conflict. In it, he cautioned against typical American overconfidence, scoffed at the "famous victories" breathlessly reported by inexperienced correspondents, and displayed an old foot soldier's seasoned contempt for the loudly lionized navy. More searchingly, he was one of the first to raise the question of America's future involvement in the Philippines. Three weeks after the commencement of hostilities, he was already asking what a victory over Spain would mean to the Filipino insurgents who had been fighting for years against the same imperial enemy. "It is possible that we shall not find him easy to get on with—that he will welcome us with that degree of hospitality to strangers that is not inconsistent with a strenuous endeavour to kick them out," Bierce warned. "It looks at this time as if we had made a brilliant conquest of Spain's white elephant, but it does not look as if we should know any too soon or any too clearly what to do with it." He perceptively saw that the Philippines, not Cuba, was the real test of American foreign policy, "whether we shall adhere to our traditional policy of self-sufficient isolation . . . or join in the general scramble for colonial expansion by treaty, purchase and conquest." The signs pointed all one way, toward a long-term involvement in the Philippines. Only an intentional "war of conquest," he said, could explain the use of ground troops against Spain, when it was obvious that the United States Navy, for all its ponderous inefficiency, was fully capable of winning the war on its own. That being the case, he advised caution. "The situation in the Philippines," he wrote in July 1898, "appears to have all the elements that are needful to a first-class international complication." When the chairman of the Senate Foreign Relations Committee piously maintained that America could not in good conscience retreat to its former policy of isolation, Bierce translated the message "into the language of common sense, that having taken a few sips of the wine of conquest and glory we like the taste of it and want more. That is well enough, or, as luck may decree, ill enough, but let us have no hypocrisy about it."[21]

The outcome of the war, after all the flag-waving parades and heart-thumping speeches, was a little anticlimactic. Bierce, who had fully expected the fighting to result in Civil War–size casualty lists, now mocked it as a "freak war" that was little more than a series of squalid jungle skirmishes. In years to come, he predicted, white-haired old veterans would have no stories to tell their grandchildren of a Cuban-style Chickamauga or Spotsylvania. From a strictly entertainment viewpoint, it was "distinctly inferior to cholera and hardly more exciting than bubonic plague." Moreover, the "Yanko-Spanko War," as he had taken to calling it, had had the deleterious effect of bringing the country into the Europeanized "great game" of imperialism. Bierce did not object to the colonization of the Philippines on purely moral grounds, as for example did his old friend Mark Twain, whose bitter 1901 essay on the subject, "To the Person Sitting in Darkness," postdated his own anti-imperialism by a good two and a half years. Rather, he questioned it on a practical level. Overestimating the capacity of the Filipino resistance fighters, Bierce worried in December 1899 that "the Philippines are a large group; there are several hundreds of islands, and of most of them we know absolutely nothing. When we reflect that for several centuries we have been hopefully suppressing the red Indians at our door, that the work is not yet complete, and that there never were a million of them all told, the task of subduing these eight or ten million Filipinos six thousand miles away seems anything but brief and easy. So far, it has been a good deal like visiting a hornet's nest uninvited when the hornets are at home. If the rest of the Filipinos are as warlike as the Aguinalderos we shall have in our new dependency a permanent military training school to take the place of the one so long supplied by the Indians." Subsequent events would prove him wrong. In a brutal, Vietnam-style guerrilla war, complete with water-torture interrogations, the burning of jungle villages, and a take-no-prisoners approach to winning native hearts and minds, the U.S. Army did manage to pacify the Philippines—at the cost of some 220,000 Filipino and 4,200 American lives. To

Bierce, it was yet another demonstration that "the entire business of being a nation is as innocent of morality as that of a thief or a pirate." Oh well, he commented, "we did not promise to be righteous in the Pacific, but only in the Caribbean."[22]

His columns on the Spanish-American War and its aftermath were the last meaningful bits of journalism that Bierce would ever write. The century was rapidly drawing to a close, and the old conflicts—personal, political, and literary—that he had devoted so much of his energy to fighting for the past three decades did not particularly engage him anymore. In mid-December 1899, after a series of quarrels with Una Hume, Lella Cotton, Edwin Markham, and other longtime friends and associates, Bierce abruptly moved back to Washington. The *Examiner* took official notice of his departure—it could scarcely have not—with a long editorial in the December 14 edition of the newspaper. The issues facing Congress, it reported, were of such "extraordinary moment" that they demanded "comment, criticism and elucidation" from the famous Prattler. At the same time, the newspaper went to some pains to distance itself from Bierce's more extreme positions, noting that "while Mr. Bierce's work is necessarily editorial in its tone, he does not always reflect 'The Examiner's' opinions or policy. There have been many instances in which he has violently opposed this paper's well-known ideas side by side with them on the editorial page." This was not exactly a ringing endorsement of Bierce's political acumen, although it was softened somewhat by praise for his "rare ability with a jest, a pun or a quip." The *Examiner* concluded that, warts and all, "the sum is what no man in America can produce today except Ambrose Bierce." Before leaving, Bierce paid a last visit to the Oakland cemetery where Lily Walsh and so many other old friends, associates, and enemies were buried. He was disappointed to find that Frank Pixley had been cremated and thus, as he later complained, he was unable to spit on his grave.[23]

Once in Washington, Bierce dutifully trudged from his apartment on Fifteenth Street to the press gallery at the Capitol, reporting on such then-current events as the Boer War (he was predictably pro-British), the Panama Canal negotiations, the Boxer Rebellion in China, the assassination of Italian King Humbert, and the "freak ideas" of Thomas Edison and Nikola Tesla. But the snap had suddenly gone out of his writing. Even the new title of his column, "The Passing Show," seemed to reflect a subtle disinterest in matters great and small. He could still produce an occasional zinger, as in his epitaph for Collis Huntington, who died in August 1900: "Here Huntington's ashes long have lain/Whose loss was our eternal gain,/For while he exercised all his powers/Whatever he gained, the loss was ours." But for the most part he showed a loss of energy that was symptomatic of his lifelong occasional bouts of depression. To his old friend Amy Cecil, who had thrown Day Bierce's fatal pistol into the ocean for him a dozen years earlier, he complained: "I'm leading a life of mere waiting—waiting for nothing in particular, except the end of it all. I've no incentive, no ambition but to go on with as little friction as possible. I fancy most observers would say that I'm having a pretty good time, and that's what I usually say myself; but may Heaven punish the malefactor who invented that deadly dull thing, a good time."[24]

The good times, such as they were, did not last long. In March 1901, Bierce rushed to New York to sit by the deathbed of his only surviving son. Leigh had come down with pneumonia after contracting a bad cold while delivering Christmas presents to the poor children of Hell's Kitchen and the Tenderloin on behalf of his current employer, the *Morning Telegraph.* True to form, he had taken the opportunity to visit a neighborhood saloon, after which time he had become "hilariously drunk" and given away all the presents before they could reach their intended recipients. Bierce, who had reconciled with Leigh a few months before, now found him "a very sick boy—a mere skeleton." Cruelly, Leigh rallied just enough "to justify at least a hope" of recovery, then relapsed and lingered another eleven days before dying, at the age of twenty-six, on March 31. "Leigh passed away this morning," Bierce stoically wired associates. His daughter, Helen, arrived from Los Angeles in time to handle the funeral arrangements. Bierce endured the service as well as he could, lecturing Helen on the need to maintain a properly dignified composure, then returned to Washington and took to his bed. Helen stayed with him while he worked through his immediate grief, but he never completely got over losing his second son. "I am hit hard; more than you can guess—am a bit broken and gone gray of it all," he wrote to George Sterling, an admission that, coming from Bierce, was tantamount to a nakedly emotional confession from anyone else. A year later, he was still counting the days since Leigh's death, and his hair, which had always been sandy blond, had now turned white.[25]

In September 1901, Bierce was again confined to his bed with another onslaught of asthma when he inadvertently became the focus of another public controversy. An almost forgotten quatrain he had written nearly two years earlier ironically became the poison seed that ruined William Randolph Hearst's growing presidential aspirations. On September 6, President McKinley was fatally shot by an unemployed millworker and self-proclaimed anarchist named Leon Czolgocz while shaking hands at a gathering in Buffalo, New York. When McKinley died of gangrene eight days later, Hearst's opponents in the press publicly accused him of virtual complicity in the President's death. Their main piece of evidence was a rather tasteless ditty Bierce had composed in February 1900 when Kentucky governor-elect William Goebel was shot and killed in a postelection quarrel. It read: "The bullet that pierced Goebel's breast/Cannot be found in all the West;/Good reason, it is speeding here/To stretch McKinley on his bier." The poem had attracted no attention then, but after the President's assassination it was seen in a different light, particularly since Hearst's newspapers had been virulently attacking

McKinley for not confronting the large trusts that were rapidly strangling American consumers. Combined with previous *Journal* editorials calling McKinley "the most hated creature on the American continent" and recommending—incredibly—that "if bad institutions and bad men can be got rid of only by killing, then the killing must be done," Bierce's luckless prophecy was used as a cudgel to assail Hearst's political aspirations.[26]

In 1904, with Hearst poised to win the governorship of New York as a springboard to the White House, Theodore Roosevelt, the current occupant, dispatched Secretary of War Elihu B. Root to the state to repeat the old charges that Hearst had contributed to McKinley's death. The ploy swung just enough votes away from the publisher to deny him the election, and with it his best chance to win the presidency. Bierce was not sorry to see Hearst kept out of the White House, but he was disgusted with Roosevelt and Root for their blatant use of his unintentionally wounding words. "If anyone thinks that Mr. Root will not go to the devil," he said, "it must be the devil himself, in whom, doubtless, the wish is father to the thought." It was particularly ironic that Roosevelt should have destroyed Hearst, since Roosevelt would never have been President in the first place without the fame he won in the Spanish-American War, which Hearst more than anyone had labored to bring about. Bierce later reluctantly visited the White House at Roosevelt's request, where, he told friends, T.R. regaled him by claiming that Bierce's short story, "A Son of the Gods," had inspired his gallant horseback ride up San Juan Hill—a ride that both he and Bierce knew had never taken place (Roosevelt had scrambled partway up the hillside on foot with the rest of the Rough Riders). He left the meeting convinced that Roosevelt was a dangerous poseur.[27]

Hearst, to his credit, never mentioned the Goebel controversy to Bierce, and even deflected calls from some of his editors to fire the columnist over the flap. Instead, he continued sending Bierce one hundred dollars a week to write whatever he wanted—which by now amounted to very little. Mostly, Bierce was content to roam about Washington on foot or on bicycle, often in the company of a young Virginian named Walter Neale, who had just started a publishing company in Washington and was consciously playing the role of Boswell to Bierce's Johnson. In his somewhat mistitled 1929 book, *Life of Ambrose Bierce*—it is actually a lengthy record of conversations between the two men, with little biographical information—Neale presents an unverifiable but more or less convincing picture of Bierce during his Washington years. As always, he had opinions on everything, from the divinity of Christ to the "indefensible" use of advertisements in newspapers and magazines. The two discussed love, marriage, sex, war, politics, religion, literature, and race—big topics that Bierce had spent the better part of four decades studying. Neale's Bierce is "every inch a man's man," strong, virile, witty, and attractive, a famous humorist who never laughed and seldom smiled, "unless a 'smile' of a kind peculiar to himself—sardonic, macabre, which would cause the onlooker to shiver slightly." Neale, who was nearly thirty years younger than Bierce, would weather his companion's notorious moods and remain a close friend and associate after relocating to New York in 1903.[28]

Another timely portrait of the artist was left by an unidentified Washington *Times* reporter who visited Bierce at his apartment in August 1902. "Mr. Bierce was found seated in his den, an apartment hung and carpeted in red and containing a Turkish couch piled high with pillows, a table full of interesting books, and a quaint little sideboard filled with a mixture of curious glasses, decanters, and a chafing dish," the newspaper reported. "He is a modest man and declares that the best thing about his work is the part he doesn't write, namely, the checks, and that even they might be better. He says that at present he is doing nothing, and adds, 'except writing.'" It is a more domesticated Bierce than one is used to seeing, but the sardonic little joke about his paychecks rings true, as does his rueful observation that he was doing nothing at present "except writing." He shared his rooms with his pet squirrel, John Henry Legs, and his pet canary, Mr. Dooley, and spent much of his time at two favorite watering holes, the Army-Navy Club and the aptly named Coffin Room, a dark, narrow bar in the basement of the Raleigh Hotel. For the first and only time in his life he began using his honorific military title, and was even listed as Major Bierce in the Washington telephone directory.[29]

Convinced that the Hearst newspapers had become "indistinguishable from circus posters," Bierce was glad to make the switch from daily to monthly journalism when Hearst bought *Cosmopolitan* magazine in the spring of 1905. His entry into magazine writing was delayed, however, by another stunning blow from California. Mollie Bierce, having somehow gotten the idea that her estranged husband wanted a divorce, obligingly filed for one in December 1904. Before the decree could become final, she died of a heart attack on April 27, 1905. Bierce, who had not seen his wife in several years (and did not want a divorce, anyway), was saddened and surprised by her death. "Death has been striking pretty close to me again, and you know how that upsets a fellow," he told Sterling, explaining that he had not yet done any writing for the magazine, since he had "not been in the mind." His nuclear family was now down to one, the twice-, soon to be thrice-married Helen, whom he called "Bib." Helping to allay some of the loneliness was the arrival of an old family friend from California, Carrie Christiansen, who moved into Bierce's apartment building on Iowa Circle, the Olympia, and began functioning as a sort of unpaid personal secretary and private nurse. Still, a deep weariness not unlike grief settled over his Washington days. "This is my birthday," he observed to one old friend. "I am 366 years old." Reading *King Lear* one night, he was struck by a desolating sorrow, a sense of "dead hands reaching everywhere."[30]

Unresolved feelings of guilt shadowed a pair of new short stories, "The Moonlit Road" and "Beyond the Wall," that Bierce wrote for *Cosmopolitan* shortly after Mollie's death. The first concerns an innocent young wife who has been strangled by her jealous husband and now haunts the earth as one of the undead who "skulk in eternal dusk among the scenes of our former lives, invisible to ourselves and one another, yet hiding forlorn in lonely places; yearning for speech with our loved ones, yet dumb, and as fearful of them as they of us. You think that we are of another world. No, we have knowledge of no world but yours, though for us it holds no sunlight, no warmth, no music, no laughter, no song of birds, nor any companionship. O God! what a thing it is to be a ghost, cowering and shivering in an altered world, a prey to apprehension and despair!" The maddened husband, by his insane act, destroys not only his and his wife's lives but also his son's, "a youth of brilliant parts and promise." It is not hard to find in the story echoes of Bierce's own truncated marriage to Mollie and the death of their son Day; and her chilly twilight world, cut off from all she had previously cared about, uncomfortably suggests the author's present state of mind.[31]

A slighter but somehow more touching story is "Beyond the Wall." In it, a wealthy trader returns to his former home in San Francisco and visits an old friend, Mohun Dampier, who has grown noticeably old since the last time he saw him. Dampier seems strangely troubled by a gentle tapping on the wall of his apartment. He explains to the narrator that ten years earlier he had met a young woman in the garden of his building and fallen head over heels in love with her. But lacking "the talent for marrying," he had been content to carry out a sort of quasi-courtship by exchanging taps on the wall between their apartments. This went on for some time, until the girl unaccountably failed to respond to one of his taps, and Dampier, in a spite, later purposely ignored her renewed tapping. The next morning, he learned that the young lady—who shared Mollie Bierce's "big black eyes"—had died the night before after a long bout with illness. Her dying wish had been to have her bed moved back beside the wall so that she could tap out one last message. Now the young girl's ghost has returned to haunt Dampier, and unable to cope with his guilty conscience, he commits suicide. Considering how Bierce had pointedly cut himself off from all contact with his wife, the tiny tapping on the wall between the too-proud Dampier and the girl with the lustrous dark eyes seems a poignant symbol of lost love and crossed communications between the unhappy, unfortunate Bierces.[32]

All of the stories that Bierce wrote for *Cosmopolitan* in one way or another concerned ghosts, including the Civil War tales "A Baffled Ambuscade," "The Other Lodgers," "Three and One Are One," and "A Resumed Identity." It is almost as though Bierce himself were leading a ghostlike existence, a feeling he underlined by revisiting his old Civil War battlefields in West Virginia and Tennessee. Autumnal West Virginia, in particular, haunted him:

"The whole region is wild and grand, and if any one of the men who in his golden youth soldiered through its valleys of sleep and over its gracious mountains will revisit it in the hazy season when it is all aflame with the autumn foliage, I promise him sentiments that he will willingly entertain and emotions that he will care to feel. Among them, I fear, will be a haunting envy of those of his comrades whose fall and burial in that enchanted land he once bewailed." He published another quatrain, this one about himself: "Ah, woe is his, with length of living cursed,/Who nearing second childhood, had no first./Behind, no glimmer, and before no ray—/A night at either end of his dark day."[33]

One brief glimmer of light came in 1906 when Doubleday, Page & Company decided to publish a collection of Bierce's demonic definitions. Bierce went up to New York for a conference with the editors, one of whom was Robert Lanier, the son of Georgia poet Sidney Lanier, the only Civil War veteran besides Bierce to achieve any literary prominence after the war. The editors liked the collection, but they were nervous about the title, *The Devil's Dictionary.* It is a measure of Bierce's eagerness to publish something in New York that he swiftly agreed to change the title to *The Cynic's Word Book.* "When it came out," he complained later, "the country already had been flooded by its imitators with a score of 'cynic' books—*The Cynic's This, The Cynic's That,* and *The Cynic's t'Other.* Most of these books were merely stupid, though some of them added the distinction of silliness. Among them, they brought the word 'cynic' into disfavor so deep that any book bearing it was discredited in advance of publication." Discredited or not, *The Cynic's Word Book* somewhat surprisingly failed to make much of a mark, and Bierce never published another book in New York. "Here in the East," he explained to Sterling, "the Devil is a sacred personage (the Fourth Person of the Trinity, as an Irishman might say) and his name must not be taken in vain." Perhaps he would have made more of a stir if he had included his own favorite, heretofore unpublished definition: "PARADISE, n. Copulation without culmination."[34]

His work with *Cosmopolitan,* too, failed to make an impression on the reading public, even after Hearst directed him to change the title of his column to "The Curmudgeon Philosopher." It was an unfortunate choice of words: Bierce was no philosopher, and in his increasingly enervated state he was scarcely a curmudgeon, although he was something of a crank. He spent much of his time sniping at homegrown socialists, newfangled inventions like the airplane, and those who dared to complain about his ridiculous over-praising of his friend Sterling's "Tennysonian" poem, "A Wine of Wizardry." He could still get off an occasional crisp one, as he did when he wondered about the possibility of someone doing an English translation of the works of Henry James. But for the most part, "The Curmudgeon Philosopher" was pretty tame stuff. Bierce complained that "the title so handicaps me that I can do nothing right," although even he admitted that much of his work was "sadly antiquated. My checks, though, are always up to date." Hearst thought so, as well; but when he attempted to get Bierce to fling some barbs in the direction of Joseph Pulitzer and the *World,* the angry columnist told *Cosmopolitan* editor Sam Chamberlain: "I don't like the job of chained bulldog to be let loose only to tear the panties off the boys who throw rocks at you. You wouldn't like it yourself in my place. Henceforth I won't bite anybody." To his friend Robert Mackay, he explained: "I'm a wage-slave for Hearst. But then the negro quarters are fairly comfortable, the corn and bacon tolerable and the overseer's whip can't reach me here in Washington. Sometimes I think I should like to be a free nigger, but I dunno'." Finally, in the spring of 1909, he resigned from the magazine, left the plantation, and severed his eventful twenty-two-year tie with William Randolph Hearst. It had been fun—of a sort—while it lasted.[35]

The catalyst for the final break was an offer from Walter Neale to publish a collected edition of Bierce's works. Greatly flattered by the proposal, which he saw as a last chance to solidify his hitherto "underground reputation," Bierce set to work at once, clipping and pasting reams of copy from yellowing stacks of old *News Letters*, *Argonauts*, *Wasps*, and *Examiners*. Disregarding his own previous warning to George Sterling that "I was a slovenly writer in those days," Bierce found it virtually impossible to discard anything he had ever written. In two months of furious work, he collected enough copy for five thick volumes. Meanwhile, Neale sent out an elaborate prospectus announcing a limited edition of 250 autographed sets, at $120 per set, to be "printed on paper of high grade, in large type, leaded; the binding will be full Levant morocco, both sides and the back decorated, bound by hand throughout, with double headbands, and lining of moire silk, with gold edges all around." The fact that Neale devoted more care to describing what was on the outside of the volumes than to what was on the inside was indicative, perhaps, of the elephantine grab bag the project would become. "The thing that saddens me," Bierce told the publisher, "is the thought of how I might have merited the praise if I had applied myself more to my art and less to pleasure." Now it was too late for that, but still Bierce cut and pasted, sadly unaware that he would have made a stronger case for himself with less, rather than more, copy.[36]

The first two volumes of *The Collected Works of Ambrose Bierce,* with an initial press run of 1,250 copies, appeared in 1909. Sales were slow. Volume one consisted of a series of would-be Swiftian satires, "Ashes of the Beacon" and "The Land Beyond the Blow," and the seminal Civil War reminiscences, "On a Mountain," "What I Saw of Shiloh," "A Little of Chickamauga," "The Crime at Pickett's Mill," "Four Days in Dixie," "What Occurred at Franklin," " 'Way Down in Alabam'," and his two accounts of his western trip with General Hazen, "Across the Plains" and "The Mirage." Elbert Hubbard, Bierce's erstwhile colleague on *Cosmopolitan,* reflected what would become a widespread critical emphasis on the books' externals when he noted: "The first volume is out, and in point of typography and binding it is beautiful as a dream when a glory of gold burnishes with brown the western sky." Volume two was devoted entirely to the great collection of short stories, *Tales of Soldiers and Civilians,* now bearing its English title, *In the Midst of Life.* New volumes came out at irregularly spaced intervals, an average of three a year, and the sumptuous bindings frequently clashed with the undifferentiated dross within. Volume three, appearing in the spring of 1910, included the collected ghost stories, *Can Such Things Be?,* along with a handful of more recent supernatural stories and a section on real-life "mysterious disappearances" that would come to have an ironic application to Bierce's own life. Volumes four and five reprinted his occasional poetry, much of it based on minor West Coast figures who, despite Bierce's claims to the contrary, could not be saved from their well-deserved anonymity. Volume six brought the ridiculous *The Monk and the Hangman's Daughter* and various collections of Aesop-like "Fantastic Fables" that he had earlier written for Tom Hood's magazine, *Fun,* and other English publications. Volume seven was devoted entirely to *The Devil's Dictionary,* printing many definitions that had been omitted from the Doubleday collection. The final volumes, eight through twelve, continued appearing, predictable as the seasons, until the autumn of 1912, when, as Bierce reported to a friend, "The completion of my 'collected works' finishes (I hope) my life's work. I am definitely 'out of it,' unless some irresistible impulse comes to me, which is not likely."[37]

Critical reception of the *Collected Works* was devastating. The twelve volumes were called variously "potatoes set in platinum," "turnips in Tiffany's window," and "pure piffle in plush pants." The London *Athenaeum,* while noting that the works had been "published in sumptuous style," complained with some justice that "the great fault or misfortune of Mr. Bierce is that, when he is not kept right by the pressure of an artistic purpose serious enough to inhibit the characteristic sallies of his intelligence, his writing is apt to be punctuated with lapses and excesses, tags of humour or extravagance or verbiage, which bring it into line, for the moment at least, with very common matter." The *Nation,* more cruelly, declared that "all that wide margins, gilt edges, and tooled leather bindings can do for these books has been done, and gentlemen whose bookrooms are papered in brown will find them a tasteful decoration. But except from the upholsterer's point of view they are not books at all, and Mr. Bierce has done an injustice to his considerable if somewhat perverse talent by marshalling its offspring in close formation." Neale, in the midst of the run, had to borrow $7,500 from a Washington bank to finish the project, and Bierce himself kicked in an extra $2,000 for company stock. But sales remained laggard, and for every old friend like Sterling who loyally ordered a collection, there were four times as many who hit up Bierce for free copies. His life work indeed seemed finished. Worse than that, it seemed irrelevant.[38]

In truth, Bierce had no one but himself to blame for the critical lambasting. A sympathetic but clear-minded editor like Percival Pollard might have been able to make some sense of the disorder by ruthlessly pruning the *Works* to half their length. An ideal collection could have included *Tales of Soldiers and Civilians; Can Such Things Be?; The Devil's Dictionary;* the wartime reminiscences "Bits of Autobiography"; "Mysterious Disappearances"; a handful of serious poems such as "A Study in Gray," "My Day of Life," "Reminded," and "Invocation"; a few representative examples of his satirical verse and fables; *The Parenticide Club;* "Jupiter Doke, Brigadier-General"; and the miscellaneous essays "A Thumb-Nail Sketch," "The Kreutzer Sonata," "Wit and Humor," and "Taking Oneself Off." A better editor than Bierce might also have convinced him to include a volume or two of his journalism, which was certainly much better and more important than he considered it. His early work on the *News Letter,* the *Argonaut,* and the *Wasp* contains some unrivaled examples of personal and political invective, while his more thoughtful columns on the Huntington funding bill, the Spanish-American War, and the annexation of the Philippines were solid and perceptive works. But Bierce did not respect his chosen profession, and his *Collected Works* cavalierly excluded his entire journalistic output.

Pollard, at any rate, would not have been able to help with the editing. He had died in December 1911 of a brain tumor, and Bierce dutifully went to Baltimore for the funeral. There he met Pollard's friend and disciple H. L. Mencken, then a thirty-one-year-old magazine editor. Between them, they made up a full 40 percent of the funeral party—Pollard was not known for the breadth of his friendships. Together, they shared a cab ride to and from the local crematorium, where, Bierce observed, "Pollard in his time has roasted many, and now he is being roasted to a turn." Mencken, whose long and contentious war with the "booboisie" would closely echo Bierce's own, was a little startled by the conversation. It was, he remembered, "a long series of gruesome and highly amusing witticisms. He had tales to tell of crematories that had caught fire and singed the mourners, of dead bibuli whose mortal remains had exploded, of widows guarding the fire all night to make sure that their husbands did not escape." Bierce suggested that they take Pollard's ashes and mold them into bullets to shoot at publishers, or else give them to the New York City Elks Lodge. They might even mail them anonymously to Ella Wheeler Wilcox, a treacly *Cosmopolitan* writer who was given to such life-affirming homilies as "All hail to life—life here, and life beyond, for earth is but the preparatory school for larger experience, for a greater usefulness!" The actual disposition of Pollard's ashes was less colorful, if equally macabre. Pollard's widow departed immediately after the service, and Mencken was left holding the bag, so to speak, which now contained not only ashes but also several larger bones, including the skull, which had not disintegrated. For months, he waited while Mrs. Pollard made up her mind what to do with her husband's remains. Finally, he attempted to mail them to Iowa, where Pollard had lived in his teens. The post office refused to accept the parcel, which they said constituted a corpse and thus could not be mailed without a permit. After much wrangling back and forth, Mencken managed to locate an undertaker who, for fifteen dollars, agreed to handle the necessary paperwork. Bierce howled with laughter at Mencken's "dead letter" and predicted that the good Christians of Iowa would quickly dig up Pollard's bones and throw them back across the state line.[39]

Funerals aside, Bierce was doing a good deal of traveling just then. Washington's current political climate, under the gigantic new President, William Howard Taft, was almost too much for a civilized man to bear. "The newspapers print page after page of lickspittle admiration of Taft, Mrs. Taft, the cub Tafts and everybody connected with the administration," Bierce complained. "I wish I could get the smell of my country out of my nose and clothing." With that in mind, in the spring of 1910, he returned to California for the first time in nearly eleven years. Arriving in San Francisco on May 19, he was shocked and saddened by the altered appearance of the city since the great earthquake four years earlier. "One does not care to look upon either the mutilated face of one's mashed friend or an upstart bearing his name," he observed. "No, my San Francisco is gone and I'll have no other." He fled the city for his brother Albert's vacation cabin on the Russian River near Guerneville. There he hiked, canoed, flirted with young women, and argued politics with Albert's son and daughter-in-law, who affected a modish socialism. He got an even larger dose of left-wing politics when he visited Sterling's recently founded artists' colony at Carmel. The minimally talented Sterling and his bohemian cohorts strode the white beaches and pine-scented hills above Point Lobos like so many sylvan wood sprites, talking of poesy and the raptures of art. It was a pose that revolted Bierce. The typical bohemian, he wrote, was "a lazy, loaferish, gluttonous, crapulent and dishonest duffer, who, according to the bent of his incapacity—the nature of the talents that heaven has liberally denied—scandalizes society, disgraces literature, debauches art, and is an irreclaimable, inexpressible and incalculable nuisance." Even worse, the privileged idlers at Carmel were "a nest of anarchists"—the worst epithet in the Biercian lexicon.[40]

Given such a view, it is not surprising that the new California artist community did not exactly welcome Bierce with open arms. Novelist Mary Austin, in particular, reacted badly to the famous visitor. Miss Austin, who liked to think of herself as a sort of white Indian, prattling on about their ancient wisdom and desert-loving ways, found the acerbic Bierce to be "a man secretly embittered by failure to achieve direct creation . . . a man of immense provocative power, always secretly—perhaps even to himself—

seeking to make good in some other's gift what he had missed. I thought him something of a posturer, tending to overweigh a slender inspiration with apocalyptic gestures." Bierce got a somewhat warmer reception from Jack London, to whom Sterling introduced him later that summer. Despite misgivings that the pair would clash over politics (London was an active socialist), California's two best-known writers hit it off famously. Bierce had learned that London's firstborn child had died a few months earlier, after living only a few days, and having lost two sons of his own, he fully sympathized with London's loss. When the two met at the Bohemian Club's annual revels in a redwood grove not far from Albert Bierce's cabin, they shook hands like old companions and quickly fell to drinking. Hours later, having compared notes on William Randolph Hearst, for whom London had covered the Russo-Japanese War, and the artists' colony at Carmel, which London abhorred for having snubbed his presumably nonartistic wife, the men headed back to Albert's camp. Along the way, Bierce went missing, and London found him sleeping peacefully in a bed of ferns at the foot of a twenty-foot embankment. Refreshed by his brief nap, Bierce invited London to stay and share another bottle of Three Star Martell cognac, and the evening concluded with the men sitting around a roaring campfire trading anecdotes with Sterling and San Francisco photographer Arnold Genthe, until "none of us quite knew what we were talking about."[41]

The meeting with London was the high point of Bierce's California trip. The increasingly precious Sterling rapidly grew tiresome, and other old friends were either retired, dead, or oddly reticent. "Where are the courageous men of the Vigilante Committee of the old days?" he wondered. "Where are those who broke the head of the mob with pick-handles in the time of Denis Kearney? I mean, where are those like them?" The answer, of course, he already knew. "They've had their moment," he wrote in a poem. "Gods! this is droll—That thieving sun is setting!" He left without saying good-bye to anyone, then stopped off for a few solitary days at the Grand Canyon, where he apparently took several snapshots of a suitably isolated spot where, he later told Walter Neale, he could kill himself in peace, secure in the knowledge that his bones would never be found. Washington, when he returned, was as bad as ever, the current Congress bearing as much resemblance to the Founding Fathers "as a flock of angels to an executive body of the Western Federation of Miners." Between recurrent bouts of asthma, the continued disappointing reception of his *Collected Works,* the death of Pollard, and a series of petty quarrels with old associates at the Army-Navy Club, Bierce was beginning to feel like one of his own ghosts, trapped between two worlds a continent apart.[42]

A second visit to California in the summer of 1912 reinforced those sentiments. For the first time in his life, he seemed old, walking with a stoop and using a cane. Much of his limited socializing was done from an armchair in the lobby of his Oakland hotel. Even a brief visit to Sterling's Carmel sideshow left him, as he wrote in the poet's guestbook, with "nothing to say." Friends had the definite sense that he was taking leave of them forever; to one, he confided that he was "sleepy for death." He paid a last visit to the cemetery at St. Helena where Mollie, Day, and Leigh were buried in an unmarked plot of raised earth surrounded by four palm trees. He gave the sexton there some money to keep up the plot, then left the little village where they had lived together as a family and returned east to his lonely apartment in Washington. He would never see California again. The cemetery sexton later recalled that he had said something about "going into Mexico."[43]

12

There Be Divers Sorts of Death

The new year of 1913 found Bierce back at his desk in Washington, writing letters to various far-flung correspondents and casting a jaundiced eye on the incoming President, Woodrow Wilson, whom he considered a better writer at least than his predecessors, if somewhat specious in his politics. The crushing defeat of former President Theodore Roosevelt, who had bolted the Republican party in favor of his own Progressive, or Bull Moose, party, filled Bierce, he told his daughter, Helen, "with a great white peace." His own peace was compounded more of resignation than of happiness. "My work is finished, and so am I," he wrote to B. J. S. Cahill in January. Other letters were less despairing, although perhaps equally distressing to their recipients. For Bierce now talked increasingly of going away, to Mexico or South America, in tones that were unmistakably fatalistic. They were, in fact, so doom-filled and portentous that one begins to suspect their author of carefully planting the seeds of a great mystery that, save for its final particulars, may not have been a mystery at all.[1]

Bierce first sounded the notes of his increasingly insistent swan song in a letter to his daughter on January 27. In it, he transferred to her the ownership of an old cemetery lot in St. Helena. "By the way," he wrote offhandedly at the end of the letter, "I do not wish to lie there. That matter is all arranged, and you will not be bothered about the mortal part of/Your Daddy." He neglected to say exactly what arrangements he had made concerning his final resting place, and Helen did not ask. A few months later, he visited her in Bloomington, Illinois, bringing with him a large cache of letters, papers, and legal documents. It was a pleasant, even affectionate, visit, with Bierce showing particular attention to Helen's two young stepsons, Henry and Victor Cowden. He seemed in good health—he told his daughter he had never felt better—but he also seemed vaguely restless and ill at ease. One evening, sitting together on Helen's veranda, father and daughter watched an old man shuffle past them down the street. "Bib, did you notice that old man?" Bierce asked after a brief silence. "I'll never be like that. Old people are cranky and fussy and infernal bores." When Helen assured him that he would always be welcome to live with her, Bierce smiled enigmatically and changed the subject. Another night, just before leaving, he told her that he intended to return to Washington and close out his affairs, then head south into Mexico. "This fighting in Mexico interests me," he said. "I want to go down and see if these Mexicans shoot straight." He would say the same thing, in much the same way, to various other friends in the weeks preceding his final departure from Washington.[2]

In May, he made a veiled, halfhearted offer to Curtis J. Kirch, editor of the Chicago-based *Lantern* magazine, to take over his editing duties for him, noting that "what your magazine needs is an editor—presumably older, preferably American, and indubitably alive. At least awake. It is your inning." Kirch, who had merely asked him to critique his magazine, did not respond. In September, he went to New York for a few days to visit friends. While there, he quarreled so bitterly with Walter Neale that he canceled a planned visit to Neale's home in Bensonhurst and returned abruptly to Washington. The cause of the quarrel is unknown, although it may have had something to do with Bierce's sudden decision to assign all his rights and royalties to Carrie Christiansen, his long-time secretary, whom Neale did not like. (In his book, Neale calls her an "ugly duckling" and implies that she and Bierce were married, an allegation for which he offers no proof.) At any rate, Bierce quickly apologized for the blowup, advising Neale to "let it go as it is" and expressing, somewhat uncharacteristically, his deep regret over the incident.[3]

On September 10, the same day he wrote to Neale to apologize, Bierce also sent letters to his niece, Lora Bierce, and to Josephine McCrackin in California, announcing his intention to visit Mexico. They were the first in a month-long series of letters to various friends and relatives, all saying essentially the same thing: that he was going into Mexico (and eventually South America), and that given the violent state of Mexican affairs, he might not be coming back. It is, of course, entirely possible that he had already decided on his baffling new trip before his quarrel with Neale—he had been thinking about it at least since his visit to Helen earlier in the year—but the timing of his formal announcement seems to suggest that the row with Neale may have been the last straw in a long series of fractured friendships and personal disappointments stretching back over the course of several years. Soon he would write George Sterling out of his life for excessive gossiping and bohemianism, addressing his old protégé as "Great Poet and Damned Scoundrel" and speaking to him, Sterling said later, like "God talking to a guttersnipe." Even his brother Albert, the last remaining link to his Indiana childhood, came in for a letter so caustic and wounding that it was said to have hastened his death by stroke a few months later. With increasing urgency, Bierce seemed to be closing all his accounts that fall, with a finality that indicated a very long journey indeed.[4]

Going to Mexico in late 1913 was a perilous undertaking—the country was then in the midst of a seven-year-long revolution that in the end would claim a million lives—but there was still something either perversely callous or purposely calculating about Bierce's letters at the time. Far from seeking to reassure his friends about his venture, the author went out of his way to alarm then with lurid speculations about his fate. Keeping in mind that Bierce was the most careful of writers, it cannot have been an accident that the central image (and in some cases the very wording) of the letters was obsessively consistent. As he put it to the gentle and aged Josephine McCrackin in his first letter to her on September 10: "I expect to go to, perhaps across, South America—possibly via Mexico, if I can get through without being stood up against a wall and shot as a Gringo. But that is better than dying in bed, is it not?" And to Lora Bierce, he wrote on October 1: "Good-bye—if you hear of my being stood up against a Mexican stone wall and shot to rags please know that I think that a pretty good way to depart this life. It beats old age, disease, or falling down the cellar stairs. To be a Gringo in Mexico—ah, that is euthanasia!" The day before, he had advised San Francisco bookstore clerk James D. Blake—scarcely a close acquaintance: "Don't write; I am leaving in a day or two for Mexico. If I can get in (and out) I shall go later to South America from some Western port. Doubtless I'm more likely to get in than out, but all good Gringos go to Heaven when shot."[5]

Was Bierce simply being morbid, or did he have an ulterior motive for writing as he did? Since he had not yet left for Mexico, he had no way of knowing with any degree of certainty how dangerous—or not—his undertaking might be. True, there was a revolution going on, and revolutions are notoriously unpredictable, especially in Latin America, but the fighting was between the Mexican people, the federal forces of President Victoriano Huerta and those of rebel leaders Venustiano Carranza, Emiliano Zapata, and Francisco "Pancho" Villa. If anything, American lives and property were being scrupulously protected: Neither side wanted the United States to intervene on behalf of the other because of some real or imagined outrage against American citizens. Even the fearsome Villa, a lifelong bandit and killer whose own handpicked biographer described him as "more of a jaguar than a man," was said to be treating all gringos with untypical courtesy and restraint. As a famous American writer, a recognizable public figure from New York to San Francisco, and a journalist with ties to the most powerful newspaper publisher in the world, Bierce (who did not lack for self-esteem) could more reasonably expect to be treated with exaggerated deference than to be hustled against the nearest adobe wall and shot. Again the suspicion lingers that, as he told McCrackin, he was going into Mexico "with a pretty definite purpose, which, however, is not at present disclosable." But what was his purpose, and why was it not disclosable? Why, for that matter, was Bierce, who had not been out of his own country for nearly forty years, suddenly so insistent about going to a land that was then in the midst of a violent revolution, one in which, it must be said, he had never expressed the first jot of interest, even while living in neighboring California for three decades?[6]

The easiest and most romantic answer is simply to take him at his word. This is what earlier biographers—with one notable exception—have done, creating in the process the now-legendary image of Bierce the gallant and quixotic old man, who, having grown restless and bored in Washington, impulsively heads down to revolutionary Mexico to drink tequila with Pancho Villa and test his Civil War–honed marksmanship on a few unfortunate *federales* before disappearing, with exquisite theatrical timing, into "the good, good darkness" of history. It is the image that Bierce himself seems to have taken great pains to create with his frequent references to being shot and disappearing forever. But again the question arises: Were these the reasonable views of a seventy-one-year-old asthmatic who knew he was embarking on a perilous trip and was simply being realistic about the dangers he was undertaking, or were they, in fact, a carefully prepared cover story designed to conceal his true purpose, which may have been less swashbuckling, if altogether more determinate. Might they even have been, as one recent investigator has suggested, a "de facto suicide note"? Did Ambrose Bierce, in actuality, go to Mexico to kill himself? For that matter, did he go to Mexico at all? Admittedly, these are difficult questions, but they are ones that must be asked, if not perhaps answered, if one is to accompany Bierce on the final leg of the sad, strange journey that was his life.[7]

His movements, from the time he left Washington on October 2 until he reached Laredo, Texas, in early November, are fairly well documented. He continued writing and sending letters to his daughter, his niece, and his secretary, Carrie Christiansen, who kept a detailed log of his messages, though at his instructions she destroyed the actual letters themselves. Interestingly— perhaps crucially—Bierce did not head directly to Mexico; he first spent nearly three arduous and weather-dampened weeks revisiting his old Civil War battlefields in the South. On two earlier occasions, he had toured some of the same battle sites, but never at such length, and his actions seem a little like those of a dying man paying a last valedictory visit to his past. That he should have wanted to see the old killing grounds again was not unusual; aging veterans of the blue and gray, in ever-thinning numbers, were forever conducting similar tours. But the fact that he took such a lengthy detour while ostensibly hell-bent on getting into Mexico strongly suggests that, for whatever reason, he did not expect to pass that way again.

According to Christiansen's itinerary, Bierce left Washington at 10:10 P.M. on the night of October 2, 1913. He was traveling alone. He arrived at his first destination, Chattanooga, at 5:00 P.M. the next afternoon, checking into the Patten Hotel on East Eleventh Street. He spent all day Saturday, October 4, walking the battle sites at Orchard Knob and Missionary Ridge, ten miles up and down the steeply wooded hillsides he had stormed under withering fire almost exactly fifty years before. The next day, he visited Chickamauga, hiking fifteen miles in the hot sun, reliving the horrific fighting in that blood-soaked north Georgia wilderness. At Snodgrass Hill, where he and his brother Albert had run into each other during General Thomas's famous stand, he made a sketch of the monument to Albert's battery, the Eighteenth Ohio Light Artillery, to send to him. Then it was on to Murfreesboro and the site of the Battle of Stones River, where Hazen's brigade had staved off disaster at Hell's Half-Acre and Bierce had gallantly rescued Lieutenant Braden under fire. No doubt he sought out the Hazen monument; like the protagonist in "A Resumed Identity," he was himself now white-haired and full of wonder at the years that had slipped so suddenly by. To Franklin then, where the pride of the Southern army had dashed itself to pieces against the hasty Union breast-works, 6,200 killed, wounded, or captured in the "devil's work" an hour before sundown on the last day of November 1864. And so to Nashville on October 10, where the ghostly remnants of that same rebel army for all intents and purposes ceased to exist before the Yankees' very eyes, while Bierce stayed in the rear and ruefully watched the black troops he had once declined to command sacrifice themselves in a tide-turning frontal assault that was "as pretty an example of courage and discipline as one could wish to see."[8]

Two days later, he left for Shiloh, looping south by steamboat to Pittsburg Landing, where he and his comrades in the Ninth Indiana had been ferried at night across the river like Charon negotiating the Styx, while wild-eyed fugitives huddled on the far bank and Bierce encountered some Union officer's white-faced little wife holding an ivory-handled revolver and vowing to do her duty "if it came to the worst." Bierce had expected to spend a day or two at Shiloh; he stayed twice that long. It was, after all, what he saw of Shiloh that made—or at least confirmed—him a writer, veteranizing him in that brotherhood of men who had seen the old world end together one rainy April morning in 1862. Their graves were still there, including twenty-one belonging to the Ninth Indiana, but only half of the three thousand Union markers had names. Bierce found a stone for T. J. Patton, the regimental adjutant, and was dismayed to see that Patton's rank had been left off his grave—for over fifty years, he had been lying there forgotten, without full military honors. The fields across the river looked the same, but the ravine of death where he had found the charred remains of hundreds of slaughtered soldiers from the

Fifty-fifth Illinois was now merely a grass-covered depression, like a fairway bunker on a well-kept golf course. For one whole day at Shiloh, Bierce did nothing but sit by himself in the sun. "And this was, O so long ago! How they come back to me—dimly and brokenly, but with what a magic spell—those years of youth when I was soldiering!"⁹

By October 20, the sun had gone away and the spell had been broken. A freakish early-autumn snowstorm blanketed west Tennessee and northern Mississippi. Bierce thrashed through the snow in a ramshackle automobile, arriving at Corinth so stiff with cold that he could barely write his name in the hotel register. The unlovely railroad town was immersed in a sea of coal dust from hundreds of engines. There was little to see, anyway; Corinth had been a "solemn farce," notable only for General Halleck's stubbornly successful avoidance of battle and Indiana governor Oliver P. Morton's disillusioning visit to the front, commemorated by Bierce in his fine story "An Affair of Outposts." The next morning, he fled south on an early train, still shadowed by a southwesterly blizzard, and pulled into Hattiesburg, Mississippi, where he had his first square meal since leaving Shiloh and his first real bath since leaving Nashville. From there, he crossed over to New Orleans, always one of his favorite cities, checking into the St. Charles Hotel on October 23 and strolling along the river among the cotton bales in now-beautiful weather. The miserable trip south, however, brought on a serious bout of asthma, so bad that Bierce was unable to lie down at night. He fought through it, though, and was soon well enough to sit down for an interview with a New Orleans *States* newspaper reporter. What he told him was duly reported under the headline, BIERCE, FAMOUS AS AUTHOR, VISITS HERE./ON WAY TO MEXICO FOR TRUTHFUL FACTS. The well-written article is important for what Bierce said, both consciously and unconsciously, about his trip. And as one of the last independent and verifiable glimpses of Bierce while he was still alive, it deserves to be quoted in full:

> *Traveling over the same ground that he had covered with General Hazen's brigade during the Civil War, Ambrose Bierce, famed writer and noted critic, has arrived in New Orleans. Not that this city was one of the places figuring in his campaigns, for he was here after and not during the war. He has come to New Orleans in a haphazard, fancy-free way, making a trip toward Mexico. The places that he has visited on the way down have become famous in song and story—places where the greatest battles were fought, where the moon shone at night on the burial corps, and where in day the sun shone bright on polished bayonets and the smoke drifted upward from the cannon mouths.*
>
> *For Mr. Bierce was at Chickamauga; he was at Shiloh; at Murfreesboro; Kenesaw [sic] Mountain, Franklin and Nashville. And then when wounded during the Atlanta campaign he was invalided home. He "has*

never amounted to much since then," he said Saturday. But his stories of the great struggle, living as deathless characterizations of the bloody episodes, stand for what he "has amounted to since then."

Perhaps it was in mourning for the dead over whose battlefields he has been wending his way toward New Orleans that Mr. Bierce was dressed in black. From head to foot he was attired in this color, except where the white cuffs and collar and shirt front showed through. He even carried a walking cane, black as ebony and unrelieved by gold or silver. But his eyes, blue and piercing as when they strove to see through the smoke at Chickamauga, retained all the fire of the indomitable fighter.

"I'm on my way to Mexico, because I like the game," he said, "I like the fighting; I want to see it. And then I don't think Americans are as oppressed there as they say they are, and I want to get at the true facts of the case. Of course, I'm not going into the country if I find it unsafe for Americans to be there, but I want to take a trip diagonally across from northeast to southwest by horseback, and then take ship for South America, go over the Andes and across that continent, if possible, and come back to America again.

"There is no family that I have to take care of; I've retired from writing and I'm going to take a rest. No, my trip isn't for local color. I've retired just the same as a merchant or businessman retires. I'm leaving the field for the younger authors."

An inquisitive question was interjected as to whether Mr. Bierce had acquired a competency only from his writings, but he did not take offense.

"My wants are few, and modest," he said, "and my royalties give me quite enough to live on. There isn't much that I need, and I spend my time in quiet travel. For the last five years I haven't done any writing. Don't you think that after a man has worked as long as I have that he deserves a rest? But perhaps after I have rested I might work some more—I can't tell, there are so many things—" and the straightforward blue eyes took on a faraway look, "there are so many things that might happen between now and when I come back. My trip might take several years, and I'm an old man now."

Except for the thick, snow-white hair no one would think him old. His hands are steady, and he stands up straight and tall—perhaps six feet."[10]

Bierce liked the article well enough to send Lora Bierce a copy of it two weeks later, along with a postscript that has puzzled biographers ever since. The letter, dated November 6 from Laredo, was actually sent November 5 from San Antonio, as Bierce made clear in a follow-up note to his niece. He had just spent a week in San Antonio, visiting the Alamo ("the shrine of each Texan's devotion"), which he said was small enough to be covered with a hat, and Fort Sam Houston, where the officers of the Third Cavalry treated him like a foreign ambassador and could hardly be dissuaded from parading the regiment in his honor. As he told Carrie Christiansen, he had known some of the officers in San Francisco and met others at the Army-Navy Club in Washington; most of them were familiar with his work. In his letter to Lora, he again advised her of his intention to cross over into Mexico, where "there is a good deal of fighting going on [but] in the character of 'innocent bystander' I ought to be fairly safe if I don't have too much money on me, don't you think?" Then he added the baffling note: "You need not believe *all* that these newspapers say of me and my purposes. I had to tell them *something*." But what had he told them? Picking through the quotes in the short *States* article, one sifts the words for a runic message. He was going to Mexico, he said, because he "like[d] the game, I like the fighting"—this from a man who fifteen years earlier had shown absolutely no interest in going to Cuba during the Spanish-American War, the greatest national conflict since the Civil War, and whose own short stories and newspaper columns, based on the most painful personal experience, had consistently depicted warfare as suicidal, dehumanizing, and implacably destructive. He was not going if he found it "unsafe"—a reservation he did not make to his friends and family— but if he went "there are so many things that might happen," and besides, he was an old man. Nevertheless, he intended to ride horseback across the entire arid, revolution-wracked countryside and then take a ship for South America, cross the forbidding Andes and the jungle-covered continent, and "if possible" return to the United States. It was, all things considered, a most unlikely scenario.[11]

The question remains: What part of the interview was his niece supposed to disbelieve? Since he had already told her about his travel plans, was she merely to disregard the part about him returning? Was Bierce in fact gently trying to tell her that he was not coming back at all? He certainly struck a gloomy note in his last letter to her on November 6: "I shall not be here long enough to hear from you, and don't know where I shall be next. Guess it doesn't matter much./Adios." This scarcely sounds like a man who intended to return at all. Looking again at the interview, one gets the impression that Bierce was putting on a little for the reporter's benefit. From his all-black clothing to his somewhat overstated jingoism ("I'm on my way to Mexico, because I like the game") to his carefully staged pause for dramatic effect ("the straightforward blue eyes took on a faraway look, 'there are so many things that might happen between now and when I come back'"), the picture he seems to be trying to project is that of a tired old man embarked on a last, dangerous journey. And while this was undoubtedly the case, the New Orleans reporter—whose profession it was to see through such poses—still seems to have found the ominous presentation a little unconvincing. The "straightforward blue eyes" are at odds with the "faraway look" they are affecting, and Bierce's characterization of himself as an old man is immediately undercut by the reporter's follow-up observation: "Except for the thick, snow-white hair no one would think him old." But why would Bierce, so proud of his physical prowess and stamina, take such pains to portray himself publicly as an aging retiree wearily leaving the field to younger men?[12]

An imaginative—to say the least—theory was put forth in 1972 by San Francisco writer Sibley Morrill, in his book *Ambrose Bierce, F. A. Mitchell-Hedges and the Crystal Skull.* Morrill contends that Bierce went to Mexico as a secret agent for the American government to monitor the nefarious doings of the Germans and Japanese, who were said to be planning either a joint Japanese-Mexican attack on the United States or a German-backed naval assault on the nearly completed Panama Canal. Bierce was a perfect candidate for spying, says Morrill, precisely because he was such an improbable choice: a prominent, loquacious, attention-attracting misanthrope of advanced years whose long-standing ties—through his membership in the Army-Navy Club—to ranking members of the military and intelligence communities gave him a perfect entrée to the clandestine world of espionage. No one would suspect an asthmatic seventy-one-year-old writer of being a secret agent, Morrill maintains, thus leaving Bierce free to roam about the countryside in the company of an English adventurer turned spy named F. A. Mitchell-Hedges (who conveniently fails to mention Bierce in his 1954 auto-biography, proving incontrovertibly—at least to Morrill—that the two were in cahoots). In this way, Bierce's letters, interviews, and much-publicized tour of Civil War battlefields were all part of a carefully thought out ruse to throw competing agents off his scent and provide the American government with a suitable cover story in the not-unlikely event that he managed to get himself killed along the way.[13]

To this point, Morrill's thesis is plausible, if rather far-fetched—the American government had more than adequate intelligence capabilities on both sides of the Mexican border without recruiting a loose cannon like Bierce to spy for them—but Morrill is just getting started. In his increasingly opaque account, Bierce and Mitchell-Hedges, having linked up with each other for unspecified reasons, head cross-country toward Guatemala, somehow finding the time along the way to buy or steal the fabled Mayan "Skull of Doom," known more prosaically as the Crystal Skull, which in the hands of the high priests of Maya was said to cause instant and invariable death. They then proceed to British Honduras, where Bierce—having presumably discharged his inconvenient spying duties—parts company with Mitchell-Hedges and spends the rest of his days investigating mysterious disappearances in the Yalbac Triangle region of the country, until at last he is transported to an underground cave by flying Mayan sorcerers and (as of 1972, at least) was still alive and well and living in Honduras.[14]

Joe Nickell, a former private detective who investigated Bierce's final days for his 1992 book, *Ambrose Bierce Is Missing and Other Historical Mysteries,* also believes that the author's New Orleans performance was a smoke screen, but one undertaken for a less supernatural reason. Following the theory first propounded by Walter Neale in his 1929 biography, Nickell sees Bierce's actions as a ploy designed to conceal his true destination—the Grand Canyon—and his true purpose—suicide. "To complete the act he needed only a distracting puff of smoke, which he conjured up in the form of a turbulent Mexico as an apparent destination," writes Nickell. "He penned final communications to further the illusion he had crossed the border, but instead the old trickster deftly slipped from sight. Perhaps—sometime before grimly cocking his revolver a few days later—he smiled wryly at the ironic thought that it was a different crossing over he was about to make." Other Bierce biographers have typically ignored Neale's version in favor of a more dramatic disappearance in Mexico. And yet given what we know of Bierce—his often-stated approval of suicide, his fascination with mysterious disappearances, his love of hoaxes, his doom-riddled letters, and his sentimental revisiting of Civil War battlefields—a strong, if circumstantial, case can be made for such a theory. It first requires setting aside eighty years' worth of mythologizing about Bierce's "probable" fate and looking anew at the situation in northern Mexico at the time of his disappearance in late December 1913, particularly with reference to the near-simultaneous disappearance of another disputatious Anglo, William S. Benton, in the same area. A closer examination of the facts surrounding the Benton case puts Bierce's disappearance in a new light by showing how difficult, if not impossible, it would have been for someone as famous as Ambrose Bierce simply to disappear in the hothouse atmosphere of revolutionary Mexico at that particular time and place.[15]

At the beginning of the revolution, Benton, a native of Scotland, was one of the wealthiest ranch owners in the state of Chihuahua. A former prospector, he had married a local girl and built his ranch, Los Remedios, into a multimillion-dollar enterprise. Prickly and proud, he was not a man accustomed to being bullied. After Pancho Villa drove the government forces out of the state in a series of battles in the fall and winter of 1913–1914, he summarily confiscated Benton's ranch and ordered the progovernment rancher to leave Mexico immediately. Benton, with more nerve than sense, confronted Villa at Juárez, where the revolutionary leader had gone to buy arms and equipment across the border in El Paso. Storming into Villa's headquarters one morning in early February 1914, Benton loudly demanded the return of his property. Villa refused, but he offered to compensate the rancher for his loss, adding, "Since you are English and I wish to avoid international incidents, I will pay you what it is worth, or what you paid for it, after which you will stay out of Mexico." This answer enraged Benton, who pulled out a pistol and attempted to shoot Villa then and there. He was overwhelmed by guards before he could pull the trigger and was then brusquely placed under arrest.[16]

Villa was now in a quandary. He did not want to antagonize the English, but he could not very well allow someone to march blithely into his headquarters and try to gun him down. After considering various alternatives, the guerrilla chieftain characteristically opted for the most murderous; he had Benton smuggled out of Juárez under cover of darkness and secretly executed. At Samalayuca, forty miles south, a small party of Villistas dug a shallow grave and Rodolfo Fierro, Villa's favorite assassin, crept up behind Benton and bashed in his head with a shovel. Then, without checking to see whether the rancher was dead or alive, the killers rolled him into the grave and unceremoniously covered him with dirt.[17]

Despite the veil of secrecy, rumors of Benton's death immediately leaked out. American consul George Carothers personally accompanied Benton's widow to Villa's headquarters to demand a full accounting of the incident. Villa protested his innocence, saying he had not even seen Benton and theatrically going through the motions of searching for the missing man throughout Juárez. Meanwhile, American citizens across the border in El Paso began saying openly that Benton had been murdered. The *New York Times* got wind of the story and loudly denounced the killing, warning that Benton's death might force the Wilson administration to intervene on the side of the Huerta government. Carothers hand-delivered to Villa a message from Secretary of State William Jennings Bryan describing the matter as a "serious affair." The British government, as well, demanded a full accounting.[18]

Faced with a potentially grave international incident, Villa finally admitted that Benton had been executed, but he insisted that the sentence had been lawfully assessed by a revolutionary court. He then wrote a letter to the *New York Times* declaring that "a court-martial sentenced Benton to death with complete justification, due to his crimes in having made an attempt on my life, as I am able to prove." Farther west, in Nogales, Villa's fellow revolutionary general Venustiano Carranza got into the act, demanding that any questions concerning Benton be directed to him as "First Chief of the Revolution." American correspondent John Reed—soon to become famous for his reporting of the Russian Revolution, which he turned into the best-selling book *Ten Days That Shook the World*—took Carranza up on his offer and traveled to his headquarters to interview him about the case. While Reed scribbled away furiously, Carranza loudly denounced American meddling and warned that "if the United States intervenes in Mexico upon this petty excuse, intervention will provoke a war which will deepen a profound hatred between the United States and the whole of Latin America!"[19]

Under mounting pressure from all sides, Villa reluctantly agreed to surrender Benton's body to an international commission. Anticipating a formal autopsy on the victim, Villa ordered his men to dig up the Englishman's body and shoot it full of bullet holes to simulate an execution by firing squad. But before this macabre postscript could take place, Carranza declared that any further investigation of the incident would represent an intolerable violation of Mexican sovereignty, and the unfortunate Benton was left mouldering in his grave. On pain of incurring a similar fate, residents of Juárez and other northern Mexican towns were expressly forbidden to speak the dead man's name.[20]

The Benton case has been routinely ignored by Bierce biographers, despite the fact that most of them have ascribed a similar fate to Bierce. This is entirely understandable, given the international uproar Benton's killing instantly provoked on both sides of the Atlantic and along the U.S.-Mexican border from Texas to California. For if the carefully concealed murder of one comparatively little-known English rancher could have become public knowledge so quickly, reaching the august pages of the *New York Times* and raising the specter of an American intervention in the Mexican Revolution, what sort of outcry might not the murder of one of America's most famous writers have occasioned? It is virtually certain that the reported death of Ambrose Bierce in early 1914 would have brought American troops pouring across the Mexican border in search of revenge, even as a perceived insult to the American flag at Tampico in March of that same year resulted in a six-month-long naval occupation of Mexico's principal port city of Veracruz, and as Villa's ill-conceived raid on Columbus, New Mexico, two years later provoked an eleven-month-long punitive expedition to Chihuahua by Brig. Gen. John J. Pershing and 6,600 American soldiers. It is equally certain that if Bierce had died during that period, either peaceably or otherwise, it would have been noticed by someone. A large contingent of foreign reporters, mainly Americans, was accompanying Villa's army at the time; Americans on both sides of the border were avidly following the progress of the war. The United States Army, through its own scouts and numerous Mexican informants, was monitoring events from its various border forts, including two facilities that Bierce himself had visited within the past few weeks. As the Benton affair conclusively demonstrates, the death of such a prominent gringo would not have gone unnoticed for long.

Instead, there was nothing: no word from Bierce, no reported sightings of him, not even a whispered rumor of his fate. Carrie Christiansen's diary, until now so full of details concerning Bierce's trip, has only two brief paragraphs purporting to show his whereabouts after November 13, 1913. The first places him "twenty or thirty miles south of Juarez" on November 28; the second has him riding into Chihuahua City on December 26 to mail a last letter stating that he was leaving for Ojinaga the next day. By now, she says, he has been "cordially received" by the revolutionaries and given credentials to travel with the army. Beyond that, as most biographers note forebodingly, "the rest is silence." Since Pancho Villa fought and won the Battle of Ojinaga on January 11, 1914, the most popular conjecture regarding Bierce's fate has been that he was killed in the battle and his body subsequently burned along with those of other victims to check an ongoing typhus epidemic. On the surface, such a conclusion seems eminently logical. In reality, it requires a rather large leap of faith.[21]

To begin with, there is absolutely no evidence that Bierce was ever at Ojinaga. Between his letter to Christiansen on December 26 and the battle on January 11, a gap of some sixteen days, the inveterate letter writer apparently communicated with no one. This in itself proves nothing; in the midst of an ongoing military campaign one might logically neglect one's personal correspondence. However, since the Villistas besieged Ojinaga for ten full days before overrunning the town, and since Ojinaga was directly across the Rio Grande from Presidio, Texas, it seems unlikely that Bierce, with time on his hands, would have failed in the interim to contact someone, if only to report his safe arrival. Nor are there any verifiable accounts of Bierce taking part in the battle itself, aside from one unsupported postwar report of "an old gringo" who supposedly was seen going into battle. Immediately after the battle, the government forces of Generals Salvador Mercado and Pascual Orozco retreated across the border to Presidio, where General Pershing personally supervised their transfer to nearby Fort Bliss for internment. Had Bierce been killed on Pershing's very doorstep, so to speak, it is altogether likely that the general would have heard about it, particularly since he also met with Villa after the battle. As it was, no reports reached Pershing of any Americans being involved in the battle—much less being killed there. Moreover, Norman Walker, a reporter for the El Paso *Herald* who covered the battle, later told investigators that he was convinced Bierce had not been present at Ojinaga.[22]

Despite the complete lack of verification, the Ojinaga scenario has been the one most frequently embraced by Bierce biographers, chiefly (one suspects) because it does away with him most swiftly and easily. Like Hamlet's ghost—though without his first-act soliloquy—Bierce is also killed offstage early in the play, and it is therefore inconvenient to have him roaming about the Mexican countryside for months or even years afterward, entirely unnoticed by American eyes, while various official and unofficial search parties fail to turn up the first scrap of hard evidence and rumors abound of ever-more-unlikely demises. In one widely accepted version, Bierce is said to have angered Villa by threatening to desert to Carranza's camp, at which point the guerrilla leader supposedly embraced Bierce warmly, bade him farewell, then turned to the killer Fierro and sent him hurrying after the American in the dark to dispatch him with a well-placed pistol shot to the head. (For ethnic and cultural reasons having to do with lingering Mexican-American antipathies, this is the version most favored in Mexico.) The main problem with this account—aside from the implausible suggestion that Bierce would have been stupid enough to openly insult the ever-dangerous Villa to his face—is one of timing. Villa and Carranza were allies, at least ostensibly, until September 1914, when the two warlords fell out over the future conduct of the revolution. Even allowing for a few months' worth of bad blood between them before the final break, such a scenario would necessarily place Bierce in Villa's camp several months after his supposed death at Ojinaga. As will be seen, this was not only improbable but also virtually impossible.[23]

By the autumn of 1913, Pancho Villa was the most famous man in Mexico, if not the world. His exploits, real and imagined, were front-page news from Dallas to Paris. Legends abounded of his Robin Hood–like good deeds, his sharing of the (stolen) wealth with the poor people of Chihuahua, and his untutored prowess at guerrilla warfare. Prominent journalists like John Reed and young adventurers like future movie star Tom Mix flocked to his side. Following the American occupation of Veracruz, Gen. Hugh Scott and consul George Carothers invited him to a much-publicized conference on the Juárez–El Paso border to explain the U.S. action and receive the former bandito's blessing. When Villa beneficently declared his support for the intervention and expressed the poignant wish for "only the closest and most friendly relations with our neighbors to the north," a relieved President Wilson described him warmly as a "high minded and noble citizen of Mexico."[24]

With his enormous sombrero, drooping mustache, and bristling bandilleros, Villa was the very image of the dashing revolutionary. Moon-faced and jolly—at least on the surface—he looked a little like a Mexican Babe Ruth, and, like Ruth, he created an image that endures to the present. A lightning rod of world attention, Villa's every move was closely scrutinized, by both the American public and its military and political leaders. If Bierce had been present in Villa's camp, he would have been immediately recognized by the traveling press. As it was, his last known interview took place in early November in San Antonio, where reporters for the local newspapers gave full play to the "prominent" and "noted" author's presence in their city and repeated his now-well-practiced story about traveling through Mexico and South America. No other journalists, including such experienced war correspondents as Floyd Gibbons, Frederick Palmer, and Gregory Mason, who were with Villa at the time, ever saw or heard of Bierce. Timothy Turner of the Associated Press later wrote a book about Villa's campaign, but he refused even to speculate about Bierce's disappearance, "being an honest man and refusing to play on my imagination." As for Villa himself, he pointedly told Carothers that he had never met Bierce, an account that Villa's last surviving wife, Señora Soledad Seanez de Villa, corroborated. University of Texas at El Paso professor Haldeen Braddy, a longtime student of the Bierce case, personally interviewed dozens of former Villistas, including Villa's widow, without turning up one authenticated sighting of the author in Villa's camp. "It is my conclusion," Braddy reported, "that the spreading belief that Bierce died in Mexico rests at present on no substantial proof whatsoever and should thus be strongly opposed." Whether or not Bierce died in Mexico, there is certainly no proof that he ever met Pancho Villa, let alone accompanied him on his well-publicized campaign in northern Mexico in 1913–1914.[25]

But if Bierce was not with Villa or his army, as legend has it, where was he? His last reported sighting, in Chihuahua around Christmas 1913, is based entirely on Carrie Christiansen's transcription of his alleged December 26 letter. Unfortunately, the letter itself has not survived, and there is strong circumstantial evidence to suggest that Bierce was never in Chihuahua. American consul Carothers, based in the city, testified later that he had never encountered Bierce there. And since Carothers was the official liaison between Villa and the American government, his lack of contact with Bierce—one of the nation's most prominent journalists, it should be repeated—places in doubt the widespread belief that Bierce received formal press credentials to accompany Villa's army. Carothers's successor, Marion Letcher, also denied ever seeing Bierce. In 1930, Letcher wrote, "I was serving at Chihuahua at the time of Mr. Bierce's disappearance and remember quite well reading references to the subject in the press, but so far as is known to me Mr. Bierce did not visit my consular district in those troublous revolutionary days. In those disturbed times it was my custom to keep a very accurate register of the movements of Americans in the district and I feel sure that had Mr. Bierce visited the State of Chihuahua for any longer period, let us say, than a few days, I would have had some record of such a visit and would now recall it. While I was at Chihuahua I had several exchanges of correspondence with a young lady in Washington [Carrie Christiansen], who was endeavoring to get some trace of Mr. Bierce through my office, and after my transfer to Washington in 1916 I had a personal interview with the same person. In response to this lady's request I investigated the subject at the time and could find no evidence that Mr. Bierce had been in Chihuahua."[26]

It is now impossible to say conclusively whether or not Bierce was ever in Chihuahua, although it seems increasingly unlikely that he joined Villa's forces there. Perhaps Letcher's qualification that "had Mr. Bierce visited the State of Chihuahua for any longer period . . . than a few days, I would have had some record of [it]" offers a clue to resolving the mystery. For it would certainly have been possible for Bierce to have gone to Chihuahua, as Christiansen says he did, without it necessarily following that he linked up with Villa's army. He might well have gone there to create a smoke screen, as Nickell has theorized, to obscure his real purpose and destination. This theory is given weight by a 1918 letter from journalist George Weeks to Bierce biographer Vincent Starrett, in which Weeks reported a conversation he had with William A. Willis of the New York *Herald* and other correspondents staying at the Hotel Sheldon in El Paso. According to Weeks, Willis told him that Bierce "had bidden them goodbye saying he was going to Mexico to offer his services to the revolutionary army, to give his life if need be, and if he was not accepted in active military life he proposed to 'crawl into some out-of-the-way hole in the mountains and die.'"[27]

On its face, such a statement would seem to argue that Bierce had indeed gone to Mexico and perished, either at Ojinaga or on some other obscure battlefield. But such a version is contradicted by Bierce's lifelong antipathy to radicals, revolutionaries, and anarchists of all stripes—each term a fair description of Pancho Villa at the time. Walter Neale, who knew Bierce better than anyone else over the last decade or so of his life, flatly rejects the notion that Bierce would ever have joined Villa's revolution. "Bierce had roundly denounced Villa time and again throughout the bandit's stormy career," writes Neale. "That Bierce could have become a member of Villa's rabble band is unthinkable." Bierce's statement to the journalists in El Paso, however, is entirely consistent with his characteristic doublespeak throughout his Mexican venture. First, he announces that he is going into Mexico, then he qualifies his statement with an ominous reference to his likely fate. When he told the porch-sitters at El Paso that he was either going to join Villa's army or else crawl off into the mountains and die, he might well have been telling them half the truth. Whether he then went south to Chihuahua for a few days, as Christiansen maintained, or immediately headed north to the Grand Canyon, as Neale and Nickell believe, is ultimately beside the point. Almost certainly, Bierce was dead by the end of January 1914. For over a month, there had been no word from him; there would be no further word in the future. Since it is unlikely that he died in Mexico, it necessarily means that he died somewhere else. But where?[28]

The only plausible countersuggestion to the Mexican scenario is Neale's assertion that Bierce killed himself in the Grand Canyon, perhaps with the same German pistol he was said to have shown friends on numerous occasions. This version has nothing to vouch for it but Neale's own word, and yet it has the great advantage of presenting both a psychologically coherent interpretation of Bierce's puzzling last days and a logical explanation for why his body was never found. As the Benton case has demonstrated, it is hardly likely that a man as famous as Ambrose Bierce could have died unnoticed in the world's reigning tinderbox—northern Mexico—either at the hands of or alongside the most notorious man in the world just then—Pancho Villa—while a whole battalion of American journalists failed utterly to notice one of the most prominent members of their own profession in their midst. Nor, according to American consular officials, could Bierce have stayed long in Chihuahua without attracting their attention. Neither is it likely that he would have gone for months or even years without contacting his friends or family, until he was killed eventually by one or another of Villa's henchmen, as alternative versions of his death have alleged. And the romantic notion that Bierce went to Mexico to court or invite death, without taking an active role in his own demise, is also unconvincing. A man who had seen as much of war's vagaries as Bierce was unlikely to trust the marksmanship of Mexican *federales* to provide him with a quick, clean death. Fanatically fastidious, he simply would not have risked a long, drawn-out death from a fecal stomach wound or a putrefying infection in some unsanitary Mexican hovel. The semisuicide, one suspects, exists only in novels and films. If Bierce was actually seeking death, he knew how to find it. The only questions were when and where.

The Neale version, supported by a modern forensic investigator, has always faced the difficult task of trying to prove a negative: that Bierce did not go to Mexico. On the surface, this would appear an insurmountable task; the sheer weight of anecdotal testimony seems to support the popular account of Bierce's crowded and romantic final days as a born-again Villista in danger-ridden northern Mexico. But, as we have seen, there is no hard evidence that Bierce ever joined Villa's army; indeed, there is good reason to doubt it. And even if he did go to Chihuahua City, there is no guarantee that he stayed there for long. It would have been a simple matter to take the Mexican National Railroad back to El Paso and switch to the Atchison, Topeka & Santa Fe for the final leg of his journey to the Grand Canyon. Once there, shielded from intruders in a cliffside cave or underneath a rocky ledge, he could have taken out his German revolver, smiled perhaps at his elaborate ruse, and lowered the curtain on a disappointing world with little ceremony and less regret. No one would have heard the shot.

There is, it must be said, no more—and no less—tangible proof for this scenario than for any other. No hiker, rafter, or patrolling park ranger at the Grand Canyon has ever found a pile of bones, a few scraps of black clothing, or a crumbling white skull with a bullet hole in the temple to indicate the author's final resting place. As Bierce himself promised, his bones have never been found. It is entirely possible that, as he told reporters in El Paso, he simply crawled off into the mountains of Mexico to die, or that, as others have suggested, he sickened with fever or asthma or heart disease and lay down unrecognized in some adobe hut to cough away his life among dark-skinned strangers. In the end, as he intended, his fate is unknown. And yet, if one were to make an educated guess, the notion that Bierce killed himself, purposively and with malice aforethought, is hard to resist. Experienced homicide detectives, when faced with a seemingly insoluble case, typically go back to the simplest explanation. Given the utter lack of eyewitnesses and the eternally missing body, logic argues that Bierce died alone, as he would have wanted, and unobserved, as he apparently took great pains to ensure. That being the case, he probably did not die in Mexico. More than that, no one can say.[29]

As the weeks lengthened into months without any further word from Bierce, his daughter, Helen, and Carrie Christiansen began contacting government officials for help in locating the missing writer. In September 1914,

Gen. Hugh Scott, army chief of staff, personally wrote to Villa confidant Felix Sommerfeld, asking him to look into the writer's disappearance on the Mexican side of the border. "The Secretary of the Interior, Mr. Franklin K. Lane, is very anxious to get news of a man by the name of Ambrose Bierce, who went to Mexico last year and his friends have heard nothing from him since last December," Scott wrote. "He went to Juárez last Fall and had credentials to permit him to pass through the Constitutionalists' territory and was accredited to the Villa forces. He did not enlist and did not take part in the activities of the campaign so far as we know." Sommerfeld subsequently went to Chihuahua and asked around, but he learned only that Bierce had left the city sometime in January for parts unknown—something else that, if true, contradicts the widespread belief that Bierce left for Ojinaga on December 27. Maj. Gen. Frederick Funston, who led the American occupation of Veracruz before assuming command of the army's entire Southern Department, conducted his own investigation into Bierce's disappearance, and likewise could turn up nothing concrete. Following the eventual rebel victory in 1917, American lawyer Samuel T. Marston, then practicing in Mexico City, also delved into the case. Marston painstakingly combed the official records of the Mexican War Department, but he found nothing relative to Bierce's disappearance. Printed notices in Mexican newspapers, circulars passed out by the Society of Mexican Pilgrims, questionnaires distributed to every British and American consular agent who held key positions during the revolution—all failed to elicit any further information. The trail, such as it was, had grown cold.[30]

In the spring of 1915, there was a brief flurry of interest after various American newspapers carried a report alleging that Bierce had made his way to England and joined the staff of British Lord Kitchener. The report apparently started when a California acquaintance of Bierce's, B. F. Mason, told the Oakland *Tribune* that he had received a letter from an English relative who claimed to have seen Bierce serving alongside Kitchener in France. Reporters descended on Helen Cowden in Bloomington, Illinois, demanding to see copies of a letter Helen had supposedly received from her father confirming the rumor. There was no letter. Carrie Christiansen had received clippings from the California papers and innocently sent them along to Helen to read, thus occasioning the run on Bloomington. As droll as it is to envision that committed Anglophile Ambrose Bierce plotting strategy with Kitchener and Haig along the Marne—for that matter, he could scarcely have done any worse—there is no real reason to believe that he survived long enough to see firsthand the horrors of the Western Front. "How my father would have enjoyed this European war," Helen wrote to Walter Neale following the incident, and knowing what we do of her father's predilection for political idiocy and gruesome death, that must qualify as a distinct understatement.[31]

In 1919, Texas journalist George F. Weeks, then publishing a newspaper in Mexico City, came out with a story purporting to show that Bierce had been

captured and executed in mid-summer 1915 by one of Villa's subcomman-
ders, Gen. Tomás Urbina. According to Weeks, Bierce had been captured
near the town of Icamole, 110 miles east of Torreón, in the company of a
Mexican peasant. The two were said to be transporting a machine gun and
ammunition on four mules, bound for Carranza's forces in Torreón. Urbina,
so the story goes, questioned the two—Bierce, who did not speak Spanish,
could not have told him very much—then had them kneel down in the dust,
arms outstretched, while a firing squad dispatched them with a single volley.
Weeks said he had gotten the story from his associate editor, Edmund
Melero, who knew Bierce slightly during the war. The story was sufficiently
intriguing to cause San Francisco *Bulletin* editor Fremont Older to send his
own reporter, James H. Wilkins, to Mexico City to interview Melero. Subsequently, Wilkins claimed to have met a friend of Melero's who served in
Urbina's army and witnessed the execution. Wilkins's account, published in
the *Bulletin* in March 1920, inflated the four-mule pack train into a regular
ammunition train and alleged that the unnamed witness had shown him a
photograph of Bierce that he had taken off his body. Unfortunately, Wilkins
provided neither the mystery man nor his picture. As for Urbina, he was also
unavailable for questioning, having met his own fate at the hands of Pancho
Villa that same fatal summer.[32]

A new spate of stories predictably followed the release in 1929 of no less
than four Ambrose Bierce biographies: by Walter Neale, Carey McWilliams,
C. Hartley Grattan, and Adolph (Danziger) De Castro. In one, apparently a
variation on the Weeks-Wilkins account, Villista forces were said to have
waylaid an ammunition train bound for President Huerta's troops at Torreón.
Some forty-five federal forces were killed in the fighting, including two Syri-
ans and a suspected Englishman named "A. Pierce." Mexican colonel Dario
Silva, formerly Pancho Villa's military secretary, told McWilliams that he had
received a report announcing the capture of the supply train in February
1914 but said that since it was around the time of the Benton affair, Villa was
understandably leery about having any more dead Englishmen turn up on his
watch, and so the report had been hastily destroyed. Since Bierce was said, in
some accounts, to have been intending to go to England after his Latin
American vacation, Silva's account is more interesting than most, but the
State Department has no record of a passport being issued to Bierce around
that time.[33]

Another intriguing but unproven story concerns an elderly American with
gray hair and asthma who supposedly attached himself to Villa's headquarters
in early 1914. The old man, who wore a beard, reportedly told members of
Villa's staff that he had been a writer in the United States and that for now
they could call him Jack Robinson—an obvious play on American slang. The
uninvited visitor studied Mexican tactics with a jaundiced eye, sneered at
their unprofessionalism, and generally made a nuisance of himself. At length,

"Robinson" supposedly quarreled with Villa and was shot by the ubiquitous Fierro at Guadalajara in November 1914. This certainly sounds like Bierce, although his hair was white, not gray, and he was never known to wear a beard. The main problem with the story is that Villa was nowhere near Guadalajara in November 1914. He was, instead, attending a convention of leading revolutionaries at Aguascalientes, one hundred miles away, after which time he met with fellow general Emiliano Zapata in Mexico City and posed for a famous photograph, sitting in the deposed president's chair at the National Palace. Flanking him in the picture were Urbina and Fierro—two of Bierce's alleged killers.[34]

Prior to her own death in December 1940, Helen Bierce Isgrigg (she had since remarried, for a third time) was besieged by mediums, psychics, and clairvoyants of all stripes claiming to know what had happened to her father. Despite the help of the spirit world, she never learned anything more. Vincent Starrett, a Chicago journalist who became acquainted with Helen while preparing a bibliography of Bierce's work, perhaps reflected the family view when he predicted that Bierce's fate "never will be known, and possibly it is better that way." An unsolved disappearance might, after all, be preferable to a known suicide.[35]

New versions of Bierce's death, each more ridiculous than the last, continued to pop up from time to time. An El Paso man told a Los Angeles newspaper that Bierce had been poisoned in his backyard—how, why, and by whom, it was never said. A paranormal investigator looking into the disappearance of one Ambrose Small postulated that since Bierce had disappeared about the same time as Small, it constituted undeniable proof that demonic forces were at work, collecting all the Ambroses of the world—which might explain why Ambrose is such a rare and unpopular name today. A rumor circulated in Buenos Aires in the early thirties that an explorer named Johnson had found a strange white man with long, flowing white hair living in the trackless jungles of Brazil's Matto Grosso. The old man, clad in jaguar skins, was being held prisoner by a tribe of Indians who believed him to be a god. Johnson, instead, believed him to be Bierce. There were also continued sightings in Mexico; Bierce was said to be living in San Luis Potosí under the name Don Ambrosio, or else had been seen drinking brandy in the Cafe Gambrinus in Mexico City. A soldier of fortune named Edward S. O'Reilly claimed to have found the missing author's grave near the village of Sierra Mojada, after hearing reports that an old man had drifted into town during the revolution searching for Villa and subsequently had been shot by some local guerrillas. Scraps of an envelope found with the body were said to bear an Oakland postmark.[36]

As recently as 1985, Mexican novelist Carlos Fuentes produced a bestselling novel, *El Gringo Viejo* (*The Old Gringo*), conflating the stories of Bierce, Benton, Urbina, and Villa into a standard love triangle involving a virginal spinster from Washington, D.C., a hot-blooded young revolutionary, and a world-weary old man hungry for death. By combining the backgrounds of Villa and Urbina and mixing in the familiar black-clad figure of "Bitter Bierce" with the postdeath firing squad Villa had once prepared for Benton, Fuentes managed to create a new version of Bierce's death that was even more stilted and unbelievable than previous accounts; but his, at least, was clearly labeled fiction. A movie version was made in 1989, with Gregory Peck starring as Bierce, Jimmy Smits as Urbina/Villa (called Arroyo in the movie), and Jane Fonda (!) as the virginal schoolmarm. It stiffed at the box office.

When all other theories fail for lack of proof, one is still left with the question of suicide. There were certainly signs that Bierce was strongly considering it: his heavily freighted letters to friends, his valedictory tour of Civil War battlefields, his promise to his daughter that she would not have to worry about burying him. If Walter Neale is to be believed (and many Bierce scholars, it should be noted, do not), Bierce had been talking about suicide for years. But even without the testimony of Neale, we have on record Bierce's own lifelong fascination with the subject, from his earliest columns in the San Francisco *News Letter* to his late essay "Taking Oneself Off," with its set of six criteria for considering the act: painful or incurable disease; the burdening of friends; the threat of permanent insanity; drunkenness or other destructive habits; the loss of friends, property, employment, or hope; and personal disgrace. Given the fact that he was then seventy-one years old and in increasingly precarious health, that he had already lost both his sons and his wife, that most of his old friends were either dead or estranged, that he was no longer writing, that his collected works had been poorly received, that the nation as a whole was turning into an intolerable haven for prohibition and women's suffrage—can anyone doubt that, in his own mind at least, he met a majority of these cruel prerequisites?

Death, at any rate, did not frighten Bierce; in one way or another, it had been his intimate companion all his life. From the deaths of his younger brother and sisters back home in Indiana to his own terrible childhood dreams, from four years of service on some of the worst Civil War battlefields to the random dangers of Reconstruction-era Alabama and the Indian- and outlaw-infested West, he had faced it personally many times. Like other soldiers who have come near to dying in battle, violent death in all its variety morbidly obsessed Bierce for the rest of his life. He attended public hangings, haunted the public morgue in San Francisco, and culled the local newspapers for ever-more-bloody and macabre accounts of murder and suicide. His own columns and stories are so filled with death that one respected critic has stated bluntly that "death is Bierce's only subject." He had seen one son lying dead at sixteen, after having blown his brains out, and another dying a sad and sordid death from pneumonia at the age of twenty-six. His best friend in England, Tom Hood, had died young; so had his critical champion Percival Pollard. His ex-wife, Mollie, was dead, and so was his Civil War mentor, William Hazen, as well as Mark Twain, Bret Harte, Joaquin Miller, his former collaborators Thomas Harcourt and William Rulofson, and his brave little protégée Lily Walsh. If death was not exactly a friend, neither was it a stranger. Whether he fell victim to a random rifle bullet at Ojinaga, or a sneaking pistol shot outside Pancho Villa's camp, or a volley of bullets from a ragtag firing squad in the middle of nowhere against a mud wall; whether he died of sickness or want in a dirt-floored hovel or, contrary to the end, crept off to the Grand Canyon and ended his life with a single all-obliterating gunshot to the head, when death came for Bierce, as it does for us all, he would assuredly have known its face.[37]

In the end, it is only fitting to give Bierce the last word—it was, after all, his life and his death. Like the wandering Arab in his story "An Inhabitant of Carcosa," he may be said, at last, to have crossed a desolate landscape and found somewhere in a ruined graveyard a timeworn tombstone bearing his own name and dates: "Ambrose Gwinnett Bierce, 1842–1914?" That concluding question mark, perhaps the most famous in literary history, still hangs in the air, unanswered and mute, while students of his life sift tirelessly for clues and ponder the wisdom of the prophet Hali: "For there be divers sorts of death—some wherein the body remaineth; and in some it vanisheth quite away with the spirit. This commonly occurreth only in solitude (such is God's will) and, none seeing the end, we say the man is lost, or gone on a long journey—which indeed he hath." It was a journey Ambrose Bierce had been preparing for all his life.[38]

Epilogue

Whether or not his disappearance was planned, Bierce's abrupt departure from the land of the living has had an overshadowing effect on his posthumous reputation. The void at the end of his story, like an unresolved chord at the end of a symphony, nags at the mind with its lack of closure, irresistibly drawing attention away from the work itself toward romantic but ultimately fruitless speculations about when, where, and how he met his fate. The man and his writings have become displaced, something Bierce, for all his studied indifference to popular success, surely never intended when he rode off into the sunset. Since then, critics and biographers have faced—not always successfully—the difficult task of separating the man from the myth, the brittle cynic from the serious artist. It is an ongoing and, one suspects, an unending process.

Lost in the immediate hubbub over Bierce's fate was any reasoned consideration of his rightful place in American letters. At the time of his disappearance, he was largely forgotten, a retired West Coast journalist who had written, it was said, a handful of grisly and morbid stories, most of them unsuitable for mixed company. He was, as his friend H. L. Mencken observed, a distinctly outré kind of writer, at best an acquired taste. It was, at any rate, too soon for most contemporary critics to manage a long-range perspective on Bierce's writings. The monumental botch of his collected works, coupled with his enduring public image as a wayward controversialist, left even the most sympathetic readers facing a literary reclamation project on a massive scale. The few personal friends remaining behind understandably shied away from such a thankless task; and the writer's many enemies were only too happy to leave him in silence, if not necessarily in peace.

The first spate of biographies, appearing in the ominous year of 1929, portrayed with varying degrees of success Bierce the man, but none paid much attention to Bierce the artist. Even Carey

McWilliams, the best of the early biographers and the one most sympathetic to Bierce's life, considered him more of a personality than an artist, "more interesting as a man than he was important as a writer." Subsequent biographers have limned him in their titles *Bitter Bierce, The Wickedest Man in San Francisco,* and *The Devil's Lexicographer,* implying by these very titles that Bierce was a sort of homegrown Aleister Crowley, a sinister figure on the extreme fringes of polite society. Similarly, the introduction to a 1946 collection of his works was entitled "Portrait of a Misanthrope." Over the years, the image has hardened and taken hold of a satanic practitioner of the blackest arts, a hater of all mankind who long before his final disappearance had taken to his cave like Timon of Athens, to scoff at and scorn the human race.

To a certain extent, Bierce himself is to blame for his image. The heartless, if hilarious, aphorisms of *The Devil's Dictionary,* the black-natured humor of *The Parenticide Club,* the frequent sensationalism of his newspaper columns, and the biting little epigrams of his poems and fables all attest to a decidedly discontented soul. The world was never Bierce's oyster, however much its irritations produced, on occasion at least, some fugitive pearls of acrid wisdom. Moreover, by moving so readily from genre to genre, he has encouraged diverse and sometimes incompatible identifications of himself as a satirist, a humorist, a naturalist, a realist, a moralist (or immoralist), a gothicist, and a fabulist. In truth, of course, no single term encompasses Bierce. Like his old Civil War commander William Rosecrans, he was "many kinds of a brilliant crank."

In recent years, there has been a move afoot to portray Bierce as an early-blooming surrealist, a spiritual godfather of the "magical realism" school of such Latin American authors as Borges, Fuentes, and Cortazar. These efforts, involving much talk of semiotics, hidden texts, *ficciónes,* and perceptual dialectics, are painstaking and respectful, although somewhat severe. In the end, they leave us with a fictional construct, "Ambrose Bierce," that bears only a glancing resemblance to the man himself. One suspects, at any rate, that the real-life author never had half so much fun writing his stories as today's academics would have us believe. *Playful* is not a word that immediately springs to mind when describing Bierce, the author or the man.

Such studies, while no doubt good for the graduate schools, miss the salient point about Bierce's work, the one thing that will always differentiate him from his more talented contemporaries Mark Twain and Stephen Crane: the personal quality of his witness. When the timeworn image of Bitter Bierce and the hothouse flowerings of Jorge Luis Bierce are stripped away, what finally remains is 1st Lt. Ambrose Bierce, Ninth Indiana Infantry, the bloodied veteran of Shiloh, Chickamauga, Pickett's Mill, and a dozen other battlefields who had experienced war on a scale—both large and small—that no other American writer had ever known in the half century preceding World War I. His true significance as an artist, in contrast to his undeniable quotability as a drawing room curmudgeon or his newfound cachet as a writer of "texts," remains grounded in his undeniable pride of place as the first American witness to modern war and the evil banality with which men die.

At the far remove of another century, it is sometimes difficult to appreciate fully just how shocking and revolutionary Bierce's message was to the genteel readers of a more innocent time, the cultivated young men and women of the Gilded Age, for whom William Dean Howells's teacup tragedies and Henry James's neurasthenic heiresses were familiar figures of a comfortable sorrow, as satisfying and nonupsetting as a good long cry. Bierce, in his own stories, never cries; he rarely even blinks. He looks at the most horrific sights with a flat perception that is almost affectless—almost, but not quite, for the sheer act of witnessing is in itself an act of profound pity, and it is in such pity, after all, as the doomed English poet Wilfred Owen reminds us, that the poetry is found.

Today, of course, the rest of the world has caught up with Bierce, and the various hells of the twentieth century now make his own amateur diabolism seem rather tame by comparison. Still, the long parade of crime and folly that has brought us just recently such diverting sights as the "ethnic cleansing" of Bosnia and the horrific tribal genocide of Rwanda would have held no surprises for Ambrose Bierce. For war, to this unreluctant warrior, had always been "a by-product of peace," and patriotism itself "combustible rubbish ready to the torch of anyone ambitious to illuminate his name." For all the variable quality of Bierce's writings and the profligate waste of his time and talent on ephemeral targets and personal grudges, the humane inhumanity of his best war stories will continue to endure—as Clifton Fadiman once observed, "Jeremiah will never be out of a job." Our own job, as readers, is to retain somehow the ability to be shocked, and by so doing, to honor anew both the poetry and the pity.

NOTES

In the hope of encouraging a wider audience for Bierce's work, wherever possible references have been made to the two best paperback collections of Bierce's fiction: *The Collected Writings of Ambrose Bierce*, Clifton Fadiman, ed., and *The Complete Short Stories of Ambrose Bierce*, Ernest Jerome Hopkins, ed. Each is more compact and readily accessible than the unwieldy twelve-volume *Collected Works of Ambrose Bierce*, which remains the source for most of Bierce's nonfiction cited below.

Chapter 1

1. Richard Ellman, *Oscar Wilde* (New York: Alfred A. Knopf, 1988), 159. San Francisco *Wasp*, March 31, 1882.

2. Ellman, *Oscar Wilde*, 165. *Wasp*, March 31, 1882. William Lyon Phelps, ed., *Letters of James Whitcomb Riley* (Indianapolis: Bobbs-Merrill, 1933), 197.

3. Paul Fatout, *Ambrose Bierce: The Devil's Lexicographer* (Norman: University of Oklahoma Press, 1951), 3.

4. "The Ancestral Bond," in *The Collected Works of Ambrose Bierce*. (New York: Neale Publishing Company, 1909–1912), 11:330. Hereafter cited as *Works*. Carey McWilliams, *Ambrose Bierce: A Biography* (New York: A. and C. Boni, 1929), 13. *The Devil's Dictionary*, in *The Collected Writings of Ambrose Bierce*, Clifton Fadiman, ed. (New York: Citadel Press, 1946), 342, 237, 211. Hereafter cited as *Writings*.

5. McWilliams, *Ambrose Bierce*, 13. David Hackett Fischer, *Albion's Seed: Four British Folkways in America* (New York: Oxford University Press, 1989), 243. Amos Otis, *Genealogical Notes of Barnstable Families* (Baltimore: Genealogical Publishing Company, 1979), 52–53. Michael Tepper, ed., *Passengers to America* (Baltimore: Genealogical Publishing Company, 1977), 125–27. Sir Leslie Stephen and Sir Sidney Lee, eds., *Dictionary of National Biography* (New York: Oxford University Press, 1921), 147.

6. "A Rational Anthem," *Works*, 5:201. *The Devil's Dictionary*, in *Writings*, 247. McWilliams, *Ambrose Bierce*, 26.

7. Fatout, *Devil's Lexicographer*, 11–12. Edward C. Starr, *A History of Cornwall, Connecticut* (New Haven: Tuttle, Morehouse and Taylor, 1926), 375–76. Theodore S. Gold, ed., *Historical Records of the Town of Cornwall, Connecticut* (Hartford: Hartford Press, 1904), 71.

8. McWilliams, *Ambrose Bierce*, 16. Donald Lines Jacobus, "The Bierce Family," Connecticut Historical Society Genealogical Manuscript Collection, 2. Fatout, *Devil's Lexicographer*, 6–9. M. E. Grenander, *Ambrose Bierce* (New York: Twayne Publishers, 1971), 15. Walter Neale, *Life of Ambrose Bierce* (New York: Neale Publishing Company, 1929), 33. Bertha Clark Pope, ed., *The Letters of Ambrose Bierce* (San Francisco: The Book Club of California, 1922), vi. Hereafter cited as *Letters*.

9. "My Favorite Murder," 793; "An Imperfect Conflagration," 803; "The Hypnotist," 810; "Oil of Dog," 800; all in *Writings*.

10. Fatout, *Devil's Lexicographer*, 14, 18. Richard O'Connor, *Ambrose Bierce: A Biography* (Boston: Little, Brown, 1967), 14–15. Richard Lingeman, *Theodore Dreiser: At the Gate of the City 1871–1907* (New York: G. P. Putnam's Sons, 1986), 61–70. "The Social Unrest," *Cosmopolitan* (July 1906), 299.

11. Fatout, *Devil's Lexicographer*, 19–24. *Wasp*, November 3, 1883.

12. Fatout, *Devil's Lexicographer*, 13, 16. San Francisco *Examiner*, November 13, 1892. "Three and Three Are One," in Ernest Jerome Hopkins, ed., *The Complete Short Stories of Ambrose Bierce* (Lincoln and London: University of Nebraska Press, 1970), 378. Hereafter cited as *Stories*. *The Fiend's Delight* (London: John Camden Hotten, 1873), 136–37.

13. *Examiner,* June 8, 1899. John Dos Passos, *The Best Times* (New York: New American Library, 1966), 232. *Wasp,* December 26, 1885. "The Love of County," *Works,* 9:255.

14. "Visions of the Night," *Works,* 10:122–33.

15. *The Devil's Dictionary,* in *Writings,* 205.

16. McWilliams, *Ambrose Bierce,* 23. San Francisco *Argonaut,* June 8, 1878. Fatout, *Devil's Lexicographer,* 19. *Cobwebs from an Empty Skull* (London: George Routledge and Sons, 1974), 149.

17. San Francisco *News Letter,* June 25, 1870.

18. Carey McWilliams, "Ambrose Bierce and His First Love," *Bookman* 35 (June 1932), 255. *News Letter,* October 2, 1869. *Examiner,* April 26, 1891. Neale, *Life of Bierce,* 66.

19. Fatout, *Devil's Lexicographer,* 15, 31, 33.

20. McWilliams, *Ambrose Bierce,* 17–18. See also George W. Knepper, ed., *Travels in the Southland, 1822–1823: The Journal of Lucius Verus Bierce* (Columbus: Ohio State University Press, 1966).

21. Knepper, *Travels in the Southland,* 12–16. McWilliams, *Ambrose Bierce,* 18–19. Louise Bilebof Ketz, ed., *Dictionary of American History* (New York: Scribner, 1976), Vol. 5: 227.

22. Knepper, *Travels in the Southland,* 17–18. Summit *Beacon,* October 12, 1842.

23. Knepper, *Travels in the Southland,* 22–26. McWilliams, *Ambrose Bierce,* 28–29.

24. Knepper, *Travels in the Southland,* viii. McWilliams, *Ambrose Bierce,* 25. Carl E. Kramer, *Capital on the Kentucky: A Two-Hundred-Year History of Frankfort and Franklin County* (Frankfort: Historic Frankfort, Inc., 1984), 140–41. Patricia L. Faust, ed., *Historical Times Illustrated Encyclopedia of the Civil War* (New York: Harper & Row, 1986), 365.

25. John E. Kleber, ed., *The Kentucky Encyclopedia* (Lexington: University Press of Kentucky, 1992), 506. Colonel James Darwin Stephens to author, August 20, 1993.

26. Fatout, *Devil's Lexicographer,* 34. Elkhart *Daily Truth,* October 7, 1922. McWilliams, "Ambrose Bierce and His First Love," 255–56.

27. Fatout, *Devil's Lexicographer,* 36. *Examiner,* May 9, 1897. McWilliams, *Ambrose Bierce,* 30.

28. McWilliams, "Ambrose Bierce and His First Love," 257.

Chapter 2

1. Daniel Aaron, *The Unwritten War: American Writers and the Civil War* (New York: Oxford University Press, 1973), 122–23.

2. Justin Kaplan, *Walt Whitman: A Life* (New York: Simon and Schuster, 1980), 261–62. Aaron, *The Unwritten War,* 72.

3. Leon Edel, *Henry James* (New York: Harper & Row, 1985), 56. Aaron, *The Unwritten War,* 96.

4. Charles D. Anderson, ed., *The Centennial Edition of the Works of Sidney Lanier* (Baltimore: Johns Hopkins Press, 1945), 7:42. Joseph Gustaitis, "South Carolina's Henry Timrod," *America's Civil War* (September 1992), 12–14. Aaron, *The Unwritten War,* 134–36.

5. Aaron, *The Unwritten War,* 91–92.

6. William Dudley Foulke, *Life of Oliver Morton* (Indianapolis and Kansas City: Bowen-Merrill Company, 1899), 1:93. William B. Weeden, *War Government, Federal and State, in Massachusetts, New York, Pennsylvania and Indiana, 1861–1865* (New York: Houghton-Mifflin, 1906), 147. Fatout, *Devil's Lexicographer,* 37–38. Howard H. Peckham, *Indiana: A Bicentennial History* (New York: W. W. Norton, 1978), 71.

7. Faust, *Illustrated Encyclopedia,* 495. James M. McPherson, *Battle Cry of Freedom* (New York: Oxford University Press, 1988), 303. Richard O. Curry and F. Gerald Ham, eds., "The Bushwhackers' War: Insurgency and Counter-Insurgency in West Virginia," *Blue & Gray* (February–March 1985), 36. McWilliams, "Ambrose Bierce and His First Love," 256.

8. Fatout, *Devil's Lexicographer,* 38. Indianapolis *Sentinel,* June 2, 1861.

9. For the Battle of Philippi, see David Mallinson, "Confused First Fight," *America's Civil War* (January 1992), 46–52.

10. Mallinson, "Confused First Fight," 48–49. "On a Mountain," *Works,* 1:227.

11. Stephen W. Sears, *George B. McClellan: The Young Napoleon* (New York: Ticknor & Fields, 1988), 80. "On a Mountain," *Works,* 1:226. Mallinson, "Confused First Fight," 51. McWilliams, *Ambrose Bierce,* 32.

12. Mallinson, "Confused First Fight," 51. *Examiner,* July 19, 1891. Roy Morris, Jr., *Sheridan: The Life and Wars of General Phil Sheridan* (New York: Crown, 1992), 231.

13. "One Kind of Officer," *Stories,* 289, 296–98.

14. "On a Mountain," *Works,* 1:225, 227.

15. Sears, *McClellan,* 83–84. McPherson, *Battle Cry,* 300.

16. Sears, *McClellan,* 86, 88.

17. McWilliams, *Ambrose Bierce,* 32. Fatout, *Devil's Lexicographer,* 39–40. Indianapolis *Journal,* July 27, 1861.

18. Sears, *McClellan,* 89–92. McPherson, *Battle Cry,* 301. Fatout, *Devil's Lexicographer,* 400.

19. Sears, *McClellan,* 91. "On a Mountain," *Works,* 1:226. McPherson, *Battle Cry,* 302.

20. "On a Mountain," *Works,* 1:228–29.

21. "On a Mountain," *Works,* 1:231–32. McWilliams, *Ambrose Bierce,* 33–34. Faust, *Illustrated Encyclopedia,* 323–24.

22. "On a Mountain," *Works,* 1:232–33. Napier Wilt, "Ambrose Bierce and the Civil War," *American Literature* 1 (November 1929), 270.

23. "On a Mountain," *Works,* 1:233. "The Coup de Grace," *Stories,* 321–22.

24. "A Horseman in the Sky," *Stories,* 357–63.

25. "On a Mountain," *Works,* 1:229. William B. Hazen, *A Narrative of Military Service* (Boston: Ticknor & Company, 1885), 21. Faust, *Illustrated Encyclopedia,* 354–55.

26. "The Crime at Pickett's Mill," *Works,* 1:284. Hazen, *Narrative,* 21–22.

27. "The Crime at Pickett's Mill," *Works,* 1:284.

28. Shelby Foote, *The Civil War: A Narrative.* (New York: Random House, 1958–74), 1:320–23.

29. Ulysses S. Grant, *Personal Memoirs of U.S. Grant.* (New York: Charles L. Webster & Company, 1885), 1:249–50. U.S. War Department, *The War of the Rebellion: A Compilation of the Official Records of the Union and Confederate Armies* (Washington, D.C.: U.S. Government Printing Office, 1880–1901), vol. 10, pt. 2, 94–95. Hereafter cited as *OR.* James Lee McDonough, *Shiloh—In Hell Before Night* (Knoxville: University of Tennessee Press, 1977), 56. Foote, *The Civil War,* 1:327–29.

30. McDonough, *Shiloh,* 92. Foote, *The Civil War,* 1:334–36.

31. McDonough, *Shiloh,* 161. Hazen, *Narrative,* 24. "What I Saw of Shiloh," *Works,* 1:240. Foote, *The Civil War,* 1:340–41. William S. McFeely, *Grant: A Biography* (New York: W. W. Norton, 1981), 115.

32. "What I Saw of Shiloh," *Works,* 1:244–45.

33. "What I Saw of Shiloh," *Works,* 1:243–44. Faust, *Illustrated Encyclopedia,* 799–800. McDonough, *Shiloh,* 210.

34. "What I Saw of Shiloh," *Works,* 1:245–48.

35. "What I Saw of Shiloh," *Works,* 1:253–55.

36. "What I Saw of Shiloh," *Works,* 1:255–57.

37. "What I Saw of Shiloh," *Works,* 1:258–62. McDonough, *Shiloh,* 156. Ernest Hemingway, "A Natural History of the Dead," in *The Short Stories of Ernest Hemingway* (New York: Charles Scribner's Sons, 1938), 441–42.

38. "What I Saw of Shiloh," *Works,* 1:263–67. Hazen, *Narrative,* 47.
39. Fatout, *Devil's Lexicographer,* 43. Hazen, *Narrative,* 36. McPherson, *Battle Cry,* 413. McDonough, *Shiloh,* 213, 225. Grant, *Memoirs,* 1:369.

Chapter 3

1. Foote, *The Civil War,* 1:375–76, 381. "What I Saw of Shiloh," *Works,* 1:237.
2. Foote, *The Civil War,* 1:376. McFeely, *Grant,* 116–20. *Examiner,* December 4, 1898.
3. William Fox, *Regimental Losses in the American Civil War: 1861–1865* (Albany: Augustus S. Bradshaw, 1898), 341. Hazen, *Narrative,* 50. Foote, *The Civil War,* 1:384–85. Lew Wallace, *An Autobiography.* (New York and London: Harper and Brothers, 1906), 2:581. "An Affair of Outposts," *Stories,* 342.
4. "An Affair of Outposts," *Stories,* 342–44.
5. "An Affair of Outposts," *Stories,* 345–49.
6. For Turchin, see Roy Morris, Jr., "The Sack of Athens," *Civil War Times Illustrated* (February 1986), 26–32.
7. *Examiner,* May 15, 1898. Elkhart *Review,* August 30, 1862.
8. Hazen, *Narrative,* 53–56. For Battle of Richmond, Kentucky, see Roy Morris, Jr., "Battle in the Bluegrass," *Civil War Times Illustrated* (December 1988), 15–23.
9. Foote, *The Civil War,* 1:714. See also James P. Jones, Jr., "'Bull' and the 'Damned Puppy': A Civil War Tragedy," *American History Illustrated* (November 1972), 12–21.
10. *Examiner,* May 8, 1898. *Examiner,* December 4, 1898. Hazen, *Narrative,* 67.
11. Foote, *The Civil War,* 1:768. "What Occurred at Franklin," *Works,* 1:326. *Examiner,* March 4, 1900. Fatout, *Devil's Lexicographer,* 46–47.
12. Fatout, *Devil's Lexicographer,* 47. *Examiner,* June 5, 1898.
13. Hazen, *Narrative,* 72. Peter Cozzens, *No Better Place to Die: The Battle of Stones River* (Urbana and Chicago: University of Illinois Press, 1990), 46.
14. Foote, *The Civil War,* 2:87. Hazen, *Narrative,* 89–90.
15. Cozzens, *No Better Place,* 151–58. Morris, *Sheridan,* 105–9.
16. Cozzens, *No Better Place,* 165–66. Hazen, *Narrative,* 75, 93. O'Connor, *Ambrose Bierce,* 30.
17. William M. Lamers, *The Edge of Glory: A Biography of General William S. Rosecrans, U.S.A.* (New York: Harcourt, Brace & World, 1961), 225. *Examiner,* October 29, 1899.
18. Cozzens, *No Better Place,* 169–71. Hazen, *Narrative,* 71, 77. Marvin E. Kroeker, "William B. Hazen: A Military Career in the Frontier West, 1855–1880," (Ph.D. dissertation, University of Oklahoma, 1987), 76–77.
19. "A Resumed Identity," *Stories,* 388–90.
20. "A Resumed Identity," *Stories,* 390–93.
21. McWilliams, *Ambrose Bierce,* 46. Grenander, *Ambrose Bierce,* 99–102.
22. Hazen, *Narrative,* 77, 95–96.
23. Ambrose Bierce Military Service Records, National Archives. San Francisco *Argonaut,* December 21, 1878.
24. O'Connor, *Ambrose Bierce,* 31. *Argonaut,* December 21, 1878.
25. Hazen, *Narrative,* 96–98. "A Baffled Ambuscade," *Stories,* 275–76.
26. "Killed at Resaca," *Stories,* 372. Grenander, *Ambrose Bierce,* 20.
27. Superintendent's Report, Kentucky Military Institute, June 16, 1859. Fatout, *Devil's Lexicographer,* 30. "George Thurston," *Stories,* 369.
28. *Examiner,* June 12, 1887. Paul Fatout, "Ambrose Bierce: Civil War Topographer," *American Literature* 36 (November 1954), 395–96. "George Thurston," *Stories,* 369.
29. Hazen, *Narrative,* 103, 114.

30. Foote, *The Civil War*, 2:675, 687. Hazen, *Narrative*, 120. "A Little of Chickamauga," *Works*, 1:270–71.

31. "A Little of Chickamauga," *Works*, 1:273. Glenn Tucker, *Chickamauga: Bloody Battle in the West* (Indianapolis: Bobbs-Merrill Company, 1961), 148–49. Hazen, *Narrative*, 121–22.

32. Hazen, *Narrative*, 122. Peter Cozzens, *This Terrible Sound: The Battle of Chickamauga* (Urbana and Chicago: University of Illinois Press, 1992), 253–55. "A Little of Chickamauga," *Works*, 1:271–72.

33. "A Little of Chickamauga," *Works*, 1:272. Cozzens, *This Terrible Sound*, 281–85, 338–40.

34. Tucker, *Chickamauga*, 203. Hazen, *Narrative*, 129–30.

35. Hazen, *Narrative*, 125. Cozzens, *This Terrible Sound*, 348. "A Little of Chickamauga," *Works*, 1:273.

36. Tucker, *Chickamauga*, 307.

37. Lamers, *Edge of Glory*, 353. Tucker, *Chickamauga*, 312–13. Cozzens, *This Terrible Sound*, 468–69.

38. "A Little of Chickamauga," *Works*, 1:274–75.

39. "A Little of Chickamauga," *Works*, 1:275–76.

40. "A Little of Chickamauga," *Works*, 1:276–77.

41. "A Little of Chickamauga," *Works*, 1:277.

42. "Chickamauga," *Stories*, 313–14.

43. "Chickamauga," *Stories*, 314–15.

44. "Chickamauga," *Stories*, 316.

45. "Chickamauga," *Stories*, 316–18.

46. Vincent Starrett, *Buried Caesars* (Chicago: Covici McGee, 1923), 60.

47. *Examiner*, April 24, 1898.

Chapter 4

1. For Dana's role, see Roy Morris, Jr., "A Bird of Evil Omen: The War Department's Charles Dana," *Civil War Times Illustrated* (January 1987), 20–29. *Examiner*, May 8, 1898.

2. McWilliams, *Ambrose Bierce*, 51–52. *OR*, vol. 30, pt. 1, 765.

3. Morris, "A Bird of Evil Omen," 29.

4. James Lee McDonough, *Chattanooga—A Death Grip on the Confederacy* (Knoxville: University of Tennessee Press, 1984), 91–93.

5. "Jupiter Doke, Brigadier-General," *Stories*, 349–51. See also G. Thomas Couser, "Writing the Civil War: Ambrose Bierce's 'Jupiter Doke, Brigadier-General,'" *Studies in American Fiction* 18 (Spring 1990), 87–98.

6. "Jupiter Doke," *Stories*, 350–53.

7. "Jupiter Doke," *Stories*, 353–55.

8. "Jupiter Doke," *Stories*, 355–56.

9. "Jupiter Doke," *Stories*, 357.

10. "The Crime at Pickett's Mill," *Works*, 1:280–81.

11. *Wasp*, February 13, 1886. McFeely, *Grant*, 147–48.

12. For the siege of Chattanooga, see Roy Morris, Jr., "All Hell Can't Stop Them," *Military History* (February 1986), 34–40. McDonough, *Chattanooga*, 96.

13. Hazen, *Narrative*, 180–235.

14. *OR*, vol. 31, pt. 1, 282, 288. Morris, *Sheridan*, 147–48.

15. *OR*, vol. 31, pt. 2, 69. Morris, "All Hell Can't Stop Them," 40.

16. McWilliams, "Ambrose Bierce and His First Love," 256. Fatout, *Devil's Lexicographer*, 49.

17. McWilliams, "Ambrose Bierce and His First Love," 257.

18. Hazen, *Narrative*, 249.

19. For McPherson's failure of nerve, see Roy Morris, Jr., and Phil Noblitt, "The History of a Failure," *Civil War Times Illustrated* (September 1988), 36–43.

20. Hazen, *Narrative*, 250. Morris and Noblitt, "The History of a Failure," 42. Albert Castel, *Decision in the West: The Atlanta Campaign of 1864* (Lawrence: University Press of Kansas, 1992), 168–69.

21. Hazen, *Narrative*, 252.

22. "Killed at Resaca," *Stories*, 372–74.

23. "Killed at Resaca," *Stories*, 375–76.

24. "Killed at Resaca," *Stories*, 376–77.

25. "Killed at Resaca," *Stories*, 376–77.

26. Richard McMurry, "Resaca: 'A Heap of Hard Fiten,'" *Civil War Times Illustrated* (December 1971), 48. "Killed at Resaca," *Stories*, 375.

27. "Killed at Resaca," *Stories*, 373–74.

28. McWilliams, "Ambrose Bierce and His First Love," 257–58.

29. O'Connor, *Ambrose Bierce*, 38.

30. Faust, *Illustrated Encyclopedia*, 373.

31. Castel, *Decision in the West*, 229–30.

32. Hazen, *Narrative*, 257. "The Crime at Pickett's Mill," *Works*, 1:284–86. Howell and Elizabeth Purdue, *Pat Cleburne: Confederate General* (Hillsboro: Hill Junior College Press, 1973), 324–28.

33. "The Crime at Pickett's Mill," *Works*, 1:287–88.

34. Purdue and Purdue, *Pat Cleburne*, 324. Castel, *Decision in the West*, 241.

35. "The Crime at Pickett's Mill," *Works*, 1:291, 294. Castel, *Decision in the West*, 240.

36. Castel, *Decision in the West*, 235. "The Crime at Pickett's Mill," *Works*, 1:279.

37. Benjamin Roundtree, ed., "Letters from a Confederate Soldier," *Georgia Review* 18 (1964), 287–88. Hazen, *Narrative*, 254, 262. Foote, *The Civil War*, 3:354.

38. Foote, *The Civil War*, 3:356. "A Son of the Gods," *Stories*, 286.

39. "One of the Missing," *Stories*, 264–74.

40. "One Officer, One Man," *Stories*, 325–29.

41. "A Son of the Gods," *Stories*, 287–89.

42. *OR*, vol. 38, pt. 1, 425. Hazen, *Narrative*, 264–65. McWilliams, *Ambrose Bierce*, 55–56. O'Connor, *Ambrose Bierce*, 41.

43. "Four Days in Dixie," *Works*, 1:307. Fatout, *Devil's Lexicographer*, 54.

44. McWilliams, *Ambrose Bierce*, 56–57.

Chapter 5

1. *OR*, vol. 38, pt. 5, 754. McPherson, *Battle Cry*, 808. *OR*, vol. 39, pt. 3, 660. John F. Marszalek, *Sherman: A Soldier's Passion for Order* (New York: Free Press, 1993), 293–98.

2. "Four Days in Dixie," *Works*, 1:307. McWilliams, *Ambrose Bierce*, 57.

3. "The Other Lodgers," *Stories*, 395–97.

4. Bierce continued to be plagued by "violent headaches and nausea" for the rest of his life, according to his pension application, and as late as November 15, 1912, he was still receiving benefits. Ambrose Bierce Pension Records, National Archives, File No. 1135804.

5. "Four Days in Dixie," *Works*, 1:297–302.

6. "Four Days in Dixie," *Works*, 1:302–5.

7. "Four Days in Dixie," *Works*, 1:305–9.

8. "Four Days in Dixie," *Works*, 1:309–10.

9. "Four Days in Dixie," *Works*, 1:310–14.

10.   *Examiner,* August 19, 1888.

11.   "What Occurred at Franklin," *Works,* 1:316–20.

12.   "What Occurred at Franklin," *Works,* 1:319–20.

13.   James Lee McDonough and Thomas L. Connelly, *Five Tragic Hours: The Battle of Franklin* (Knoxville: University of Tennessee Press, 1983), 157. Purdue and Purdue, *Pat Cleburne,* 420.

14.   "What Occurred at Franklin," *Works,* 1:319–24. Sam R. Watkins, *Co. "Aytch"* (New York: Collier Books, 1962), 235.

15.   "The Major's Tale," *Stories,* 384–88.

16.   *Wasp,* July 14, 1883. *Examiner,* June 5, 1898. *OR,* vol. 45, pt. 1, 508.

17.   *OR,* vol. 45, pt. 1, 293. Bierce Service Records, National Archives. *Examiner,* August 17, 1890.

18.   "'Way Down in Alabam'," *Works,* 1:328–29. Fatout, *Devil's Lexicographer,* 59. Matthew C. O'Brien, "Ambrose Bierce and the Civil War: 1865," *American Literature* 48 (November 1976), 378. Robert Selph Henry, *The Story of Reconstruction* (Indianapolis: Bobbs-Merrill, 1938), 63. See also Walter L. Fleming, *Documentary History of Reconstruction,* vol. 1 (Cleveland: Arthur H. Clark Company, 1906), 25–33.

19.   "'Way Down in Alabam'," *Works,* 1:329–31. Henry, *Story of Reconstruction,* 62. Walter L. Fleming, *Civil War and Reconstruction in Alabama* (New York: Columbia University Press, 1905), 291–99. James E. Sefton, *United States Army and Reconstruction, 1865–1877* (Baton Rouge: Louisiana State University Press, 1967), 39–40.

20.   "'Way Down in Alabam'," *Works,* 1:333.

21.   "'Way Down in Alabam'," *Works,* 1:328, 332–34. Robert G. Rogge, "Heartland Hammered Furiously," *America's Civil War* (May 1988), 18–24.

22.   "'Way Down in Alabam'," *Works,* 1:328–29, 335–37.

23.   "'Way Down in Alabam'," *Works,* 1:337–40.

24.   "'Way Down in Alabam'," *Works,* 1:340–44.

25.   "'Way Down in Alabam'," *Works,* 1:344–48.

26.   Fleming, *Civil War and Reconstruction,* 292–93, 301. Sefton, *United States Army,* 39. Henry, *Story of Reconstruction,* 64. "'Way Down in Alabam'," *Works,* 1:335. E. Merton Coulter, *The South During Reconstruction* (Baton Rouge: Louisiana State University Press, 1947), 8.

27.   Kroeker, "William B. Hazen," 105–6. Fatout, *Devil's Lexicographer,* 66. "Across the Plains," *Works,* 1:361–63.

28.   "Across the Plains," *Works,* 1:363. Kroeker, "William B. Hazen," 109. Robert M. Utley, *The Indian Frontier and the American West, 1846–1890* (Albuquerque: University of New Mexico Press, 1984), 99–100.

29.   Kroeker, "William B. Hazen," 110, 117–18.

30.   Kroeker, "William B. Hazen," 112. "A Sole Survivor," *Works,* 1:387.

31.   "Across the Plains," *Works,* 1:361, 364–65. For the Fetterman massacre, see Kevin D. Randle, "Reckless Pursuit Halted," *Military History* (August 1986), 20–25.

32.   Kroeker, "William B. Hazen," 112–13. Evan S. Connell, *Son of the Morning Star* (San Francisco: North Point Press, 1984), 1–4. Juliana Clayton, "Lieutenant's Ghastly Discovery," *Wild West* (August 1992), 26–32.

33.   "A Sole Survivor," *Works,* 1:387. Rosalind Lock, "Jim Beckwourth," *Wild West* (June 1993), 8, 78–79. William Gardner Bell, "Attack Outside Fort's Walls," *Wild West* (June 1993), 40.

34.   "Across the Plains," *Works,* 1:365.

35.   "Across the Plains," *Works,* 1:368.

36.   "Across the Plains," *Works,* 1:364, 368–69. Kroeker, "William B. Hazen," 115. Fatout, *Devil's Lexicographer,* 70. *Argonaut,* May 31, 1879. *Wasp,* April 30, 1881.

37.   Kroeker, "William B. Hazen," 120–21. "Across the Plains," *Works,* 1:369.

38. Fatout, *Devil's Lexicographer*, 72. McWilliams, *Ambrose Bierce*, 76–77. "Across the Plains," *Works*, 1:369.

39. Robert M. Utley, *Cavalier in Buckskin: George Armstrong Custer and the Western Military Frontier* (Norman: University of Oklahoma Press, 1988), 40. Grenander, *Ambrose Bierce*, 29.

Chapter 6

1. For San Francisco history, see Oscar Lewis, *San Francisco: Mission to Metropolis* (Berkeley: Howell-North, 1966), 41–64. Doris Muscatine, *Old San Francisco: The Biography of a City* (New York: Putnam's, 1975), 250–55.

2. Lewis, *Mission to Metropolis*, 64.

3. Muscatine, *Old San Francisco*, 202–5.

4. Oscar Lewis, *This Was San Francisco* (New York: David McKay, 1962), 175–76.

5. Lewis, *This Was San Francisco*, 169, 179–80.

6. McWilliams, *Ambrose Bierce*, 80–82. Fatout, *Devil's Lexicographer*, 74.

7. McWilliams, *Ambrose Bierce*, 80.

8. McWilliams, *Ambrose Bierce*, 79–80. Muscatine, *Old San Francisco*, 158.

9. Muscatine, *Old San Francisco*, 169. Lewis, *Mission to Metropolis*, 2–3.

10. Jon Guttman, "Emperor Norton I," *Wild West* (February 1989), 8, 55–58.

11. Guttman, "Emperor Norton I," 58. Muscatine, *Old San Francisco*, 170.

12. Lewis, *Mission to Metropolis*, 70, 94.

13. Lewis, *Mission to Metropolis*, 71–74. Muscatine, *Old San Francisco*, 161. Franklin Walker, *San Francisco's Literary Frontier* (New York: Alfred A. Knopf, 1939), 246–47.

14. Walker, *Literary Frontier*, 243, 247–48. Muscatine, *Old San Francisco*, 160.

15. Lewis, *Mission to Metropolis*, 70. Fatout, *Devil's Lexicographer*, 75–76. *Write It Right*, in *The Devil's Advocate: An Ambrose Bierce Reader*, ed. Brian St. Pierre (San Francisco: Chronicle Books, 1987), 221.

16. Richard Saunders, *Ambrose Bierce: The Making of a Misanthrope* (San Francisco: Chronicle Books, 1985), 12. O'Connor, *Ambrose Bierce*, 66–67. Muscatine, *Old San Francisco*, 394. Lewis, *This Was San Francisco*, 173–74.

17. *Argonaut*, March 9, 1878. McWilliams, *Ambrose Bierce*, 81. Fatout, *Devil's Lexicographer*, 55, 76–77.

18. Walker, *Literary Frontier*, 241–42.

19. Fatout, *Devil's Lexicographer*, 76.

20. Fatout, *Devil's Lexicographer*, 78. Walker, *Literary Frontier*, 248–49.

21. Fatout, *Devil's Lexicographer*, 79–80. McWilliams, *Ambrose Bierce*, 87–88. Justin Kaplan, *Mr. Clemens and Mark Twain* (New York: Simon and Schuster, 1966), 13, 69, 75. *Examiner*, November 8, 1889.

22. Fatout, *Devil's Lexicographer*, 79–80.

23. *News Letter*, December 5, 1868. O'Connor, *Ambrose Bierce*, 72.

24. *News Letter*, February 4, 1871. *News Letter*, August 28, 1869. *News Letter*, February 11, 1871.

25. *News Letter*, December 18, 1869. *News Letter*, July 17, 1869. *News Letter*, May 15, 1869.

26. *News Letter*, October 8, 1870. Walker, *Literary Frontier*, 253. *News Letter*, July 24, 1869. *News Letter*, August 6, 1870.

27. *News Letter*, February 13, 1869. *News Letter*, May 29, 1869. *News Letter*, December 3, 1870.

28. *News Letter*, December 26, 1868. *News Letter*, January 20, 1872.

29. *News Letter*, April 23, 1870. *News Letter*, May 8, 1869. *News Letter*, January 7, 1871.

30. *News Letter,* April 10, 1869.

31. *News Letter,* January 6, 1872.

32. *News Letter,* February 6, 1869. O'Connor, *Ambrose Bierce,* 72. *News Letter,* November 18, 1871.

33. *News Letter,* November 18, 1871. *News Letter,* May 29, 1869. *News Letter,* October 23, 1869. Walker, *Literary Frontier,* 254.

34. *News Letter,* June 5, 1869. Walker, *Literary Frontier,* 252–53.

35. *News Letter,* November 27, 1869. O'Connor, *Ambrose Bierce,* 75. Walker, *Literary Frontier,* 240, 250. McWilliams, *Ambrose Bierce,* 87. Fatout, *Devil's Lexicographer,* 90.

36. Fatout, *Devil's Lexicographer,* 90. *News Letter,* May 21, 1870. *News Letter,* September 4, 1869. *News Letter,* July 15, 1871.

37. *News Letter,* July 30, 1870. *News Letter,* March 9, 1872. *News Letter,* February 19, 1870. *News Letter,* June 18, 1870. *News Letter,* August 27, 1870.

38. *News Letter,* April 23, 1870.

39. *News Letter,* August 6, 1870. *News Letter,* April 8, 1871. *News Letter,* September 24, 1870.

40. *News Letter,* April 8, 1871. *News Letter,* January 27, 1872.

41. Walker, *Literary Frontier,* 258. *Examiner,* March 3, 1889. *News Letter,* August 27, 1870.

42. Grenander, *Ambrose Bierce,* 32–33. *Overland Monthly,* March 1871. *Overland Monthly,* June 1871.

43. *Overland Monthly,* January 1871.

44. Grenander, *Ambrose Bierce,* 33. Kaplan, *Mr. Clemens and Mark Twain,* 131. "The Haunted Valley," *Stories,* 117–21.

45. "The Haunted Valley," *Stories,* 122–26.

46. "The Haunted Valley," *Stories,* 117, 119, 123, 125.

47. "The Haunted Valley," *Stories,* 122, 124, 126.

48. *The Devil's Dictionary,* in *Writings,* 248. O'Connor, *Ambrose Bierce,* 75.

49. Neale, *Life of Bierce,* 140–42.

50. McWilliams, *Ambrose Bierce,* 90–92. *News Letter,* March 18, 1871.

Chapter 7

1. Anderson, *Works of Sidney Lanier,* 5:138, 8:12.

2. McWilliams, *Ambrose Bierce,* 90–91. O'Connor, *Ambrose Bierce,* 78. Fatout, *Devil's Lexicographer,* 92.

3. Grenander, *Ambrose Bierce,* 34. McWilliams, *Ambrose Bierce,* 91–92.

4. *News Letter,* February 5, 1870. McWilliams, *Ambrose Bierce,* 91–92. *The Devil's Dictionary,* in *Writings,* 297, 325. O'Connor, *Ambrose Bierce,* 79.

5. O'Connor, *Ambrose Bierce,* 81. *News Letter,* January 16, 1869. McWilliams, *Ambrose Bierce,* 92, 94.

6. McWilliams, *Ambrose Bierce,* 93. O'Connor, *Ambrose Bierce,* 81. *News Letter,* December 30, 1871.

7. Neale, *Life of Bierce,* 115–16, 123.

8. Neale, *Life of Bierce,* 118.

9. "The Kreutzer Sonata," *Works,* 10:160–61.

10. *News Letter,* March 9, 1872.

11. McWilliams, *Ambrose Bierce,* 94.

12. Fatout, *Devil's Lexicographer,* 94–95. "My Favorite Murder," *Stories,* 454. Maurice Frink, "A Sidelight on Ambrose Bierce," *Book Notes* (August 1923), 154.

13.   McWilliams, *Ambrose Bierce,* 95. Grenander, *Ambrose Bierce,* 36. *Weekly Alta California,* August 24, 1872.

14.   Grenander, *Ambrose Bierce,* 36. M. E. Grenander, "Ambrose Bierce and Charles Warren Stoddard: Some Unpublished Correspondence," *Huntington Library Quarterly* 23 (May 1960), 261–64. *Weekly Alta California,* July 27, 1872.

15.   Fatout, *Devil's Lexicographer,* 98. For Joaquin Miller, see M. M. Marberry, *Splendid Poseur: Joaquin Miller—American Poet* (New York: Thomas Y. Crowell, 1953).

16.   McWilliams, *Ambrose Bierce,* 97. M. E. Grenander, "Ambrose Bierce and *Cobwebs from an Empty Skull:* A Note on BAL 1100 and 1107," *Papers of the Bibliographical Society of America* 69 (1975), 404. Fatout, *Devil's Lexicographer,* 97. M. E. Grenander, "Ambrose Bierce, John Camden Hotten, *The Fiend's Delight,* and *Nuggets and Dust,*" *Huntington Library Quarterly* 28 (August 1965), 355.

17.   Grenander, "Ambrose Bierce and *Cobwebs from an Empty Skull,*" 404–5.

18.   Stephen and Lee, *Dictionary of National Biography,* 664–67. Fatout, *Devil's Lexicographer,* 98. *Wasp,* February 14, 1885.

19.   Stephen and Lee, *Dictionary of National Biography,* 719, 769, 876–77. "A Sole Survivor," *Works,* 1:388–89.

20.   "Working for an Empress," *Works,* 1:349. *New York Times,* February 25, 1911. McWilliams, *Ambrose Bierce,* 109. Fatout, *Devil's Lexicographer,* 99.

21.   Grenander, "Ambrose Bierce, John Camden Hotten," 355. M. E. Grenander, "California's Albion: Mark Twain, Ambrose Bierce, Tom Hood, John Camden Hotten, and Andrew Chatto," *Papers of the Bibliographical Society of America* 72 (1978), 457–62.

22.   Steven Marcus, *The Other Victorians: A Study of Sexuality and Pornography in Mid-Nineteenth-Century England* (New York: Basic Books, 1964), 67–73. Grenander, "California's Albion," 460.

23.   Marcus, *The Other Victorians,* 68. Grenander, "Ambrose Bierce, John Camden Hotten," 56–57. Grenander, "California's Albion," 458.

24.   McWilliams, *Ambrose Bierce,* 98–100.

25.   McWilliams, *Ambrose Bierce,* 100.

26.   Grenander, "Ambrose Bierce, John Camden Hotten," 357–59.

27.   Grenander, "Ambrose Bierce, John Camden Hotten," 359–60. McWilliams, *Ambrose Bierce,* 98–99. *Nuggets and Dust* (London: Chatto and Windus, 1872), 124. Neale, *Life of Bierce,* 121. *Examiner,* September 4, 1887.

28.   Grenander, "Ambrose Bierce, John Camden Hotten," 362–66. Fatout, *Devil's Lexicographer,* 101–2. *The Fiend's Delight,* 75. O'Connor, *Ambrose Bierce,* 87–88.

29.   "Mortality in the Foothills," *Works,* 12:316. McWilliams, *Ambrose Bierce,* 99, 107. Grenander, "Ambrose Bierce, John Camden Hotten," 365.

30.   Grenander, "Ambrose Bierce, John Camden Hotten," 365. "A Sole Survivor," *Works,* 1:391–93. O'Connor, *Ambrose Bierce,* 93–94.

31.   McWilliams, *Ambrose Bierce,* 101–2. Fatout, *Devil's Lexicographer,* 106. Neale, *Life of Bierce,* 133.

32.   Grenander, "Ambrose Bierce and Charles Warren Stoddard," 267. McWilliams, *Ambrose Bierce,* 102–3.

33.   Grenander, "Ambrose Bierce, John Camden Hotten," 368. Grenander, *Ambrose Bierce,* 39. "D.T.," in *Nuggets and Dust,* 17–20.

34.   "A Working Girl's Story," in *Nuggets and Dust,* 20–22.

35.   *Nuggets and Dust,* 134, 137, 140, 150, 170.

36.   McWilliams, *Ambrose Bierce,* 100–101. M. E. Grenander, "A London Letter of Joaquin Miller to Ambrose Bierce," *Yale University Library Gazette* 46 (October 1971), 113. Grenander, "Ambrose Bierce and Charles Warren Stoddard," 267, 275.

37. McWilliams, *Ambrose Bierce,* 107–12. Grenander, "Ambrose Bierce and Charles Warren Stoddard," 280. Alyn Brodsky, *Imperial Charade: A Biography of Emperor Napoleon III* (Indianapolis and New York: Bobbs-Merrill, 1978), 273. "Working for an Empress," *Works,* 1:357.

38. "Working for an Empress," *Works,* 1:350–51. Fatout, *Devil's Lexicographer,* 109.

39. Fatout, *Devil's Lexicographer,* 112. Byron Farwell, *Queen Victoria's Little Wars* (New York: Norton, 1972), 190–91. "Working for an Empress," *Works,* 1:353.

40. "Working for an Empress," *Works,* 1:354–55, 358. McWilliams, *Ambrose Bierce,* 112–13.

41. O'Connor, *Ambrose Bierce,* 101. Grenander, "Ambrose Bierce and Charles Warren Stoddard," 278. Fatout, *Devil's Lexicographer,* 113–14. McWilliams, *Ambrose Bierce,* 106.

42. McWilliams, *Ambrose Bierce,* 104–5. "The Damned Thing," *Stories,* 104.

43. McWilliams, *Ambrose Bierce,* 113–14. *Argonaut,* February 9, 1879. *Argonaut,* November 9, 1878.

Chapter 8

1. McFeely, *Grant,* 393–94. Lewis, *Mission to Metropolis,* 150–54.

2. Lewis, *Mission to Metropolis,* 147–50. Muscatine, *Old San Francisco,* 304–16. O'Connor, *Ambrose Bierce,* 105.

3. Saunders, *Ambrose Bierce,* 24–25. McWilliams, *Ambrose Bierce,* 120. Fatout, *Devil's Lexicographer,* 116–19. *The Devil's Dictionary,* in *Writings,* 207. *Examiner,* October 14, 1888.

4. Lewis, *Mission to Metropolis,* 135–38. McWilliams, *Ambrose Bierce,* 120–21.

5. Lewis, *Mission to Metropolis,* 139. Muscatine, *Old San Francisco,* 389–90. McWilliams, *Ambrose Bierce,* 122.

6. O'Connor, *Ambrose Bierce,* 108–9. *Argonaut,* March 25, 1877. McWilliams, *Ambrose Bierce,* 123. *Argonaut,* June 9, 1877.

7. McWilliams, *Ambrose Bierce,* 124–25. *Argonaut,* November 16, 1878.

8. *Argonaut,* May 5, 1877. *Argonaut,* June 2, 1877. *Argonaut,* October 27, 1877.

9. *Argonaut,* July 20, 1878. *Argonaut,* June 26, 1878. *Argonaut,* April 28, 1877.

10. Fatout, *Devil's Lexicographer,* 118, 127. "A Revolt of the Gods," *Stories,* 424. *The Devil's Dictionary,* in *Writings,* 318.

11. *Argonaut,* April 1, 1877. *Argonaut,* April 25, 1877. McWilliams, *Ambrose Bierce,* 129.

12. McWilliams, *Ambrose Bierce,* 121. Saunders, *Ambrose Bierce,* 26. O'Connor, *Ambrose Bierce,* 113. Lois Rather, *Bittersweet: Ambrose Bierce and Women* (Oakland: Rather Press, 1975), 47–48.

13. McWilliams, *Ambrose Bierce,* 127. *Argonaut,* June 23, 1877. Fatout, *Devil's Lexicographer,* 143. *Examiner,* February 5, 1888.

14. For the Great Strike of 1877, see Nell Irvin Painter, *Standing at Armageddon* (New York and London: W. W. Norton, 1987), 15–18. McWilliams, *Ambrose Bierce,* 134–35.

15. Lewis, *Mission to Metropolis,* 139–41.

16. Lewis, *Mission to Metropolis,* 141–42. Muscatine, *Old San Francisco,* 403–4. O'Connor, *Ambrose Bierce,* 106.

17. Lewis, *Mission to Metropolis,* 142. Muscatine, *Old San Francisco,* 330. O'Connor, *Ambrose Bierce,* 106. *Argonaut,* November 3, 1877.

18. O'Connor, *Ambrose Bierce,* 117. Page Smith, *The Rise of Industrial America* (New York: McGraw-Hill, 1984), 188.

19. *Argonaut,* May 24, 1879. *Argonaut,* February 16, 1878.

20. *Argonaut,* May 18, 1878. O'Connor, *Ambrose Bierce,* 110.

21. O'Connor, *Ambrose Bierce,* 109. Franklin Walker, *Ambrose Bierce: The Wickedest Man in San Francisco* (San Francisco: Colt Press, 1941), 21.

22. Rather, *Bittersweet*, 40. *Argonaut*, October 5, 1878.

23. McWilliams, *Ambrose Bierce*, 126. *Argonaut*, October 12, 1878. Muscatine, *Old San Francisco*, 163.

24. McWilliams, *Ambrose Bierce*, 133–34. *Argonaut*, February 2, 1878.

25. Rather, *Bittersweet*, 48–49. O'Connor, *Ambrose Bierce*, 118. *Argonaut*, April 22, 1877. *Argonaut*, April 27, 1878.

26. "The Night Doings at 'Deadman's,'" *Stories*, 177–84.

27. "The Famous Gilson Bequest," *Stories*, 236–43.

28. "The Famous Gilson Bequest," *Stories*, 241.

29. "The Famous Gilson Bequest," *Stories*, 237–38, 242.

30. Fatout, *Devil's Lexicographer*, 126–27. Grenander, "Ambrose Bierce and Charles Warren Stoddard," 289–91.

31. Kaplan, *Mr. Clemens and Mark Twain*, 209–11.

32. *Argonaut*, January 5, 1878.

33. McWilliams, *Ambrose Bierce*, 219. *The Devil's Dictionary*, in *Writings*, 338.

34. "On with the Dance," *Works*, 8:268. *Wasp*, February 17, 1883. W. D. Howells, "Criticism and Fiction," in George McMichael, ed., *Anthology of American Literature*, vol. 2 (New York: Macmillan, 1980), 599.

35. McWilliams, *Ambrose Bierce*, 144–46.

36. McWilliams, *Ambrose Bierce*, 142, 145. Fatout, *Devil's Lexicographer*, 132.

37. O'Connor, *Ambrose Bierce*, 124–26. "A Sole Survivor," *Works*, 1:394–95.

38. "A Sole Survivor," *Works*, 1:396–97.

39. McWilliams, *Ambrose Bierce*, 145–46. Fatout, *Devil's Lexicographer*, 133. O'Connor, *Ambrose Bierce*, 129.

Chapter 9

1. Fatout, *Devil's Lexicographer*, 134. *Examiner*, January 24, 1897. McWilliams, *Ambrose Bierce*, 157.

2. McWilliams, *Ambrose Bierce*, 154–55.

3. Fatout, *Devil's Lexicographer*, 138. *Wasp*, April 9, 1881.

4. Saunders, *Ambrose Bierce*, 38. *Wasp*, November 22, 1884. *Wasp*, September 23, 1882. Walker, *Wickedest Man*, 19.

5. *Wasp*, May 3, 1884. *Wasp*, October 14, 1882.

6. Saunders, *Ambrose Bierce*, 36–37.

7. *Wasp*, April 2, 1881. *Wasp*, July 15, 1882. *Wasp*, October 18, 1884.

8. *Wasp*, October 7, 1882. Ernest Jerome Hopkins, ed., *The Ambrose Bierce Satanic Reader* (Garden City: Doubleday and Company, 1968), 195.

9. *Wasp*, December 23, 1882. *Wasp*, July 19, 1884.

10. *Wasp*, October 21, 1881. McWilliams, *Ambrose Bierce*, 161–62. Fatout, *Devil's Lexicographer*, 137.

11. *Wasp*, September 23, 1882. "The Shadow on the Dial," *Works*, 11:36–37.

12. Allan Peskin, *Garfield* (Kent: Kent State University Press, 1978), 601–7.

13. Walker, *Wickedest Man*, 28. *Wasp*, June 24, 1881. *Wasp*, September 23, 1881.

14. "The Game of Politics," *Works*, 11:78–79. *Wasp*, August 2, 1884. Walker, *Wickedest Man*, 30.

15. Gerald F. Linderman, *Embattled Courage: The Experience of Combat in the American Civil War* (New York: Free Press, 1987), 266, 271. Nina Silber, *The Romance of Reunion: Northerners and the South, 1865–1900* (Chapel Hill: University of North Carolina Press, 1993), 106–22.

16. "What I Saw of Shiloh," *Works*, 1:269. *Wasp*, February 28, 1885.

17. "What I Saw of Shiloh," *Works,* 1:269. *Wasp,* December 12, 1885. "The Game of Politics," *Works,* 11:73. "Election Day," *Works,* 4:270–71.

18. McWilliams, *Ambrose Bierce,* 155. *The Devil's Dictionary,* in *Writings,* 323, 328, 332, 325, 326, 330, 327, 329.

19. *The Devil's Dictionary,* in *Writings,* 188. "Wit and Humor," *Works,* 10:100–1. "To Train a Writer," *Works,* 10:77. B. S. Field, Jr., "Ambrose Bierce as Comic," *Western Humanities Review* 31 (1977), 175.

20. *The Devil's Dictionary,* in *Writings,* 207, 383, 361, 299, 293, 225, 211, 233, 207, 266, 218, 354, 323, 247, 347, 261, 387, 317, 379, 207, 195, 237, 208.

21. Robert F. Richards, *Concise Dictionary of American Literature* (New York: Philosophical Library, 1955), 15. *The Devil's Dictionary,* in *Writings,* 260, 265, 280, 273, 194, 390, 385–86, 304, 387, 388, 355.

22. *The Devil's Dictionary,* in *Writings,* 205, 211, 322, 342, 237, 210, 261, 218, 221, 245, 219, 314, 390, 307.

23. *Wasp,* March 17, 1882. O'Connor, *Ambrose Bierce,* 137–38.

24. *Wasp,* May 29, 1886. McWilliams, *Ambrose Bierce,* 156–57. *Wasp,* August 26, 1881.

25. *Wasp,* March 31, 1882. "To Oscar Wilde," *Works,* 4:145.

26. McWilliams, *Ambrose Bierce,* 162–64.

27. McWilliams, *Ambrose Bierce,* 161. *Wasp,* May 5, 1882. *Wasp,* March 28, 1885. O'Connor, *Ambrose Bierce,* 145–46.

28. McWilliams, *Ambrose Bierce,* 162, 173. Fatout, *Devil's Lexicographer,* 139. Helen Bierce, "Ambrose Bierce at Home," *American Mercury* 30 (December 1933), 453.

29. McWilliams, *Ambrose Bierce,* 164. "Californian Summer Pictures," *Works,* 5:276. *Wasp,* July 8, 1881.

30. "A Study in Gray," *Works,* 4:259–60.

31. McWilliams, *Ambrose Bierce,* 155, 165–66. *Examiner,* July 11, 1897.

32. "Epigrams," *Works,* 8:350. "The Opposing Sex," *Works,* 11:291. Walker, *Wickedest Man,* 37.

33. Walker, *Wickedest Man,* 38.

34. "An Imperfect Conflagration," *Stories,* 405.

35. "An Imperfect Conflagration," *Stories,* 406–7.

36. Stuart C. Woodruff, *The Short Stories of Ambrose Bierce: A Study in Polarity* (Pittsburgh: University of Pittsburgh Press, 1964), 117.

37. "Taking Oneself Off," *Works,* 11:340–43.

38. Fatout, *Devil's Lexicographer,* 148. *Wasp,* December 5, 1885.

39. Fatout, *Devil's Lexicographer,* 151. Helen Bierce, "Ambrose Bierce at Home," 453, 455.

40. Fatout, *Devil's Lexicographer,* 152–53.

41. "A Thumbnail Sketch," *Works,* 12:305.

42. McWilliams, *Ambrose Bierce,* 174.

Chapter 10

1. William A. Swanberg, *Citizen Hearst* (New York: Charles Scribner's Sons, 1961), 33, 41.

2. Swanberg, *Citizen Hearst,* 4, 32, 34–37. O'Connor, *Ambrose Bierce,* 153–54.

3. O'Connor, *Ambrose Bierce,* 155. Swanberg, *Citizen Hearst,* 71.

4. Swanberg, *Citizen Hearst,* 59–60. *Examiner,* May 16, 1887.

5. Swanberg, *Citizen Hearst,* 42–47.

6. Swanberg, *Citizen Hearst,* 60, 106. Adolph DeCastro, *Portrait of Ambrose Bierce* (New York: Century Company, 1929), 92.

7. Swanberg, *Citizen Hearst*, 66–67.

8. "A Thumbnail Sketch," *Works*, 12:312.

9. "A Thumbnail Sketch," *Works*, 12:307.

10. "A Thumbnail Sketch," *Works*, 12:314–15.

11. *Examiner*, November 18, 1894. *Examiner*, July 27, 1890. *Examiner*, July 14, 1889. O'Connor, *Ambrose Bierce*, 159.

12. *Examiner*, May 10, 1891. *Examiner*, April 29, 1894. *Examiner*, November 27, 1892. *Examiner*, October 23, 1892. *Examiner*, September 18, 1887.

13. *Examiner*, July 6, 1890. *Examiner*, June 3, 1894. *Examiner*, April 29, 1894.

14. McWilliams, *Ambrose Bierce*, 81. "Invocation," *Works*, 4:31–39.

15. McWilliams, *Ambrose Bierce*, 188–89. Fatout, *Devil's Lexicographer*, 165.

16. Hazen, *Narrative*, xxiv, 265. Fatout, *Devil's Lexicographer*, 159–60.

17. For Confederate flags controversy, see Morris, *Sheridan*, 383. "The Confederate Flags," *Works*, 4:337.

18. Saunders, *Ambrose Bierce*, 50.

19. *Examiner*, December 11, 1887. *Examiner*, December 9, 1888. *Examiner*, May 22, 1892. *Examiner*, August 31, 1890.

20. Helen Bierce, "Ambrose Bierce at Home," 455–56. "Oneiromancy," *Works*, 4:363.

21. Helen Bierce, "Ambrose Bierce at Home," 455–56. McWilliams, *Ambrose Bierce*, 189. "Epigrams," *Works*, 8:347.

22. McWilliams, *Ambrose Bierce*, 191–92. Fatout, *Devil's Lexicographer*, 170–72.

23. Fatout, *Devil's Lexicographer*, 172–74. *Examiner*, July 27, 1889. Chico *Enterprise*, July 26, 1889.

24. McWilliams, *Ambrose Bierce*, 192–94. Fatout, *Devil's Lexicographer*, 174–75. *Enterprise*, July 27, 1889.

25. McWilliams, *Ambrose Bierce*, 194. Saunders, *Ambrose Bierce*, 57.

26. *Argonaut*, August 5, 1889.

27. *Examiner*, August 25, 1889.

28. McWilliams, *Ambrose Bierce*, 193. Lawrence Berkove, "Ambrose Bierce's Concern with Mind and Man," (Ph.D. dissertation, University of Pennsylvania, 1962), 72–74. "Epigrams," *Works*, 8:363.

29. *Examiner*, September 3, 1889. *Examiner*, October 13, 1889. "The Affair at Coulter's Notch," *Stories*, 267–77. *Examiner*, October 4, 1889.

30. "The Affair at Coulter's Notch," *Stories*, 278–83.

31. "The Kreutzer Sonata," *Works*, 10:150, 152.

32. "The Kreutzer Sonata," *Works*, 10:153–54.

33. Emily Leider, "'Your Picture Hangs in My Salon': The Letters of Gertrude Atherton to Ambrose Bierce," *California History* (Winter 1981–82), 336. "A Watcher by the Dead," *Stories*, 72–81.

34. Gertrude Atherton, *Adventures of a Novelist* (New York: Liveright, 1923), 202–5. Leider, "'Your Picture Hangs in My Salon,'" 338.

35. Atherton, *Adventures of a Novelist*, 205.

36. Leider, "'Your Picture Hangs in My Salon,'" 342–43.

37. *Examiner*, March 23, 1890. *Examiner*, October 4, 1891. McWilliams, *Ambrose Bierce*, 183. George Sterling, "The Shadow Maker," *American Mercury* 6 (September 1925), 14. O'Connor, *Ambrose Bierce*, 192.

38. *Examiner*, January 22, 1899. For the Bierce-Markham feud, see J. S. Goldstein, "Edwin Markham, Ambrose Bierce, and 'The Man with the Hoe,'" *Modern Language Notes* 58 (March 1943), 165–75. O'Connor, *Ambrose Bierce*, 191.

39. McWilliams, *Ambrose Bierce*, 249–51. Grenander, *Ambrose Bierce*, 64–65.

40. John Berryman, *Stephen Crane* (New York: World Publishing Company, 1962), 170.

41. "An Occurrence at Owl Creek Bridge," *Stories,* 305–13.

42. "An Occurrence at Owl Creek Bridge," *Stories,* 307. e. e. cummings, "Plato Told Him," in *Anthology of American Literature,* vol. 2, George McMichael, ed. (New York: Macmillan, 1980), 1224. See also F. J. Logan, "The Wry Seriousness of 'Owl Creek Bridge,'" *American Literary Realism* 10 (Spring 1977), 101–13.

43. "An Occurrence at Owl Creek Bridge," *Stories,* 308–9.

44. "An Occurrence at Owl Creek Bridge," *Stories,* 309. Peter Stoicheff, "'Something Uncanny': The Dream Structure in Ambrose Bierce's 'An Occurrence at Owl Creek Bridge,'" *Studies in Short Fiction* 30 (Summer 1993), 355–65.

45. McWilliams, *Ambrose Bierce,* 210, 212–14.

46. Grenander, *Ambrose Bierce,* 59–61. *The Monk and the Hangman's Daughter,* in *Works,* 6:19–162.

47. Grenander, *Ambrose Bierce,* 59–60. Fatout, *Devil's Lexicographer,* 192–93. *McEwen's Letter,* May 25, 1895. McWilliams, *Ambrose Bierce,* 214.

48. O'Connor, *Ambrose Bierce,* 207–9.

49. Joseph W. Slade, "'Putting You in the Papers': Ambrose Bierce's Letters to Edwin Markham," *Prospects* 1 (1975), 340. "The Jew," *Works,* 9:373–81.

50. O'Connor, *Ambrose Bierce,* 209. *Examiner,* October 20, 1895. *Examiner,* November 8, 1895.

51. *Examiner,* January 21, 1894. DeCastro, *Portrait of Bierce,* 216.

Chapter 11

1. McWilliams, *Ambrose Bierce,* 237. Fatout, *Devil's Lexicographer,* 214.

2. Fatout, *Devil's Lexicographer,* 214. Grenander, *Ambrose Bierce,* 65. *Examiner,* July 26, 1896.

3. *Examiner,* February 1, 1896. McWilliams, *Ambrose Bierce,* 239.

4. O'Connor, *Ambrose Bierce,* 228–31. Fatout, *Devil's Lexicographer,* 215, 218.

5. Hopkins, *Ambrose Bierce Satanic Reader,* 220. *Examiner,* February 14, 1896. *Examiner,* February 29, 1896.

6. McWilliams, *Ambrose Bierce,* 240–41. Fatout, *Devil's Lexicographer,* 219.

7. Fatout, *Devil's Lexicographer,* 217–18. O'Connor, *Ambrose Bierce,* 231–32. McWilliams, *Ambrose Bierce,* 239. *Examiner,* March 21, 1896.

8. Fatout, *Devil's Lexicographer,* 219. *Examiner,* January 10, 1897. Hopkins, *Ambrose Bierce Satanic Reader,* 221. O'Connor, *Ambrose Bierce,* 232.

9. McWilliams, *Ambrose Bierce,* 243–44. AB to J. H. E. Partington, March 26, 1893, in Pope, *Letters,* 27–28. Fatout, *Devil's Lexicographer,* 237.

10. AB to S. O. Howes, May 14, 1899, quoted in McWilliams, *Ambrose Bierce,* 259. O'Connor, *Ambrose Bierce,* 235. McWilliams, *Ambrose Bierce,* 245–46.

11. McWilliams, *Ambrose Bierce,* 244–45. *Examiner,* January 10, 1897.

12. O'Connor, *Ambrose Bierce,* 230, 233–34, 236. *Examiner,* January 17, 1897.

13. McWilliams, *Ambrose Bierce,* 249–53. Fatout, *Devil's Lexicographer,* 231–32.

14. New York *Journal,* October 11, 1895. Swanberg, *Citizen Hearst,* 107–10.

15. Swanberg, *Citizen Hearst,* 113–43.

16. *Examiner,* March 17, 1895. "A Thumbnail Sketch," *Works,* 12:305.

17. *Examiner,* April 24 1898. "Civilization," *Works,* 11:59. *Examiner,* July 31, 1898. *Examiner,* July 10, 1898.

18. *Examiner,* May 9, 1898. *Examiner,* May 12, 1895. *Examiner,* April 3, 1898. G. J. A. O'Toole, *The Spanish War: An American Epic* (New York and London: W. W. Norton, 1984), 53–54.

19.   Gerald F. Linderman, *The Mirror of War: American Society and the Spanish-American War* (Ann Arbor: University of Michigan Press, 1974), 128, 138–39.

20.   *Examiner,* August 7, 1898. *Examiner,* September 4, 1898. *Examiner,* April 7, 1898. *Examiner,* November 6, 1898.

21.   *Examiner,* May 8, 1898. *Examiner,* May 29, 1898. *Examiner,* July 17, 1898.

22.   *Examiner,* February 19, 1899. *Examiner,* December 3, 1899. *Examiner,* December 4, 1898.

23.   McWilliams, *Ambrose Bierce,* 260–63. Fatout, *Devil's Lexicographer,* 235–36. *Examiner,* December 14, 1899. AB to Amy Cecil, January 2, 1901, quoted in McWilliams, *Ambrose Bierce,* 270.

24.   McWilliams, *Ambrose Bierce,* 265. Fatout, *Devil's Lexicographer,* 239.

25.   McWilliams, *Ambrose Bierce,* 269–70. Fatout, *Devil's Lexicographer,* 243–44. AB to George Sterling, May 2, 1901, in Pope, *Letters,* 46. Neale, *Life of Bierce,* 53.

26.   Fatout, *Devil's Lexicographer,* 246–47. *Examiner,* February 4, 1900. Swanberg, *Citizen Hearst,* 191–94. "A Thumbnail Sketch," *Works,* 12:308–9.

27.   O'Connor, *Ambrose Bierce,* 257–58. "A Thumbnail Sketch," *Works,* 12:310. Neale, *Life of Bierce,* 112–13.

28.   "A Thumbnail Sketch," *Works,* 12:310. Neale, *Life of Bierce,* 60, 209.

29.   McWilliams, *Ambrose Bierce,* 275.

30.   McWilliams, *Ambrose Bierce,* 272–73, 277, 292. AB to George Sterling, May 16, 1905, in Pope, *Letters,* 110. "Reminded," *Works,* 4:190.

31.   "The Moonlit Road," *Stories,* 136–44.

32.   "Beyond the Wall," *Stories,* 193–200.

33.   Fatout, *Devil's Lexicographer,* 262. "Epigrams," *Works,* 8:361.

34.   McWilliams, *Ambrose Bierce,* 289. Fatout, *Devil's Lexicographer,* 272. Preface to *The Devil's Dictionary,* in *Writings,* 188. AB to George Sterling, May 6, 1906, in Pope, *Letters,* 120.

35.   Fatout, *Devil's Lexicographer,* 268. O'Connor, *Ambrose Bierce,* 276–79. John C. Stubbs, "Ambrose Bierce's Contributions to *Cosmopolitan:* An Annotated Bibliography," *American Literary Realism* 4 (Winter 1971), 58–59. McWilliams, *Ambrose Bierce,* 295. AB to Robert Mackay, August 20, 1906, Huntington Library.

36.   Neale, *Life of Bierce,* 414–21. Fatout, *Devil's Lexicographer,* 281–82. AB to George Sterling, February 21, 1907, in Pope, *Letters,* 131. AB to Walter Neale, October 25, 1908, Huntington Library.

37.   Fatout, *Devil's Lexicographer,* 288. AB to Ruth Robertson, November 3, 1912, University of Southern California.

38.   Neale, *Life of Bierce,* 419, 424, 426. London *Athenaeum,* September 16, 1911. *Nation,* August 31, 1911.

39.   M. E. Grenander, "H. L. Mencken to Ambrose Bierce," *Book Club of California Quarterly News Letter* 22 (Winter 1956), 5–6. McWilliams, *Ambrose Bierce,* 286. New York *World,* March 1, 1925. Fred Hobson, *Mencken: A Life* (New York: Random House, 1994), 112.

40.   McWilliams, *Ambrose Bierce,* 298, 302. AB to George Sterling, June 11, 1906, in Pope, *Letters,* 121. Fatout, *Devil's Lexicographer,* 289. Kevin Starr, *Americans and the California Dream* (New York: Oxford University Press, 1973), 267–73. O'Connor, *Ambrose Bierce,* 288–89.

41.   Mary Austin, "George Sterling at Carmel," *American Mercury* 41 (May 1927), 67–68. Fatout, *Devil's Lexicographer,* 291. Saunders, *Ambrose Bierce,* 89–92. O'Connor, *Ambrose Bierce,* 289–90.

42.   McWilliams, *Ambrose Bierce,* 298, 304. "My Day of Life," *Works,* 4:344. Neale, *Life of Bierce,* 431–32.

43.   McWilliams, *Ambrose Bierce,* 312–14.

Chapter 12

1. AB to Helen Cowden, November 6, 1912, in M. E. Grenander, "Seven Ambrose Bierce Letters," *Yale University Library Gazette* 32 (July 1957), 13. AB to B. J. S. Cahill, January 20, 1913, in Pope, *Letters,* 189.

2. AB to Helen Cowden, January 27, 1913, in Grenander, "Seven Ambrose Bierce Letters," 15. McWilliams, *Ambrose Bierce,* 315–16.

3. AB to Curtis J. Kirch, May 22, 1913, in Pope, *Letters,* 193. Neale, *Life of Bierce,* 446–47.

4. AB to Lora Bierce, September 10, 1913, in Pope, *Letters,* 194. AB to Josephine McCrackin, September 10, 1913, in Pope, *Letters,* 195. O'Connor, *Ambrose Bierce,* 298.

5. AB to Josephine McCrackin, September 10, 1913, in Pope, *Letters,* 195. AB to Lora Bierce, September 29, 1913, in Pope, *Letters,* 196–97. AB to James D. Blake, September 29, 1913, in Grenander, "Seven Ambrose Bierce Letters," 15–16.

6. John S. D. Eisenhower, *Intervention: The U.S. and the Mexican Revolution, 1913–1917* (New York: W. W. Norton, 1993), 79. Martin Luis Guzman, *The Eagle and the Serpent* (New York: Alfred A. Knopf, 1930), 44. AB to Josephine McCrackin, September 13, 1913, in Pope, *Letters,* 196.

7. Joe Nickell, *Ambrose Bierce Is Missing and Other Historical Mysteries* (Lexington: University Press of Kentucky, 1992), 23.

8. Carey McWilliams, "The Mystery of Ambrose Bierce," *American Mercury* 22 (March 1931), 335. *Examiner,* June 5, 1898.

9. McWilliams, "Mystery of Ambrose Bierce," 336. McWilliams, *Ambrose Bierce,* 321. "What I Saw of Shiloh," *Works,* 1:268.

10. McWilliams, "Mystery of Ambrose Bierce," 336. Pope, *Letters,* xiv–xvi.

11. AB to Lora Bierce, November 5, 1913, in Pope, *Letters,* 197. McWilliams, "Mystery of Ambrose Bierce," 336.

12. AB to Lora Bierce, November 6, 1913, in Pope, *Letters,* 198.

13. Sibley S. Morrill, *Ambrose Bierce, F. A. Mitchell-Hedges and the Crystal Skull* (San Francisco: Cadleon Press, 1972), 44–57.

14. Morrill, *Ambrose Bierce,* 60–79.

15. Nickell, *Ambrose Bierce Is Missing,* 29–31. Neale, *Life of Bierce,* 429–49.

16. Eisenhower, *Intervention,* 72–73. See also Ronald Atkin, *Revolution: Mexico, 1910–1920* (New York: John Daly Company, 1970), 167–73.

17. Eisenhower, *Intervention,* 74.

18. Eisenhower, *Intervention,* 74–75.

19. Eisenhower, *Intervention,* 75–77.

20. Eisenhower, *Intervention,* 78.

21. McWilliams, "Mystery of Ambrose Bierce," 337. Grenander, *Ambrose Bierce,* 74–75.

22. McWilliams, "Mystery of Ambrose Bierce," 333. Eisenhower, *Intervention,* 59.

23. Eisenhower, *Intervention,* 181.

24. Eisenhower, *Intervention,* 54, 128.

25. Ambrose Bierce Papers, Stanford University. O'Connor, *Ambrose Bierce,* 306–7. Dale L. Walker, "A Last Laugh for Ambrose Bierce," *American West* 10 (November 1973), 63.

26. O'Connor, *Ambrose Bierce,* 306–7. McWilliams, "Mystery of Ambrose Bierce," 334–35.

27. Nickell, *Ambrose Bierce Is Missing,* 31–33. William A. Willis to Vincent Starrett, January 31, 1918, Ambrose Bierce Papers, Stanford University.

28. Neale, *Life of Bierce,* 432–33.

29. Robert L. Arnberger, superintendent, Grand Canyon National Park, to author, January 27, 1995.

30.   McWilliams, "Mystery of Ambrose Bierce," 334–35. Walker, "Last Laugh for Ambrose Bierce," 38.

31.   McWilliams, *Ambrose Bierce,* 328. Neale, *Life of Bierce,* 434–36.

32.   McWilliams, *Ambrose Bierce,* 327–28. Starrett, *Buried Caesars,* 63–64.

33.   McWilliams, "Mystery of Ambrose Bierce," 331–32.

34.   McWilliams, "Mystery of Ambrose Bierce," 333–34. Eisenhower, *Intervention,* 158–68.

35.   Starrett, *Buried Caesars,* 68.

36.   McWilliams, "Mystery of Ambrose Bierce," 330–33. Starrett, *Buried Caesars,* 67. Dale Walker, "Last Laugh for Ambrose Bierce," 39. O'Connor, *Ambrose Bierce,* 297.

37.   Edmund Wilson, *Patriotic Gore: Studies in the Literature of the American Civil War* (New York: Oxford University Press, 1962), 622.

38.   "An Inhabitant of Carcosa," *Stories,* 51.

BIBLIOGRAPHY

Manuscripts

Boston Public Library
Brigham Young University
Brooklyn Public Library
California State Library
Connecticut Historical Society
Dartmouth College
Elkhart Public Library
Ella Strong Denison Library
Filson Club
Harvard University
Huntington Library
University of Illinois
Indiana Historical Society
Kentucky Historical Society
Knox College
Library of Congress

University of Louisville
Marietta College
University of Michigan
Middlebury College
New-York Historical Society
Oakland Public Library
Princeton University
University of Oregon
University of Pennsylvania
University of Rochester
University of Southern California
Stanford University
Syracuse University
University of Virginia
Wagner College
Yale University

Newspapers

Chico *Enterprise*
Elkhart *Daily Truth*
Elkhart *Review*
Indianapolis *Journal*
Indianapolis *Sentinel*
New York Times

San Francisco *Argonaut*
San Francisco *Examiner*
San Francisco *News Letter*
San Francisco *Wasp*
Washington *Times*
Weekly Alta California

Government Documents

U.S. War Department. *The War of the Rebellion: A Compilation of the Official Records of the Union and Confederate Armies.* 128 vols. Washington, D.C.: U.S. Government Printing Office, 1880–1901.
Ambrose Bierce Military Service Records and Pension Records, National Archives, Washington, D.C.

Books by Ambrose Bierce

Bierce, Ambrose. *Black Beetles in Amber.* San Francisco: Western Authors Publishing Company, 1892.
————. *Can Such Things Be?* New York: Cassell Publishing Company, 1893.
———— [Dod Grile, pseud.]. *Cobwebs from an Empty Skull.* London: George Routledge and Sons, 1974.
————. *The Collected Works of Ambrose Bierce.* 12 vols. New York: Neale Publishing Company, 1909–1912.
————. *The Cynic's Word Book.* New York: Doubleday, Page and Company, 1906.
———— [William Herman, pseud.]. *The Dance of Death.* San Francisco: Henry Keller and Company, 1877.

———. *Fantastic Fables.* New York: G. P. Putnam's Sons, 1899.

——— [Dod Grile, pseud.]. *The Fiend's Delight.* London: John Camden Hotten, 1873.

——— [with C. A. Danziger]. *The Monk and the Hangman's Daughter.* Chicago: F. J. Schulte, 1892.

——— [Dod Grile, pseud.]. *Nuggets and Dust.* London: Chatto and Windus, 1872.

———. *The Shadow on the Dial and Other Essays.* San Francisco: A. M. Robertson, 1909.

———. *Shapes of Clay.* San Francisco: W. E. Wood, 1903.

———. *Tales of Soldiers and Civilians.* San Francisco: E. L. G. Steele, 1892.

———. *Write It Right.* New York: Neale Publishing Company, 1909.

Books, Articles, and Dissertations

Aaron, Daniel. "Ambrose Bierce and the American Civil War." In *Critical Essays on Ambrose Bierce,* edited by Cathy N. Davidson. Boston: G. K. Hall, 1982.

———. *The Unwritten War: American Writers and the Civil War.* New York: Oxford University Press, 1973.

Anderson, Charles D., ed. *The Centennial Edition of the Works of Sidney Lanier.* 10 vols. Baltimore: Johns Hopkins Press, 1945.

Anderson, D. D. "Can Ohio and the Midwest Claim Ambrose Bierce?" *Ohioana* 16 (Summer 1973), 84–89.

———. "The Old Northwest." In *Critical Essays on Ambrose Bierce,* edited by Cathy N. Davidson. Boston: G. K. Hall, 1982.

Andrews, W. L. "Some New Ambrose Bierce Fables." *American Literary Realism* 8 (Autumn 1975), 349–52.

Atherton, Gertrude. *Adventures of a Novelist.* New York: Liveright, 1923.

———. "The Literary Development of California." *Cosmopolitan* 10 (January 1891), 269–78.

Atkin, Ronald. *Revolution: Mexico, 1910–1920.* New York: John Daly Co., 1970.

Austin, Mary. "George Sterling at Carmel." *American Mercury* 41 (May 1927), 65–72.

Bachtzhold, Howard G. *Mark Twain and John Bull: The British Connection.* Bloomington and London: Indiana University Press, 1970.

Bahr, Howard W. "Ambrose Bierce and Realism." *Southern Quarterly* 1 (July 1963), 309–31.

Beer, Thomas. *The Mauve Decade.* New York: Alfred A. Knopf, 1926.

Bell, William Gardner. "Attack Outside Fort's Walls." *Wild West* (June 1993), 38–44.

Berkove, Lawrence. "Ambrose Bierce's Concern with Mind and Man." Ph.D. dissertation, University of Pennsylvania, 1962.

———. *Ambrose Bierce: Skepticism and Dissent. Selected Journalism from 1898–1901.* Ann Arbor: Delmas Books, 1980.

———. "Arms and the Man: Ambrose Bierce's Response to War." *Michigan Academician* 1 (1969), 21–30.

———. "'Hades in Trouble': A Rediscovered Story by Ambrose Bierce." *American Literary Realism* 25, 67–84.

———. "The Heart Has Its Reasons: Ambrose Bierce's Successful Failure at Philosophy." In *Critical Essays on Ambrose Bierce,* edited by Cathy N. Davidson. Boston: G. K. Hall, 1982.

———. "The Man with the Burning Pen: Ambrose Bierce as Journalist." *Journal of Popular Culture* 15 (February 1981), 34–40.

———. "A Strange Adventure: The Story Behind a Bierce Tale." *American Literary Realism* 14 (1981), 70–76.

Berryman, John. *Stephen Crane.* New York: World Publishing Company, 1962.

Bierce, Helen. "Ambrose Bierce at Home." *American Mercury* 30 (December 1933), 453–58.

Braddy, Haldeen. "Ambrose Bierce and de Maupassant." *American Notes & Queries* 1 (April–May 1941), 67–68.

———. "Trailing Ambrose Bierce." *American Notes & Queries* 1 (April–May 1941), 4–5, 20.

Brazil, John R. "Behind the Bitterness: Ambrose Bierce in Text and Context." *American Literary Realism* 13 (1980), 225–37.

Brodsky, Alyn. *Imperial Charade: A Biography of Emperor Napoleon III.* Indianapolis and New York: Bobbs-Merrill, 1978.

Brooks, Van Wyck. *The Confident Years: 1885–1915.* New York: E. P. Dutton, 1952.

———. *Emerson and Others.* New York: E. P. Dutton, 1927.

Castel, Albert. *Decision in the West: The Atlanta Campaign of 1864.* Lawrence: University Press of Kansas, 1992.

Clayton, Juliana. "Lieutenant's Ghastly Discovery." *Wild West* (August 1992), 26–32.

Conlogue, William. "A Haunting Memory: Ambrose Bierce and the Ravine of the Dead." *Studies in Short Fiction,* 28 (Winter 1991), 21–29.

Connell, Evan S. *Son of the Morning Star.* San Francisco: North Point Press, 1984.

Cooper, A. B. "Ambrose Bierce, an Appraisal." *Bookman* 33 (July 1911), 471–78.

Cornish, Dudley Warner. *The Sable Arm: Black Troops in the U.S. Army, 1861–1865.* Lawrence: University of Kansas Press, 1956.

Coulter, E. Merton. *The South During Reconstruction.* Baton Rouge: Louisiana State University Press, 1947.

Couser, Thomas G. "Writing the Civil War: Ambrose Bierce's 'Jupiter Doke, Brigadier-General.'" *Studies in American Fiction* 18 (Spring 1990), 87–98.

Cozzens, Peter. *No Better Place to Die: The Battle of Stones River.* Urbana and Chicago: University of Illinois Press, 1990.

———. *This Terrible Sound: The Battle of Chickamauga.* Urbana and Chicago: University of Illinois Press, 1992.

Crane, J. K. "Crossing the Bar Twice: Post-Mortem Consciousness." *Studies in Short Fiction* 6 (1968), 361–65.

Curry, Richard O., and F. Gerald Ham, eds. "The Bushwhackers' War: Insurgency and Counter-Insurgency in West Virginia." *Blue & Gray* (February–March 1985), 30–37.

Davidson, Cathy N., ed. *Critical Essays on Ambrose Bierce.* Boston: G. K. Hall, 1982.

———. *The Experimental Fictions of Ambrose Bierce.* Lincoln: University of Nebraska Press, 1984.

———. "Literary Semantics and the Fiction of Ambrose Bierce." *ETC: A Review of General Semantics* 31 (1974), 263–71.

DeCastro, Adolph. "Ambrose Bierce as He Really Was." *American Parade* 1 (October 1926), 28–44.

———. *Portrait of Ambrose Bierce.* New York: Century Company, 1929.

DeGregorio, William A. *The Complete Book of U.S. Presidents.* New York: Dembner Books, 1984.

Dimeo, Steven. "Psychological Symbolism in Three Early Tales of Invisibility." *Riverside Quarterly* 5 (1971), 20–27.

Dos Passos, John. *The Best Times.* New York: New American Library, 1966.

Dunbar, J. R. "Letters of George Sterling to Carey McWilliams." *California Historical Society Quarterly* 46 (Summer 1967), 235–52.

Edel, Leon. *Henry James.* New York: Harper & Row, 1985.

Eisenhower, John S. D. *Intervention: The U.S. and the Mexican Revolution, 1913–1917.* New York: W. W. Norton, 1993.

Ellman, Richard. *Oscar Wilde.* New York: Alfred A. Knopf, 1988.

Fadiman, Clifton, ed. *The Collected Writings of Ambrose Bierce.* New York: Citadel Press, 1946.

Farwell, Byron. *Queen Victoria's Little Wars.* New York: W. W. Norton, 1972.

Fatout, Paul. "Ambrose Bierce." *American Literary Realism* 1 (Fall 1967), 13–19.

———. *Ambrose Bierce and the Black Hills.* Norman: University of Oklahoma Press, 1956.

———. "Ambrose Bierce: Civil War Topographer." *American Literature* 36 (November 1954), 391–400.

———. *Ambrose Bierce: The Devil's Lexicographer.* Norman: University of Oklahoma Press, 1951.

Faust, Patricia L., ed. *Historical Times Illustrated Encyclopedia of the Civil War.* New York: Harper & Row, 1986.

Field, B. S., Jr. "Ambrose Bierce as Comic." *Western Humanities Review* 31 (1977), 173–80.

Fischer, David Hackett. *Albion's Seed: Four British Folkways in America.* New York: Oxford University Press, 1989.

Fleming, Walter L. *Civil War and Reconstruction in Alabama.* New York: Columbia University Press, 1905.

———. *Documentary History of Reconstruction.* Vol. 1. Cleveland: Arthur H. Clark Company, 1906.

Follett, Wilson. "Ambrose Bierce—An Analysis of the Perverse Wit That Shaped His Work." *Bookman* 68 (November 1928), 284–89.

———. "Ambrose, Son of Marcus Aurelius." *Atlantic Monthly* (July 1937), 32–42.

Foote, Shelby. *The Civil War: A Narrative.* 3 vols. New York: Random House, 1958–74.

Fortenberry, G. E. "Ambrose Bierce: A Critical Bibliography of Secondary Comment." *American Literary Realism* 4 (Winter 1971), 11–16.

Foulke, William Dudley. *Life of Oliver Morton.* Vol 1. Indianapolis and Kansas City: Bowen-Merrill Company, 1899.

Fox, William. *Regimental Losses in the American Civil War: 1861–1865.* Albany: Augustus S. Bradshaw, 1898.

Francedese, Janet M. "Ambrose Bierce as Journalist." Ph.D. dissertation, New York University, 1977.

Fraser, J. M. "Points South: Ambrose Bierce, Jorge Luis Borges." *Studies in 20th-Century Literature* 1 (1977), 173–81.

Frink, Maurice. "A Sidelight on Ambrose Bierce." *Book Notes* (August 1923), 154.

Fuentes, Carlos. *The Old Gringo.* New York: Farrar, Straus and Giroux, 1985.

Gold, Theodore S., ed. *Historical Records of the Town of Cornwall, Connecticut.* Hartford: Hartford Press, 1904.

Goldstein, J. S. "Edwin Markham, Ambrose Bierce, and 'The Man with the Hoe.'" *Modern Language Notes* 58 (March 1943), 165–75.

Grant, Ulysses S. *Personal Memoirs of U.S. Grant.* 2 vols. New York: Charles L. Webster & Company, 1885.

Grattan, C. Hartley. *Bitter Bierce: A Mystery of American Letters.* New York: Doubleday, 1929.

Grenander, M. E. *Ambrose Bierce.* New York: Twayne Publishers, 1971.

———. "Ambrose Bierce and Charles Warren Stoddard: Some Unpublished Correspondence." *Huntington Library Quarterly* 23 (May 1960), 261–92.

———. "Ambrose Bierce and *Cobwebs from an Empty Skull:* A Note on BAL 1100 and 1107." *Papers of the Bibliographical Society of America* 69 (1975), 403–6.

———. "Ambrose Bierce, John Camden Hotten, *The Fiend's Delight,* and *Nuggets and Dust.*" *Huntington Library Quarterly* 28 (August 1965), 353–71.

———. "Bierce's Turn of the Screw: Tales of Ironical Terror." *Western Humanities Review* 11 (Summer 1957), 257–63.

———. "California's Albion: Mark Twain, Ambrose Bierce, Tom Hood, John Camden Hotten, and Andrew Chatto." *Papers of the Bibliographical Society of America* 72 (1978), 457–62.

———. "H. L. Mencken to Ambrose Bierce." *Book Club of California Quarterly News Letter* 22 (Winter 1956), 5–10.

———. "A London Letter of Joaquin Miller to Ambrose Bierce." *Yale University Library Gazette* 46 (October 1971), 109–16.

———. "Seven Ambrose Bierce Letters." *Yale University Library Gazette* 32 (July 1957), 12–18.

Guelzo, Allen C. "Bierce's Civil War." *Civil War Times Illustrated* (September 1981), 36–45.

Gustaitis, Joseph. "South Carolina's Henry Timrod." *America's Civil War* (September 1992), 10–14.

Guttman, Jon. "Emperor Norton I." *Wild West* (February 1989), 8, 55–58.

Guzman, Martin Luis. *The Eagle and the Serpent.* New York: Alfred A. Knopf, 1930.

Harding, Ruth Guthrie. "Mr. Boythorn Bierce." *Bookman* 61 (August 1925), 636–43.

Harris, Leon. "Satan's Lexicographer." *American Heritage* 28 (April 1972), 57–63.

Hartwell, Ronald. "What Hemingway Learned from Ambrose Bierce." *Research Studies* 38 (December 1970), 309–11.

Hazen, William B. *A Narrative of Military Service.* Boston: Ticknor & Company, 1885.

Hemingway, Ernest. *The Short Stories of Ernest Hemingway.* New York: Charles Scribner's Sons, 1938.

Henry, Robert Selph. *The Story of Reconstruction.* Indianapolis: Bobbs-Merrill, 1938.

Highsmith, James Milton. "The Forms of Burlesque in *The Devil's Dictionary.*" *Satire Newsletter* (Spring 1970), 115–27.

Hobson, Fred. *Mencken: A Life.* New York: Random House, 1994.

Hopkins, Ernest Jerome, ed. *The Ambrose Bierce Satanic Reader.* Garden City: Doubleday and Company, 1968.

———. *The Complete Short Stories of Ambrose Bierce.* Lincoln and London: University of Nebraska Press, 1970.

Jacobus, Donald Lines. "The Bierce Family." Connecticut Historical Society Genealogical Manuscript Collection.

Jones, Idwal. "San Francisco: An Elegy." *American Mercury* 20 (August 1925), 477–84.

Jones, James P., Jr. "'Bull' and the 'Damned Puppy': A Civil War Tragedy." *American History Illustrated* (November 1972), 12–21.

Kaplan, Justin. *Mr. Clemens and Mark Twain.* New York: Simon and Schuster, 1966.

———. *Walt Whitman: A Life.* New York: Simon and Schuster, 1980.

Kelly, Dennis. "Atlanta Campaign: Mountains to Pass, A River to Cross." *Blue & Gray* (June 1989), 8–30, 46–58.

Ketz, Louise Bilebof, ed. *Dictionary of American History.* Vol. 5. New York: Scribner, 1976.

Kleber, John E., ed. *The Kentucky Encyclopedia.* Lexington: University Press of Kentucky, 1992.

Klein, Marcus. "San Francisco and Her Hateful Ambrose Bierce." *Hudson Review* 7 (August 1954), 392–407.

Knepper, George W., ed. *Travels in the Southland, 1822–1823: The Journal of Lucius Verus Bierce.* Columbus: Ohio State University Press, 1966.

Knight, Melinda. "Cultural Radicalism in the American Fin de Siècle: The Emergence of an Oppositional Literary Culture." Ph.D. dissertation, New York University, 1992.

Kramer, Carl E. *Capital on the Kentucky: A Two-Hundred-Year History of Frankfort and Franklin County.* Frankfort: Historic Frankfort, Inc., 1984.

Kroeker, Marvin E. "William B. Hazen: A Military Career in the Frontier West, 1855–1880." Ph.D. dissertation, University of Oklahoma, 1987.

Lamers, William M. *The Edge of Glory: A Biography of General William S. Rosecrans, U.S.A.* New York: Harcourt, Brace & World, 1961.

Leider, Emily. "'Your Picture Hangs in My Salon': The Letters of Gertrude Atherton to Ambrose Bierce." *California History* (Winter 1981–82), 333–49.

Lewis, Oscar. *San Francisco: Mission to Metropolis.* Berkeley: Howell-North, 1966.

————. *This Was San Francisco.* New York: David McKay, 1962.

Linderman, Gerald F. *Embattled Courage: The Experience of Combat in the American Civil War.* New York: Free Press, 1987.

————. *The Mirror of War: American Society and the Spanish-American War.* Ann Arbor: University of Michigan Press, 1974.

Lingeman, Richard. *Theodore Dreiser: At the Gate of the City 1871–1907.* New York: G. P. Putnam's Sons, 1986.

Lock, Rosalind. "Jim Beckwourth." *Wild West* (June 1993), 8, 78–79.

Logan, F. J. "The Wry Seriousness of 'Owl Creek Bridge.'" *American Literary Realism* 10 (Spring 1977), 101–13.

Mahoney, Tom. "The End of Ambrose Bierce." *Esquire* (February 1936), 62, 149–50.

Mallinson, David. "Confused First Fight." *America's Civil War* (January 1992), 46–52.

Malone, Dumas, ed. *Dictionary of American Biography.* Vol. 5. New York: Charles Scribner's Sons, 1932.

Marberry, M. M. *Splendid Poseur: Joaquin Miller—American Poet.* New York: Thomas Y. Crowell, 1953.

Marcus, F. H. "Film and Fiction: 'An Occurrence at Owl Creek Bridge.'" *California English Journal* 7 (1971), 14–23.

Marcus, Steven. *The Other Victorians: A Study of Sexuality and Pornography in Mid-Nineteenth-Century England.* New York: Basic Books, 1964.

Mariani, Giorgio. "Ambrose Bierce's Civil War Stories and the Critique of the Martial Spirit." *Studies in American Fiction* 19 (Autumn 1991), 221–28.

Marszalek, John F. *Sherman: A Soldier's Passion for Order.* New York: Free Press, 1993.

Martin, Jay. "Ambrose Bierce." *The Comic Imagination of American Literature,* edited by Louis D. Rubin, Jr. New Brunswick: Rutgers University Press, 1973.

McCann, William, ed. *Ambrose Bierce's Civil War.* Los Angeles, Chicago, and New York: Henry Regnery Company, 1956.

McDonough, James Lee. *Chattanooga—A Death Grip on the Confederacy.* Knoxville: University of Tennessee Press, 1984.

————. *Shiloh—In Hell Before Night.* Knoxville: University of Tennessee Press, 1977.

McDonough, James Lee, and Thomas L. Connelly. *Five Tragic Hours: The Battle of Franklin.* Knoxville: University of Tennessee Press, 1983.

McFeely, William S. *Grant: A Biography.* New York: W. W. Norton, 1981.

McGinty, Brian. "His Bones Were Never Found." *American History Illustrated* (January–February 1990), 52–57.

McMichael, George, ed. *Anthology of American Literature.* Vol. 2. New York: Macmillan, 1980.

McMurry, Richard. "Resaca: 'A Heap of Hard Fiten.'" *Civil War Times Illustrated* (December 1971), 20–28, 43–49.

McPherson, James M. *Battle Cry of Freedom.* New York: Oxford University Press, 1988.

McWilliams, Carey. *Ambrose Bierce: A Biography.* New York: A. and C. Boni, 1929.

————. "Ambrose Bierce and His First Love." *Bookman* 35 (June 1932), 254–59.

————. "The Mystery of Ambrose Bierce." *American Mercury* 22 (March 1931), 330–37.

Mencken, H. L. *A Book of Prefaces.* New York: Alfred A. Knopf, 1917.

————. "The Ambrose Bierce Mystery." *American Mercury* 18 (September 1929), 124–26.

————. *Prejudices, Sixth Series.* New York: Alfred A. Knopf, 1927.

Millard, Bailey. "Personal Memories of Bierce." *Bookman* 40 (February 1915), 653–58.

Miller, Arthur M. "The Influence of Edgar Allan Poe on Ambrose Bierce." *American Literature* 4 (May 1932), 130–50.

Monaghan, Frank. "Ambrose Bierce and the Authorship of *The Monk and the Hangman's Daughter.*" *American Literature* 2 (January 1932), 337–49.

Morrill, Sibley S. *Ambrose Bierce, F. A. Mitchell-Hedges and the Crystal Skull.* San Francisco: Cadleon Press, 1972.

Morris, Roy, Jr. "All Hell Can't Stop Them." *Military History* (February 1986), 34–40.

———. "Battle in the Bluegrass." *Civil War Times Illustrated* (December 1988), 15–23.

———. "A Bird of Evil Omen: The War Department's Charles Dana." *Civil War Times Illustrated* (January 1987), 20–29.

———. "The Sack of Athens." *Civil War Times Illustrated* (February 1986), 26–32.

———. *Sheridan: The Life and Wars of General Phil Sheridan.* New York: Crown, 1992.

Morris, Roy, Jr., and Phil Noblitt. "The History of a Failure." *Civil War Times Illustrated* (September 1988), 36–43.

Muscatine, Doris. *Old San Francisco: The Biography of a City.* New York: Putnam's, 1975.

Nations, Leroy J. "Ambrose Bierce: The Gray Wolf of American Letters." *South Atlantic Quarterly* 25 (1926), 253–58.

Neale, Walter. *Life of Ambrose Bierce.* New York: Neale Publishing Company, 1929.

Nickell, Joe. *Ambrose Bierce Is Missing and Other Historical Mysteries.* Lexington: University Press of Kentucky, 1992.

O'Brien, Matthew C. "Ambrose Bierce and the Civil War: 1865." *American Literature* 48 (November 1976), 377–81.

O'Connor, Richard J. *Ambrose Bierce: A Biography.* Boston: Little, Brown, 1967.

Otis, Amos. "Bearse." *Genealogical Notes of Barnstable Families.* Baltimore: Genealogical Publishing Company, 1979.

O'Toole, G. J. A. *The Spanish War: An American Epic.* New York and London: W. W. Norton, 1984.

Owens, David M. "Bierce and Biography: The Location of Owl Creek Bridge." *American Literary Realism* 26 (Spring 1994), 82–89.

Painter, Nell Irvin. *Standing at Armageddon.* New York and London: W. W. Norton, 1987.

Partridge, Eric. "Ambrose Bierce." *London Mercury* 16 (October 1927), 625–38.

Peckham, Howard H. *Indiana: A Bicentennial History.* New York: W. W. Norton, 1978.

Peskin, Allan. *Garfield.* Kent: Kent State University Press, 1978.

Phelps, William Lyon, ed. *Letters of James Whitcomb Riley.* Indianapolis: Bobbs-Merrill, 1933.

Pollard, Percival. *Their Day in Court.* New York: Neale Publishing Company, 1909.

Pope, Bertha Clark, ed. *The Letters of Ambrose Bierce.* San Francisco: The Book Club of California, 1922.

Powers, James G. "Freud and Farquhar: An Occurrence at Owl Creek Bridge?" *Studies in Short Fiction* 19 (Summer 1982), 278–81.

Purdue, Howell and Elizabeth. *Pat Cleburne: Confederate General.* Hillsboro: Hill Junior College Press, 1973.

Randle, Kevin D. "Reckless Pursuit Halted." *Military History* (August 1986), 20–25.

Rather, Lois. *Bittersweet: Ambrose Bierce and Women.* Oakland: Rather Press, 1975.

Reed, Ishmael. "On Ambrose Bierce's *Tales of Soldiers and Civilians.*" In *Classics of Civil War Fiction,* edited by David Madden and Peggy Bach. Oxford: University Press of Mississippi, 1991, 37–43.

Richards, Robert F. *Concise Dictionary of American Literature.* New York: Philosphical Library, 1955.

Rogge, Robert G. "Heartland Hammered Furiously." *America's Civil War* (May 1988), 18–25.

Roth, Russell. "Ambrose Bierce's 'Detestable Creature.'" *Western American Literature* 9 (November 1974), 169–76.

Roundtree, Benjamin, ed. "Letters from a Confederate Soldier." *Georgia Review* 18 (1964), 287–88.

Saunders, Richard. *Ambrose Bierce: The Making of a Misanthrope*. San Francisco: Chronicle Books, 1985.

Schaefer, Michael Wingfield. "'Just What War Is': Realism in the Civil War Writings of John W. De Forest and Ambrose Bierce." Ph.D. dissertation, University of North Carolina, 1990.

Sears, Stephen W. *George B. McClellan: The Young Napoleon*. New York: Ticknor & Fields, 1988.

Secrest, Philip. "Scene of Awful Carnage." *Civil War Times Illustrated* (June 1971), 5–9, 45–49.

Sefton, James E. *United States Army and Reconstruction, 1865–1877*. Baton Rouge: Louisiana State University Press, 1967.

Silber, Nina. *The Romance of Reunion: Northerners and the South, 1865–1900*. Chapel Hill: University of North Carolina Press, 1993.

Slade, Joseph W. "'Putting You in the Papers': Ambrose Bierce's Letters to Edwin Markham." *Prospects* 1 (1975), 335–68.

Smith, Page. *The Rise of Industrial America*. New York: McGraw-Hill, 1984.

Solomon, Eric. "The Bitterness of Battle: Ambrose Bierce's War Fiction." *Midwest Quarterly* 5 (1963–64), 147–65.

Starr, Edward C. *A History of Cornwall, Connecticut*. New Haven: Tuttle, Morehouse and Taylor, 1926.

Starr, Kevin. *Americans and the California Dream*. New York: Oxford University Press, 1973.

Starrett, Vincent. *Buried Caesars*. Chicago: Covici McGee, 1923.

Stein, W. B. "Bierce's 'The Death of Halpin Frayser': The Poetics of Gothic Consciousness." *Emerson Society Quarterly* 18 (1972), 115–22.

Stephen, Sir Leslie, and Sir Sidney Lee, eds. *Dictionary of National Biography*. New York: Oxford University Press, 1921.

Sterling, George. "The Shadow Maker." *American Mercury* 6 (September 1925), 10–19.

Stoicheff, Peter. "'Something Uncanny': The Dream Structure of Ambrose Bierce's 'An Occurrence at Owl Creek Bridge.'" *Studies in Short Fiction* 30 (Summer 1993), 355–65.

St. Pierre, Brian, ed. *The Devil's Advocate: An Ambrose Bierce Reader*. San Francisco: Chronicle Books, 1987.

Stubbs. John C. "Ambrose Bierce's Contributions to *Cosmopolitan:* An Annotated Bibliography." *American Literary Realism* 4 (Winter 1971), 57–59.

Suhr, Robert Collins. "Storming Through the Ice." *America's Civil War* (May 1989), 26–33.

Superintendent's Report, Kentucky Military Institute, June 16, 1859.

Swanberg, William A. *Citizen Hearst*. New York: Charles Scribner's Sons, 1961.

Tepper, Michael, ed. *Passengers to America*. Baltimore: Genealogical Publishing Company, 1977.

Thomas, Jeffrey. "Ambrose Bierce." *American Literary Realism* 8 (Summer 1975), 198–201.

Tucker, Glenn. *Chickamauga: Bloody Battle in the West*. Indianapolis: Bobbs-Merrill Company, 1961.

Utley, Robert M. *Cavalier in Buckskin: George Armstrong Custer and the Western Military Frontier*. Norman: University of Oklahoma Press, 1988.

———. *The Indian Frontier and the American West, 1846–1890*. Albuquerque: University of New Mexico Press, 1984.

Walker, Dale L. "A Last Laugh for Ambrose Bierce." *American West* 10 (November 1973), 34–39, 63.

Walker, Franklin. *Ambrose Bierce: The Wickedest Man in San Francisco*. San Francisco: Colt Press, 1941.

———. *San Francisco's Literary Frontier*. New York: Alfred A. Knopf, 1939.

Wallace, Lew. *An Autobiography*. 2 vols. New York and London: Harper and Brothers, 1906.

Watkins, Sam R. *Co. "Aytch."* New York: Collier Books, 1962.

Watson, Bruce. "Who Was It Wrote *The Devil's Dictionary*?" *Smithsonian* (March 1992), 103–114.

Weeden, William B. *War Government, Federal and State, in Massachusetts, New York, Pennsylvania and Indiana, 1861–1865*. New York: Houghton-Mifflin, 1906.

Weimer, David R. "Ambrose Bierce and the Art of War." In *Essays in Literary History,* edited by Rudolf Kirk and C. F. Main. New York: Russell and Russell, 1965.

West, George. "The California Literati." *American Mercury* 8 (July 1926), 281–86.

Wiggins, R. A. "Ambrose Bierce: A Romantic in the Age of Realism." *American Literary Realism* 4 (Winter 1971), 1–10.

Williams, Stanley T. "Ambrose Bierce and Bret Harte." *American Literature* 17 (May 1945), 179–80.

Wilson, Edmund. *Patriotic Gore: Studies in the Literature of the American Civil War*. New York: Oxford University Press, 1962.

Wilt, Napier. "Ambrose Bierce and the Civil War." *American Literature* 1 (November 1929), 260–85.

Woodruff, Stuart C. *The Short Stories of Ambrose Bierce: A Study in Polarity*. Pittsburgh: University of Pittsburgh Press, 1964.

Zinn, Howard. *A People's History of the United States*. New York: Harper & Row, 1980.

Index